CW01203312

THE INSTITUTIONS
OF MEANING

THE INSTITUTIONS OF MEANING

A Defense of Anthropological Holism

Vincent Descombes

Translated by
Stephen Adam Schwartz

Harvard University Press

Cambridge, Massachusetts
London, England
2014

Copyright © 2014 by the President and Fellows of Harvard College
All rights reserved
Printed in the United States of America

Originally published as *Les institutions du sens*, copyright © 1996 Les Éditions de Minuit
www.leseditionsdeminuit.fr

Cataloging-in-Publication Data available from the Library of Congress

ISBN: 978-0-674-72878-3 (alk. paper)

Contents

Preface to the English Translation xi

PART I

INTENTIONALIST CONCEPTIONS OF MIND

1. The Intentionality of the Mental 3

    1.1.—The distinctive quality of psychological descriptions is to be expressed in intentional language. Any language that has a logic analogous to that of verbs of declaration is an intentional language.   3

    1.2.—The psychological description of a person is as much the description of his environment as of his states. Thus, Achilles's anger is only comprehensible when set in Achilles's world.   7

    1.3.—How are we to explain this intentional character of a mode of description? There are two possibilities: by means of a thesis regarding the transitive structure of consciousness (Brentano) or through an anthropological holism of the mental (Wittgenstein).   9

    1.4.—The Scholastic conception of intentionality holds that the intention of a term is comparable to the direction of an arrow that a bowman sends toward the object aimed at. This image illustrates the fact that there are two possible relations between the thinking subject and the object of thought: an intentional relation (aiming at it) and a real relation (physically touching it).   12

    1.5.—Wittgenstein evokes the distinction between these two relations to an object in an aphorism regarding the thief that can be looked for when he is not present, but who can be hanged only if he is present.   20

1.6.—"All consciousness is consciousness of something": Brentano's now-classic formulation seems to assimilate verbs of consciousness to the transitivity of action verbs. ... 23

1.7.—The transitivity of an intentional verb is paradoxical since such verbs must necessarily take a direct object, even if there is nothing in the world that is the object of the intentional act signified by the verb. ... 26

1.8.—If intentional verbs were really transitive, they would have an intentional passive form that would describe a real change in the object they aim at. ... 32

1.9.—Several French philosophers have sought to give substance to the idea of a real history of the intentional object by, for example, taking up Kojève's claim that the word is "the murder of the thing" (Lacan) or by developing a form of social constructivism (Foucault). These theories rest on an illegitimate assimilation of intentional relations to real relations. ... 36

2. The Paradox of the Intentional Object 47

2.1.—What Husserl calls "the paradox of the intentional object" is the fact that the perceived tree, taken as such, unlike the tree itself, does not have the natural powers of a physical thing (it can *be seen to be burning up,* but it cannot *burn up*). How is this doubling of the tree—into both an object of physical actions and an object of mental operations—to be avoided? ... 47

2.2.—According to Husserl, the only tree that can be seen in the garden is the intentional object. ... 55

2.3.—Intentional objects are not entities endowed with a specific mode of existence. It is meaningful to ask "Where is the tree perceived?" but meaningless to ask "Where is the perceived tree?" ... 59

3. A Holistic Conception of Intentionality 65

3.1.—The question of the intentional passive is about knowing the conditions in which an active intentional form ("Romeo loves Juliet") can be changed into an intentional passive form ("Juliet is loved by Romeo"). ... 65

3.2.—Intentional logic examines the function of intentional operators such as "It is said that . . ." or "It is believed by N that . . ." It shows that the intentional relation of the mental act to the object (when the object exists) necessarily depends on a real relation. ... 66

3.3.—"To look for" forms a system with "to find" (Wittgenstein). The verb "to look for" is always intentional, while the verb "to find" assumes that the intentional object sought coincides with the real object. Indeed, one cannot find what one is looking for under a certain description without at once finding the object under all of the descriptions applicable to it, including those that did not form part of the definition of the object sought. ... 77

3.4.—Mental holism, which allows us to solve the Husserlian paradox of the intentional object, is not simply a rejection of psychical atomism. It is a holism that can be called "anthropological" in order to stress that it places the mind within the context of collective habits and common institutions. ... 86

PART II

THE ANTHROPOLOGICAL HOLISM OF THE MENTAL

4. The Question of Holism 95

    4.1.—The question of mental holism is first raised regarding signs and subsequently about the mind manifested by those signs. Can there be an isolated sign? That is impossible, according to the holistic conception of meaning.   95

    4.2.—Meaning holism appears incompatible with the fact of communication: how could one understand someone's speech if his words were only intelligible when resituated within the whole of his language?   98

    4.3.—Pierre Duhem maintained that the theories put forward by the experimental sciences were global in character. In the case of a conflict with experience, the entire construction is rejected and not an isolated hypothesis.   103

    4.4.—Semantic holism does not bear on the confirmation of theories, but on the way in which units of meaning are to be defined. Quine maintains that the unit of meaning is not the sentence, but the whole set of sentences that constitute the discourse of a theory. For him, this discourse is a collective whole made up of sentences.   109

    4.5.—Collectivist holism consists in conceiving the whole as a collection of individuals that together possess collective attributes.   113

    4.6.—Structural holism consists in conceiving the whole as a system of parts that depend upon one another in virtue of the relations that define them.   115

5. The Illusion of Collective Individuals 123

    5.1.—A collective whole cannot be defined both as a collective being consisting of a plurality of individuals and as a higher-order individual.   124

    5.2.—A proposition is collective if it has a collective subject. Nevertheless, a collective subject is not the name of a collective individual but a logical construction that allows the predicate to be related to several individuals by saying that *together* they are doing something or have a certain status.   129

    5.3.—Methodological individualism is right to hold that collective individuals are fictions. However, concrete totalities are precisely not made up of individuals that are independent from one another, but of interdependent parts.   136

    5.4.—Logical atomism cannot account for real complexity.   143

    5.5.—Nominalist analysis cannot account for the diachronic identity of complex beings.   149

6. The Order of Meaning 155

    6.1.—There are three philosophies of structural analysis: *structural holism* seeks to understand the interdependence of the parts of a whole; *formalism* seeks purely formal characteristics that remain invariant between one domain and   156 another; *structural causalism* seeks to reveal the action of the form of a productive process upon the product.

6.2.—A description of a whole made up of parts is not a description of several individuals through the attributes they collectively possess; it is a description of a thing as it presents itself in one or another of its parts. 160

6.3.—The material description of a meaningful totality is not sufficient to identify it. One must also describe the order that the elements must have for the whole to be meaningful. Formal description provides this order of meaning. 166

6.4.—A holistic analysis distinguishes two levels. At the higher level, the whole is identified in relation to other totalities. At the lower level, it is described in its internal differentiation into parts. At no point does a holistic analysis end up with individual elements. 176

7. The Logic of Relations 186

7.1.—What are called *internal* relations are relations that enter into the reality of their terms. William James carried out a pluralist critique of the monistic idea of a universe organized entirely by internal relations: individuals must exist before they can have relations. 186

7.2.—Russell criticizes the monistic doctrine that the relation between two objects expresses the *intrinsic* reality of those objects and characterizes the *whole* of which those objects are the parts. He sets against this doctrine the fact that a change in the relation is not necessarily an intrinsic change. 189

7.3.—An intrinsic change is a change in the thing; an extrinsic change is a change in the environment exterior to the thing. 196

7.4.—The monism of internal relations and the pluralism of external relations do not distinguish between essences and accidents. This is why their discussion is general: either all relations are internal or none is. However, the distinction between internal and external must be relative to a description. 198

7.5.—Leibniz did not seek to eliminate relational propositions (as Russell believes), but to analyze them in their logical complexity. 202

8. The Subject of Triadic Relations. 211

8.1.—What Peirce calls a *real relation* is a relation whose description is irreducible to the conjunction of several propositions asserting facts that are independent from one another. When the description of a relation can be analyzed as such a conjunction, it is a relation of *reason*. 211

8.2.—Peirce does not merely note the irreducibility of relations to qualities, but he shows that within the very category of relations, triadic relations (grounded in intentional actions) are irreducible to dyadic relations (grounded on natural actions). 219

8.3.—Like Hegelian philosophers, Peirce criticizes the way in which logic is traditionally expounded. But the reform he advocates is both analytic and holistic and not dialectical. 226

9. Essays on the Gift............................238

9.1.—The act of giving something to someone is an irreducibly triadic fact: the three terms of the relation are linked to one another in virtue of a rule. The description of the gift cannot separate the link between the people and the thing given from the link between the people who are the giver and the recipient. 238

9.2.—Mauss, in his study of the obligatory exchange of gifts, aims to describe institutions as a system. Lévi-Strauss believes that such a description is insufficient and that ideological facts can only be explained by facts that are intellectual without being intentional. 246

9.3.—The structures of the mind cannot be conceived as the mechanisms of psychical functioning. They are schemata for the production of a meaningful order of human affairs. The anthropologist must account not only for the way in which individuals establish relations of equality among themselves by means of schemata of reciprocity but also for the way they establish relations of order among different statuses. 259

10. Objective Mind...............................270

10.1.—The philosophies of language that want to stay within the speech acts of speakers run up against the problem of determining an impersonal meaning of discourse. If there is no impersonal meaning of words, communication would be nothing but perpetual misunderstanding. 271

10.2.—Phenomenologists accept the idea of an impersonal mind in the sense of *objectified mind,* as when an author's thought can be contained in an object (his text). However, in order to account for communication, more is required: impersonal meanings must precede and provide the measure for personal meanings. 284

10.3.—Institutions constitute an *objective mind* because they rest on ideas. These ideas are common, not because they are in fact shared by a great many individuals, but because they are authoritative. 295

10.4.—The subject of the institutions of social life is not the individual but the system formed by the partners in a triadic relation and their common object. 303

11. Distinguishing Thoughts 314

11.1.—The fact of having the same thought as someone else would be similar to the fact of having the same car if thoughts could be individuated in the same way that we individuate cars. This is not the case: thoughts are identified contextually, by their content. 314

11.2.—One could call a *reflexive personal thought* a thought by which the thinking subject conceives of itself according to a description. To compare the reflexive personal thoughts of two subjects is to bring out an intersubjective identity or difference. 323

11.3.—A *social thought* is a personal thought by which two (or more) subjects conceive of themselves as the members of a system founded on their relation. 329

Thus, people thinking about an appointment they have with one another are having the same social thought.

11.4.—What would a translator do if he were working in a condition of radical ignorance of the language he was to translate from? It would be fruitless to engage in multiple observations of the natural circumstances in which sentences are uttered. Rather, he must establish a relation of interlocution with the people whose discourse he is to translate and do so by conforming to the local institutions of meaning. 335

Works Cited 341

Index 351

Preface to the English Translation

I am delighted that this book, which was published in France in 1996, is now appearing in English translation. The experience of rereading the book more than fifteen years after its initial publication spurs me to two lines of reflection: one regarding the overall intention of the book (I) and another about the questions opened up by the book but which it did not attempt to answer (II).

I

What was my intention in writing *The Institutions of Meaning*? To answer this, it is best to recall the circumstances that led to its composition.

My earliest drafts of this book derived from the notes to courses I taught, beginning in the middle of the 1980s, first at Johns Hopkins University and later at Emory University. One of these courses concerned Montesquieu's *The Spirit of the Laws*. This course allowed me to relate the idea of a "spirit of the laws" to two other ideas: on the one hand to draw links between this notion, which is really a "spirit of institutions"[1] and the

---

1. In the Second Part of *A Defence of "The Spirit of the Laws,"* Montesquieu defines his object of study as follows: "Those who have some insight will see at the first glance that the objects of this work are the laws, the various customs, and manners of all the nations on earth. It may be said that the subject is of prodigious extent, as it comprehends all the institutions received among mankind." Montesquieu, *A Defence of "The Spirit of the*

Hegelian concept of "objective mind" or "objective spirit"; on the other, links between Montesquieu's idea and a similar idea within twentieth-century social anthropology (which I knew principally through my readings of the works of Marcel Mauss, Claude Lévi-Strauss, and Louis Dumont). Montesquieu's inspired idea, which Hegel recognized and praised, is that the "mores" and "manners" of a people are institutions and that these institutions form a *totality* whose principle one might come to understand.

Another course I taught around that time bore upon the structuralist episode within French thought during the second half of the twentieth century. At the time, my American students were especially intrigued by the paradoxes put forward by a strain of thought known as "poststructuralism." This current was felt to be the cutting edge of French philosophy. I drew attention to the fact that it would be difficult to claim to have grasped the essentials of poststructuralism if one remained ignorant of or indifferent to structuralism itself (as was sometimes the case among my interlocutors). And I succeeded—at least I think I did—in awakening in some of my interlocutors an interest in structural analysis as it is practiced in the human sciences.

Both courses required me to speak about the merits of a "holistic" conception of the forms of human life and thus to enter into the classical debate about the status of the human sciences. One must refer to this debate if one wants to understand where the technical term "holism" comes from, even though this term does not appear in the vocabulary of classical philosophers or even in the work of Durkheim, Mauss, and Lévi-Strauss, who did, however, invoke the principle by which "the whole is more than the sum of its parts."

Yet within the American context in which I found myself at the time, the term "holism" was being used in a remarkable variety of ways. What was the relation between the holism of the sociologists I was teaching and

---

Laws," in *The Complete Works of M. de Montesquieu,* vol. 5 (London, 1777), 243 [translation modified]. In the title of his treatise, the word "law" must therefore be taken in the broad sense so as to include not only legislation proper but also "customs" and "manners" that are, as he puts it, a kind of legislation without a legislator: "Mores and manners are usages that laws have not established, or that they have not been able, or have not wanted, to establish." Montesquieu, *The Spirit of the Laws,* ed. and trans. Anne M. Cohler, Basia C. Miller, and Harold S. Stone (Cambridge: Cambridge University Press, 1989), 317.

"holism" as understood by philosophers such as W. V. O. Quine or Donald Davidson?

One might well claim that there is in fact no meaningful relation among the different uses of the term and therefore no way to compare the "mental holism" discussed by American philosophers with the "holism" of symbolic systems dealt with by structural anthropology. But such claims fail to consider that the structural analysis of human institutions—as practiced by Lévi-Strauss or Dumont when, for example, they compare different kinship systems—is ultimately meant to be an analysis of the structures *of the human mind*. More generally, the philosophy of the human sciences is a philosophy of the sciences of the mind. It is thus the task of a philosophy of mind to answer the question: how can the human sciences be *sciences* if they bear upon phenomena that differ from those of the natural sciences in that they comprise a dimension of *meaning*?

This question is one that has been asked since at least the middle of the nineteenth century: what is the status of disciplines such as history, philology, linguistics, ethnology, sociology, and political economy? In nineteenth-century France, these sciences were called "*sciences morales*" [moral sciences], which the Germans translated as *Geisteswissenschaften* [sciences of the mind]. The term "sciences of the mind" has the virtue of emphasizing the essential point: if we are to determine the way in which such scholarly disciplines are sciences, it will not be enough to ask methodological questions; we will also have to spell out our conception of mind by developing a philosophy of mind.

It might be objected that one ought not confuse the object of a "philosophy of mind" in the contemporary (English) sense of the term and what was meant by spirit or mind (*Geist*) in Dilthey's era. One might add that English requires us to choose between two translations of the French word *esprit*: are we referring to the mental capacities of an individual (mind) or to a pure spirit?

I do not believe that we should be deterred by such objections. First, it is worth pointing out that Gilbert Ryle's classic book *The Concept of Mind* has been translated into German as *Der Begriff des Geistes*.[2] Second, and moving in the other direction, it is striking that an excellent English

---

2. Gilbert Ryle, *The Concept of Mind* (1949; Chicago: University of Chicago Press, 2000). Gilbert Ryle, *Der Begriff des Geistes,* trans. Kurt Baier (Stuttgart: Reclam, 1986).

translator of the relevant part of Hegel's *Encyclopaedia of the Philosophical Sciences,* William Wallace, renders the notion of *der objektive Geist* as "objective mind."[3] The vocabulary therefore presents no insurmountable obstacle to the idea of asking the philosophy of mind to clarify the relations between the human sciences and the natural sciences.

Moreover, by returning to the origins of the debate regarding the "moral sciences," we come to a better understanding of why the stakes are those of a philosophy of mind.

In the nineteenth century, it was possible to believe that psychology, the basis for all of the human sciences, was on the verge of attaining the enviable status of an experimental science, thereby joining the natural sciences. Its object would then be the discovery of the psychological laws governing the formation and combination of elementary psychical units, or *representative ideas*. In other words, the common conception of mental life at the time was both atomistic and associationist.

In the twentieth century, in the wake of the revitalization of philosophical logic by Frege, Russell, and Wittgenstein, philosophers began to treat psychological concepts in an entirely different way. Philosophy of mind effected what has been called its "linguistic turn." Although it is certainly the case, as has often been pointed out, that the phrase "linguistic turn" means many different things to different people—thereby leading to numerous misunderstandings—I understand it in the following way, which I derive from Wittgenstein and which is the only sense of this phrase that is at issue in this book.

Peter Geach, in his book *Mental Acts,* raised the question of how we can know if a thinking subject possesses a certain concept or not.[4] What can serve as a criterion allowing us to decide, for example, whether a child of a given age possesses the concept of *self* or of *negation*? Geach answers by

---

3. G. W. F. Hegel, *Hegel's Philosophy of Mind, Being Part Three of the Encyclopaedia of the Philosophical Sciences,* trans. William Wallace (1894; Oxford: Clarendon Press, 1971). [Translator's note: The translation of *der objektive Geist* as "objective mind" has been preserved in the recent revised translation: G. W. F. Hegel, *Hegel's Philosophy of Mind: A Revised Version of the Wallace and Miller Translation (Hegel's Encyclopaedia of the Philosophical Sciences),* trans. William Wallace and A. V. Miller, rev. Michael Inwood (Oxford: Oxford University Press, 2006).]

4. P. T. Geach, *Mental Acts: Their Content and Their Objects* (London: Routledge and Kegan Paul, 1957), 12.

turning to the linguistic expression of our thoughts. He points out that there is a parallel between *judging* and *saying*. Some languages, he notes, use the same verb to attribute a judgment (i.e., a mental act) to someone as they do to attribute speech (i.e., a speech act) to him. As a result, reporting a judgment in indirect style (e.g., "he thought it was time to go home") and reporting speech directly (e.g., "he said, 'it is time to go home'") come down to the same thing. A judgment, then, consists in exercising one's conceptual capacities. As Geach puts it:

> It will be a *sufficient* condition for James having the concept of *so-and-so* that he should have mastered the intelligent use (including the use in made-up sentences) of a word for *so-and-so* in some language. Thus: if somebody knows how to use the English word "red," he has a concept of red; if he knows how to use the first-person pronoun, he has a concept of *self*; if he knows how to use the negative construction in some language, he has a concept of negation.[5]

Geach is careful to specify that the thesis in question is not about the psychological genesis of conceptual capacities (e.g., does the child first learn to speak or to think?), nor does it claim to posit a *necessary* condition for the possession of a concept, as if the knowing use of words were the only way in which a subject's intellectual capacities could be expressed. In fact, they are also expressed in his behavior, his actions, and his attitudes (Geach gives the example of a chess match conducted in silence and in which one or both of the participants might well be aphasic).[6] The possession of a concept is thus not to be *defined* by linguistic competence; rather, linguistic competence—the possibility of using the word in a linguistic construction—becomes one of the most incontrovertible criteria for the possession of a concept. In other words, as Robert Brandom recently put it, the "linguistic turn" conceived in this way consists in judging the conceptual capacities of a thinking subject in terms of her linguistic capacities.[7]

A direct consequence of the linguistic turn in the philosophy of mind was to transfer into the domain of the mental a conflict between two opposing schools in the philosophy of language. On the one hand, *semantic*

---

5. Ibid., 12–13.
6. Ibid., 13.
7. Robert B. Brandom, *Perspectives on Pragmatism: Classical, Recent and Contemporary* (Cambridge, MA: Harvard University Press, 2011), 22.

atomism applied to discourse analysis the principle that the composite presupposes the simple. It maintains that the meaning of a complex symbol (e.g., a proposition) arises from the different meanings attached to the simple symbols of which it is composed. As for these simple symbols, they must acquire their respective meanings independently of one another, out of the immediate interface between mind and the external world. For example, it is maintained that a given sound becomes the name of an object by being vested with a nominative function via an act of ostensive definition. On the other hand, *semantic holism*—for example, that of Ferdinand de Saussure—maintains that the concept of a sign is the epitome of a holistic concept, meaning that the concept of a sign apprehends its object only insofar as it sees it as part of a whole: only within a system can something function as a sign. Another way of putting it is that it is only in virtue of its relations to other signs within a meaningful totality that something can be used as a sign. As Wittgenstein remarked, I can certainly invent a new sign—for example in order to name a particular painful sensation that I am feeling right now—but I am able to name this current sensation only if my language already has a place prepared for this sign, i.e., only if I have already mastered a technique for applying certain words as "names of sensations."[8]

Semantic holism is, of course, a rejection of semantic atomism. It also entails mental holism, i.e., the rejection of atomistic and associationist conceptions in psychology. However, there are several ways to reject an atomistic approach to a particular domain, be it language, mental life, or social life. Thus, philosophy of language must decide whether to embrace a strict semantic holism such as that expressed by Frege's context principle—i.e., it is only within the context of a proposition that words have semantic functions of reference or predication—or, alternatively, to go further and adopt an anthropological holism such as the view Wittgenstein defended (without, of course, giving the idea this doctrinal label) with his model of language games. That model holds that to practice a language game (for example, the "game" of assertion or of giving orders and

---

8. Ludwig Wittgenstein, *Philosophical Investigations,* rev. 4th ed., ed. P. M. S. Hacker and Joachim Schulte, trans. G. E. M. Anscombe, P. M. S. Hacker, and Joachim Schulte (1953; Oxford: Wiley-Blackwell, 2009), § 257 (98).

executing them) is to participate in a "form of life," that is, a certain organization of common life with its presuppositions, techniques, and customs—in a word, its *institutions*.⁹

An explanation of what is covered by the term "anthropological holism" requires a return to the domain of the human sciences, those sciences that take phenomena of mind as their object. And to do this is to notice that the philosophy of the human sciences has constantly discussed the question of how those sciences ought to conceive of the relation between a *whole* and its *parts*. As a general rule, one must decide what comes first in the determination of a phenomenon falling into the domain of such sciences: does the whole present itself as the result of a composition of parts, or is it that the parts can only be defined through the internal differentiation of a totality that is already given?

In *The Mind's Provisions*, I sought to establish that our ordinary psychological concepts can be applied to an individual only in the conditions required by anthropological holism, i.e., by taking into account the historical and institutional context for that individual's activities.[10] As a result, I concluded that we should reject as incoherent the program ("methodological solipsism") that sought to redefine psychological concepts by giving them a more restricted domain of application. These redefined concepts would describe pure internal states of the individual (i.e., narrow mental states), which would allow them to be given a causal function in the movement of the organism. In reality, as I argued, one cannot conceive of an individual state that is at once an *internal* state (meaning that it is given independently of its context) and an *intentional* state (meaning

---

9. I have borrowed the term "anthropological holism" from Fodor and LePore, who use it to characterize Wittgenstein's position. They define it as follows: "Anthropological holism is distinct from semantic holism only insofar as it concerns the relation between language and its intentional background—that is, the relation between language and the cultural background of beliefs, institutions, practices, conventions, and so forth upon which, according to anthropological holists, language is ontologically dependent." Jerry Fodor and Ernest LePore, *Holism: A Shopper's Guide* (Oxford: Blackwell, 1992), 6.

10. Vincent Descombes, *The Mind's Provisions: A Critique of Cognitivism*, trans. Stephen Adam Schwartz (Princeton: Princeton University Press, 2001).

that it is identifiable by a content to be specified in terms borrowed from the environment in which the individual lives). For example, one cannot identify out of context a state that would consist in thinking that it would be enjoyable to play a game of chess or that one must go to the bank, because these contents are meaningful only if the subject that thinks these things is situated in a surrounding environment that includes games of chess and bank accounts. Such thoughts cannot be redefined as the "internal" mental states of an individual subject if they have the intentional content by which we specify them.

That book led to a question that it left unresolved but that this book will attempt to answer. From a philosophical point of view, the question of what it is to think or to have a given thought can be asked in the following way: what is it to have the same thought as (or a different thought from) someone else? In other words, how do we identify thoughts?

This question is central for a philosophy of the social sciences. As Georg Simmel said, "One does not need to be a Caesar in order to understand Caesar."[11] Indeed, we are here confronted with something like a test for judging the quality of a philosophy of mind. Every philosophy of mind that requires me to identify with you in order to be able to claim that I understand you should be rejected. It would amount to the following reasoning:

- Only Caesar can understand Caesar.
- We understand what Caesar is saying when he says in his language "the die is cast" (*alea jacta est*).
- As a result, we must all, at least from time to time, be capable of becoming Caesar.

The work of the historian, the anthropologist, the sociologist, and the linguist is well and truly destined to allow us to understand what people thought and said in other languages and within other forms of life. If carrying out such work necessarily involved making my person coincide with that of the actors I seek to interpret, the work would be doomed from the start either to failure or to offering entirely arbitrary interpretations.

---

11. Georg Simmel, *The Problems of the Philosophy of History: An Epistemological Essay*, 2nd ed., ed. and trans. Guy Oakes (1892; New York: Free Press, 1977), 94.

PREFACE TO THE ENGLISH TRANSLATION   xix

* * *

In *The Institutions of Meaning*, I had an opportunity to discuss the principal episodes in the history of reflection about the problems raised by anthropological holism within the human sciences. These episodes are as follows:

At the time of the debate about the method of the "moral sciences," it was generally accepted that a discipline studying phenomena of a semantic kind would necessarily include a "circle of the part and the whole," or a "hermeneutic circle." Thus, for a text to be explained, one must already have an idea of the meaning of the whole in order to begin to assign meanings to the different parts of that whole. The same observation was later made within American philosophy. An ethnologist approaching a completely new territory confronts a problem of "radical translation" (Quine): how is it that the circle is not a vicious one? Is an understanding attained in this way not simply an interpretation of dubious value? These questions require a philosophical clarification for, in fact, it does not prove impossible for people to read new texts or to learn a completely novel language by being immersed in it.

Another debate, also ostensibly about method (much like Dilthey's dispute with positivism), involved two opposing schools in social philosophy: one claiming that society is more than a set of individuals and another that says that it cannot be anything other than such a set. This debate took an analytic form after the partisans of "methodological individualism" followed Karl Popper in his program of reducing social totalities to mere "logical constructions," which amounts to turning the word "society" into an oblique way of referring to the individuals forming the group. Here we must remember that the adjective "methodological," which is consistently used to indicate the object of debate, is misleading. It is not about limiting oneself to questions of method while leaving the so-called "ontological" question in suspense: the debate involves opposing positions regarding the mode of existence of collective entities.

It is noteworthy that the sociological holism of Durkheim and the entire French School of Sociology that follows him was, at root, a sociology of mind. For Durkheim, what grounds the separate reality of the social are collective representations, above all the great conceptual systems for the classification of things and events. Yet Durkheim never managed to offer a clear explanation of how such collective representations could be present within the thoughts of individuals. By referring to a "collective consciousness," he opened himself up to an objection that was not long in coming—that he had turned society into a great collective individual with its own states of consciousness separate from the individuals that constitute it. On this point, a leap forward was made when social anthropology successfully defined the program of a structural approach to social reality as opposed to a purely genetic approach or a naturalistic (e.g., functionalist) one. After recalling how Gestalt theory triumphed over associationism in psychology, Lévi-Strauss characterized the philosophical change involved:

The same change in attitudes is beginning to appear in the study of human institutions, which are also structures whose whole—in other words the regulating principle—can be given before the parts, that is, that complex whole constituted by the institution's terminology, its consequences and implications, the customs through which it is expressed and the beliefs to which it gives rise.[12]

Thus, the structuralism defended by Lévi-Strauss appears as a particularly sophisticated form of sociological holism. Nevertheless, this structuralism clearly calls for philosophical clarification since it immediately raises this question: how can the whole be given before the parts? This would be impossible if we had not understood that the whole can precede itself in the form of a "regulating principle" and thus as a rule governing the differentiation of the parts according to distinctive oppositions and relations of complementarity within the whole. This is, of course, the basic form of the structural analysis of symbolic systems of any kind.

One need only recall these different debates to notice that the term "holism" covers different and perhaps incompatible positions. It is therefore appropriate to ask the question of anthropological holism as such: in what sense is there a priority of the whole over the parts in the anthropological domain? I have sought to answer this question in five steps:

---

12. Claude Lévi-Strauss, *The Elementary Structures of Kinship*, rev. ed., ed. Rodney Needham, trans. James Harle Bell, John Richard von Sturmer, and Rodney Needham (Boston: Beacon Press, 1969), 100–101 [translation modified].

(1) As a way of introducing the ideas that are today brought together under the name "mental holism," I begin with an idea that is broadly accepted in the contemporary philosophy of mind: that the distinctive logical feature of our concepts of the mental is their intentionality. To think is to think *about something* or to think *that something*. But how are we to characterize such relations between a mental act and its object since, as we know, the existence of the act does not depend on the existence of its object even though we use the object to identify the act? To use Wittgenstein's example: the sheriff can look for the horse thief even when, in reality, this thief does not exist and the horses in question have not been stolen. I have tried to demonstrate that one cannot explain what the intentional relations of mental acts consist in until two dimensions have been introduced.

The first is the holistic dimension of a system of psychological concepts within which they are able to present the characteristic of intentionality. As Wittgenstein points out: if "looking for something" is intentional even in the absence of its object, this is because "to look for" is to seek *to find* and "to find" is necessarily a verb that is really transitive.[13] Or, to take another example: "thinking of Smith" is intentional only because to think of Smith is to think of someone who *is in fact called* Smith and because one can, in certain conditions and through a transitive act, attract the attention of Smith by shouting "Smith!"

The second is the institutional dimension of an objective mind: thus, to speak of someone by calling him "Smith" is, from the perspective of the practice of a language, to designate someone that everyone is able to identify thanks to the institution of the legal name that determines who is called "Smith." It might be objected that there are lots of people named "Smith." This is true, but in our normal use of proper names, we have ways of overcoming possible misunderstandings. Once again, it is the institution that gives meaning to a remark such as this one: "Though this person *is* named Smith, he is not the right Smith, the one I am looking for."

(2) Is such a mental holism an anthropological holism? Several American philosophers, following Quine, have developed a holism that invites us to think of totalities as indivisible collections of elements. A whole is then something like what, in commercial terms, is called a "lot"—i.e., various

---

13. Ludwig Wittgenstein, *Philosophical Remarks,* ed. Rush Rhees, trans. Raymond Hargreaves and Roger White (Oxford: Blackwell, 1975), § 28 (67–68).

articles that cannot be sold separately. One must buy the whole (one might well say "the whole pile") or forgo the purchase. The same is true of the holism that Quine believes has an effect on the verification of scientific theories: we understand that a theory consists in a discourse made up of several sentences, but the discourse as a whole is what must be evaluated by confronting it with our experience, since it is impossible to isolate one or another sentence so as to verify it independently of the others.

Such a holism of the collection (or "collectivist" holism) asks us to understand the word "totality" as a kind of indivisible block that cannot be further broken down despite being made up of several elements. The logical form that corresponds to this is that of a proposition in which the predicate is applied collectively to several subjects, as when one says of the members of parliament—taken collectively—that they have passed a law with a majority of votes, which means that some of them have approved it only in their role as members of the legislative body making the decision and not by their individual vote. In such conditions, it is difficult to see the totality in question as a real one. To believe that a "collective" is something more than a plurality of individuals is to be led astray by the mirage of a collective individual. The criticisms raised by methodological individualism against such a hypostasis are fully justified. But this is not the only conceivable holism.

Collectivist holism makes an indivisible whole out of a plurality. It presupposes no particular relation among the elements of this whole other than the similarity of all being members of the same collection. Yet, the holism that we need in the human sciences is a conception of the relation between the whole and its parts that will explain why and how holistic analysis is possible. The words "holistic analysis" are those that Louis Dumont used to refer to what he hoped to retain from structural analysis for the uses of social anthropology. A holistic analysis consists in the revelation of the relations of dependence among the parts within the whole (as a result, for example, of the differentiation of this whole by various distinctive oppositions). In order to come to a satisfactory redefinition of the holist position, what was required was a properly philosophical evaluation of the structuralist program in the social sciences. This is what I sought to do in two steps: first, by introducing the notion of a *real* system (as opposed to a merely *nominal* system); second, by going back over an ambiguity within French structuralism as it was theorized in the 1950s.

(3) This involved, first, determining whether anthropology can do without the notion of a real totality. In order to do this, I found it useful to go back to the debates at the beginnings of logical atomism and thus, in a sense, at the origin of analytic philosophy—the "revolt" of several self-proclaimed "realists" against neo-Hegelian holism (or "monism," as it was called in Russell's era). In the same period, William James upheld an empiricist pluralism in opposition to the idealist doctrine of internal relations. It was therefore appropriate for me to ask: what can be done with a notion such as that of an *internal relation*?

It seemed to me that the logic of relations could be used to defend the idea that there are relations that constitute real systems formed by the two terms related. As Charles Sanders Peirce showed, this can take place in one of two ways: in a dyadic mode (in which case one is dealing with a "dynamic system" formed by an active subject and a passive object) or in a polyadic mode (which results in a "normative system" requiring *at least* three terms—for example, in the case of a transaction such as *giving*, the system formed by the giver, the thing given, and the recipient).

(4) Thus, the notion of a triadic relation (which necessarily includes a normative dimension) opens up for us the field of those systems dealt with in the human sciences. Such systems are normative ones. This means that the "regulating principle" referred to by Lévi-Strauss in the text cited above must be understood in the sense of a rule governing behavior. It cannot be any sort of mechanism (even a "mental" one) to maintain the regular functioning of a natural system. It follows that what we should retain from structuralism is the idea that the structures of the mind have the characteristics of the normative principles that animate institutions. As a result, we will have to reject various hybrid notions such as those of "symbolic efficacy" or the "structural unconscious." Such notions belong to the regime of dyadic relations, while they nevertheless seek to explain the meaning of our behavior (if only as "meaning effects"). The theorists who have advanced such notions are in reality playing a double game involving both a naturalistic explanation through mechanisms (which are indifferent to meaning) and an explanation through meaning itself.

(5) If we understand structural holism in this way, we will be able to develop it into a theory of objective mind. As has been shown by authors such as Raymond Aron and Charles Taylor, the phenomenological notion of "objectified mind" is insufficient for the descriptive investigation of the

human world. As the term suggests, an objectified mind is the external result, the material trace of the subjective acts that precede it. For example, the speech act carried out by a speaking subject is "objectified" in the form of a text that reports it *verbatim,* and this text is the objectified version in that it appears on a page in a book or engraved in the marble of a monument. To understand this objectified mind is to move from the material inscription to the speech act and from the speech act to the meaningful intention of a subject. By definition, an objectified mind cannot precede the acts of which it is the objectification. It therefore cannot feature as a totality that can be given before its parts. However, to account for social life, we cannot do without the sociological concept of an "objective mind" (another name for Durkheim's "collective representations") or some other equivalent of this Hegelian notion. Indeed, cooperation among the members of a society presupposes the existence of institutions that provide their acts with a common context from which they derive their "objective" meaning, the meaning these acts must have for everyone, including for those who are their originators.

This notion of an institutional context that is necessary for the meaning of an act to be determined, even for the act's originator, provides us with the answer to the question with which this investigation began: how is it possible to know whether two people are or are not thinking the same thing or having the same thought? This is a fundamental question for every philosophy of mind. For if we cannot explain how to identify or differentiate the thoughts of two people, then we also will be unable to state what thoughts an individual has or, for that matter, what our own thoughts are. The answer to this question is that we cannot say whether two people are thinking the same thing unless we have ways of determining in an impersonal way what each of them has said (or could have said) in order to express his thought. This impersonal, anonymous determination is precisely what is made possible by the institutions of meaning in which they participate—for example, their common language and common forms of life.

II

The book thus ends with the response to the initial question asked: what is it to *have the same thought*? Is it possible to determine whether two people have the same thought? This response consists in invoking institutions (such as our linguistic practices), ways of acting and thinking that have been established outside of the individual and that serve as models to guide her in her conduct.

This response also raises new questions that the present book does not seek to answer, though some of its readers believed that it did answer them implicitly. These readers maintained that one cannot speak of objective mind—rather than of a merely "objectified" mind—without subjecting the activities of individuals to established rules. This would amount, according to these critics, to denying that an individual subject is able to have truly personal thoughts. His thoughts would be dictated by the institutions. As a result, according to this view, the individual may well believe himself to be the thinker of his own thoughts, but in reality it is the language or the system of the signifier that thinks within him.

This reading and the objection to which it leads were surprising to me since they repeat an error that I thought I had thoroughly condemned not only in this book but also in *The Mind's Provisions*—an error that goes some way to explaining the sterility of the semiological variant of French structuralism that came to prominence through slogans such as "the unconscious is structured like a language." This error originates in the ambiguity of the term "language" in English (or *langage* in French). One would have to make clear whether one means language in the sense of *discourse* or *parole* (as when the fox speaks to the crow in flattering language[14]) or in the sense of language as code or *langue*. Structural analysis applies to signifying systems, to systems of rules, and therefore to languages [*langues*] in this latter sense. But the fact that a language [*langue*] has a syntactical structure that is binding on all its speakers in no way allows one to anticipate what people are going to say in that language or whether their utterances will be unremarkable rather than inventive or the converse.

14. [Translator's note: The reference here is to La Fontaine's fable "Le Corbeau et le renard" [The Crow and the Fox]: "Maître Corbeau sur un arbre perché / Tenait dans son bec un fromage. / Maître Renard, par l'odeur alléché, / Lui tint à peu près ce langage. . . ." [Perched on a treetop, Master Crow / Was clutching in his bill a cheese, / When Master Fox, sniffing the fragrant breeze, / Came by and, more or less, addressed him so. . . .]. Jean de La Fontaine, "The Crow and the Fox" in *The Complete Fables of Jean de La Fontaine,* trans. Norman R. Shapiro (Urbana, IL: University of Illinois Press, 2007), 5.]

* * *

There remains the question of how "subjective mind" is situated within the surrounding social environment that constitutes an "objective mind" for it—or, to put it another way, how the individual subject relates to the various rules and practices that make up its instituted environment.

I began to answer this question in two subsequent books that elaborate upon the same concept of mind presented in *The Institutions of Meaning*. Where is this concept to be found? Once again, I sought it in the philosophy of intentional action, which allowed me to bring together, using a terminology derived in part from Wittgenstein, an Aristotelian inspiration (not unlike the inspiration for Elizabeth Anscombe's revival of the meaning of the "practical syllogism") and a Hegelian one.[15]

How does the individual stand as a thinking subject—i.e., as an agent of actions that are properly human—when this agent undertakes an action that presupposes the application of instituted rules? This is the question I sought to clarify in *Le Complément de sujet: Enquête sur le fait d'agir de soi-même* [The Subject as Complement: An Inquiry Into the Fact of Acting on One's Own].[16] Does the autonomy of a human agent require that he be the author of the rule that he applies? Can I be autonomous even where I apply a rule that is common to us and was followed by our ancestors? The philosophers who see this as impossible are those who define human autonomy as a form of self-legislation. Yet it is possible to demonstrate, with support from the grammar of action, that self-legislation is a variant of the self-positing by which the metaphysics of the subject (of the *Ego*) defines the ontological status of an autonomous agent. The only way an individual could at once be both the legislator and subject to the legislation would be for her to be split into two people (as in Kant): a transcendental one and

---

15. Elizabeth Anscombe, *Intention* (1957; Cambridge, MA: Harvard University Press, 2000). For the Hegelian inspiration, see the important article by Charles Taylor, "Hegel's Philosophy of Mind," where he writes: "Self-conscious understanding is the fruit of an interiorization of what was originally external. . . . This understanding of conscious self-possession . . . involves seeing our mental life fundamentally in the category of action." Charles Taylor, "Hegel's Philosophy of Mind" in his *Human Agency and Language: Philosophical Papers 1* (Cambridge: Cambridge University Press, 1985), 85.

16. Vincent Descombes, *Le complément de sujet: Enquête sur le fait d'agir de soi-même* (Paris: Gallimard, 2004).

an empirical one. If we set aside this dogma of the self-positing subject, we are left to define autonomy by returning to the domain of rule learning. As long as the pupil is unable to play on her own or appreciate the play of others on her own (both from the point of view of the correctness of the moves made by the players and from the point of view of the abilities evinced by these moves), she has not yet entered into the game and can only participate in it under the tutelage or protection of a player with more expertise. The moment when she can get by on her own is the moment of her autonomy. But to say that she can now play on her own in no way means that she is *subjugated* by the rules of the game as she has learned them. She remains free, if the fancy strikes her, to invent variations or, indeed, entirely unanticipated forms of the initial game. It is precisely now—and only now—that she can do this.

On another issue, the analysis put forward in *The Institutions of Meaning* may well leave the reader unsatisfied. It has been pointed out that the notion of "institutions" is quite general and that there are several varieties of rules, several forms of normativity. This is true. Thus, to take the example that played a central role in structural anthropology, we cannot conflate the rule that *forbids* incest—the prohibition of an act that remains possible—with the rule that *defines* kinship relations and thereby also the possibilities of matrimonial alliance. The boy is forbidden to sleep with his sister (or, within the Oedipal scenario, with his mother), but it is *impossible* rather than forbidden for him to marry her. Nevertheless, to arrive at a less monolithic view on established rules and models of conduct (i.e., institutions) will require us to appeal to the distinctions among the various modalities that can be expressed by the same verbs "to be able to" [*pouvoir*] and "to have to" [*devoir*].[17] These are questions that I

---

17. So, for example, a distinction will have to be drawn between logical (or grammatical) impossibilities where one cannot even describe what carrying out the impossible action would consist in, on the one hand, and physical (or juridical) impossibilities, on the other. The requirement for such distinctions is brought out well in a passage from Wittgenstein's *Blue Book*:

[W]hen one says "You can't count through the whole series of cardinal numbers," one doesn't state a fact about human frailty but about a convention which we have made. Our statement is not comparable, though, always falsely compared, with such a one as "it is impossible for a human being to

addressed more thoroughly in a later book, *Le raisonnement de l'ours* [The Bear's Reasoning].[18]

If I were today to undertake a revision of the present book, I would be able to make use of several recent developments in philosophy, particularly those arising from the fruitful encounter between two distinct currents of philosophy: American pragmatism and German idealism.

Since the publication of this book in France, pragmatism has flourished within the United States. In the 1990s, this school of thought was already showing signs of a revival. At the time, Richard Rorty was drawing inspiration from John Dewey and Wilfrid Sellars, while Hilary Putnam suggested we reread William James. However, both at the time were principally preoccupied with epistemological questions surrounding the justification of our beliefs or the definition of truth. It is not these issues that concern me in the present book but rather questions in the philosophy of mind and of language. This is why I have instead turned to Charles Sanders Peirce and his logic of relations.

Thus, if I were writing this book today, I could make use of the work of what is sometimes referred to as the Pittsburgh School. I could make a place for the concept of a "second nature" that John McDowell has done much to renew.[19] This would allow me to enrich the notion of objective mind, which the present book has already reinterpreted in a broader sense than one finds in Hegel, since the notion elucidated here, like Dilthey's conception, includes language and, more generally, the different components of a culture. It would also allow me to spell out the relations between objective mind and the subjective minds of individuals.

---

swim across the Atlantic"; but it *is* analogous to a statement like "there is no goal in an endurance race." And this is one of the things which the person feels dimly who is not satisfied with the explanation that though you can't know . . . you can conjecture. . . .

Ludwig Wittgenstein, *The Blue and Brown Books: Preliminary Studies for the "Philosophical Investigations,"* 2nd ed. (Oxford: Blackwell, 1969), 53–54.

18. Vincent Descombes, *Le raisonnement de l'ours et autres essais de philosophie pratique* (Paris: Les Éditions du Seuil, 2007).

19. John McDowell, *Mind and World* (Cambridge, MA: Harvard University Press, 1994).

I could also appeal to Robert Brandom's analyses in *Making It Explicit*.[20] Indeed, our respective points of view are entirely complementary. Brandom generally uses the word "institution" to designate the *act of instituting*: there is an institution whenever someone confers a status upon someone else or recognizes someone else as having a status arising out of the normative commitments that result from what they say and do. In the present book, the word "institution" designates, in a way consistent with the definitions proposed by Durkheim and Mauss, the "ways of acting and thinking" that individuals, in coming to the world and acting within it, find already established and already defined. Thus defined in its sociological sense, an institution is the established rule in virtue of which our conduct—in the appropriate context—has a given meaning. And it is this rule that defines the various statuses that we recognize one another as having, whether they be, for example, the relation between a *giver* and a *recipient* (in the case of a gift) or that between the *owner* of something and all those who are *excluded* from its possession or use (in the case of the distinctive opposition that defines the institution of private property). It is clear that the two uses of the word "institution" must join up: if there are preestablished rules, they must have been established by some means (thereby bringing the verbal sense of the word to the fore); but if instituting acts have taken place, it must be possible to identify what has thus been established (and here it is the nominal sense of the word that matters).

But, in reality, one would have to write a new book in order to develop further the notion of objective mind—or any equivalent notion that might be proposed—in these different directions.

---

20. Robert Brandom, *Making It Explicit: Reasoning, Representing, and Discursive Commitment* (Cambridge, MA: Harvard University Press, 1994).

THE INSTITUTIONS
OF MEANING

PART I

Intentionalist Conceptions of Mind

I

The Intentionality of the Mental

This book aims to present and defend a holistic conception of mind. As the words "intentionality" and "intentionalist" are specialized philosophical terms, they will require a more thorough explanation than a mere definition might provide. In this chapter, I hope to provide the necessary technical vocabulary. But before doing that, I should provide some justification for the effort that will be required to come to a sufficiently clear notion of intentionality.

1.1. Intentional Terms

Why should our approach to contentious questions about the mind proceed by way of considerations of intentionality? There are two reasons, both of which derive from the state of such questions in contemporary philosophy.

First reason: it is generally accepted that the description of everything that entails mental life—of opinions, attitudes, and behavior (insofar as an intelligible order can be discerned in it) and even of mores and institutions—must be carried out in what are called "intentional terms." What, then, is a description in intentional terms? To begin to address this question, we should first note that intentional terms are opposed to natural terms. Intentional terms allow us to state how things present themselves to someone. This "someone" need not be a particular someone; it could be a general function or an anonymous entity such as "the public" or "our ancestors" or "the tradition." Natural terms, on the other hand, allow us to state how things are in themselves. Thus, a description of what is happening when what is happening is that *it is raining* will require a descriptive discourse that makes use of natural terms. But a description of what is happening when what is happening is that *it is said to be raining* (or that it is believed to be raining or affirmed to be raining or that rain is hoped for or feared or needed or announced, etc.) will require a descriptive discourse in intentional terms. In this example, the intentional term is the semantic verb "to say that."

That it is raining is a meteorological fact. *That it is said to be raining* is a fact that falls within the purview of the sciences of the mind—linguistics, for example. There is also a formal criterion by which intentional descriptions of the sort given in the sciences of the mind can be recognized: they use what is called indirect discourse, a grammatical form used after declarative verbs and verbs of opinion, perception, or attitude. The construction that allows one to report the *content* of someone's words or thoughts (without necessarily reproducing the words verbatim or the exact form of expression, if any, that the thoughts were given) is, in Latin, called *oratio obliqua*. This construction allowed logicians claim that what is distinctive about intentional verbs such as "to judge that," "to say that," "to believe that," and "to wish that" is that they create an *oblique context* within discourse. Everything that appears within such a context (everything in the sentence that appears in the object clause governed by the intentional verb) tells us not of the world but of what someone thinks or says or believes or wishes about it.

I have set in opposition two types of events: natural events and intentional events. This opposition can be easily transposed into other ontological categories: natural abilities and intentional abilities, natural relations and intentional relations. Are intentional events also mental events? Yes, they are, but only if we hold mental events to be those that are meaningful. Thus, to say that it is raining is an intentional event (and therefore mental in this sense), not because it comprises an *interior* part (thought) added to the *exterior* part (language), but because I have done something other than describe the event of the speech act as a speech act if I have failed to mention that the words uttered meant something. What serves here as the criterion of the mental is not interiority but rather signification. In other words, mind is not found first in our heads and then, derivatively or as an effect, in signs. To make this claim is not to deny that there are interior mental acts or unexpressed mental episodes. It is only to point out that, from the perspective of meaning or intentionality, the interior is not to be privileged—there is a complete equivalence between the interior and the exterior. For example, it will not do to contrast the crudeness of (exterior, material) language with the subtlety of ideas. Books are "mental goods" (Mallarmé) but not because they are exterior signs that refer back to interior ideas in the way that smoke refers to the fire that produces it or, more generally, in the way the work refers back to the worker.[1] The ideas of a thinker are to be sought in the thinker's book, for the only way we have of identifying and analyzing an idea is to identify and analyze the expression it may be given.

That is the first reason: without using the language of intentions, as philosophers know, it is impossible to talk about the meaning of a sentence, the aims of an undertaking, the motives for an action, or the rules observed in social life. Here is the second reason: the language of intentions is as such irreducible to naturalistic language. The recognition of this point, if it were correctly understood, would have important consequences, since it would entail the abandonment of the great positivist project of *a unified science of all phenomena,* which was, of course, meant to include psychology. But if the intentional mode of description can never be eliminated in favor of the naturalistic mode, the sciences of the mind will never form part of the unified science of all phenomena. There would therefore be no such unified science of all phenomena, *unless,* that is, we decreed that the only phenomena worthy of the name are those that can be described in natural terms and that, therefore, only natural terms allow one to formulate genuine descriptions. The human sciences [*Geisteswissenschaften*] would then be something other than the sort of inquiries subject to factual proof that we call "sciences." They would instead be mere personal constructions or free interpretations.

---

1. Stéphane Mallarmé, "Displays," in *Divagations,* trans. Barbara Johnson (Cambridge, MA: Harvard University Press, 2007), 221 (translation modified). [Translator's note: The phrase from Mallarmé here translated as "mental goods" (*la denrée mentale*) is the title Descombes gave in French to the companion book to *The Institutions of Meaning.* That volume has been translated into English as *The Mind's Provisions: A Critique of Cognitivism,* trans. Stephen Adam Schwartz (Princeton: Princeton University Press, 2001).]

Today, philosophers generally concede that intentional language is untranslatable as such into a language that would use only natural terms. Those philosophers who remain committed to the positivist project will then have to find a way to evade this obstacle to a naturalistic psychology. Many have sought to do this using theories of automatic calculating machines (theories of artificial intelligence).[2] For it is true that such machines can be described in two different ways, both as the machines that they are and as if they were the human calculators that they stand in for. Why not reverse the procedure in order to provide two descriptions of an intelligent being? One, in intentional terms, would apply to such a being insofar as it speaks, has goals and ideas, etc. The other, in natural terms, would apply to the mechanical functioning of a machine capable of replacing him. The coordination of these two levels of description would allow us not to *reduce* the intentional to the natural—for the gap between them cannot be bridged—but to locate the former in the latter. Yet such a program would appear to presuppose an atomistic conception of the mental. Otherwise, it would be impossible to coordinate the two levels systematically. It is for this reason that one might well maintain that those in favor of this "research program" are involved in a rearguard action.

I have claimed that naturalist or positivist philosophers could accept the irreducibility of intentionality without having to concede that their program has failed. All they need to do is refuse to acknowledge that intentional utterances are authentically descriptive. To say that *it is raining* might then be the beginning of a scientific inquiry, but to say that *it is said (by someone) to be raining* would be, at best, the beginning of an interpretation. Why would it be an interpretation of natural facts rather than a fact of a different order, an intentional fact? The rationale for this arises out of what is called "mental holism." It is a relatively simple matter to state what one has rejected in claiming that the phenomena of mind are "holistic" and thereby have the character of totalities or complex systems. In doing so, one is rejecting the idea that mental life is made up of atoms of psychic life such as associationist psychology's *mental images* or the *signifiers* posited by theories of the structural unconscious.[3] Once atomism has been rejected, it

---

2. I discuss this naturalistic program in *The Mind's Provisions*.

3. The psychology of the association of ideas spoke of "laws" or "principles" of association; ideas would be combined according to their links of contiguity, resemblance, or

remains to be seen whether one has thereby also rejected any intelligible concept of mind or whether a new concept might be forged that takes into account the impossibility of building the mind up through the combination of representational elements in associative chains. This question, which the present book seeks to answer, will be taken up again at the end of Chapter 3. But first we must clarify the notion of intentionality itself. For example, is there only one possible conception of the property of intentionality? Are there not rather (at least) two intentionalisms, one derived from the philosophical tradition of Brentano and Husserl and another to be sought in the work of philosophers such as Peirce and Wittgenstein?

1.2. Achilles's Psychology

It is important that I explain what distinguishes an intentionalist conception of mind from other conceptions that have been put forward. To propose a conception of mind is not to practice psychology. Philosophy of mind describes neither behaviors nor operations but explains what it is to provide a description of the life or activity of a being from the point of view of the mind. More simply put, we are looking to determine what is distinctive about explanations of a "psychological" type.

I put the word "psychological" in quotation marks for a reason. Psychological attributions are peculiar in that they have two dimensions that can be differentiated: act and content.[4] If we consider a psychological attribution to be the attribution of an *act*, we will think of it as being something individual and even personal. In order for there to be anger, for example, there must be someone who is angry. To speak about Achilles's

---

contrast in the psychological subject's experience. These principles are the same as those used by those characters in novels—such as Sherlock Holmes or Poe's Dupin—whose uncommon powers of penetration allow them to discern the course of others' thoughts. Similarly, although the theories of the structural unconscious borrow the names of their psychological mechanisms from rhetorical tropes (metaphor, metonymy), they would appear to involve the same sort of mechanical association by resemblance or contiguity as in Frazer's *Golden Bough* or Freud's work.

4. The same would be true if the attribution were not that of a mental act (such as thinking about something) but of a state (such as being aware of something) or of a disposition to act or perceive things in a particular way. In all these cases, a distinction must be drawn within the psychological fact under consideration, between the *fact* of the state or disposition and its *content*.

anger is to speak about his "psychology," even if the ancient Greeks would not have put it that way. Achilles has physical attributes (his size, his age, his strength). He also has psychological attributes (for example, he is quick to anger). To speak in this way is to put in place a logico-philosophical (or metaphysical) schema of attributes and their subjects for the description of beings such as Achilles. This schema is not formally any different than that for the description of everyday things: the door and its height, the wall and its color, the water and its coolness, the radiator and its heating power.

But if we consider psychological attribution now from the point of view of its *content,* things present themselves in an entirely different way. From the point of view of content, what is attributed to Achilles when Homer says he is angry is not comparable to a quality or a state. In order to say that Achilles is angry, we have to talk about the content of this anger. But in order to render this content, we will have to go beyond the person of Achilles. We will have to talk about Achilles's place among Greek warriors, about Agamemnon, about Briseus, etc. The description of the angry Achilles requires that we discuss the features of his *pathos*.

Contemporary philosophers claim that a concept such as *anger* is an intentional concept in that one cannot be simply irritated—one must be irritated or angry *with someone*. More generally, the description of a person is intentional if it requires us to specify not only the person's act or state but to do so with reference to an object. I will come back shortly to the reasons for calling Achilles's anger an intention. For now we should note that the intentionality of Achilles's anger does not inhere in some voluntary or deliberate quality of that anger. It inheres rather in the fact that the anger concerns or has as its object *Agamemnon*—not Agamemnon *per se,* but Agamemnon insofar as he has taken some of the plunder that belongs to Achilles. The remarkable thing here is that, because its content can only be stated in public or impersonal terms, Achilles's anger is not a simple state of Achilles. Generally, the content of psychological descriptions is to a great extent impersonal. To take another example: when I think about the door to my house, my concept of it may well be different from yours. But it is not a concept of a door at all if it is nothing but a wholly personal attribute.

Considering together the two observations just made brings a problem to light. On the one hand, the concept of mind calls for individuation since mind is manifest in living persons. On the other hand, the concept of mind cannot be treated as though it were entirely the concept of a personal attribute. While people exhibit mind in their own behavior, the *content* of what they exhibit is largely impersonal. The concept of intention seems to call for us to locate mind in the intentional subject (in his head), but it quickly becomes apparent that that is not its place. It is rather that the subject, in order to acquire a mind, must be situated within a milieu that would have been described in classical French as "moral" or in German as "spiritual" [*geistig*].⁵ This moral milieu is formed by institutions as providers of meanings that individual subjects can make their own.

These remarks provide an indication as to why this book in the philosophy of mind has in its title the word "institutions," which more readily calls to mind the philosophy of law or of sociology than of psychology. The thesis of this book will be precisely that the *objective mind* of institutions precedes and makes possible the *subjective mind* of particular persons, although both of these terms will of course need to be made clear. This is the defining thesis of what I will call *anthropological holism*.

1.3. Brentano's Thesis

In one sense, the phrase "the intentionalist conception of the mind" means nothing more than the expression "the contemporary conception of the mind." Currently, as I have mentioned, the thesis of the intentionality of mind is broadly accepted. It has therefore ceased to be a thesis altogether, for want of a rival. Nevertheless, the agreement of philosophers about this

---

5. Hegel himself pointed out the equivalence between the philosophical French word *moral* and the German *geistig* in § 503 of the *Encyclopaedia of the Philosophical Sciences*. "Moral" is here not to be taken in the narrow sense of what is good or honorable from the point of view of morality: "In the French language 'le moral' is contrasted with 'le physique', and means the spiritual [*das Geistige*], intellectual in general" G. W. F. Hegel, *Hegel's Philosophy of Mind: A Revised Version of the Wallace and Miller Translation (Hegel's Encyclopaedia of the Philosophical Sciences)*, trans. William Wallace and A. V. Miller, rev. Michael Inwood (Oxford: Oxford University Press, 2006), § 503 (224). It is worth noting that William Wallace, the original English translator of this text in 1894 rendered *das Geistige* by "the mental": G. W. F. Hegel, *Hegel's Philosophy of Mind, Being Part Three of the Encyclopaedia of Philosophical Sciences,* trans. William Wallace (1894; Oxford: Clarendon Press, 1971), § 503 (248).

matter remains trivial and obtains only on condition that the infamous property of intentionality is not explained.

There is a school of thought that understands intentionality according to a doctrine called "Brentano's Thesis." Brentano, as one might imagine, never spoke about anything called Brentano's Thesis, but he did write that the domain of the mental (in other words, of psychology in his view) could be delineated using the property of intentionality as a criterion. Take any attribute: if it is intentional, it is mental; and if it is mental, it is intentional. But the thesis is not and, moreover, could not be limited to that claim. In order to claim that what is intentional is *ipso facto* mental, one must also say something about the nonintentional. If an attribute is not intentional, then what is it? The answer is that it is *physical*. This gives rise to the counterpart of the thesis regarding the mental: nothing that is intentional is physical and nothing that is physical is intentional. The question that we must now ask is whether this philosophy is the only intentionalist conception of the mind that one might propose.

A remark by the philosopher J. N. Findlay captures well the essence of Brentano's Thesis. Findlay says that what assures that intentionality is the mark of mind is that we cannot imagine a purely physical thing having a relation to anything but itself: "Whether stones refer to objects or not, it is impossible to say, but, if they do, they undoubtedly have, or are, minds."[6] We do not know whether stones have activities or states by which they refer to the world that surrounds them (and this we do not know, apparently, because one would have to *be* the stone in order to verify that it is not endowed with intentionality). Nevertheless, we know in advance that, if they do so refer—if they open themselves on their own to objects outside of them—then they have mental properties. Findlay's example of the stone is not chosen at random but meant to be the very embodiment of material weight, inertia, and indifference to the external world. Stones are at the opposite pole from mind, which is to say that the tenor of the problem would have been utterly changed if the philosopher had taken as his example, say, a bird or a house pet.

6. J. N. Findlay, *Meinong's Theory of Objects and Values,* 2nd ed. (1933; Oxford: Clarendon Press, 1963), 6. This general notion of reference as reference to some other thing is often used to explain Brentano's conception of intentionality. This notion must not be confused with Frege's concept of *Bedeutung,* despite the latter having been translated into English as "reference."

I will refer to Brentano's conception of intention as a *Cartesian* one, but not in order to trace its historical lineage. Descartes, to my knowledge, never used the word "intentionality."[7] Nevertheless, once Brentano's Thesis has been understood in this way, it satisfies the great Cartesian principle that insists that operations of the mind (*mens*) must be distinguished from operations of the body.

Brentano's Thesis invites us to think that subjects can relate to objects or engage with them in two different ways: physically or mentally. If I drive my car, the relationship is physical, but if I merely think about or admire my car, the relationship is mental or intentional. The philosopher's aim is to bring out the difference between these two types of acts or operations.

Every intentionalist conception of the mind will set the intentional and the physical in opposition, as I myself have done in my discussion of the two modes of description. Yet, it would be wrong to rush to the conclusion that such an opposition is necessarily of a Cartesian, or dualist, variety. Consider again the example of Achilles's anger. It evidently has a physical aspect. Does that mean that his anger is the conjunction of a physical event, which is a function of the body, and a mental event, which is a function of the mind? If anger is to be defined through the conjunction of two events, are these events not rather (1) an event felt to be an insult and (2) a forthcoming event in which amends are made? Confronted with the Cartesian conception, it is possible to define a non-Cartesian position on the intentionality of mental concepts. The elements of such a conception can be found in the work of authors such as Peirce and Wittgenstein.[8]

---

7. By contrast, the Scholastic notion of an "objective reality of the idea," which was later taken up by Descartes, belongs to the history of the theory of the mode of (intentional) presence of objects to the mind. The things we speak and think about are objects of discourse or of thought: they have *esse objectivum* or *realitas objectiva*. This of course is not sufficient to endow them with reality or being properly so called (*realitas formalis*). Concerning the way the history of the concept of intention has been understood by Husserl and Heidegger, see Jean-François Courtine "Histoire et destin phénoménologique de l'*intentio*" in *L'intentionalité en question: Entre phénoménologie et sciences cognitives,* ed. Dominique Janicaud (Paris: J. Vrin, 1994), 13–36.

8. These are the authors whose work inspired Hilary Putnam, in *Reason, Truth and History* (Cambridge: Cambridge University Press, 1981), to criticize several contemporary theories of intentionality and meaning for their mentalism and solipsism.

In a non-Cartesian conception of intentionality, the difference between a naturalistic description and an intentionalist description is not that the former speaks only about physical operations where the latter speaks about nonphysical (i.e., immaterial) ones. Rather, it is a difference in the way the subject is integrated within its environment. The naturalistic description sometimes describes states internal to the subject and sometimes describes its interactions. In the former, the external milieu plays no role. In the latter, the milieu is limited to the immediate environment. An intentionalist description of Achilles, by contrast, recounts an episode in the story of Achilles, an episode that is itself part of the history of the Trojan War. The intentionalist description is thus one that gives Achilles a milieu that is broader than that of his physical interactions. But for Achilles to have a broader milieu than the limited one of his immediate interventions does not mean that he has the power to act *at a distance* or to experience telepathic effects. It remains to be seen what positive meaning an intentionalist description of Achilles might have.

1.4. The Intention of Terms

Let us begin with the word "intention." This word, in its ordinary use, comes from the vocabulary of action. But its philosophical use also derives from logic. A lawyer pleads that his client has indeed committed the acts of which he is accused but has done them unintentionally. An action can thus be carried out with or without an intention to do so. When a logician, on the other hand, uses the term "intention," he is referring to the meaning of a term.[9] What is the relationship between these two uses of the word? The answer can be found by a return to an image that governs the transition between the practical and the logical realms.[10] For a medieval

---

9. It follows that, from a logical point of view, all semantic terms have an intention. Needless to say, not all terms are intentional in the practical sense indicated above. Every semantic term signifies something (has an intention). In order to say what the term signifies, we make use not of natural terms but of intentional terms such as "says," "signifies," "refers to," "describes," "represents," etc.

10. Philosophers who defend the Brentanian intentionalist conception and who see intentionality as an intrinsic property of certain of the subject's states or acts tend to deny that there is any link between practical and logical intentions, as does, for example, John Searle in the opening pages of his *Intentionality: An Essay in Philosophy of Mind*

logician, as Peter Geach explains, the intention of a term is *quod anima intendit,* what the mind aims at in the use of the term.[11] The image that underpins this use of the verb is that of an archer who aims his bow (*intendere arcum*) at a target. Just as the archer moves his bow with an intention, the term that figures in a proposition is also used with an intention. The intention of the archer is to hit the target with his arrow. By means of an easily intelligible shift, we may speak of the "arrow's intention," giving us two intentions: that of the archer and that of the arrow.

To say that the archer has an intention is not to claim that he has some sort of mental activity that would be superadded to his manipulation of the bow. Rather, it is to say that he makes use of the means he deems appropriate to attain his own ends. The archer does not aim twice, once physically and again mentally. In reality, practical intentionality is not an activity at all; in order to have a goal, one need not have given oneself over to some sort of separate mental activity of "intending" or "aiming at" something. To have an intention in doing something is rather to do what one does and to do it with an aim such that there is an *intentional relation* between one's present activity and the anticipated result. The idea shared by the practical and logical uses of the concept of intention is that of an intentional relation.

To say that the arrow has an intention obviously does not mean that it desires or hopes to attain its ends and that it uses various means to do so. The orientation of the arrow relative to its target cannot be expressed in such animistic terms. The arrow does not have an intention in the way an agent or a subject of action would. It has an intention insofar as it is an element of the action and thereby enters into an intentional structure of means and ends. By calling this a "structure," we emphasize that it is a set of relations, at a minimum the contrast between what is attempted and

---

(Cambridge: Cambridge University Press, 1983), vii–viii. Here, I plan to defend the contrary thesis, upheld by critics of Cartesian philosophy of mind such as Charles Sanders Peirce, who stress the unity of the concept of intention. See Christiane Chauviré, *Peirce et la signification: Introduction à la logique du vague* (Paris: Presses Universitaires de France, 1994), 72–74. In *The Mind's Provisions,* I began with intentionality in the practical sense. Here, I aim to present intentionalism starting from its logical sense.

11. P. T. Geach, *Reference and Generality: An Examination of Some Medieval and Modern Theories,* 3rd ed. (1962; Ithaca: Cornell University Press, 1980), 181.

what is achieved. The arrow thus has an intention because it is destined (in this case, by the archer) to hit the target (if the shot is successful).

It might be claimed that the linguistic usage of medieval logicians is distant and irrelevant to today's usage. Yet Brentano himself, in the famous passage cited by virtually everyone who writes about intentionality, does claim to be using a Scholastic term.[12] Even so, he does not make explicit reference to logicians but rather to the psychological doctrines of the *verbum mentis*. Peirce, however, uses precisely the notion of an intentional relation in introducing a logical theory of the proposition. This theory is firmly within modern logic (of which Peirce was, of course, one of the founders).

Peirce wrote several articles in Baldwin's *Dictionary of Philosophy and Psychology,* including the article entitled "Subject."[13] For a logician such as Peirce, the subject in question is the subject of a proposition. More precisely, the "subject" is that part of the proposition that conveys what the entire proposition bears upon, i.e., what contemporary philosophers would call the *object* of the proposition.[14] This should be borne in mind in what follows.

12. Here is the passage to which Brentano owes his notoriety: "Every mental phenomenon is characterized by what the Scholastics of the Middle Ages called the intentional (or mental) inexistence of an object, and what we might call, though not wholly unambiguously, reference to a content, direction towards an object (which is not to be understood here as meaning a thing), or immanent objectivity. Every mental phenomenon includes something as object within itself, although they do not all do so in the same way. In presentation something is presented, in judgement something is affirmed or denied, in love loved, in hate hated, in desire desired and so on." Franz Brentano, *Psychology from an Empirical Standpoint* (1874), ed. Oskar Kraus and Linda L. McAlister, trans. Antos C. Rancurello, D. B. Terrell, and Linda L. McAlister (New York: Routledge, 1995), 68.
13. Charles Sanders Peirce, *Collected Papers of Charles Sanders Peirce*, vol. 2: *Elements of Logic,* ed. Charles Hartshorne and Paul Weiss (Cambridge, MA: Harvard University Press, 1932), § 357 (205–208).
14. Peirce resolutely uses the terms "subject" and "object" in their initial logical sense and not in the way that modern idealistic philosophers use them. For him, a subject is never a psychological creature or hypostasized self-consciousness, but always a logical subject—i.e., the part of the proposition charged with the referential function. As for the object, it is always for him an object of thought. On the logic of the proposition in Peirce, see Claudine Tiercelin, *La pensée-signe: Études sur C. S. Peirce* (Nîmes: Éditions Jacquéline Chambon, 1993), 280–306, as well as Chauviré, *Peirce et la signification,* 157–184.

Peirce begins the text with an explanation of the word "proposition," after having abstractly defined it as a sign that "separately indicates its object."[15] In order to make this definition usable, Peirce provides some surprising examples. If we maintain that portraits and weather vanes are propositions, where is the subject in such cases? Insofar as a portrait states something, it states what someone looks like. The subject in such a portrait would be the name of the person depicted added to the image. Everything else would be the predicate. The words "Portrait of Mister N" written below the portrait would thus be the logical subject of such a proposition-painting. Insofar as a weather vane states something, it states which way the wind is blowing. How does it do this? It is able to do this because it is constructed in such a way as to visibly indicate the wind's direction to us. A weather vane has a real relation to the wind and it is this real relation—determined by its construction—that distinctly indicates its reference.

It might be objected that although the apparatus of the weather vane has been constructed so that the action of the wind determines the position of the pointer (which is the predicative part of the proposition), the portrait is not bestowed with a real relation to the original by adding the inscription "Portrait of Mister N" to it. The relation between the weather vane and the wind is real because it is natural and, indeed, causal in that the wind acts on the weather vane. The young woman whose portrait and inscription state that they are her portrait (by naming her) has no natural power to act upon the portrait. Only the painter or viewer provides the painted canvas with a relation to the young woman. This relation is therefore an intentional relation.

This is correct. The portrait has no direct real relation with the original. Where the original ages in the way living beings do, the portrait ages in the way that painted canvases do. The addition of the name of the original does not put the predicate of the proposition in a relation of direct dependence with what it is meant to portray (the visual appearance of the original). More generally, the proper noun has no real relation with the original. Yes, says Peirce, but the name *did* have such a relation, and that is sufficient for the needs of communication in signs. For Peirce, the linguistic class of nouns is derived from pronouns. In his view, pronouns do

---

15. Ibid.

not replace nouns—nouns are put in the place of pronouns to allow us to speak about things in their absence. If there is no direct relation between a portrait and its original, there is in the portrait an indication (the inscription below the portrait) that posits that there was such a relation, that the image in the painting is that of the person named, just as the name inscribed is the name that was given to the person by means of a real relating of the naming sign and the person to be named. In other words, the relation of reference is a physical relation; even if it is no longer a physical relation in the current use of the signs in question, the important thing is that it *was*.

Both cases are propositions because we can distinguish two elements of the sign: one part that plays the role of a predicate and another part that is a real relation or, failing that, takes the place of a real relation to something else. The examination of the portrait as sign prepared the way in Peirce's analysis for the examination of propositions properly so called, those made up of words. Such propositions also do not have as subjects an element that is in a real relation with an object. But they necessarily contain an element that can be considered to replace this real relation. Peirce goes on to give a third example that serves to mediate between his previous examples, on the one hand, and the kinds of classical examples one finds in treatises on logic, on the other: a baby points at a flower and says "pretty." Peirce's analysis is to distinguish two elements in this speech act; the word "pretty" is a symbol, for the word must be used and understood as a sign in order to have any kind of signifying power.[16] The relationship between this adjective and the flower is an intentional relation (here, the intention to describe). In contrast, the relationship between the pointing finger and the flower is a real relation—the arm is in fact pointed toward the flower even if it turns out that this gesture was not intended to indicate the object to which the adjective applies. Thus, in this case of the finger pointing at the flower, two relations will have to be distinguished: (1) a real relation that does not depend on whether a signifying function is given to the gesture; (2) an intentional relation, which the gesture acquires

---

16. Peirce's analysis recalls that of Rabelais. Gargantua, admiring the handiwork of his mare who has cleared a vast forest above Orleans, declares "Je trouve beau ce" [I find beautiful that], "and *Beauce* has been its name ever since." Rabelais, *Gargantua and Pantagruel,* trans. M. A. Screech (New York: Penguin Books, 2006), 256.

when it is intended and understood as a sign that informs us of the identity of the subject of the proposition.

More generally, an intentional relation in discourse is a relation by which this discourse refers to the world. This relation is definitively underwritten by the fact that something is inserted into the discourse whose function might almost be said to be to insert the *thing itself* into *language*. Needless to say, this introduction of the thing into discourse is merely an appearance, for it is only in language that contact is made between the predicate and the thing (for example, in the association of the noun and the verb). Contact is made in language, but it is not made in the predicative part of the proposition. Nothing in the predicate indicates that it is intended by the author of the proposition to describe one thing rather than another. This information must be provided elsewhere, in a discrete part or, as Peirce puts it, "separately." There are words and linguistic constructions that have this function of ensuring that the predicate applies to one thing rather than another. They can do this because they make use of a real relation in order to base an intentional relation on it.

The key to all of this is the distinction between a real connection to things and a connection that is only intentional. The weather vane has a real or natural relation to the wind. The portrait has an intentional relationship with the original just as does the proposition with its object (via the noun).

The principle of every intentionalist philosophy is the opposition between these two relations. This opposition will therefore be prominent in the work of every intentionalist. Consider, for example, what Husserl says in a paragraph that bears upon "the spiritual ego in its comportment toward the surrounding world."[17] In the *cogito,* the ego is brought into a relation with its world, i.e., with things and with men. This relation is in no way a real relation; it is an intentional relation to a real object.[18] The

---

17. Edmund Husserl, *Ideas Pertaining to a Pure Phenomenology and to a Phenomenological Philosophy, Second Book: Studies in the Phenomenology of Constitution,* trans. Richard Rojcewicz and André Schuwer (Dordrecht: Kluwer Academic Publishers, 1989), § 55 (226).

18. "This relation is not immediately a *real relation but an intentional relation* to something real." Ibid., 226–227 [emphasis in original].

difference, for Husserl, is this: I am the one who has an intentional relation with the object, which is given to me, appears to me, is noticed by me, etc. A real relation is above all a causal relation between an object and me, i.e., me as this human being, this body, this flesh. "The real relation collapses if the thing does not exist; the intentional relation, however, remains."[19] Let us suppose that the object of the intentional relation does exist. I will have two *parallel* relations to this (real) object: a real relation and an intentional relation.[20] The relation to a real object is, according to Husserl, a psychophysical fact. But such a fact is inconsequential for anyone describing intentional relations, which are not affected by the unreality of the object.

Every intentionalist philosophy, as I say, will set these two types of relation in opposition to each other, but it remains to be seen whether the distinction is defined in the same way. As we have seen, for Husserl, a subject can have both types of relation (in parallel) to a real object but only an intentional relation to an unreal object. For Peirce, things present themselves somewhat differently. Here is how he applies the distinction between the real and the unreal to a phenomenon such as dreams:

> "Real" is a word invented in the thirteenth century to signify having Properties, i.e., characters sufficing to identify their subject, and possessing these whether they be anywise attributed to it by any single man or group of men, or not. Thus, the substance of a dream is not Real, since it was such as it was, merely in that a dreamer so dreamed it; but the fact of the dream is Real, if it was dreamed; since if so, its date, the name of the dreamer, etc. make up a set of circumstances sufficient to distinguish it from all other events; and these belong to it, i.e., would be true if predicated of it, whether A, B, or C actually ascertains them or not. The "Actual" is that which is met with in the past, present, or future.[21]

The dream is real, but the characters who present themselves to me in the dream are unreal. Because they are unreal, I cannot have any relation

---

19. Ibid., 227.
20. "[E]ach time the Object does exist a real relation runs 'parallel' to the intentional relation. . . ." Ibid.
21. Charles Sanders Peirce, *Collected Papers of Charles Sanders Peirce*, vol. 6: *Scientific Metaphysics*, ed. Charles Hartshorne and Paul Weiss (Cambridge, MA: Harvard University Press, 1935), § 453 (311).

to them, not even an intentional one. Intentional relations must be with real objects. Otherwise, there might well be *the intention of a relation* to something, but there cannot be a *relation of intention* to it.

Husserl claims that, in the case of a real object, the subject of the mental act can simultaneously have real and intentional relations to the object. In this case, the intentional relation is "parallel" to the real relation. I do not want to give the impression of encumbering what is, after all, a mere analogy with more than it can be made to support. But it so happens that the figure of two parallel lines allows us to ask a central question for any reflection about intentionality. If the two relations are parallel to each other, does that not suggest that they never meet (at least if the image is taken from Euclidean geometry)? This is apparently how Husserl understood the matter: the intentional relation does not depend on the real relation, is not affected by it, and can survive its absence. But, if the two never meet, in what way are they relations to the same object? Should we not rather say that the real relation is the relation to a real object and the intentional relation is a relation to an intentional object? As we will see, Husserl strenuously criticizes any doubling of the object that would prevent us from having intentional relations to real objects. We should therefore look to his work for a way of avoiding this doubling (see the discussion below on the ideality of the object).

For his part, Peirce would have to say that the two relations to the object are not parallel precisely because they must meet in the object. In order for the weather vane to indicate the direction *of the wind* it must be in a real relation with the wind. Similarly, in order for the proposition that claims that "Socrates is seated" to bear upon Socrates, a real link between the name "Socrates" and the person of Socrates must be supposed. More generally, the predicate of a proposition is supposed to describe an object, but the link between the predicate and that object is purely intentional. In other words, when used in an empty way—i.e., without being applied to one thing rather than another—the predicate is nothing but the *intention* to describe an object (no object has as yet been described). In order for the proposition to bear on the object aimed at, it must contain an element that identifies what is intended. By itself, the proposition about Socrates wants to say something about someone, but it will not speak to *you* about anyone at all unless you already know who Socrates is. The proposition tells you *who is seated*: Socrates. But the proposition does not tell you *who Socrates is*. You will have to have learned this by some other means and cannot discover it by analyzing the propositional sign. This point is fundamental for Peirce. He illustrates it using the example of a geographical map. A map is the description of a territory and is thus essentially predicative. But a map tells you nothing about the position of real objects for as long as you are unable to find on the map the point where you are and at least one other point so as to orient it.

Describe and describe and describe, and you never can describe a date, a position.... It would, certainly, in one sense be extravagant to say that we can never tell what we are talking about; yet, in another sense, it is quite true.[22]

Has Peirce here discovered what Arthur Prior calls a "defect of language"?[23] It is not one as far as ordinary communication, which is always contextual, is concerned. It might seem to be a defect, though, if one had hoped that the sign would be sufficient to determine entirely its object and therefore to posit its own relation to the object. The defect exists only if one holds a dyadic conception of the semantic relation (see below, chapter 4, section 4).

We will therefore have to ask whether intentional relations can subsist without a real relation, as the Brentanians and Husserlians claim.

1.5. Intentional Presence

In an article that did much to revive the theme of intentionality among those schools of contemporary philosophy that had not been influenced by phenomenology, Roderick Chisholm begins by citing Wittgenstein's remark that "I can look for him when he is not there, but not hang him when he is not there."[24] This remark obviously alludes to the adage about the difference between hanging a thief in the flesh and hanging him in

---

22. Charles Sanders Peirce, *Collected Papers of Charles Sanders Peirce,* vol. 3: *Exact Logic,* ed. Charles Hartshorne and Paul Weiss (Cambridge, MA: Harvard University Press, 1933), § 419 (260).
23. A. N. Prior, *Objects of Thought,* ed. P. T. Geach and A. J. P. Kenny (Oxford: Oxford University Press, 1971), 147.
24. Roderick Chisholm, "Sentences About Believing," *Proceedings of the Aristotelian Society* 56 (1955–1956): 125. The citation of Wittgenstein is from Ludwig Wittgenstein, *Philosophical Investigations,* rev. 4th ed., ed. P. M. S. Hacker and Joachim Schulte, trans.

effigy. There is a difference between what I can do to a thief when he is within my grasp and what I can do to him when he is out of reach. The latter actions, bearing upon the absent thief, are purely intentional. Even if Wittgenstein did not use the word "intentional" here, Chisholm is perfectly correct to claim that this sentence seeks to bring out what is proper to intentional verbs such as "to look for" as opposed to "to hang." Yet the entire difficulty is one of knowing whether this way of distinguishing the intentional and the nonintentional corresponds to the distinction drawn in Brentano's Thesis. Chisholm's commentary immediately following the citation from Wittgenstein is interesting in this regard.

> The first of these activities, Brentano would have said, is *intentional*; it may take as its object something which does not exist. But the second activity is "merely physical"; it cannot be performed unless the object is there to work with.[25]

Whether deliberately or not, Chisholm's gloss slightly distorts what Wittgenstein said in such a way as to make it accord with Brentano's Thesis. Wittgenstein speaks of a thief who is sought because he is elsewhere. Chisholm moves from this object, which cannot be found *here,* to a nonexistent object, one that could not be found no matter where we might happen to be. The epitome of an intentional activity would then be not the search for an object (to be found wherever it may be) but rather fiction or error, thinking directed to beings that do not exist (e.g., Pegasus, a square circle, etc.).[26] On might respond that, of course, a transition from absent objects to nonexistent objects is possible. The victim of a hoax

---

G. E. M. Anscombe, P. M. S. Hacker, and Joachim Schulte (1953; Oxford: Wiley-Blackwell, 2009), § 462 (141). Chisholm's text is the one referred to by Quine in *Word and Object*. The importance of Quine's commentary on Chisholm's text for this entire debate derives from the fact that these two thinkers have diametrically opposed philosophies of mind. They nevertheless agree on one point: intentional descriptions are irreducible to physical descriptions. This is the consensus I alluded to earlier. See Willard van Orman Quine, *Word and Object* (Cambridge, MA: MIT Press, 1960), § 45 (216–222).

25. Chisholm, "Sentences About Believing," 125.

26. All of the philosophers of the School of Brentano (Brentano himself, Meinong, Twardowski, Husserl), give a great deal of attention to examples involving what they call *irrealia*—mythical entities, legendary characters, impossible objects, etc. In this they seemed to some to give philosophical support to Symbolist and Post-Symbolist literary movements that see fiction as the emblem of the superiority of mind over nature. This encounter took place in France in the writings of Sartre, Blanchot, and Derrida on Mallarmé.

might well seek someone that cannot be found and for the simple reason that the description provided is of an imaginary person. This is why, the response continues, the distinction Wittgenstein makes does not exclude the possibility that the search might be for something that does not exist. Nevertheless, this response must be set aside. When we learn that our search has no object (because of the nonexistence of the person we are looking for), we give up our search. Now imagine that we were discussing Pegasus and that someone reminds us that Pegasus is a mythical horse; that would hardly be a reason to stop our conversation.

But there are more serious issues. I can look for my thief when he is not here. But how could I search for my thief if he does not exist? Who would "my thief" be if my thief turns out to be nobody? In order to assign an object to an intentional activity, is it not necessary, as Peirce maintains, that it be supported by a real relation?

Wittgenstein's sentence does not juxtapose a merely physical activity (hanging the thief) with an activity that is not physical—or not only physical and therefore mental (looking for the thief). Hanging and looking for are both physical activities. Wittgenstein did not say that looking for is an activity distinct from hanging in that it is carried out (or can be carried out) in one's head where hanging is necessarily an external activity. It is true that one can look "in one's head" for the location of a file (i.e., one tries to remember where one put it). Looking for a thief, however, is an external activity. It is nonetheless an intentional activity.

The meaning of Wittgenstein's aphorism is rather this: I can recount an episode of hanging by speaking only of what is present at the very instant when the activity is recognized. However, I cannot give a complete (intelligible) description of what a detective is doing if I fail to say who he is looking for, and this requires me to add something absent to what is present.

When the sheriff is looking for the horse thief named Smith, there is no *direct* relation between the sheriff and Smith. Rather, there is a direct relation between the sheriff and various things in his vicinity—his horse, his map, those around him—a relation that he establishes with the aim of being in a position to get his hands on Smith. The relation between searching and the sought object passes through the anticipation of a situation where the search is successful (the sheriff is in close contact with Smith) or is unsuccessful (there is no contact with Smith).

What is at issue is the mode of presence of Smith in the search and the hanging, respectively. In order for Smith to be present in the scene of Smith's hanging, he must be naturally present—i.e., in person, in flesh and blood. In the scene where Smith is being looked for, it hardly matters whether Smith is naturally present or not. What matters is that he is believed to be absent. But it would also seem to be necessary that Smith be present in another way; otherwise nothing would allow the scene to be described as a search *for Smith*. In what way is he present when he is not really present? To speak of Smith's intentional presence in the scene is a way of saying that (1) none of the natural elements that make up the scene is the man we are looking for and (2) what is effectively present in the scene is the search for someone named Smith. In other words, the man is not there; the only things that are there are the people who are looking for him. Nevertheless, we cannot do without the mention of Smith, who is not there. Let it not be said that Smith is indirectly present in the form of some external or even cerebral effigy. *He is not there at all.* It is pointless to say that the sheriff has in his possession a photograph or a description of Smith, for they do nothing to provide Smith with a natural presence. In fact, they add nothing at all, for the photograph is only that of Smith by virtue of having been connected to Smith by an intentional relation.

It is clear, then, that to say that the thief has an intentional presence is not to suggest that a new way for something to be present has been discovered. All that one is saying is that the description of the scene is not complete as long as it is limited to what is naturally present.

What has to be added in order to give Smith an intentional presence in a scene where he has no natural presence? Classical intentionalism, as exemplified by Brentano's Thesis, maintains that what must be added are mental acts endowed with an intrinsic power to be directed at objects, without any dependence on the real presence of those objects here or anywhere else. How are we to understand this claim?

1.6. All Consciousness Is Consciousness of Something

I have claimed that Brentano's Thesis posits a criterion for the mental. Everything intentional is mental and everything mental is intentional. It matters little how this criterion was devised—whether it began with the mental to find that it was intentional or, conversely, with the intentional to realize that it was always mental. What matters for us is that the thesis proposes a criterion that is absolutely general in scope. It basically tells us this: look at as many cases of the mental as you please, and you will see that they are all cases of intentionality; take as many cases of intentionality as you like, and you will have to admit that they are all instances of the mental.

What, then, is intentionality when it is seen as a property that is characteristic of all mental acts and states and only of mental acts and states? In the philosophical literature, three formulas for intentionality have been proposed.

(I) *All consciousness is consciousness of something.* Modern philosophers regularly refer to any and every mental form as "consciousness." For example, when someone sees a tree, what is said to happen is that she has visual consciousness of a tree or, better still, that she *is* a visual consciousness of a tree, as the Cartesians would say. And if someone remembers an upcoming appointment, he has (or is) a memorial consciousness of an appointment. These two examples make plain that every attribution of a mental event is the attribution of an event that is related to an object. More generally, to have a representation is to have a representation of something.

(II) *All consciousness is directed toward an object.* Or, put another way, to be conscious is to go beyond oneself toward an object. For example, to imagine is to imagine something other than one's own thought, or it is to be present, in one's thought, to something other than one's thought.

(III) *In all consciousness, something is presented to the subject.* For example, in every representation something is represented, in every instance of love something is loved, and so on. Every mental act is about something other than the act itself.

Each of these formulas commits us to conceiving intentionality according to a particular category. To know which category in each case, it is useful to pay some attention to the grammatical form in which the thesis is expressed.

According to the first formula, intentionality is something like a *transitive state* of the conscious subject. As a result, mental phenomena will be defined as intentional states.

The second formula sees intentionality as a *kind of activity* and no longer just as a relation. Consciousness, it is maintained, is the way in which the conscious subject exists and behaves and is present; it cannot *be* without *being outside itself* among things. Such a formula is preferred by those philosophers who see the intentionality of mental acts as a mark of the *ekstasis* or *transcendence* of the subject. Where natural things exist by remaining in themselves, the subject exists by ceaselessly projecting itself outside of itself.

The third formula associates a fact expressed in the passive voice with the fact in the active voice that was emphasized in the second formula. When someone perceives, something is perceived. When someone imagines, something is imagined. When someone loves, something is loved.

To sum up, formula I tells us that what is intentional are the subject's mental states. Formula II tells us that what is intentional is primarily the being or mode of being of the subject. And formula III tells us that what is intentional is the being or mode of being of the objects of thought.

All of these formulas present two difficulties. First, they define intentionality by means of a certain *transitivity*. If we were to take them at face value, we would have to maintain that every transitive action is a mental phenomenon. Second, the transitivity here ascribed to mental phenomena is far from clear. In what way can it be said that being imagined *happens to the Eiffel Tower* when someone imagines the Eiffel Tower? In what way is this an event that affects it? When the Eiffel Tower is repainted, the painters' activities really affect the Eiffel Tower, but the activity of simply thinking about it does not affect it at all. Nothing happens to it. This is another application of the previously discussed adage that one can initiate an intentional activity that bears on someone in his absence. Let us consider an objection made by Anthony Kenny. After citing the famous page from Brentano, Kenny makes the following comment:

> In reading this passage we feel a certain difficulty. It is true that where there is love then *something* is loved, if there is to be hatred then *something* must be hated; but is it not also true that if heating takes place then *something* is heated and if cutting takes place then *something* is cut? "Heat" and "cut" are not psychological verbs: how then can Brentano say that object-directedness is peculiar to psychological phenomena? He appears to have taken a feature common to all grammatically transitive verbs as being a peculiarity of psychological verbs.[27]

27. Anthony Kenny, *Action, Emotion and Will*, 2nd ed. (1963; London: Routledge, 2003), 136.

The question one would like to ask those who subscribe to Brentano's Thesis is a grammatical one: Does your definition of intentionality not simply conflate it with transitivity, as your formula seems to imply, so that not only are the verbs of intentional acts transitive but all transitive verbs are then verbs of intentional acts and therefore mental? If so, what do you do with verbs that are not psychological? In a footnote, Kenny cites a page from Husserl's *Ideas,* claiming that it might be taken as a response to this question. On this page, Husserl provides a list of examples of intentional "experiences." There we find not only "psychological phenomena" such as those mentioned by Brentano, but also action itself. Husserl writes that "perceiving is the perceiving of something" and judging is the judging of something. He finishes his series of examples with acting and doing: "Acting concerns action, doing concerns the deed" (*Handeln geht auf Handlung, Tun auf Tat*).[28] To do is to do something; all doing is in relation first with what is to be done before eventually being done. Kenny wonders, then, whether Husserl has failed to consider that any action that has an object is, by this definition, accurately characterized by its intentionality.

If this were so, we would have to conclude that, for the phenomenologist, to heat is not necessarily to heat something and to cut is not necessarily to cut something. If a verb's transitivity is the mark of the mental, there can be transitivity only where there is a (conscious) mental direction toward the object of the action. The suggestion might seem disconcerting, but it would be precipitous of us to dismiss it out of hand. In order to see this, let us take up Michael Dummett's commentary on Brentano's definitions.

1.7. The Unconditional Transitivity of the Mental

In a study comparing the ideas of Husserl and Frege on perception, Dummett is led to address "Brentano's celebrated . . . thesis on intentionality."[29] In the course of explaining the doctrine, Dummett finds

---

28. Edmund Husserl, *Ideas: General Introduction to Pure Phenomenology,* trans. W. R. Boyce Gibson (1931; New York: Collier, 1962), § 84 (223).
29. Michael Dummett, "Thought and Perception: The Views of Two Philosophical Innovators," in his *Frege and Other Philosophers* (Oxford: Oxford University Press, 1991), 264.

Brentano's formulation of it lacking and suggests a correction. He does this with the aim of making the account clearer, not to put forward his own ideas on the subject. The result of this correction is thus not a thesis about intentionality that can be ascribed to Michael Dummett but rather Brentano's Thesis on intentionality as Brentano should have formulated it (in Dummett's view) had he taken some possible objections into account. What objections? Precisely the sort of grammatical objections that Kenny raises.[30]

Dummett first notes that Brentano's distinction is poorly drawn. Under "psychical phenomena," Brentano provides a list of mental acts signified by transitive verbs. The list comprises the following: "any idea or presentation which we acquire either through sense perception or imagination." To be more specific, it includes such things as "hearing a sound, seeing a colored object, feeling warmth or cold"; also "thinking of a general concept" as well as judgment, recollection, expectation, inference, conviction and opinion, doubt. Finally, it includes emotions: "joy, sorrow, fear, hope, courage, despair, anger, love, hate, desire, act of will, intention, astonishment, admiration, contempt."[31] All of these phenomena have an object.

When it comes to "physical phenomena," Brentano refers to perceptible qualities: "a color, a figure, a landscape which I see, a chord which I hear, warmth, cold, odor which I sense; as well as similar images which appear in the imagination."[32] None of these have an object intrinsically. Dummett makes the following remark:

Since his "physical phenomena" are not acts in even the most general sense, and cannot be referred to by transitive verbs, it would be literally ungrammatical to speak of them as having, and therefore, equally, as lacking, objects. What Brentano means is best seen by contrast with what we should ordinarily call a physical act, for instance that of kicking a football. The object of such a physical act is extrinsic to it *qua* physical act.[33]

---

30. In what follows, I will not speculate about whether the reformulation is justified within the context of a historical exegesis of the totality of Brentano's writings. It is sufficient for my purposes that the reformulation is philosophically justified looking only at the authoritative formulation as it appears most often in the literature on intentionality. My aim is only to understand the thesis on the transitivity of mental acts.
31. Brentano, *Psychology*, 60.
32. Ibid., 61.
33. Dummett, "Thought and Perception," 264.

Here again the discussion moves into grammatical terrain. Dummett's criticism of Brentano is essentially that he has compared *adjectives* (qualities) with *transitive verbs* (acts). According to Dummett, what Brentano should have compared were transitive and intransitive verbs. This would have immediately led him to consider the ineluctable objection that there are also verbs of physical action that are transitive. To imagine is to imagine something, for example, a flowering pear tree. But to kick is to kick something, for example, a ball. By Brentano's criterion, every transitive verb would denote an intentional act and every act would be a psychical one! To kick a ball would be a mental and not a physical action. This objection confronts the Brentanian with a paradox that arises from his own definitions.

Dummett's reformulation allows the Brentanian to respond simply by accepting the paradox. By adopting Dummett's reformulation, he can respond to Kenny's objection by saying that, indeed, the grammar of an ordinary language contains transitive verbs that are in no way intentional, such as "to kick" or "to heat" alongside other transitive intentional verbs such as "to imagine" and "to love." But the transitivity is not the same in the two cases. If we now draw a distinction between the contingent transitivity of the verbs of physical action and the necessary transitivity of the verbs of mental operations, it is then true to say that, in a sense, only the psychological verbs are truly transitive.

In what sense? In the sense that they are *intrinsically* transitive. This is what Dummett's remarkable example of kicking a football shows. Dummett continues:

> Up to the point of contact, the act of kicking the football would have been exactly the same if the ball had not been there: it is only to the intention underlying the act that the object is intrinsic, in that I should not have had precisely the same intention if I had meant just to make a kicking motion without impact. In a different terminology, the relation of a physical act to its object is external, that of a mental act to its object internal.[34]

The response attributed by Dummett to his (corrected) Brentano-Husserlian philosopher is thus that, contrary to what was believed outside

---

34. Ibid., 264–265.

THE INTENTIONALITY OF THE MENTAL

of the circle of philosophers, verbs signifying a physical action carried out on an object are not the most exemplary transitive verbs. There are verbs that are more transitive still. The argument can be delineated as follows:

1. The description of a physical action such as kicking a ball *qua* just such an action of kicking a ball *is not* a strictly physical description of that action.[35] Indeed, this action could be carried out in just the same way, up to the moment of impact with the ball, without there even being a ball present. The mention of the ball is thus external to the physical reality of the action. The kicker cannot swing his leg or move his foot if there is no leg to swing or foot to be moved; the physical action therefore takes place where the leg and the foot are and not where the ball happens to be. And for as long as the ball has not been touched, it is indifferent to whatever might happen to the foot. If the ball could undergo some modification simply because a foot had been moved in its direction and without physical contact, the ball would be an animate being possessed with the means to detect movements in its vicinity and the ability to be disturbed by them.

2. In everyday language, there is of course such a thing as the physical action of kicking a ball. But we must be careful here. When we express ourselves in this way, we bring various physical episodes together under an intention; we speak for example of a foot that will soon strike the ball. In order to provide a strictly physical description, one would have to break down the action in a (Cartesian) dualist way: on the one hand, the *physical* component of the action (the gesticulation, which is only contingently linked to its effects on what surrounds it); on the other, the intentional or *mental* component.

3. The description of the kicker as performing the act of kicking the ball is thus a hybrid description. It could even be said that it makes use of illegitimate concepts, since it mixes up the mental and the physical, the intention and the impact. One might speak here of a Cartesian philosophy of intentionality, not in order to suggest that it has been derived from

---

35. *A* ball, and not precisely *this* ball rather than another. Dummett sets in opposition the intention to effectively carry out the kick and that of only going through the motions without touching the ball. He does not take up a further distinction between the intention to kick this ball in front of me and the intention to kick any object of the football type that happens to be located at the end of my foot's trajectory.

Descartes's writings or even elaborated under his influence, but just as a way of saying that it respects the great principle of dividing the vocabulary of human affairs into two separate parts, with one lexicon for operations of the body and another for operations of the mind.

4. Dummett's reasoning supporting the Brentanian criterion for the mental is based on a consideration of the temporality proper to different types of actions. When we speak of the action of kicking a ball, we are describing a process by its result. If the ball has not yet been kicked, the process is identified by the result it will have in a moment. In order to be perfectly accurate, one would have to say, "the result that it *may* have in a moment." Between the current moment and the moment still to come of the impact of the kicker's foot upon the ball, there is a gap that one's imagination can fill with all manner of interruption. During the interval between the present action and the result to come, the ball could at any time be annihilated (for example, through the intervention of a higher power who, like a Homeric divinity, would deprive the kicker of the fruit of his efforts).

Since any change tending toward a result can be interrupted and since, therefore, it can tend toward a result that in the end will not obtain, it follows that one cannot speak of purely physical tendencies. To do so would be to attribute to natural movements an aim or the intellectual anticipation of their results in the way one does for intentional movements of which we say that they have failed to produce the result intended when, precisely, this result does not come about. Physical movement is never oriented, for in that case it would have to aim at its result *regardless of what happens*. But to aim at a result no matter what in fact happens is precisely what we call an intentional aiming at the object. Here we again find the Cartesian demand that the properly physical universe be stripped of anything that resembles a tendency to, propensity for, or a continuity of movement.

To recapitulate: Brentano's Thesis cannot be a thesis on the characteristic property of the mental without being a thesis on the difference between the mental and the nonmental. It is therefore a thesis concerning every sort of thing and in that sense a metaphysical thesis. After the clarifications we have just offered, this metaphysical thesis could be expressed in the following way: every action expressed by a transitive verb bears on an object, and there are two ways for an action to have an object.

Some actions have an object if the world is willing to grant them one. We will not say of them (in the present) that they *have* an object but will say (after the fact) that they *had* an object. Physical actions never have an object (in the present); they will have had an object (after the fact) if they interfere with the movements of other physical bodies. More precisely, physical actions only have an object during the brief moment of impact or contact. Since we can consider the entire movement of the foot minus the final impact with the ball, we can therefore detach it from its object. The external world furnishes the object to this act; nothing in the movement of the foot requires that there be a ball at the end of its trajectory. The world, not the act, determines what the object is. The relation remains an external one.

Other actions have an object even if they have no external object. In other words, they have an object by themselves, whether the world provides an object for the act or not. In these cases, we determine the object by looking at the act itself, not by looking at the world.

So it is that mental acts turn out to be all the more transitive if the world does not consent to provide them with anything that might serve as a real object (it is from this that the predilection for cases of mental aiming at fictive or impossible objects derives). The criterion of the mental is then still its intentionality, but redefined as an *unconditional* transitivity.

And if the intentionality of mental acts is an unconditional transitivity, the relation between the intentional act and the object is in one way or another guaranteed by the very nature of the act. The intentional relation to the object needs no real relation; it attains its object by itself. In the Brentanian-Husserlian-Cartesian philosophy of intentionality, intentional relations can and must remain *parallel* to real relations.

The question is then that of the doubling of the object: how can two relations link the subject of the act to the *same* object if they are parallel? How is it that there are not, for intrinsically transitive acts, two objects—first, regardless of what happens, an intentional object and, second, a contingent real object dependent on the vagaries of the external world? This is the question of what might be called "the intentional passive."

1.8. The Intentional Passive

The doctrine of the unconditional transitivity of the mental can be understood as an attempt to provide a solution to a difficulty encountered by the classical doctrine of intentionality. This classical doctrine can be found in the work of Antoine Arnauld and Claude Lancelot, the *General and Rational Grammar* of 1660, which is better known as the *Port-Royal Grammar*. The ideas that interest us are introduced in Chapter XVIII of the Second Part. After mentioning the traditional division of verbs into the three categories of active, passive, and neuter, they write:

> What are properly called *active* verbs are those which signify an action to which is opposed a passion, like *to beat, to be beaten; to love, to be loved*. Either these actions are directed towards a *subject*, in which case they are *real actions*, such as for example *to beat, to break, to kill, to slander*. Or else they are directed only at an *object*, in which case they are called *intentional actions*, such as for example, *to love, to know, to see*.[36]

It follows that we will have to distinguish between two sorts of accusative, two kinds of direction or end to a transitive verb: a subject or an object. The words "subject" and "object" are taken in their traditional sense, which the authors explain in the section devoted to what they call the "accusative":

> OF THE ACCUSATIVE CASE
>
> Those verbs which signify actions which are transmitted beyond the agent, such as to beat, to break, to heal, to love, to hate, have subjects which receive these actions, or objects which these actions concern. For if one beats, one beats someone; if one loves, one loves something, etc. And thus these verbs require that they be followed by a noun which will be either the subject or the object of the action which the verbs signify. It is this which has caused a new ending, called the *accusative*, to be given to nouns in languages which have cases. For example, *amo Deum* (I love God), *Caesar vicit Pompeium* (Caesar conquered Pompey).[37]

---

36. Antoine Arnauld and Claude Lancelot, *General and Rational Grammar: The Port-Royal Grammar*, ed. and trans. Jacques Rieux and Bernard E. Rollin (The Hague: Mouton, 1975), 142–143.

37. Ibid., 83–84.

It is remarkable that, for them, the "subject of an action" is not the agent (i.e., what for us is the subject par excellence), but the patient who receives the action, what is beaten in the action of beating or cured by the action of curing. Their distinctions are, then, these:

1) A *real* action terminates in a *subject*. It cannot be carried out if there is not something else that is, as a result of the action itself, the seat of a change. The correspondence between the active and passive forms is then this: when we describe what happens in the active, we express the change as something done by the agent. By contrast, a description in the passive expresses this same change by presenting it as the *passion* that the thing receiving the action undergoes. The patient-subject must *receive* something from the agent—namely, the change that it undergoes.

2) An *intentional* action only terminates in an *object*. This means that the thing that it "concerns" is in no way changed by being taken as the object of an intentional act. It is not the subject of any real change. It is therefore only an object of thought or of speech (whence derives the theory, taken up by Descartes, of the "objective reality" of things in the ideas that we have of them).

From this point of view, intentional actions resemble actions signified by *neuter verbs*. Neuter verbs, as Arnauld and Lancelot explain in the same chapter, are also called "intransitive verbs." Some among their number do not signify actions but rather qualities (such as the Latin *albet*, "it is white"). Other neuter verbs do signify actions:

[T]he other neuter verbs signify actions, but ones which do not pass on to a subject different from him who acts, or which does not concern another object, such as the verbs *to dine, to sup, to walk, to speak*.[38]

Here, the authors have quite clearly distinguished three different types of action. Properly immanent action is that which does not move from an agent to a patient in the way that real action does. Intentional action, by contrast, is an entirely separate category; it is neither immanent nor transitive. This suggests that the philosophies of intentionality had succumbed to the temptation to reduce the number of types of action from three to two. One way do this would be to reduce intentional actions to immanent

38. Ibid., 145.

actions by arguing that they do not establish a real relation to "a subject different from him who acts." This is the sort of reduction criticized by the phenomenologists, following Husserl, who denounced the assimilation of the object of an intentional relation to an immanent object situated in the head. This reduction must fail in their view, because an immanent action is quite incapable of "concerning another object."

The originality of intentional actions can also be misunderstood in another way: by trying to turn them into pure and simple transitive actions. This is the temptation to which Brentanians and Husserlians risk falling prey. One might even claim, along with Dummett, that they have already fallen prey to it, since the transitivity of mental acts implies the intransitivity of physical acts; there would then be only two kinds of action—intransitive (physical) action and transitive (mental) action.

Nevertheless, the classical doctrine seems unsatisfactory in that it does not really explain the status of the action that "concerns" an object. Intentional verbs must signify transitive actions and thus must have the same syntax as verbs of physical action. Yet transitive action does not pass into the thing with regard to which the agent acts, but is limited to "concerning" that thing. Intentional action is thus a kind of transitive action but one in which nothing passes from the agent to the patient. An action arises out of or seems to arise out of the subject, but nothing is received by the object. This *nothing* that must be transmitted beyond what acts and into the object is precisely what is signified in utterances in the passive voice. Thus, intentional action is something real for the subject of the relation. What corresponds to it, as one would expect since the relation is transitive, is a passion on the side of the object of the relation. And yet, this passion is nothing.

Here we must draw a distinction between the respective points of view of the grammarian and the philosopher. For the linguist, the problem of intentional passions presents no difficulties. In every language in which it is possible to say that Romeo loves Juliet, it is also possible to say that Juliet is loved by Romeo. The solution is easy because we are dealing with grammatical passions. So, from the linguistic point of view, passion is not to love but to be loved, since "to love" is the active form of the verb and "to be loved" is the passive.

The philosopher may also wonder about the grammar of statements of passion, but his grammar is philosophical. The *Port-Royal Grammar* is also philosophical, since it draws a distinction (one that the French language does not) between transitive verbs of real action and transitive verbs of intentional action. It is in the role of philosopher-grammarians that we ask whether intentional verbs possess an authentic intentional passive. How are we to account for the *intentional passive* that the philosopher makes use of when he says that, for example, in love *something is loved* and in imagination *something is imagined*?

For the classical doctrine as exemplified in the *Port-Royal Grammar,* intentional actions are more quasi-transitive than transitive. They have an object, but this object is not affected by the action. They therefore form what would seem to be an illegitimate category: the verb of intentional action is transitive, like the verb of real action, but intentional action is immanent, like intransitive action. Things are somewhat different, though, if we follow Brentano's Thesis in insisting that mental acts are not immanent and that they move out of the subject and are directed toward the object. The interpretation of Brentano's Thesis to which Dummett's discussion has led us can be found among all Husserlians, since they contest the error of seeing the intentional object as an object immanent to the mind, i.e., contained within it.[39] Intentional action must be authentically transitive, must pass beyond the subject to reach the object itself. It is pointless to make intentional action terminate in anything other than the thing itself—that is, to make it terminate in an observed object to be distinguished from the subject of real changes.

If mental action must move outside of the subject in the name of its unconditional transitivity, it must be something outside of the subject (just as physical action is outside of the acting subject since it is something that, by the very fact of it occurring, the patient undergoes). It can no longer be claimed that nothing whatever happens to the intentional object. It can equally no longer be claimed that intentional passion is but the

---

39. One does find in the work of Husserl and some of his commentators a polemic against Brentano's theory of intentionality. According to this critique, Brentano turned the intentional relation to the object into a relation to an object contained within the mind. In fact, this critique is unjustified. Stanislas Breton, in a comparative study of three great philosophies of intentionality (those of the Scholastics, of Brentano, and of Husserl) shows that all of them insist on the same point: the relation cannot be with some mental intermediary but must be with the thing itself. See his *Conscience et intentionnalité* (Paris: Vitte, 1956), especially 43–45.

shadow of intentional action, i.e., nothing on the side of the object. The problem that thus arises for the partisan of the transitive or ecstatic character of intentional acts is one of providing a plausible reality for intentional passions.

1.9. The Idea of an Intentional History

Contemporary French philosophy has developed the idea of an intentional history of the object, although the terminology it uses to describe it is somewhat different. By this I am referring to the idea that the history of certain objects should not be conceived as the positive history of a reality independent of humans and that imposes itself on them as a given. The intentional history of an object is that of a reality constituted in and by the thoughts of human actors. These thoughts are the conceptual systems put to work in discourse—in "discursive practices"—as well as in actions. The principle of this philosophy of history is that discursive events are not only linguistic events but are also events belonging to the thing itself. *Things* change (directly) as a result of human *discourse*. The history of these things, as soon as we speak about them, becomes the history of the things we speak about and therefore depends, according to this view, on what we say about them.

The various facets of this idea of an intentional history are by now familiar, even though it was not under this name that they became known to the public. I need therefore only briefly evoke some of the expressions of this idea while taking care to note that each is indeed an application of the principle according to which intentionality is a transitivity. This principle of the unconditional transitivity of the mental allows us to conceive of a historical narrative that is philosophical rather than positive in that it overcomes the separation of the (human) subject and the object. The object's link to the subject is an internal link, an intrinsic relation such that humanity cannot change its ideas or its language without also changing the *world* by that very fact.

What then are the objects whose history must take an intentional form? For a dialectical philosophy of history—if we mean by that a philosophy that seeks in universal history the destiny of the relation between the thinking subject and the objects of his thought—the objects whose history must be thought of as intentional are *all objects* of whatever sort.

The epitome of an intentional event, as we saw when we looked at the medieval origins of the logical use of the word *intentio,* is the imposition of a name on a thing. If we were to express this act from the side of the object, we might say that things *enter* into the language. The issue now is how to conceive of this entry into language as an event in the history of the thing itself or, if you will, how to conceive the history of this thing as ceasing to be independent from the history of signs and this from the very moment where the thing becomes an object of discourse.

Such an idea has become familiar to a broad public under the lapidary formulation given to it by Jacques Lacan: *the symbol is the murder of the thing.*[40] The idea itself comes from Alexandre Kojève's lessons on Hegel's *Phenomenology of Spirit.*[41] It consists in describing the event of providing a common noun for a thing as one affecting the thing itself. This might seem bizarre at first. How can dogs, for example, not be utterly indifferent to the fact of being called "dogs" rather than something else? Is this dialectical form of thinking not, as its critics sometimes contend, a kind of "prelogical mentality"? It is nonetheless worth giving this idea a closer look. How do we ordinarily describe the event of naming seen as an event in the history of the animal who speaks (man) and not in that of the animal spoken about (dog)? The rise of language is seen as an expression of the power of abstraction. Where pure subjects of perception have only animalistic relations to things such as dogs, the situation is quite different for humans who have acquired language. The former may encounter this or that dog; if he recognizes the type *dog* in the canine individual he confronts, he does so without being able to posit this type as separate or for itself. Once language has been acquired, he is able to conceptualize *what a dog is* and to do so without thinking of one or another individual of the species. The imposition of the common noun on a class of things thus

---

40. "Thus the symbol manifests itself first of all as the murder of the thing, and this death constitutes in the subject the eternalization of his desire." Jacques Lacan, "The Function and Field of Speech and Language in Psychoanalysis," in *Écrits: A Selection,* trans. Alan Sheridan (1966; New York: Routledge, 1977), 77.

41. Alexandre Kojève, *Introduction à la lecture de Hegel,* ed. Raymond Queneau (Paris: Gallimard, 1947). [Translator's note: A partial English translation is available as *Introduction to the Reading of Hegel: Lectures on the Phenomenology of Spirit,* ed. Raymond Queneau and Allan Bloom, trans. James H. Nichols, Jr. (1969; Ithaca, NY: Cornell University Press, 1980).]

liberates a universal. In saying this we continue to describe the change in the mental powers of the subject as a change in the object by saying that the universal has been freed from the metaphysical constraint of having to present itself within the limits of a particular individual. The man armed with the concept *dog* can see beyond the particular. Rather than apprehending *universalia in re,* he apprehends them *post rem,* in discourse and in thought.

Kojève presents the exercise of this intellectual power of abstraction as having grave consequences for the individuals that make up the species of dogs. His thesis rests on a somewhat original theory of universals that sets up a pure and simple identity between the *real* essence (the type, the natural kind) and the *nominal* essence (the conditions that *we* put in place for the application of a word to a given thing). When the first man gave the name "dog" (or its equivalent in Adamite language) to dogs, the essence of dogs became the meaning of the word "dog." By means of some speculative word play, Kojève can then move from the theme of abstraction to the theme of annihilation. To extract the universal "dog" from the empirical individual dogs that are given to perception is like making these empirical individuals vanish so as to retain only the universal.

> Without the intervention of the Understanding, the essence "dog" would exist only in and through real dogs, which would in return determine it in a univocal manner by their very existence. And this is why we can say that the relationship between the dog and the essence "dog" is "natural" or "immediate." But when, thanks to the absolute power of the Understanding, the essence becomes meaning and is incarnated in a *word,* there is no longer any "natural" relationship between it and its support; otherwise, words that have nothing in common among them insofar as [they are] phonetic or graphic spatio-temporal entities (*dog, chien, Hund,* etc.) . . . could not serve as support for one sole and selfsame essence, having all one single selfsame meaning.[42]

Kojève clearly subscribes unreservedly to what Quine will later call the myth of meaning. First the essence (or meaning) is borne by an organism

---

42. Kojève, "The Idea of Death in the Philosophy of Hegel," trans. Joseph J. Carpino, in *Hegel and Contemporary Continental Philosophy,* ed. Dennis King Keenan (Albany: State University of New York Press, 2004), 42. The French text is from Kojève, *Introduction à la lecture de Hegel,* 545.

that is its natural support. Then, the essence is borne by a word, which is its symbolic support. The word is thus for Kojève a material support with which an ideal entity, the meaning, has been arbitrarily associated.

In his interpretation of the function of the sign in Hegel, Kojève's personal contribution is to put the stress on what is "negative" in this exercise—that it is an annihilation, a suppression. In doing so, he evokes the famous passage from the Preface to the *Phenomenology of Spirit*, in which Hegel took up the defense of the understanding against the attacks of the Romantics, who condemned the understanding for being able only to abstract or dissect and for thereby being incapable of grasping the organic unity and living totality.[43] Hegel responded that spirit is strong enough to remain undaunted by the work of analysis or the "negative." Spirit does not retreat before the apparent death that abstraction is, because it knows that it will find real unity at a higher level.

Kojève interprets Hegel's position on the operation of abstraction as equivalent to a kind of death sentence or sacrifice. Because the abstraction that frees the universal is also the suppression of all particular and individuating aspects of the thing, it takes on, in Hegel's reading, the appearance of a murder.

This interpretation is obviously arbitrary. In Hegel's text, there is nothing murderous about conception or intellection, the first operation of the mind. Understanding is compared rather to a re-creation or rebirth by which the thing enters into the spiritual universe. Moreover, Kojève himself, in another commentary, discerns this power in an intellect that produces the universal "table" from the perception of a table.[44] But by

---

43. G. W. F. Hegel, *The Phenomenology of Spirit*, trans. A. V. Miller (Oxford: Clarendon Press, 1977), § 32 (18–19).

44. "When I perceive this table, I do not *perceive* that it is a *table*; it is not my perception that reveals to me that *this* table is an instantiation of *tables*. However, the real table is not only a 'thing' with a perceptible form, but also a 'table': i.e., a determinate thing that is called by the word 'table.' Sensations and Perceptions are not all that exists; there are also *words* that have a meaning, that is, *concepts*. The word or the concept, by leaving the specific and determinate content of the perceptible thing intact, separates this content from the *hic* and *nunc* of the Sensation of this thing's being" (Kojève, *Introduction à la lecture de Hegel*, 314). This passage demonstrates quite well the extent to which this theory rests on a representationism. Against the empiricists, Kojève insists that there are not just sensations and perceptions, there are also concepts. But he forgets to add that there are also real tables and not just possible perceptions of tables (if, indeed, this is how we are to understand the idea of a "perceptible table").

systematically drawing his examples of naming from living species, Kojève manages to make his view seem plausible. As long as the universal (which Kojève calls "Meaning" or "Essence") is naturally present, this presence is that of a living animal.

But when Meaning (Essence) "dog" passes into the *word* "dog" . . . the Meaning (Essence) *dies*: the word "dog" does not run, drink, and eat; in it the Meaning (Essence) *ceases* to live—that is, it *dies*. And that is why the *conceptual* understanding of empirical reality is equivalent to a *murder*.[45]

Kojève, it is true, goes on to say that these claims must be taken in a special, speculative way. Hegel is aware that it is not necessary to condemn the dog to death to conceive that it is a dog. What was at issue was only the contrast between empirical individuals (who are born and who die) and our concept, which is that of the type and therefore applies to all, without taking into account their individual differences or the vicissitudes of their existences.

Nevertheless, in a note, Kojève says that the literal and brutal reading of Hegel must not be dismissed: "Let us note, however, that a conceptual or 'scientific' understanding of the dog actually leads, sooner or later, to its *dissection*."[46] There are then two interpretations to be made of the aphorism according to which the symbol is the murder of the thing, two readings that could be set in opposition, by borrowing terms from Pascal: the interpretation of the *spiritual* Hegelians and that of the *carnal* Hegelians.

It is the carnal interpretation that Lacan takes up with brio in one of his seminars from 1954.[47] When the name is imposed on the thing, it is in order to dominate the thing, which thereby loses its independence. Its survival now depends on us, who speak about it. Lacan's chosen example is the word "elephant." One might believe that the history of elephants has nothing to do with the history of the word "elephant," but this would be an error. Thanks to this word, the elephant enters into human deliberations,

---

45. Kojève, *Introduction to the Reading of Hegel*, 140; *Introduction à la lecture de Hegel*, 372–373.

46. Kojève, *Introduction to the Reading of Hegel*, 141; *Introduction à la lecture de Hegel*, 373.

47. Jacques Lacan, *The Seminar of Jacques Lacan, Book I: Freud's Papers on Technique 1953–1954*, ed. Jacques-Alain Miller, trans. John Forrester (New York: Norton, 1988), 178.

which have led to decisions concerning elephants. Rewriting Lacan's claim using the opposition between the natural and the intentional, we will say that the fate of elephants depends more on their intentional history—their history in the minds and speech of humans—than on their natural history.

> With nothing more than the word *elephant* and the way in which men use it, propitious or unpropitious things, auspicious or inauspicious things, in any event catastrophic things have happened to elephants long before anyone raised a bow or a gun to them.[48]

The idea that intentional events are endured by the objects that they concern might seem crude or primitive. I believe that this idea is a profound one, but in the way that a myth is profound. Just as in a myth, the speculative idea here seeks to say everything by means of a striking turn of phrase. Unfortunately, there arises out of this no elucidation of the way in which intentional events—actions carried out by subjects—can also be held to be passions that objects really undergo. Here the myth seeks to provide a single answer to several questions that philosophers normally see as distinct. And the philosophers are right to do so, since it is their job to clarify by drawing the required distinctions.

The first question is that of the psychological operation of abstraction, which is traditionally raised in the following terms: how does one move beyond *images* of things in order to arrive at their *concepts*? The use of language—of symbols—is testimony to the fact that such a move does occur. Yet it cannot be explained by extracting "resemblances" or "points in common" from mental images. We must therefore recognize the intervention of an active intellect in the creation of concepts.

Another question is this: how is it that the human subject does not relate to other humans as counterparts (as beings whose external appearance reflects back to him his own *image*) but rather as partners in dialogical relations involving the exchange of *symbols*? The myth conflates the two parts of this question into one, which it presents as the operation of moving beyond the "imaginary" toward the "symbolic."[49]

48. Ibid.
49. It is worth noting that the front cover of this volume of Lacan's seminar in the original edition published by the Seuil publishing house is not illustrated by an inscription reading "ELEPHANT" but by a photograph of an elephant facing the reader. A final

Finally, a third question is whether concepts purely and simply reproduce a real order of things—the order of natural kinds—or whether, by contrast, they are created by the subject. If they are created, the order of things that they allow us to conceive is itself a created order, a historical order. In this case, it can be said that the things so ordered have an intentional history. But nowhere here is it a question of murder or annihilation; everything takes place within an intellectual order or, to use the title of one of Michel Foucault's books, an *order of discourse*.

Let us now consider the *spiritual* interpretation of the neo-Hegelian speculation on intentional history.

A first example of the spiritual interpretation can be sought in phenomenology. The history of the number *pi* and the history of figures such as the circle or the trapezoid are necessarily intentional histories. They are the histories of the intentions directed toward these objects (although the philosophy of mathematics will have to determine whether they are more appropriately described as *intuitions* or as *constructions*). It might be wondered whether such an idea provides the principles with which to conceive not *all* history but at least the history of everything phenomenal, everything that takes on meaning in the thought and life of humans.

In his introductory text to his French translation of Husserl's *The Origin of Geometry,* Jacques Derrida brought together the neo-Hegelian theme of the concept's eradication of the empirical thing and Husserl's phenomenological reduction. In doing so, he meant to suggest that phenomenology ought to take what was elsewhere called a "linguistic turn." Is the reduction not performed by the simple act of speaking, since language takes us out of the natural world and into the world of meanings (of "essences")? Husserl could then be understood in a linguistic rather than a transcendental way: intentional events are discursive events. In other words, discourse affects, in one way or another, the object on which it bears. It nullifies it as an (ephemeral) empirical object and recovers it as an ideality.

---

note in the text informs us that, at the end of his course, "Jacques Lacan has figurines representing elephants handed out" (Ibid., 287). The passage to the symbolic would appear not to lead to the word and still less to discourse.

On this, Derrida points out that what Husserl prefers to call "objects" have a status that is analogous to that of numbers. Here is Derrida's explanation of what Husserl understands by an intentional relation to an object:

The mathematical object seems to be the privileged example and most permanent thread guiding Husserl's reflection. This is because the mathematical object is *ideal*. Its being is thoroughly transparent and exhausted by its phenomenality. Absolutely objective, i.e., totally rid of empirical subjectivity, it nevertheless is only what it appears to be.[50]

This sense of the term "object" is clearly the condition for Derrida's entire attempt to conceive history itself as an intentional history. He also cites the passage in which Husserl gives the word—the word "lion," for example—a similar kind of objective status. Just as it is the same number three every time one speaks about three units, it is the same word "lion" in use every time the word is written, uttered, etc.[51] There is thus a kind of *neutralization* of empirical existence in favor of an ideality (empirical existence being that of the instances of the word—*tokens*—and ideal existence being that of the *type*). In a footnote, Derrida compares this neutralization to the annihilation of which Hegel wrote, referring to two passages from Hegel cited in two commentaries, one by Maurice Blanchot and the other from Jean Hyppolite.[52] The conjunction of these two references allows Derrida to add the name of Mallarmé, whom Blanchot had interpreted in a Hegelian (or, more precisely, Kojèvian) way, to the other authorities invoked.[53]

---

50. Jacques Derrida, *Edmund Husserl's "Origin of Geometry": An Introduction,* trans. John P. Leavey, Jr. (Lincoln, NE: University of Nebraska Press, 1989), 27.
51. Ibid., 67.
52. Ibid. The citations of Hegel can be found in: Maurice Blanchot, "Literature and the Right to Death" (1949), trans. Lydia Davis, in *The Work of Fire,* trans. Charlotte Mandell (Stanford, CA: Stanford University Press, 1995), 322; Jean Hyppolite, *Logic and Existence* (1953), trans. Leonard Lawlor and Amit Sen (Albany, NY: State University of New York Press, 1997), 32.
53. The intentional event of speech substitutes the poet's words for the ordinary image of the thing, as if the poet were speaking not of the flower but of the archetypal Idea of the flower. "I say: a flower!" It is a marvelous event that is capable of "transposing a fact of nature into its almost complete and vibratory disappearance with the play of the word."

Derrida adds that, for Husserl, such a linguistic neutralization could never be sufficient to change things into pure intentional objects. While there is certainly something ideal about the English word "lion," its ideality is not that of the meaning common to all words used to designate lions in the different actual languages. As for that meaning, it is also an ideality, but not an ideality equivalent to the species of lions, which are contingent creatures. The empirical lion is neither the word "lion" nor the meaning of this word. It is a natural reality.[54] It does not therefore appear possible to turn the history of lions into an intentional history. To do so would be to treat animals like geometric figures, like pure idealities. On the other hand, in the case of the objects of geometry, the history can only be an intentional one. This intentional history, according to Husserl's *The Origin of Geometry,* is a discursive one. Derrida continues:

> Whether geometry can be spoken about is not, then, the extrinsic and accidental possibility of a fall into the body of speech or of a slip into a historical movement. Speech is no longer simply the expression (*Aüßerung*) of what, without it, would *already* be an object: caught again in its primordial purity, speech *constitutes* the object and is a concrete juridical condition of truth.[55]

Intentional history must be the history of entities that are intentional through and through, like numbers and geometrical objects. If the history of discourse is to be simultaneously and necessarily the history of what this discourse talks about, it will be necessary for the thing to be totally created or recreated within language.

Another expression of the idea of an intentional history of some objects can be found in the work of Michel Foucault. Ian Hacking has shown

---

Thus, poetry can evoke without designating, "without the bother of a nearby or concrete reminder." The critics who have commented on this text in the light of the Hegelian doctrine of abstraction have not paid sufficient attention to the fact that, although Mallarmé does speak of an emanation of "the pure notion" or of the "idea" that is "absent from every bouquet," this idea is also "delicate" [*suave*] and it awakens "musically." This implies that we have in no way left the sensible realm for the abstraction of the concept. Stéphane Mallarmé, "Crisis of Verse," trans. Mary Ann Caws in *Selected Poetry and Prose,* ed. Mary Ann Caws (New York: New Directions, 1982), 75–76.

54. Derrida, *Introduction,* 71.
55. Ibid., 77.

that Foucault practiced a certain "dynamic nominalism" in his studies on the human sciences.[56] It is a nominalism in the sense that concepts are held to be pure human creations destined to serve certain needs; among things, there are no natural kinds that correspond to our concepts. We create the categories in which we describe the world. This philosophy of universals, Hacking points out, is untenable when one attempts to apply it to the concepts of natural science: it would amount to denying that, within a science, word and object can be distinguished. But if this distinction could not be drawn, one would be unable to proceed with experiments (i.e., bringing about natural changes in things, changes that are not purely intentional or simple changes in the descriptive vocabulary or the system of concepts). Nevertheless, says Hacking, this philosophy does have something plausible about it if it is applied, as it is in Foucault's work, to the social sciences. There, science constructs its object and it is not always easy—the nominalist will claim that it is impossible—to distinguish the word from the thing, intentional changes from real ones. There must then be a difference. It is impossible to imagine writing the history of cholera, say, as an intentional history, as the victims must have had a real relationship with the virus. By contrast, it is not inconceivable that an intentional history of madness might be written, one in which the insane would be present only as people to be described and classed. Here the intentional history can subsequently be extended by a real history insofar as real passions follow from intentional passions. Indeed, everything here arises directly or indirectly out of the discourse on the object. If a new conceptual system is produced (on the side of intentions) for thinking about madness or crime or the limits of personal life, that very fact suffices to produce new phenomena. Whence the "dynamic" character of this nominalism: with the arrival of a new conceptual scheme, not only are individuals placed in new "categories"—as happened when those with nervous illnesses were reclassified as *neurotics* suffering from psychological complexes—but it also happens that new phenomena are produced. For example, Hacking notes, cases of multiple personality, which were extremely rare in France before 1875, became more and more common after the theory was put forth.[57] It is as if the

56. Ian Hacking, "Five Parables," in *Philosophy in History,* ed. Richard Rorty, J. B. Schneewind, and Quentin Skinner (Cambridge: Cambridge University Press, 1984), 103–124.
57. Ibid., 123.

concept were necessary for the production of this disorder in an individual to occur.

Here again, it would seem that an inappropriate shortcut has been taken. There is surely something to the idea of an intentional history of madness. If we understand a "positivist history" to be one that takes no account of the fact that people *speak* and thereby *give meaning* to mental illness, that they have *conceptions* of it that are themselves historical, then such a positivist history will have to be deemed lacking. But an authentic dynamic nominalism should maintain that the intentional event coincides with the real event—that, for example, people effectively become mad or criminals solely in virtue of being described as mad or criminals (i.e., in virtue of having applied to them the entire conceptual system summed up by the words "madness" and "crime" in a given era). To maintain this, however, would be to give the authors of a discourse a strange demiurgic power over the phenomena of madness or criminal conduct. So, as soon as psychologists produce a new concept of intelligence—"intelligence is whatever my test measures"—they will have *produced* new aptitudes and not just a new system for classifying individuals. In fact, the nominalism that Hacking finds plausible is more moderate. It does not claim that psychiatrists produce hysterics solely by producing theories of hysteria; it says that psychiatrists, by producing concepts of hysteria, put into circulation classifications and symptoms that can thereafter be taken up by the general public. As a result, the intentional event alone is not sufficient to produce neurosis: there must also be people to hear what doctors have to say about the illness and to produce the symptoms described. In such situations, the entire passage from the intentional—the discursive events—to the real rests in the end on the activity by which these people take up the categories and meanings drawn up by the scientists.

It would therefore seem that the philosophers have not been successful in giving a meaning to the idea of an authentic intentional history of the things of this world. Either the history is nothing more than a history of ideas and not things, or it is not really an intentional history, a history of the intentional passion of the world that we talk about.

2

The Paradox of the Intentional Object

2.1. The Cogito as Action outside of Oneself

The question remains: do we have the right to use the intentional passive form? Grammatically, we do. What about logically?

What is the phenomenological response? It appears at first glance to have as its principal aim to explain to us the legitimacy of the use of the intentional passive. It says that things are indeed what are perceived, conceived, loved, and hoped for. When there is perception, something is perceived and what is perceived is, for example, the house, not an image or idea of the house. When there is love, something is loved: it is Juliet that Romeo loves, not some idea that he has of her.

The first generation of French phenomenologists, as it happens, put the emphasis on this aspect of intentionality. Reading the earliest texts of Sartre or Merleau-Ponty, it becomes clear that Husserlian phenomenology was for them the bearer of a message of liberation from traditional theories of knowledge. As a result of these hopes for phenomenology, the heart of the intentionalist thesis was not the fact that thought might be directed toward fictions (e.g., we are capable of thinking about Pegasus). It was rather the reverse: for the "existential" phenomenology of the time, such possibilities must be put into perspective if they are not to end up confirming representationist theories that conceive of the mental as a self-contained sphere, isolated from the world. For these French interpreters the intentionality of consciousness implies that man is constitutively oriented toward the things themselves, and this remains the case even where his thought is directed toward chimeras or myths. In this ecstatic conception of intentionality, to be human is to be present to the things themselves. A phenomenology thus concerned with conceiving the *cogito* as *action outside of oneself* will have to show how dreams, the imagination, delirium, and illusion are also forms of presence to the world and how thinking about Pegasus is not to cease relating to something other than oneself.

As a result, it is not at all insignificant that we can say, in all good logical and philosophical conscience, that things are perceived and that they are loved. The use of the intentional passive is not only legitimate, it is crucial, since it will allow us to affirm the ecstatic or transitive nature of consciousness. In order for consciousness to be a presence to the thing, the thing itself must *receive* this act of the presence of the subject by itself becoming present to consciousness.

But if this is how the phenomenologist hopes to understand the use of the intentional passive, he will have to tell us more. Indeed, we will ask him what exactly it is that happens to the thing when it is the object of an intentional passion. If nothing whatsoever happens to the thing as a result of the intentional action, we may as well say that this passive form says nothing and exists only within a linguistic perspective.

The phenomenological response seems to me to be as follows: something well and truly does happen to the thing when it becomes an intentional object. Its intentional passion is not, of course, a real passion (in the way baldly proclaimed by the neo-Hegelian version of intentionalism). Nothing real happens to it. But what happens to it is not nothing—what happens to it is that it *appears*. What can the action of the subject do to the thing if it does nothing real and in no way touches it? It can make it show itself, present itself, and be given to someone. The intentional event consists, then, on the object's side, in a donation or a manifestation.

We can restate this view by looking at the Port-Royal distinction between the subject-patient and the observed object: when a thing is the object of a thought or feeling, nothing happens to the *subject* (patient) of the natural relation, but something happens to the *object* of the intentional relation.

For example, the phenomenologist might say, "When I perceive a cube, the following happens: an intentional object is constituted for me in the successive acts of perceptual fixation."[1] Each of these perceptive acts is limited to one "side" or "angle" of the thing. The cube itself is never given to perception with all of its six sides at the same time. Nevertheless, each of the perceptions of a side is the perception of a side of a six-sided cube. There is thus at work in this experience an intention directed toward the six-sided cube, one that organizes all of the perceptive operations. On the side of the subject of this intentional correlation, we will find acts whose progression we will have to describe. On the side of the object, we will find a progressive movement of manifestation or of *constitution* of the cube, if the object is a cube, or of the house if it is a house. This movement is precisely the intentional passion that we express in the grammatical form of the intentional passive.

The Port-Royal grammarians drew a distinction between the subject (which undergoes real action) and the object (which is "observed" by intentional action). But care is required: the authors' vocabulary is not a post-Kantian one here. For them, there are not beings that are simple objects (things) and other beings with the superior status of subjects (us). Instead, there are two points of view, two aspects, and two ways of considering a single selfsame thing: as the subject of its changes (when it changes as a result of action on it by another thing) and as object of an intentional act. When the maniac explains his crime of passion by saying, "Your Honor, I killed her because I loved her," he moves from a point of view in which the murdered person is a *subject* of change to one in which she is an *object* of love.

Does the phenomenologist also draw a similar distinction? What I see or what appears to me is the thing itself. Even so, what is constituted by my experience can only be an object; it cannot be a subject of real passions. To perceive a house from every angle may well be to *constitute* it as an object, but in no event can it be to *construct* it as a subject (capable of being inhabited, heated, furnished, etc.). A distinction must therefore be made between the thing as something that can undergo an action (e.g., I repaint a wall of my house) and the thing as it can be constituted in my perception (e.g., a house appears to me).

Husserl takes up precisely this question in his famous paradox of the tree that cannot burn up. Husserl himself calls it the "paradox of the

---

1. See, for example, Edmund Husserl, *Cartesian Meditations,* trans. Dorion Cairns (The Hague: Martinus Nijhoff, 1960), § 17 (39–41).

intentional object" in *The Crisis of European Sciences and Transcendental Phenomenology* as a way of explaining a passage in his *Ideas* that, he says, readers might find unsettling.² There is a tree that can burn up—the tree considered as a natural thing, a botanical reality. This tree is not the phenomenologist's concern. The tree that interests the psychologist who seeks to describe a subject's experience and nothing but a subject's experience is the tree as an object of a perceptual experience, the intentional tree. This perceived tree, unlike the other, cannot burn up.³

The reader is indeed quite likely to find this declaration unsettling. Does Husserl mean to say that it is impossible to see a tree burn up? Certainly not. It is obviously possible to *see* a tree burn up. The perceived tree can be perceived in flames. What is not possible is for it *to be* in flames. Yes, but how can I perceive a tree that cannot be in flames, that cannot burn up, that has no chemical composition? If the thing I see is not combustible, it is quite simply not a tree. This explains the legitimate sense that Husserl's claim is a paradox.

Husserl's response is valid for both the descriptive psychology of experience (as opposed to a naturalistic psychology) and for first philosophy (taking first philosophy to be the attempt to uncover the order in which things constitute themselves in our experience, proceeding from the most derived to the most originary). Let us stick to the response given by Husserl's hypothetical psychologist, who seeks to describe a perceptual experience. The response is that the psychologist is not at all interested in knowing whether the thing the psychological subject sees *is* or *is not* a tree. What interests him is knowing whether the subject *sees* a tree or not, meaning whether the subject has the experience of seeing a tree. The psychologist thus never deals with the tree *simpliciter* (the tree capable of burning up, to take up Husserl's striking turn of phrase). He deals only

---

2. Edmund Husserl, *The Crisis of European Sciences and Transcendental Phenomenology,* trans. David Carr (Evanston: Northwestern University Press, 1970), § 70 (241).

3. "The tree *plain and simple,* the thing in nature, is as different as it can be from this *perceived tree as such,* which as perceptual meaning belongs to the perception, and that inseparably. The tree plain and simple can burn away, resolve itself into its chemical elements, and so forth. But the meaning—the meaning of *this* perception, something that belongs necessarily to its essence—cannot burn away; it has no chemical elements, no forces, no real properties." Edmund Husserl, *Ideas: General Introduction to Pure Phenomenology,* trans. W. R. Boyce Gibson (1931; New York: Collier, 1962), § 89 (240).

with what shows itself in experience to be a tree, what shows itself as a tree. His goal must be to describe the syntheses by which a tree is constituted for the conscious subject in the sequence of her mental acts.

Husserl's psychologist has thereby adopted the attitude that has since come to be called "methodological solipsism." Indeed, Husserl himself was responsible for providing the fullest and most systematic elaboration of the principles of such a method.[4]

In *The Crisis of European Sciences,* Husserl returns to this point so as to declare that the crisis is merely apparent. Taken out of its context, the claim made in *Ideas* might have seemed paradoxical, but on reflection it is not:

[O]ne can say of a simple tree that it burns up, but a perceived tree "as such" cannot burn up; that is, it is absurd to say this of it, for one is expecting a component of a pure perception . . . to do something which can have meaning only for a wooden body: to burn up.[5]

Husserl does little more in what follows than to remind the reader of the context of what he claimed in *Ideas*. The psychologist, in order to describe experience and nothing but experience, carries out an abstraction. He brackets the natural relations between his psychological subject and the things that surround him (above all, the causal actions of these things on the subject's organism). Thereafter, the tree as a natural thing susceptible to burning up will no longer be an issue. Does this abstraction result in the sort of "psychical givens" so dear to the theorist of the association of ideas? No, because the objects given to the subject have in no way disappeared. In fact, *nothing* has disappeared once one has suspended natural relations. In this way, the perceptions remain perceptions of the tree. The psychologist will therefore be obliged to speak of the tree in order to speak of this perception.

But which tree are we referring to here? The error of the naturalistic psychologist is to believe that it is nothing but the tree *simpliciter*. But this

---

4. The same objections can therefore be made to this solipsism as can be made to more recent versions of the doctrine. Husserl tells us that the psychologist need never wonder if the perceived trees exist or not. This is highly debatable. Is a psychology of apprenticeship or of deception not obliged to be concerned with precisely the difference between seeing things where they are and seeing them where they are not?

5. Husserl, *Crisis of European Sciences,* §70 (242).

tree is no longer at issue. The object that must be taken into account after the abstraction or reduction is the tree as it is experienced (in perception, in the imagination, in memory, etc.). The difference is marked by a gap that the philosopher will highlight: the intentional tree of the psychologist cannot serve as a passive subject in sentences using physical or causal verbs of action. This tree cannot be destroyed by fire, cannot be cut, etc.

The tree as it is perceived cannot be on the receiving end of physical actions carried out by the natural agents around it. So what can be done to it? The response would seem to be that one can do only one thing to it: one can make it *appear*. It is therefore a subject of intentional passions.

This thesis is difficult to put forward in a fully satisfactory way, but we might have an easier time understanding it if we take note of the fact that Husserl has raised a problem in descriptive philosophy as well as a problem in descriptive psychology.

A problem in descriptive *psychology* is, for example, the problem of knowing how to distinguish perception from hallucination: is there a difference in lived experience between the two rather than a simple difference in the consequences? Is there an experience in which the object is given in the mode of perceptual presence and another in which it is given in the mode of hallucinatory presence? More generally, the task of descriptive psychology is to inventory the forms of consciousness and their systematic relations.

The problem in descriptive *philosophy* is that of knowing what distinguishes a description of a tree from a description of a perception of a tree, given that one must speak about the tree—or, rather, speak as if one were speaking of the tree *tout court*—in order to speak about the case of perception insofar as it is a perception of the tree and not of the church steeple or the cloud. More generally: in what way can a description of intentional acts be a description of the intentional acts themselves, given that it must pass through an identification of the objects of those intentional acts? Husserl tells us that what enters into the psychologist's description are terms one would use while in the "natural attitude" (tree, branch, flowers, garden, etc.), but not with the same meaning. The use of quotation marks allows this difference to be marked.

Every intentionalist philosophy of mind must ask the question of the status of the intentional object, a question raised by Husserl: what, then, is this tree that cannot burn up? For our aim in all of this is precisely to know what makes a description intentional, i.e., not a description of the tree (by its natural dispositions or chemical composition) but of the intentional event (the perception of the tree or the discourse about the tree).

This description of the perception of the tree is carried out in a way that seems to *double up* the description of the tree. Straight off, this makes us uneasy, for we have the impression of being given two incompatible descriptions of the tree. In the natural description of the tree, we are told that the tree is characterized by a variety of natural powers (e.g., that it can be chopped down, cut up, burned up). In the intentional description, we are told that the tree in question no longer has all these properties at the same time that it retains other such properties (e.g., its visible properties: color, external form, etc.).

Husserl's conception is not always easy to work out, especially because of the odd vocabulary he devised. Yet the paradox of intentional objects was not something invented by Husserlian phenomenology. We find a closely related version of it in Proust, with regard to what paintings show. Here is how Proust's narrator describes the paintings painted by the fictional painter Elstir. It is as if, we are told, Elstir were carrying out in his studio a "new creation of the world." He dips into "the chaos made of all things we see" in order to extract and deposit on "rectangles of canvas" here an ocean wave and there a young man dressed in a white twill jacket.

> The young man's jacket and the splash of the wave had taken on a new dignity, in virtue of the fact that they continued to exist, though now deprived of what they were believed to consist in, the wave being now unable to wet anyone, and the jacket unable to be worn.[6]

Reading this passage, one cannot help noticing that, although the text is Proust's, but for the style it could easily be Husserl's. The phenomenologist's reduction might here be called the carrying out of a new creation of the (visible) world. What the phenomenologist calls the "natural attitude" is also apparent in this passage and inheres in the prejudices by which one looks at the painting and seeks something other than the pure visual presence of visible things. Finally, Proust speaks of the new dignity that

---

6. Marcel Proust, *In the Shadow of Young Girls in Flower*, trans. James Grieve, ed. Christopher Prendergast (New York: Viking, 2004), 415.

things acquire in the painter's actions: they are still there even though they no longer have a natural presence. The wave can no longer soak us nor the jacket clothe us. But the jacket and the wave remain present, in a painted presence that is analogous to the presence to mind that the phenomenologist seeks to describe.

What, then, is the descriptive problem common to both the psychologist describing experience as such and the historian of painting describing a picture? It is necessary to both that something be introduced that is neither the tree (in the garden) nor the act of perceiving it—something like the wave painted by Elstir, which is no longer a wave in the sea yet without being reduced to a mere section of the painting. The painted wave is not a natural reality (it cannot splash us); nor is it a real element of the painting considered as a physical entity. To better grasp this, one might imagine a painting whose physical makeup must be restored in order to salvage the painted wave. And if this seems hard to imagine for a painting, one need only replace the painting by a mosaic. One can imagine a mosaic that reproduces Hokusai's famous cresting wave. Over the years, this mosaic has been so abraded that the wave no longer appears. A conservator is then tasked with repairing the missing material parts of the whole so that the wave reappears.

We want to be able to offer a description of the painting (or of our perception, or of a novel) that says *what appears* in the painting (or in our experience or in the novel). If what appears is a wave, we want to be able to talk about that wave. If this wave is reproduced in multiple copies, like the famous Hokusai print, we want to be able to say that the same wave appears in all of them. In all such speech, the wave and the young man's jacket are what a phenomenologist would call "idealities." We cannot enter into contact with these beings. They are ideal objects in much the same way that numbers are. To say that a painting depicts a crashing wave does not mean that it is a portrait of a crashing wave nor does it mean that it is the portrait of some other sort of purely visual wave. It means that there are two ways of identifying the painting or of being able to know if it is the same painting, for example, as one that has been encountered before: by *individuating* it according to its materials (canvas, pigments, glazes, etc.) or by *specifying* it according to its iconic reality, by what it shows. The requirement that old paintings periodically be restored demonstrates that one must do more than conserve the materials that make up the painting in order to conserve the painting's iconic reality. When we identify a painting's iconic content, we describe it but we do not individuate it. The painting of a young man in a white jacket is not individuated by its relation to the object—the young man—in the way that a car might be individuated by its relation to its owner. Indeed, we can identify the owner in ways other than by the description "current owner of this car," whereas we only know the young man by virtue of the painting of him, unless we happen to come across independent means of identifying him (on this, see our discussion of Peirce's analysis of the portrait, in chapter 1).

2.2. Where Do We See the Tree in the Garden?

Are there two worlds—a world of natural trees and another of intentional trees? Similarly, are there waves on the sea, which one encounters at the seaside, on the one hand, and painted waves, which are in paintings, on the other? Husserl emphatically rejects any idea of a doubling of the tree or of a conflict between the real tree and the perceived tree. He repeatedly comes back to the question, perhaps because he sees as constant the temptation to reduce the intentional to the immanent—i.e., to turn the intentional object into a purely mental object. In *Ideas,* just after having written the paradoxical sentence we cited above, Husserl cautions the reader against such a misunderstanding. Doubtless the intentional tree is given (constituted) in and by intention, while the natural tree is given by nature. But it would be an error to set them in opposition by assigning the natural tree to the external world and the intentional tree to lived experience, i.e., to mental life. If we understand the difference between the real object (whose existence is bracketed in the *epoché*) and the intentional object in this way

we are beset by the difficulty that now *two* realities must confront each other whereas only *one* of these is present and possible. I perceive the thing, the object of nature, the tree there in the garden; that and nothing else is the real object of the perceiving "intention."[7]

We should therefore not seek the perceived tree anywhere but where trees are found, e.g., in the garden (if it is a tree in the garden). These

---

7. Husserl, *Ideas,* § 90 (243).

declarations would appear to leave no room for doubt. They have, moreover, been the inspiration for some eloquent passages in the works of French phenomenologists. Sartre, for example, acclaimed this return to things and the expulsion of intentional objects outside of the private realm. In Husserl's thought, he claimed, the real world is returned to us since the tree that we see is *there,* in the external world.

To speak of there being two trees here, one corresponding to the subject of real passions and the other to the subject of intentional passions, would indeed result in there being one tree too many. One of them will have to go. Which one will it be?

One might think that the superfluous tree is the one that attempted to place itself between the subject of the act of perception and the natural tree. Where is the tree that I perceive? It is in the garden. It is in the garden because that is where it grew. In these conditions, the intentional object of perception can only be the natural tree and, as a result, cannot in any way be some other (intentional) tree. On the other hand, the perceptual act has a distinctive orientation or meaning—a content, but not an object—that results in this act bearing on this tree and not, say, on the house or on the cloud. This interpretation has been proposed several times, particularly by philosophers keen to bring Husserl's analysis closer to Frege's.[8] It has in its favor that it considerably simplifies the armature of distinctions that an intentional relation would require us to put in place. For Frege, semantic relations are triadic, as we know. For example, a proper noun: it is a *sign*; this sign designates an *object* and has a referential relation to what it names; it has this reference in virtue of its *sense* [*Sinn*]. For Frege, the sense or meaning is the way in which the name presents the object. Two proper nouns can present the same object in different ways (same reference [*Bedeutung*], different sense [*Sinn*]). The idea that inspires the partisans of a syncretic fusion of phenomenology and analytic philosophy is that of

---

8. This interpretation was proposed, notably, by Dagfinn Føllesdal in a series of articles. See especially his "Husserl's Notion of Noema," *The Journal of Philosophy* 66, no. 20 (1969): 680–687. This article was translated into French for an issue of the journal *Les études philosophiques* (January–March 1995) devoted to the convergence between phenomenology and analytic philosophy. In the same issue, François Rivenc's study "Husserl avec et contre Frege" (13–38) demonstrates convincingly that any such convergence is illusory. The most extensive presentation of the "convergence" interpretation to my knowledge is that of David Woodruff Smith and Ronald McIntyre, *Husserl and Intentionality: A Study of Mind, Meaning, and Language* (Dordrecht: D. Reidel, 1982).

applying this Fregean analysis of the semantic relation to what Husserl says about the intentional relation: there is an *act* that possesses a *meaning* (it is, for example, a "perception-of-a-cube"); in virtue of its meaning (*Noema*), the act must bear upon this or that *object*. Perhaps, but is what Husserl calls an object the same thing that Frege calls an object? This is not possible, for Husserl believes that our intentional acts can be directed at nonexistent objects, whereas Frege sees names that apply to nothing real as names that are devoid of objects.

If phenomenology could be naturalized in the way that the philosophers of the syncretic school hope, the intentional passions of the object would have to attach to a thing that is in other respects the subject of real passions. But that would mean that an imaginary object would not be subject to intentional passions (it would not be able to appear or be constituted in the syntheses of a consciousness). Husserl undeniably wants to be able to say that Jupiter and Pegasus are constituted by intentional designs [*visées intentionelles*]; they are therefore subject to intentional passions, even though they can undergo no real action on our part.

But what is then to be made of Husserl's many declarations on the absurdity of distinguishing intentional from real objects? Does Husserl not say that the intentional object is the tree perceived "there, in the garden"? Could there be any clearer statement of his unwillingness to draw a distinction between a tree in the garden and an intentional tree?

Yes, but do these declarations state what the partisans of the syncretic reading want them to state, namely *that the intentional object is none other than the object itself*? I believe they mean precisely the opposite, that *the object itself is none other than the intentional object*. They do not mean that there are no objects other than the objects that there really are (the objects that are really objects, or, in the language of Port-Royal, the subjects of real passions). They mean, conversely, that there are no objects other than intentional objects, the objects toward which consciousness is directed. In other words (and this should not surprise us), what prevents the phenomenological response from being synthesized with Fregean semantics and thereby contributing to a grand naturalistic theory of the mind is that this response is an *idealist* one. When all is said and done, phenomenology invites us to allow intentional objects to be constituted in intentional acts and then to proceed to the constitution of physical things (subjects of real passions) on the backdrop or ground provided by intentional objects (subjects of intentional passions).

* * *

Consider some of the declarations that are so often invoked to support the identity of the intentional object and the object itself. What do they say? One might take a look at the *Logical Investigations,* a work well known for having been published prior to Husserl's official turn towards idealism. Take, for example, the following passage from the Fifth Investigation:

> It is a serious error to draw a real [*reell*] distinction between "merely immanent" or "intentional" objects, on the one hand, and "transcendent," "actual" [*wirklich*] objects, which may correspond to them on the other . . . It need only be said to be acknowledged *that the intentional object of a presentation is the same as its actual [wirklicher] object, and on occasion as its external object, and that it is absurd to distinguish between them.* The transcendent object would not be the object of *this* presentation, if it was not *its* intentional object.[9]

This text is so frequently cited and interpreted by Husserl's commentators that one can almost hear their sighs of relief. The fear was of slipping back into a representationist doctrine that separates the subject from the thing by inserting a mediating representation between them, but this citation comforts them that such is not the case: the perception of the tree bears on the tree and on nothing else, there is nothing immanent or mental interposed. Husserl himself wrote as much and did so in capital letters in the original German edition: the intentional object is no different than the object that intention is concerned with. Therefore, these commentators conclude, the intentional tree is nothing but the real tree in the garden, the tree that can burn up.

Nevertheless, this syncretic reading rests on a mistake.[10] For Husserl, there can be a relation to the object even when the object does not exist. Husserl stresses this point: nothing changes for the phenomenologist of conscious intentions if the object at which they are directed does not exist.

---

9. Edmund Husserl, *Logical Investigations,* vol. 2, trans. J. N. Findlay, ed. Dermot Moran (London: Routledge, 2001), 126–127 (italics in the text; in the original German text, the words translated as "the same" and "absurd" are not only in italics but in all-uppercase letters).

10. David Bell has demonstrated as much in his *Husserl* (London: Routledge, 1990), 133–140.

Husserl treats in exactly the same way a relation to the object *Jupiter* [the god] as he does a relation to the object *Bismarck* or a relation to the object *Cologne cathedral* as he does a relation to the object *Tower of Babel.*[11]

2.3. The Ideality of the Object

Experts in the phenomenological tradition had already concluded that the lesson to be drawn from Husserl is nothing other than the thesis of the ideality of objects. I will cite a commentary by Jean Beaufret that is useful here because it bears on precisely the problem that occupies us, that of knowing whether there is one tree or two (one for the real relation and the other for the intentional one).

Beaufret presents Husserl's reasoning as follows. The phenomenologist's concern is to be rid of the idea that the immanent object is the solution to the problem posed by mental acts insofar as they bear upon objects without really acting on them. The immanent object is a representationist solution to the problem of knowing how it is that my perception is the perception of an apple tree and my imagination is the imagination of a winged horse. In both cases I enter into a relation with a representation, an idea that presents me with, in one case, an apple tree and, in the other, a winged horse. The only difference is that the winged horse does not exist, while the apple tree does exist (perhaps). Husserl's objection, according to Beaufret, amounts to this: two apple trees, each as real as the other (one as a botanical thing growing in the garden and the other as an image emerging in my head), do not result in the perception of an apple tree. It serves no purpose to double up the object, because doing so does not move the explanation forward.

Husserl's solution is simply to place the intentional object in the garden: the perceived apple tree is in the garden. Thus, in Beaufret's view, Husserl's solution is to get rid of the external apple tree; it is superfluous here because it has been posited to be extraneous to consciousness, which could only indirectly infer its presence through an inductive process. Nevertheless, Husserl's solution is not a classical idealism, for Husserl does not locate the apple tree within consciousness (where it could only appear as a mental object, which would be *insufficient,* Beaufret claims, to explain the perception

---

11. The examples are Husserl's. See *Logical Investigations,* vol. 2, 99.

of the apple tree). It is, rather, a phenomenological idealism in which the object of consciousness is to be sought in the external world. It clearly remains an idealist response since the apple tree has been derealized. It loses something (in appearance)—its reality outside of consciousness (i.e., natural reality, the reality it has when it bypasses consciousness so as to be what it is). But it also gains something: presence to consciousness, which neither the external apple tree of common sense nor the image of the apple tree of naturalistic psychology possesses.

It is therefore in a sense derealized, that is, stripped of its existence outside of consciousness. But in another sense it is much more real than a simple image within us, since it is there *before* us in the garden. The true apple tree is thus no more *within* consciousness than it is *outside* of it, and this is what makes it all the more present to consciousness.[12]

Phenomenology understood in this way is opposed to common sense. Beaufret continues: "There is no other reality of things than their intentional reality," and this is as true for the apple tree in the garden as it is for "the abstract ideality of the seven regular solids."[13] The same status is thus given to apple trees as to "idealities" such as numbers or geometrical figures.

It is worth noting that the intentional reality of an object can only be its intentional passion, that is, the reality that it receives from an intentional action directed toward it or that constitutes it. This means that, in the course of explaining Husserl's thought, Beaufret is led to adopt almost the exact formula put forward by his teacher at the Sorbonne, Léon Brunschvicg (from whom he no doubt felt he had broken): the history of Egypt is the history of Egyptology. Brunschvicg might just as well have said that Egypt's only reality is its intentional reality, the reality it receives because historian-subjects constitute it through their attentions and intentions toward it. (Beaufret's students would take up this idealist motif in turn; but while subscribing to Brunschvicg's paradox, they would also have come up with their own formulations, talking about how discursive practices construct, with different truth and reality effects, the historical entity called Egypt.)

It is difficult to see in something's "reduction" to its intentional reality anything but a philosophical witticism designed to wake up the drowsy

12. Jean Beaufret, "Note sur Husserl et Heidegger," in *De l'existentialisme à Heidegger: Introduction aux philosophies de l'existence,* 2nd ed. (1971; Paris: J. Vrin, 1986), 122.
13. Ibid.

reader. It of course means that the apple trees would be nothing to us if we did not perceive them in one way or another. But to say that their reality is entirely intentional says more than that because it amounts to saying that the apple tree has no natural activities such as growing, nourishing itself, or growing apples. Or perhaps it means that its only natural activities are those that we constitute by the sequence of our intentions when we intend the meaning of (the words) "apple tree." It is as if we were told that there is no other reality to war than what the newspapers say about it (i.e., its "media reality"). It seems to me that our first reaction to this "reduction" would be to interpret it charitably: the newspaper readers back home only know about the war what the papers are authorized to say about it. We would thereby understand that there are no doubt aspects of the war that we know nothing about. Yet it would be surprising, to say the least, if we were expected to understand this reduction as an ontological thesis to the effect that there is no battle but only journalists writing articles about battles and that the battle is nothing but an intentional object constituted in and by their journalistic practices.

Beaufret seems to be saying that we can do without the exterior apple tree (the apple tree of common sense), for the intentional apple tree (the perceived apple tree) can be placed exactly where common sense places it—in the garden. We thus lose nothing through the reduction since there is still an apple tree in the garden. Yet we gain something, since the apple tree in the garden is the apple tree present to mind (the intentional apple tree), whereas the exterior apple tree could only be represented by the subject by means of mental doubles that were insufficient for the task.

This solution seems unsatisfactory because it rests on an ambiguity. What is meant by "the perceived tree is in the garden"? Should one not instead say, "the tree is perceived in the garden"? Here we must decide between two ways of expressing the expulsion of the intentional object outside of the lived experience of consciousness:

(1) The perceived tree is in the garden.
(2) The tree is perceived in the garden.

A statement such as 2 could be a response to an ordinary question: "Where did you see a tree?" Answer: "I saw it in the garden" (i.e., when looking in the garden I saw a tree there). But what is the question to which statement 1 might be the answer? It could be a question in the philosophy of mind: where is the tree perceived? Is it in the eye or the brain or in the garden? In other words, where does the act of perceiving take place? But this is not the problem raised by the phenomenologist. His question is a different one. He seems to want to situate something—the perceived tree. He asks, "Where does one find this perceived tree, that is, the tree as an intentional object?" This question assumes that there is an entity, the perceived tree, to which characteristics can be attributed—for example, that of being located in the garden. According to Beaufret, then, Husserl means to say that the perceived tree is in front of me (and not in the trivial sense according to which the tree, when it is perceived by me, is in front of me). It is situated before me in the garden and not in my head.

It goes without saying that a tree that is in the garden can be perceived in the garden. But the *perceived tree* is to be found neither in the garden, nor in someone's head, nor anywhere else, for there exists no such thing as a *perceived tree*. To speak about a "perceived tree" is, in the current parlance, to speak about the tree *under a description*. Here we will have to provide a short explanation about the logic of the locution "an object under a description."

The logic of this locution is familiar to philosophers of action. It is therefore useful to look to them for its explanation. Take Aristotle's example of a fortuitous meeting. Here is a man walking to the market to shop. He is surprised to encounter there a man who owes him money and whom he has not been able to contact. We will say that his walk is intentional under the description "going to the market to shop" but that it is not intentional under the description "going to meet the man who owes him money." As for the walk as such, independent of any description, it is neither intentional nor unintentional. Elizabeth Anscombe, with whom this indispensable distinction originates, was at pains to point out that it was not an innovation but rather a recasting of the classical distinction between the thing considered in itself and the thing considered from this or that point of view (i.e., *as* this or that).[14] Here we rediscover the distinction employed by Husserl according to which the tree *simpliciter* is

---

14. The distinction is one that she puts to work in her book *Intention* (Oxford: Blackwell, 1957). She later clarified the logic of the expression "*x* under the description *d*" in the article "Under a Description," *Noûs* 13, no. 2 (1979): 219–233.

distinguished from the tree as something perceived in much the same way that a walk in itself can be distinguished from a walk taken as the act of going shopping. Anscombe insists that the locution "*qua* + description" introduces a property that belongs to the predicate and not the subject of the proposition. Transposing her example, a single individual might receive a salary in her capacity as an employee, an honorarium in her capacity as a lecturer, and a fee in her capacity as a singer. She receives, then, a salary, an honorarium, and a fee, but in different capacities. As an artist she receives the fee, as a lecturer or under the description "lecturer" she receives the honorarium, etc. She can therefore without contradiction be both badly paid (as an employee) and well paid (as a singer).

But if this is so, the Port-Royal grammarians turn out to have been right: the difference between the subject of real passions and the object of intentions (i.e., the subject of intentional passions) is a difference between two points of view of the same thing. There is therefore not, on the one hand, a tree *simpliciter* (to be constituted by the objectivization of the perceived tree) and a perceived tree that cannot burn up, on the other. Rather, there is a tree that can sometimes be considered through those of its properties that fit under a description of the perception of a tree (those that constitute the tree's *visibility*), but that can also be considered under other descriptions or other aspects. Husserl, for his part, seems to be saying that it is possible to formulate propositions that bear upon the perceived tree, the tree insofar as it is perceived; the perceived tree, he claims, cannot burn up. If this claim bore upon the intentional object, we would have to ascribe to it the logical subject "the tree *qua* something perceived." This logical subject would be given the predicate ". . . cannot burn up." Such an analysis is quite simply untenable. The form of the attribution "x, *qua* A, is B" should be understood thus: "x is A and it is in virtue of the fact that it is A that x is B." It is then immediately clear that the words "x, *qua* A" do not comprise a logical unit but are instead a propositional fragment that, taken alone, have no meaning since they are equivalent to an incomplete formula: "x, insofar as it is A . . ."[15]

---

15. Bell, *Husserl*, 98–99 and 180–181. On this point Bell follows Peter M. Simons, "The Formalisation of Husserl's Theory of Whole and Parts" in *Parts and Moments: Studies in Logic and Formal Ontology*, ed. Barry Smith (Munich: Philosophia Verlag, 1982), 131–133.

But if the words "the object *qua* something perceived" are not a logical unit that can serve as the subject of a declarative proposition, then the phenomenologist's entire idealist solution collapses. This means that one cannot eliminate the exterior apple tree and replace it with the intentional object even if one subsequently constitutes, by means of a kind of Galilean objectivization, an "exterior" apple tree out of the apple tree of the life-world. It is not possible because, as a rule, there are no intentional objects. Intentional objects are objects under an intentional description. In order to make reference to them, to speak about the apple tree in the garden (of this perception as being that of the apple tree), one must first make reference to the apple tree itself.

If the phenomenological answer is as I have attempted to reconstitute it, this response fails to provide a status to the grammatical form of the intentional passive. There are, as we have seen, two conditions that any such response must satisfy. The phenomenological response only satisfies one: it gives a meaning to the intentional passion of the object. It does so by adopting an idealist theory of the object whose entire reality thereby becomes intentional. Recall that this is the solution with which Sartre's *Being and Nothingness* begins: "Modern thought has realized considerable progress by reducing the existent to the series of appearances which manifest it."[16] But the other condition is not satisfied; there is no authentic relation between an active subject and a passive object. One can (perhaps) say who the active subject is—each of us is supposed to be his own source of intentions. But what is the initiator of, for example, the tree before me? Which tree is at issue? What is the "existent" whose entire being inheres in the series of its manifestations? In order to answer this, one has to make reference to it. But to make reference to it presupposes the establishment of a real relation to something in order to then apprehend the way in which the thing thus identified comes to be an object of intention. This is precisely what phenomenology does not allow us to do.

---

16. Jean-Paul Sartre, *Being and Nothingness: A Phenomenological Essay on Ontology*, trans. Hazel E. Barnes (New York: Washington Square Press, 1956), 3.

3

A Holistic Conception of Intentionality

3.1. On the Correct Use of the Intentional Passive

We have just considered one of the most elaborate solutions yet provided to the problem that concerns us. It is perhaps worthwhile to take our bearings before seeing whether there might not be some other solution.

All intentionalist philosophies of mind draw a distinction between natural relations (of a thing to other things; for example, of a living thing to the things around it) and intentional relations (first of a sign to an object and then, by extension, of an act to an object).

The School of Brentano (by which we mean not Brentano's disciples so much as all those who define intentionality in accordance with "Brentano's Thesis") is distinct in speaking of intentional relations to objects that may not exist. This is because it understands the irreducibility of intentional relations to real relations as a kind of separation. There can be an intentional relation to an object in the absence of any real relation. This possibility is illustrated by cases of fictional, imaginary, or even impossible beings.

Whence a first paradox, the paradox of unconditional transitivity: there is an intentional relation to the object even when there is no object with which to enter into a relation. And a second paradox, which Husserl expressed in speaking about the tree that cannot burn up: even when there is a real tree, this tree only interests us if it is the intentional tree, the tree that, as such, cannot burn (even if it can *be seen* to be burning up!).

Phenomenology *seems* to say that one can use the intentional passive and give it a real value. And this is perhaps what phenomenologists *believe* they are saying when they insist that the phenomenological reduction seeks only to allow us to describe the fact of the appearance of the things themselves. The things themselves are what appear to us, what we perceive. But, in reality, phenomenology ends up saying something completely different. What it says is that one cannot use the intentional passive if one makes its grammatical subject the object of a real relation. The grammatical subject must be the object of an intentional relation. Nothing, then, distinguishes the case of Jupiter from that of Bismarck. However, in an authentic intentional passive, the subject of the verb is a *thing* (a subject of real changes) taken as an *intentional object*. In order to use the intentional passive "is loved" or "is perceived," one must be able to say who is loved (Juliet) or what is perceived (one of the trees in the garden). Here we once again find Peirce's idea: however numerous and systematic our descriptions may be, they do not provide a relation to the object. The intention of a relation to something is insufficient to establish an intentional relation to something.

There then remain two possibilities: (1) intentional relations are not relations at all—they are pseudo-relations, pure appearances, and unable to engender an intentional passive; (2) intentional relations are not independent relations that one might find between an act (taken in itself) and an object but are rather fragments of a greater system that unites internal relations to external relations (this would be the holistic conception). In both cases one ceases treating intentional verbs as transitive verbs. In the first hypothesis one is resigned to saying that they are intransitive, in the second hypothesis that they are neither intransitive like verbs for states of affairs nor transitive like verbs of real action.

3.2. Intentional Logic

The difficulty that concerns us is a logical or, if you prefer, logico-philosophical (i.e., metaphysical) one: knowing whether we have the right to use a form of expression that linguistics manuals do not recognize but whose existence has been brought out by philosophical grammar—the intentional passive.

I borrow the notion of "intentional logic" from Arthur Prior, who defines it as follows:

Having in mind the scholastic view that all mental acts have an intention or reference to an object, I propose to use the phrase "intentional logic" for the study of statements formed by such operators as "It is believed that," "It is supposed that," "It is desired that," "It is feared that," "It is asserted that."[1]

What justifies, in Prior's view, the idea of such an intentional logic is that it allows one to speak about the common logical form of a large number of propositions formed along the lines of "it is believed that." All intentional verbs can be expressed in the form of an operator or a *mode* applied to a proposition (what is traditionally called the *dictum* of the modal proposition). If one can speak of a mode and a dictum here, it is because there are parallels between such intentional operators and more familiar logical modes (e.g., "it is possible that," "it is necessary that"). Prior reminds us that the idea of an affinity among all such operators is not a recent one. Logicians noticed the existence of such parallels quite some time ago.[2] Yet a new impetus for this sort of analysis arose from Quine's identical critical treatment of both classical modal concepts and verbs of propositional attitude.[3] Modalities and intentional verbs have in common that they form contexts that are semantically opaque (from the perspective of their reference to objects). Opacity here means that although we do find in the reported sentence (the *dictum*) a term that the person who originally uttered it meant to refer to this or that object, the context in which the term is used prevents us from grasping this reference. It is as if we were unable to see *what* he is speaking to us about or whether he is speaking *about something* in the world. We are constrained to remain with his intention to speak to us about something that we have no way of identifying other than by that very intention. As we can see, the logician's

---

1. A. N. Prior, *Time and Modality, Being the John Locke Lectures for 1955–6 Delivered in the University of Oxford* (Oxford: Clarendon Press, 1957), 84.
2. See Arthur N. Prior, *Formal Logic* (Oxford: Oxford University Press, 1962), 215–220, as well as "The Ethical Copula" in his *Papers in Logic and Ethics,* ed. P. T. Geach and A. J. P. Kenny (Amherst: University of Massachusetts Press, 1976), 9–24.
3. See primarily Willard van Orman Quine, "Reference and Modality," in *From a Logical Point of View* (Cambridge, MA: Harvard University Press, 1953), 139–159; "Quantifiers and Propositional Attitudes," in *The Ways of Paradox and Other Essays* (Cambridge, MA: Harvard University Press, 1976), 185–196; *Word and Object* (Cambridge, MA: MIT Press, 1960), § 30 (140–145), §§ 41–45 (194–220); and "Intensions Revisited," in *Theories and Things* (Cambridge, MA: Harvard University Press, 1981), 113–123.

semantic opacity has the same effects as does the phenomenologists' "reduction" (*epoché*).

I have highlighted Prior's somewhat dated essay here, not because it offers a perspective on what is called "the semantic opacity of oblique contexts" that is markedly different from what one might find in the work of other logicians, but because Prior's presentation is unusual. It happens that Prior attacks the problem of referential opacity in the form that has been our concern from the start. His analysis might help us to find, within the scope of logical analysis, the essence of the theses that we presented above in a phenomenological mode.

Indeed, as we will see, the question Prior asks (even if he does not refer to an "intentional passive") is this one: when do we have the right to move from the intentional active to the intentional passive?

An intentional logic must first ask this: what does the intentional proposition speak about? The statement "the museum is closed" bears on the museum, but on what does the intentional proposition "it is said that the museum is closed" bear?

For some logicians, the intentional operator "it is said that" completely changes the status of the sentence that follows this operator. The semantic opacity, they claim, is explained by the fact that the operator operates on a sentence. In this view, the statement "it is said that the museum is closed" speaks of a sentence (a reality made of words) and says something about that sentence. It says of the sentence that it is a sentence uttered by people (an implicit "they") and would therefore in no way be about the museum and whether it is closed.

If this were the case, it would mean that intentionality is not at all relational. It is the very principle of intentionalism that intentionality is not a *real* relation. But the conclusion to be drawn from a logical analysis of intentional propositions would be, according to these logicians, even more radical. We would have to conclude that intentional relations are pseudo-relations—i.e., not even "quasi-relations" (as Brentano himself called them). In an intentional proposition, there would be no relation whatever to anything at all. One would never get outside of language (or the mental act). We would have to believe that intentional verbs have the appearance of verbs taking an object but are in fact intransitive.

A HOLISTIC CONCEPTION OF INTENTIONALITY

This logicians' thesis reminds us of the psychological theory of "mental data" that Husserl criticized, according to which the apple tree is not mental data and therefore psychology is not concerned with apple trees unless they are doubled so as to take the form of mental data. Similarly, here, the museum is not a discursive datum, a thing said, and therefore we need not bother ourselves with anything but the words "the museum." To this position, Husserl quite rightly retorted that if the perception is of an apple tree, the psychologist should study perception of an apple tree and not of some psychic entity that takes the place of an apple tree within the subject's mental life. The logicians' thesis gives rise to an analogous objection: if the words "the museum" are in the sentence in order to refer to the museum, these words and their referential relations concern us. Putting the phrase in quotation marks when it is cited or reported cannot mean that this phrase is no longer about the museum or its being closed.

In order to establish this, Prior compares intentional logic to tense logic.[4] Here are two statements that differ only in their linguistic tenses (these examples date from 1956; this is important since what is at issue is the logic of tenses):

(1) Professor Carnap is flying to the moon.
(2) Professor Carnap will fly to the moon.

Everyone accepts that these two propositions bear on Professor Carnap and that there is no problem of ambiguity in the propositions' references to things in the world (Carnap, the moon). We can develop a logic of tenses that expresses temporal differences by means of operators. For example, in order to state something about the future, one might say:

(3) It will be the case that Professor Carnap is flying to the moon.

For the logician, this formulation has the virtue of conveying that the speaker is declaring today that a statement that is not true today (because Professor Carnap was not flying to the moon at the moment when Prior came up with this example) will be true at some point in the future. The

---

4. Prior, *Time and Modality*, 8–9.

logical form is thus that of a temporal operator applied to a dictum. This application of an operator to the initial proposition in no way changes the fact that proposition 3 is about Carnap.

Now we need only establish a parallel between the proposition that has been rendered modal by the temporal operator, on the one hand, and a proposition made modal by an intentional operator, on the other. Prior invites us to consider the following together:

(3) It will be the case that Professor Carnap is flying to the moon.
(4) It is believed that Professor Carnap is flying to the moon.

Because the complex proposition 3 refers to Carnap and because proposition 4 presents the same logical complexity of an operator applied to a dictum, nothing prevents us from concluding that the intentional proposition speaks of Carnap. The simple fact that an operator has been applied to a dictum does not suffice to suspend or cancel the reference to Carnap. If one maintains that the opacity of proposition 4 rules out any reference to Carnap, one will then have to explain with reasoning drawn from the intentionality of the operator why it is that proposition 4 cannot be paraphrased as follows: there is someone named Carnap, and this person named Carnap is the object of a belief to the effect that he is flying to the moon. This paraphrase is none other than our form of the intentional passive. Can we say of the object that the subject wishes to speak about that it is *about it* that certain things have been said? If we cannot, the form of the intentional passive is illegitimate. If we can, it is legitimate.

I believe we should embrace unreservedly Prior's conclusions here. When *it is said* that Carnap will fly to the moon, Carnap is *someone about whom it is said* that he will fly to the moon. To deny it would be to deny that there are proper names or deny that the words classed as proper names can perform their function as proper names in our discourse. Were it said in a history class that Caesar crossed the Rubicon, the students could not be presumed to have noted a fact about Caesar. On the day of the test, they could refuse to answer questions bearing upon Julius Caesar, claiming that the individual mentioned in the test is not among those they know by acquaintance. "Perhaps you want to ask us about the history lessons we were given by Professor Malet. We can tell you what he said. But our logic of intentional propositions prevents us from being able to tell whether he was speaking about someone and who that someone might have been. Because it is now our turn to recount what the professor said, our answer can only bear upon Professor Malet's utterances." The examiner, for her part, could not write in her report that the history professor, according to his students' testimony, had never mentioned Caesar crossing the Rubicon. The examiner might deem the students' answers to be poor, but she cannot say that they attributed to someone (the professor) statements about someone (Julius Caesar). In short, proper names would be incapable of filling their assumed function, which is to allow us to speak of things in their absence, thereby enabling a witness to report to an interlocutor what he heard said about a third person.

Here we have obtained a first result. The analysis of this example shows how an intentional relation can be obtained. The two conditions recognized above have been satisfied. First, there is a relation to something; this relation is assured by the fact that the sentence contains the name by which the person in question is known. Prior's example is really about Carnap. Second, the entire reality attributed to the subject of the intentional passive is an intentional reality. Proposition 4, of course, does not say that Carnap really is flying to the moon; it says *of him* that this is what someone else said about him. Carnap is the one mentioned, but the statement tells us nothing about Carnap himself. An intentional passion has therefore been attributed by this form of the intentional passive.[5]

Does Prior's demonstration mean that we should reject the thesis of the referential opacity of oblique contexts? That would be an overly hasty conclusion. The examples given above all make use of a *proper name* to assign a reference to what is said in the proposition. But consider now the status of an intentional proposition containing a *definite description*. Here are

---

5. The conjunction of these two conditions comes down to saying that the context created by the intentional operator is well and truly intentional. This also implies that it must be nonextensional. It is nevertheless true and noteworthy that one cannot specify *what is believed* or *what is said* in a language other than the one used by the person whose opinions or statements are being reported. When George IV wanted to know if Walter Scott was the author of *Waverley,* his question did bear upon Walter Scott. Nevertheless, his question was precisely that question and not whether Walter Scott was the same man as Walter Scott or whether the author of *Ivanhoe* was also the author of *Waverley.*

Prior's examples and, here again, he himself uses the form of the intentional passive:

(7) Sid believes that Walter's horse has wings.
(8) Walter's horse is believed by Sid to have wings.[6]

An unbridgeable gap separates the active form 7 from the passive 8, which confirms the distinction drawn by philosophical grammar between verbs of real action and verbs of intentional action. It is impossible to get to 8 from 7 by means of additions bearing on Walter's horse or Sid.

Prior uses several arguments to develop this irreducibility of the passive to the active. First, the belief reported in the intentional proposition gives Sid responsibility for identifying Walter's horse. It is his belief that determines what he takes to be Walter's horse. By contrast, when we declare that Walter does indeed have a horse, we are the ones speaking. The entire problem is knowing whether the words "Walter's horse" when spoken by Sid apply to the same animal that we refer to in that way. As Prior puts it, it would likely serve no purpose to bring Sid to (the actual) horse that belongs to Walter and say, "See, it has no wings." Sid would not contradict himself if he said, "It is true that this horse has no wings, but this is not Walter's horse." He would of course be incorrect, but he would have said nothing illogical.

Here again we find a phenomenological argument: it is pointless to say that the apple tree exists and that it is not a representation. We do not learn that the perception is that of the apple tree by being otherwise informed of its existence. Instead, we ought to learn it through perception itself. But if perception designates its own object, in vain would it seek to bear on the apple tree itself—the apple tree as such that can burn up—for in the end it can only bear upon the intentional tree.

It is just as pointless to leave Sid with the task of identifying his intentional object with the real object by saying:

(9) Sid believes that Walter's horse is Walter's horse.

Here again, Sid is the one doing the speaking. Far from underwriting the coincidence between his intentional object and the real horse belonging

6. Prior, *Time and Modality*, 66–67.

to Walter, statement 9 is trivially true.[7] How could Sid believe anything different? This example does not move us forward.

Here we find another point stressed by Husserl: it is *absurd* to say that the intentional object is something other than the real object, but that does not allow us to give the intentional relation the character of a real relation.

In the end, Prior concludes that the only addition that allows us to move from 7 to 8 is this:

(10) Walter's horse is believed by Sid to be Walter's horse.

This example demonstrates the failure of all these reductions, since it is a proposition in the intentional passive. We must therefore already possess an intentional passive in order to move from Sid's intentional action regarding Walter's horse to a statement in the passive that says of Walter's horse the intentional relation it has for Sid.

This logical analysis leads to the conclusion that one cannot arrive at the intentional passive other than from the intentional passive. In other words, oblique contexts are indeed opaque in their reference. But what are the philosophical stakes of this conclusion? At first glance, it would seem to support those who maintain that intentional description is only possible from a solipsistic point of view. Even when we seem to be speaking about objects, we are in fact speaking about intentional objects and therefore, in reality, about subjects that experience, live through, or carry out intentional operations. And if this is so, the intentional phenomenon that is effectively given to us is not a relation between me, on the one hand, and the apple tree, on the other (or between Sid, on one side, and a horse on the other) but is a whole comprising consciousness and its intentional object, an *ego-cogito-cogitatum*. The logician holding forth about semantic opacity would appear to do nothing but confirm the phenomenologist's views on the effects of the reduction. Just as the phenomenologist is unable to find in the subject's perceptive intention an apple tree able to burn up

---

7. Statement 9 puts words in the speaker's mouth that can only be taken as *de dicto*: Walter's horse, whichever it turns out to be, is certainly Walter's horse.

(but only the intention of such an apple tree), the logician cannot extract from the *dictum,* by means of logical analysis, a part of the proposition that serves to refer to a thing in the world.

I do not believe that we can leave things there. In fact, all that we can conclude is that there can be no legitimate passage from the intentional active to the intentional passive for as long as we are speaking of objects by means of definite descriptions (e.g., "Walter's horse," "the apple tree in the garden"). But this is something we already understood; a real relation is required in order to be able to identify the object through a referential relation.

The time has come to bring together Prior's two demonstrations. When Sid says, "Walter's horse has wings," it has not been said *of Walter's horse* that it has wings, nor has it been said *of a horse* (perhaps another horse). But when it is said that Professor Carnap will fly to the moon, it is said *of Professor Carnap* that he will fly to the moon. It follows that the form of the intentional passive is not to be ruled out as such. What is to be ruled out is the hasty move to this form from insufficient premises or situations that do not allow it. We have already remarked that, in Prior's examples, in one case the proposition is one where the object of reference has been named, and in the other the object has been merely described. If this object has merely been described, it has not really been identified, for the reference—in the strict sense of the *relation* of reference—requires, as Peirce insists, a real or positive connection and cannot arise out of a pure combination of descriptions.

Let us return to the example of Sid attempting to defend his absurd belief by means of the following claim: yes, this horse has no wings, but it is not Walter's horse. The intentional logic of the belief recognizes that the truth conditions of the statement expressing the belief are insufficient to identify *what is believed,* the propositional object of the belief. Sid has not contradicted himself by saying at one and the same time that the horse he is being shown has no wings and that Walter's horse does have wings, as long as he refuses to say that they are the same horse.

He does not contradict himself only because we grant him the privilege of specifying what he means by the words "Walter's horse." As long as he maintains this prerogative, our logic will remain a logic of *subjective* belief, as it were—a belief whose content can only be provided by Sid. The conclusion to the logical analysis of the expression of this belief is that a subjective belief as such remains indeterminate. Sid can speak as long as he likes; we will not know what he believes, because we do not know what or who he is talking about, or at least we will not know it so long as we limit ourselves to an isolated expression of this belief or so long as we imagine we might be able to grasp it in the form of a proposition.

Now consider the case where Sid believes that Walter's horse is faster than the others and will win the race. Yet far from being faster, Walter's horse finishes last. Could Sid, having bet on this slow horse, refuse to pay by claiming, as above, that "yes, the horse that you are pointing to did lose the race, but I retain the prerogative of saying which horse is Walter's and I can assure you that, in my view, that is not Walter's horse." Could he argue from phenomenological privilege (the *ego* determines the intentional object) or logical privilege (the context of my declaration having been opaque, you do not have the right to say that my horse lost)? Of course not. In a race, only *identified* horses take part. The issue of intentional objects does not arise. This is then a situation where the intentional passive is entirely legitimate. Sid said that Walter's horse was going to win the race and even bet accordingly, and *here*—a real relation established by the index finger pointed at the animal—is Walter's horse that Sid claimed would win.

To use some terminology that we will introduce in chapter 10, one might say that we are not locked into a logic of *subjective mind* and that it is possible to consider things from the point of view of *objective mind*. An objective mind is not one composed of identifiable objects (for example, of "propositions in themselves" or "ideal objects"). Nor is it some sort of superior power that would think in our place and perform intellectual operations within us and without our knowledge and whose results we could do no more than record. Objective mind is present wherever it is possible to confront someone with what he ought to know. In order for such a thing to be conceivable, a distinction must be drawn between the personal use of signs and an impersonal usage that has the force of law. In short, the idea of objective mind is that I can confront someone with a law that is his law, not necessarily because he knows it explicitly, but because *all are presumed to know the law* [*nul n'est censé ignorer la loi*].

The notion of "reference" should be understood as deriving from the verbs "to refer to" and "to make reference to." Like many semantic verbs, these verbs have two usages. In their *personal* usage, they tell us what the speaker has in mind, as when someone is speaking about something. This usage corresponds exactly to the view of consciousness or language as closed upon itself: there is no question of apple trees or horses, only of apple tree perceptions and horse beliefs, with the result that we do not know exactly what is at issue and any move to the passive is thereby ruled out. In the *impersonal* usage, these verbs tell us what the statement itself refers to. If the statement contains the words "Professor Carnap," it bears upon the person so named. When Sid bets on Walter's horse, his subjective beliefs may diverge from those of his entourage, but the institution of betting is built upon the impersonal usage of language, not its personal usage. What constitutes the impersonal usage—the norm—is obviously not something that can be decided once and for all but, rather, depends on the context. The important thing is that with this usage we exit the subjective perspective but without leaving the realm of intentionality. What makes the move to the intentional passive possible is therefore the way in which the *institution* of the proper name requires each of us to submit his intentional relations to the test of real relations.

Peirce would appear to have been right: intentional relations are assuredly *irreducible* to real relations, but they nevertheless depend on a real relation in order to establish themselves.[8] We must therefore understand how an intentional relation to an object can be based on a real relation to an object.

We have thus far been considering two lines of response to the question of the status of intentional verbs. The Brentanians tell us that they are *transitive* verbs and that, indeed, they are more transitive than other such verbs because they are unconditionally so. The consequence of this view, however, is that such transitivity cannot be an authentic transition to something other than the act itself. Intentionality, it will then be claimed, is not a relation but rather a quasi-relation, since it may turn out to be a relation to a "something" that does not exist.

As a result, the Brentanian response becomes indistinguishable from the view of those philosophers who see in the semantic opacity of intentional verbs a reason to think that these verbs are, in reality, intransitive.

---

8. This is Peirce's idea of a pragmatics of assertion. See Christiane Chauviré, *Peirce et la signification: Introduction à la logique du vague* (Paris: Presses Universitaires de France, 1994), 142–152, and Claudine Tiercelin, *La pensée-signe: Études sur C. S. Peirce* (Nîmes: Éditions Jacquéline Chambon, 1993), 302–306.

These two responses, which in the end are indistinguishable from each other, are both inadequate. They seem to require intentional verbs to be both intransitive and transitive: intransitive so as to avoid any possible confusion between intentional relations and real relations; transitive so that we are able to ask questions that, in themselves, do not appear to be unintelligible—e.g., who is loved by A? whom is A thinking about? who is lauded by A?

We want to be able to ask such questions. We therefore want to be able to use the intentional passive. But we want it to be an intentional passive and a not a real passive. How can we satisfy these requirements? It is necessary and sufficient that intentional verbs be *both* transitive and intransitive. If that condition proved contradictory, a dialectical solution would be required. Yet I do not believe it to be contradictory because it can be understood in the following way: an intentional verb, by itself, *is not* transitive; nevertheless, it must not be classed among the intransitive verbs, for it can *become* transitive, not by itself but through its association with another verb that is usually transitive. Instead of speaking of an extraordinary transitivity (which is ultimately unintelligible) of intentional verbs, we would then have to say that these verbs are bestowed with an ordinary transitivity (that they do not possess in themselves) by virtue of their internal link with other verbs that *are* transitive in the ordinary way.

The proposed solution is this: intentional verbs are transitive because they are intentional *in a system* that must contain transitive verbs (that are really transitive). In other words, intentionality is a property that is conferred upon some acts or processes in virtue of their integration within a more general system. This response boils down to saying that the intentionality of the mental is nothing but an aspect of the holism of the mental.

3.3. A Holistic Conception of Intentionality

We would like to understand how it is that the form of the intentional passive is sometimes legitimate even though it is not universally so. An example from Wittgenstein might help us here. Someone is in his room waiting for someone. In *The Blue Book,* the example appears in the form of the following question: "What happens if from 4 till 4:30 A expects B to come to his room?"[9]

This example concerns two people, A and B, and therefore two stories. We are only concerned with A's biographical line; it is A's intention that this line should cut across B's at a single point, but it remains to be seen if the expected event will occur. Thus, the episode that belongs to A's history involves B without anything in B's history betraying this fact. If we say that B is expected by A, the entire reality stated in this passive form is intentional. It is possible that B knows or suspects that his visit is expected by A. But if he knows or suspects it, he does so by himself and not in any way as a result of the fact that A is expecting him. In reality, it is conceivable that A expects B without B knowing that he is expected. The activity of expecting B only concerns A's movements and does not affect B at all. If it did, it would be magic.

The two elements of our problem of the intentional passive are present in Wittgenstein's example:

(1) There is, as there should be, a relation between A and B in the sense that it is a visit by B that is expected and not a visit by someone else. Indeed, there is a determinate response to the question "whom are you expecting?" The *passive* is thus legitimate: B is expected, not C.
(2) A engages in conduct that concerns B, but A does nothing to B. Expecting is not a physical action and therefore not really transitive. The passive "B is expected by A" is well and truly an *intentional* passive.

The problem is therefore once again knowing what this passive form means. In what way is B expected by A when B experiences nothing as the object of such expectation?

9. Ludwig Wittgenstein, *The Blue and Brown Books: Preliminary Studies for the "Philosophical Investigations,"* 2nd ed. (Oxford: Blackwell, 1969), 20. It is not my intention in what follows to provide an exegesis of Wittgenstein's writings. As a result, I am not concerned here with what Wittgenstein's theory of intentionality might or might not be. One suspects that Wittgenstein himself would be averse to even speaking of a "theory." My sole aim is to make use of some of Wittgenstein's analyses to show that one can speak about intentionality without assimilating it to a paradoxical transitivity. On the evolution of Wittgenstein's views on intentionality, see Jacques Bouveresse, *Le mythe de l'intériorité: Expérience, signification et langage privé chez Wittgenstein,* 2nd rev. ed. (1976; Paris: Les Éditions de Minuit, 1987), 279–302.

A HOLISTIC CONCEPTION OF INTENTIONALITY

This example moves us away from the sorts of cases normally discussed in the literature. It brings out a complexity of the intentional act that is lost in both the preferred examples of the Austrians (for example, thinking about fictive objects such as Pegasus or a mountain of gold) and those of the phenomenologists (such as perceiving a cube through all of its sides). This example spurs me to make four remarks:

First, is expecting a physical or a mental act?

The example is openly non-Cartesian. Recall that Dummett, in the course of illustrating Brentano's Thesis, invited us to draw a Cartesian distinction between kicking a ball, which is clearly a movement of the body, and forming the intention to kick a ball, which appears to be a pure operation of the mind or consciousness. The same cannot be done with the example where A expects B's visit from 4:00 to 4:30. Is it a physical or mental activity? It is impossible to determine.

It cannot be said that it is a *physical* activity, because there are no gestures or movements specific to the behavior of expecting. One can imagine all kinds of comportments that are compatible with the description "A is expecting B's visit." In fact, expecting this visit is not so much a matter of doing this or that as it is of doing nothing that might prevent the visit, not undertaking any activity that would render the subject A unable to welcome B at the moment he arrives. Expecting is physical in the sense that it requires that certain physical conditions be fulfilled: if the visit is to take place in my room, and if my conduct is that of expecting Smith in my room, I will have to be in that room (not elsewhere) and physically available for the visit. But expecting is not physical in the sense where it would suffice to perform certain movements or gestures to be in the process of expecting the anticipated visit. The physical conditions of expecting are necessary conditions, not sufficient ones.

Nevertheless, expecting is no more a *form of consciousness* than it is a physical activity. It is not necessary for A to think constantly of B—he need only make sure not to stray from the room and to open the door at the appropriate moment. But, in order to remember not to stray from the room, A need not, at every instant, recall his expected meeting. All that is required is that A give himself these instructions and that he remain in his room in light of them. One can easily imagine that, during the entire period of waiting, his power of attention will be focused on other things—reading a novel, for example—and that he ceases reading his novel at 5:00 only to confirm that he waited until 4:30 and beyond for nothing. When did he stop waiting? At 4:30 or at 5:00? The question has no determinate answer because, although there are scheduled dates and times for the visit, there are no dates and times for the expecting, which is not a state in the strict sense.

Second, what exactly is intentional about expecting?

Every case of expecting is the expecting of something. But of what? Wittgenstein's example brings out the hazards of an ambiguity: we speak of expecting B, but we also speak of expecting B's visit. The first form suggests a transitive act, a "transcendence of consciousness" that projects itself toward B wherever he may be. The second form is more suggestive of a projection from the present to the future, which is neither here nor elsewhere. The appeal of this example is that it invites us to ask, "What is relational about expecting?" In this example, the expecting bears on something that B is supposed to do. There are then two activities at issue: what A does and what B is supposed to do.

In the traditional conception, what we call "intentionality" is the property of an act or a state. An act is intentional if it presents a certain structure, which some describe as a structure of consciousness (*cogitatio-cogitatum, noesis-noema*) and others as a structure analogous to that of a speech act. But, in our example, intentionality is not the structure of *an act*; it is the structure of at least *two activities*.

To expect something is not a relation between a subject and an expected object. To expect is a relation appropriately posited between what a subject is doing now (for example, reading the newspaper) and another activity that is supposed or hoped to occur—in our example, seeing the expected person enter the room. The expected person is the person expected by A to come into view at any moment between 4:00 and 4:30, provided that A remains, as agreed, in his room. This intentional structure between acts is a structure of *subordination*. The two acts—one actually carried out and the other anticipated—are not simply linked. One serves as the measure of the other: the future event is what gives its meaning to the present activity.

* * *

But—third question—how is it that B is the person expected? How can it be said that the intention to welcome him in the near future applies to B and not to someone else?

The case of someone expecting another person's visit requires that both have the necessary conceptual resources. These resources are necessary to participation in the institution of *meeting*. One cannot arrange a meeting for tomorrow with one's dog, nor with a member of a tribe that has no clocks and is therefore unconcerned by the hour of the day. One must have a form of life that provides such resources.

It might be objected that this example is flawed for being too complex. To analyze it, one has to put together all of the intentional objects of all of the intentions that enter into the behavior of expecting, when one ought to have begun with these more elementary intentions themselves. According to this objection, the intentionality that ought to have been considered is the intentionality intrinsic to cogitative acts such as, for example, *thinking of Smith*. Where in such intentions would one locate activities external to the subject and their subordination to other acts or other events? Where is there room for the social, historical, and institutional context that is assumed when we describe an activity as being that of expecting someone with whom one has made an appointment?

The answer is that every intentional operation, when clearly expressed, reveals itself to have a similar complexity to that of the case of *expecting*. Every intentional act is intentional in a context. Every intentional act that seeks to bear transitively upon an object requires another act to determine that object.

What distinguishes thinking of Smith and thinking of Brown? What distinguishes thinking of John Smith and thinking of Bill Smith? Consider the case where I know nothing of the person with whom I have an appointment other than that his name is Smith (a name in my appointment book). I have an appointment with a person named Smith. The traditional conception asks us to look for some contact with the object of the intention, contact that must be established in nonphysical and noncausal ways. Intentionality, in this view, is *presentational*: intention presents me with its object. Intention would thereby have the power of establishing a real relation solely on the basis of an intentional relation. But, asks Wittgenstein, by what miracle can the intention to think of Smith bring my thought into contact with the right Smith and not some other Smith, wherever he may be?[10]

These examples suggest another response than that of a power of direct presentation proper to mental acts. How can I think about Smith? In other words, how can I make it so that, when I am thinking of Smith, my thought bears on the right Smith and not on his homonym? How can I invoke or *summon* Smith in my thought? How, as Wittgenstein asks, do I call *him* to mind?[11] The answer is within the question: in order to summon him in our thoughts, we do what we would do in life—*we call him by his name*. Here as elsewhere, Wittgenstein exteriorizes the mental not because he denies the existence of interior acts but because he denies that interior acts have powers that the same acts would not when exteriorized in language.

My ability to target Smith's person in my thought cannot go beyond my ability to explain to you who Smith is—for example, my ability to explain to you who it is that I call by the name "Smith." Imagine that one asks at a hotel's reception desk, "Mr. Smith, please." But the name is a common one and it so happens that the hotel has two guests by that name. "Which one would you like to see?" It happens that I know nothing of Mr. Smith other than that I am to meet him at his hotel. There are then two possibilities, depending on what I want. If I only want to make contact with a person named Smith, anybody named Smith will do. When the receptionist puts me through to the room of one of the guests named Smith, my intention to get in touch with (a) Smith has been fulfilled. Of course, this is not how we normally understand the case. We are normally not satisfied to end up in contact with anybody who happens to be named Smith. We want the right one. But what do we mean by "the right one"? *Something else will have to be said about it.* This example is enough to show that the very act of thinking of Smith is a contextual one.

---

10. Ludwig Wittgenstein, *Philosophical Investigations,* rev. 4th ed., ed. P. M. S. Hacker and Joachim Schulte, trans. G. E. M. Anscombe, P. M. S. Hacker, and Joachim Schulte (1953; Oxford: Wiley-Blackwell, 2009), § 668 (177) and following.

11. "How does he call HIM to mind?" Ibid., § 691 (181). See also Peter Geach's commentary in *Mental Acts: Their Content and Their Objects* (London: Routledge and Kegan Paul, 1957), 73.

* * *

Finally, the last remark I would like to make about Wittgenstein's example is that it provides an excellent illustration of the following point: there are systematic relations among the various intentional verbs. In Wittgenstein's *Philosophical Remarks,* we also find this typically intentionalist idea: "Expecting is connected with looking for [*die Erwartung hängt mit dem Suchen zusammen*]. I know what I am looking for, without what I am looking for having to exist."[12]

Wittgenstein's thought here comes close to a cherished idea of Husserl's that has been considerably developed within phenomenology: every mental act must form part of a teleological chain. If I perceive a cube, I perceive in reality three of its faces, but I expect it to have three other faces on the side that I do not see. The present act does not *guarantee* that there will be three other faces to be seen. Rather, it *requires* that the three other faces be where they are expected if the object that I see is indeed a cube. Similarly, I see the façade of a house from the garden and immediately expect it to have the other facades, an interior, etc. However, Husserl posits these internal relations as being among pure intentional acts. Indeed, he asks us to separate radically (via the *epoché*) intentional relations from real relations. The latter are not nullified but must be constituted subsequently out of intentional acts. A real relation will then be a relation held or posited to be real by an intention. By contrast, Wittgenstein's example invites us to reconceive the system of intentional acts. *Expecting* and *looking for* are intentional, but they are internally related to *receiving* (or not) what one expects, *finding* (or not) what one is looking for. And this is where we leave the intentional to return to the real relation that must have been presupposed in order to say what it was that was expected or looked for. The solution to the problem that phenomenology left unresolved lies therefore in the internal relation between the intentional relation (e.g., *expecting*) and the real relation (e.g., *receiving*).

Consider the relation between *looking for* and *finding*. "To look for" is clearly an intentional verb. It is a verb that forms a system with "to find," just as "to expect" forms a system with "to receive." But what of the verb

12. Ludwig Wittgenstein, *Philosophical Remarks,* ed. Rush Rhees, trans. Raymond Hargreaves and Roger White (Oxford: Blackwell, 1975), § 28 (67–68).

"to find" itself? It is noteworthy that this verb is not necessarily intentional. Sometimes, one finds the thing one was looking for. It also sometimes happens that one finds *without looking for*. On this point, the French nineteenth-century Littré dictionary gives some useful explanations. "To find" [*trouver*] is to

> Encounter [*rencontrer*] someone or something either that one is looking for or that one is not looking for. "Ah! Lord Géronimo, how fortunate to find you here as I was just on my way to your house to look for you." (Molière, *The Forced Marriage,* Scene 1)

The example from Molière clearly shows the two acceptations. Sganarelle finds Lord Géronimo where he was not looking for him (thus, without looking for him "here"), but that is all for the good since he was looking for him (elsewhere). Yet, at the end of the entry for "to find," where synonyms are provided, Littré explains the semantic contrast between "to find" and "to encounter" [*rencontrer*]: "'to find' does not exclude the idea of looking for but 'to encounter' does." At first, this gives the impression that the explanation provided for "to find" contradicts that provided for the verb "to encounter." On the one hand, the definition of "to find" gives us to understand that an encounter can be intentional or not; one can encounter something that one was looking for, or one can encounter something that one was not looking for (one happens upon it). On the other hand, we are subsequently told that the idea of an encounter excludes the idea of looking for. If there is an encounter, it must be with something that one was not looking for, a contact without intention. On the one hand, I can encounter Smith when Smith is precisely the person I was looking for. On the other, it would be enough to know that I *encountered* Smith to understand that I was in Smith's presence without having been looking for him.

It seems to me that the explanations in Littré are in no way contradictory and that they account perfectly well for our use of the concepts of looking for and finding, on condition that we introduce a distinction—the distinction of intentionality—which could be expressed as follows:

It is possible to find without having looked for.
It is impossible to find without encountering.

The first proposition amounts to saying that it is possible merely to encounter, to have an encounter with something without having undertaken to look for it. The second proposition is to be understood as follows: it is impossible merely to find—meaning to find only and uniquely what one was looking for without finding at the same time (as in a simple encounter) what one was not looking for.

To put it in another terminology, we will say that looking for is necessarily "under a description" (*secundum quid*) but that an encounter is necessarily an encounter with an object *tout court* (*simpliciter*). These propositions clearly bear upon the intentional object (what one was looking for, what one found). They are not meant to suggest that two people have been found where only one was sought. What is at issue is the *aspect* under which what is looked for is looked for and the aspect under which it is found. The found object is necessarily richer than the object sought, and that is why it is also an encountered object. Oedipus is looking for Laius's murderer. When he finds him, he also finds someone he was not looking for, namely Oedipus himself.

The conclusion to be drawn from this systematic link is that to speak of the intentionality of the mental is a way of speaking of the holism of the mental. An intentional verb is not intentional in isolation; it is intentional by virtue of its integration within a system of intentional verbs. Among these intentional verbs, a distinction must be made between strictly intentional verbs such as "to look for" and verbs that are sometimes intentional, such as "to find." One might say that the former have a *full-time* intentionality, meaning that they are never directly transitive and that, at least in philosophical grammar, they are not constructed with a direct object (however they may be constructed in a given language). The latter verbs possess a *part-time* intentionality, and that is what allows them to provide the entire group of intentional verbs with a contact with or positive connection to reality. This contact should be conceived as a reciprocally real relation between two clearly individuated entities.

The verbs that are strictly intentional *are not transitive*. Thus, to look for Smith is to look for someone, and to think of Smith is to think of someone. But, as everyone acknowledges, if I am merely looking for someone, there is not necessarily someone who is the person I am looking for. The move to the passive is impossible, and this is a sign that there is no action here outside oneself. It often will happen that the intentional activity remains intransitive. No real relation is then necessary to it. For example, the search for a person able to fill a certain role or satisfy a requirement is at first also a search to find out if such a person exists.

Nevertheless, things are quite different on those occasions when we are able to say that our intentional activity truly bears upon a particular object. In such cases, we want to be able to move to the form of the intentional passive. When I am looking for *Smith,* I am not looking for *a* Smith, whether he exists or not (in much the same way that, for the Brentanians, our thoughts about Pegasus bear on Pegasus even though Pegasus is a legendary creature). This means that I am looking for Smith and no one else, even if I am unable to tell you anything about him other than that he left a message under that name. If I subsequently learn that the Smith in question is nothing but the result of a mystification or confusion, I will be unable to specify the object of my search.

Intentional verbs are systematically linked, in virtue of their meaning, to other verbs. For example, to seek someone is to seek to find someone, while to think of someone in particular is to think of that someone in a particular context. If this context is that provided by a system of names, the purely intentional verb "to think of" followed by a proper name enters into an internal relation with verbs such as "to name," "to call," and so forth. These latter verbs include a transitive (nonintentional) use; there are people called "Smith" (i.e., who bear the name "Smith," which they were given). As a result, the passive form is natural—these people are called by the name they were given. It can happen that they are summoned using this name. And in this way we see the intentional passive used in a way that is entirely intelligible.

3.4. Mental Holism

Today, philosophers speak of "mental holism" in two related senses that merit being distinguished from each other: (1) to indicate a condition that bears upon the psychological description of the subject of an action (what is holistic in this case are the concepts used in this description); (2) to indicate that the description of someone's state of mind is not the description of an internal state and that it is not possible to describe the state of mind in which a subject acts, responds, or exists by abstracting that subject from its social and historical world. In both cases, holism is above all the rejection of atomism, the idea that we will one day be able to reconstruct the mental lives of people by combining psychical atoms by means of principles governing the association of ideas or the succession of signifiers. However, the implications of holism differ somewhat depending on whether the thesis is pushed toward an anthropological holism (as in the second sense above).

Mental holism is first the name given to the stumbling block that proved to mark the downfall of the plausible and intelligent version of the behaviorist program put forward by philosophers such as Gilbert Ryle. Let us suppose that a psychologist wants to reduce a state of mind to external behavior—for example, the fact of someone believing that it might rain. A belief, it will be recognized, is not the same thing as a judgment. Someone may believe that it might rain without necessarily having formed an explicit judgment (whether aloud or in her mind) on the matter. There is thus no reason to look for her belief in the form of an entity that would be present in her head (in the form of a cogitative content currently present to her mind). Our psychologist will follow Ryle and will define belief as a disposition to do certain things when certain circumstances present themselves. He will say, then, that if N goes out with an umbrella, she believes it will rain, and if she goes out without an umbrella, she believes that rain is unlikely. This behavior would then provide us with a test allowing us to decide whether N believes it will rain or not.

It is easy enough to show that this psychological schema is simplistic. By asking us to reduce belief to such a disposition (to take an umbrella if it threatens to rain and not to take one if it does not), the reductive psychologist acts as if someone going out with an umbrella could not have any other motive than to use it to shelter her from the rain. But N may be taking her umbrella in order to give it back to its owner, and she might leave the umbrella at the house because she prefers to have her hands unencumbered while walking, even if she is convinced that a downpour is on the way.

In short, belief is indeed something that will manifest itself in behavior, but the psychologist cannot identify a given mental state (believing that it is going to rain) unless he also concerns himself with the other thoughts and desires of the person involved. Here we may speak of a *psychological mental holism*.

It is worth pointing out that what is dubious is not the idea of giving implicit beliefs the status of *dispositions* rather than of current states of mind or, as Ryle put it, of episodes of mental life. Ryle is to be credited for having rehabilitated modal notions of powers and capacities.[13] For many philosophers, it was surprising to realize that attributions of capacities (personal powers) could not be analyzed as if they were statements announcing the possibility of a fact. So, for example, the mental attribution of a capacity such as "I can now read a text in Greek" cannot be assimilated to "It is possible for me to read a text in Greek now." In order to be able to read a text in Greek now (in the sense of a capacity), I need only *know* Greek. By contrast, in order for it to be possible that I read a text in Greek now, it is sufficient that doing so not be logically excluded (for example by the fact that the text I am reading is written in French).

In fact, the weak point of the theory presented in *The Concept of Mind* is to be found elsewhere. Ryle claims to be able to eliminate the mind/body problem by showing that there is a *logical* difference between psychological and physical descriptions. The difference that he puts forward is that between the concept of an *episode* and that of a *disposition*. But the difference between the dispositional and the actual is not a difference between the mental and the physical. Ryle's own examples show this: when it comes time to analyze statements of dispositions, he speaks of elastic objects, brittle glass, and soluble sugar.[14]

Peter Geach has made a more radical objection to all forms of behaviorism.[15] The objections he raises to Ryle's view are those of a mental

---

13. I call it a rehabilitation because Ryle's readers who were versed in Scholastic terminology had no difficulty in finding the Scholastic *habitus* in Ryle's concept of "dispositions." Thus, Anthony Kenny, tasked with translating into English the section of Aquinas's *Summa Theologica* devoted to the *habitus* (1a2æ, q. 49–54), translated the title *De habitibus in generali* as *On Dispositions in General*. In his Introduction, Kenny explains that the Latin word *habitus* would not be appropriately translated "habit" and that, conversely, the Latin *dispositio* does not correspond to what we understand today as a disposition but rather to a state. Anthony Kenny, Introduction to *Summa Theologiae*, vol. 22, *Dispositions for Human Acts (1a2æ, 49–54)*, by Thomas Aquinas, trans. Anthony Kenny (New York: McGraw-Hill, 1964), xxi.

14. Gilbert Ryle, *The Concept of Mind* (1949; Chicago: University of Chicago Press, 2000) 31, 102.

15. Geach, *Mental Acts,* 8.

holism that is not only psychological (linking actions and dispositions of mind) but also *anthropological*. Ryle gave the example of a gardener. If the gardener believes that it is going to rain, he will not bother to water his lettuce plants.[16] But, in this example, Ryle is not discussing a pure psychological subject. His example is a gardener, which implicitly introduces an anthropological context to the description. The term presents us with an actor who has specific needs and goals to be attained. If we observe that the gardener does not water his lettuce, we may conclude that he is convinced that it is going to rain. This is true, but only on condition that he behaves as a good and decent gardener. If we learn that he is discontented and often negligent, we will not be so sure about our ability to apply our test of the gardener's intentions. This holism is anthropological. In referring to someone as a gardener, we give ourselves the right to dispense with any further enquiry into the subject's person. We know what a gardener is. An entire world of institutions is presupposed by the term, and it is in this context that we consider any incident that might arise. The anthropology in question here is of course a *social* anthropology.

At the time, Geach did not use the word "holism" (whether in a psychological or an anthropological sense). Moreover, the position he defended in his book would surely not be considered holistic in the sense in which the term came to be understood, after Quine, by most American philosophers (see chapter 4, below). Indeed, Geach writes later in his text that there is one characteristic behavior that can serve as a criterion for the attribution of a belief: the behavior consisting in expressing one's belief in a declaration. Of course, the gardener who declares that he is not watering his lettuce because it is going to rain might well be lying. Nevertheless, says Geach, lying is necessarily the exception and not the rule. As a result, it is possible to say of someone who says, "I believe it is going to rain" that he is someone who believes it is going to rain. There is no need to know anything more about his opinions. One need only know the *language* he understands and in which he responds.

A philosopher defending holism in the sense given to it by Quine and Davidson might say that we have to *interpret* the linguistic behavior of the gardener—in exactly the same way that we have to interpret his behavior with the watering can and the lettuce—and that only by adopting a

16. Ryle, *The Concept of Mind*, 175.

hypothesis regarding the totality of his opinions and desires can we come to understand his utterances in one way or another.

This simple example reveals the central problem to which the rest of this book is devoted: knowing that we cannot identify mental entities one by one (based on exterior behavior), must we conclude that it is impossible to understand a declaration from a person whose worldview and aspirations are unknown to us?

Anthropological holism is nicely captured by Wittgenstein's aphorism "If a lion could talk, we wouldn't be able to understand it."[17] We must understand something of a being's form of life before we can understand the meaning of its statements. The expression "form of life" here should call to mind at one and the same time a psychological core of needs, desires, and natural reactions as well as a historical core of institutions and customs— in other words, mores that are made up of both natural tendencies and transmitted ways of doing things without it being possible to draw an absolutely clear line between the natural and the institutional. This is a result of the extraordinary entanglement of the two, which led Pascal to say that one ought to speak of a second nature (with regard to institutions) and a first institution (when speaking of nature).[18]

With the question of anthropological holism, we return to the theme of the inquiry I began in *The Mind's Provisions*. There, I concluded that an atomistic analysis of the mental is impossible and that this impossibility is a conceptual or metaphysical one; atomistic psychologies require us to enumerate the subject's intentions, ideas, opinions, and desires. In order to enumerate them, we have to be able to identify them by means of an individuation, in the way that one does for apples or marbles. It follows that the analysis of the mind will have to be holistic. Or, rather, it would be better to say that the analysis will either be holistic or there will be no analysis of the mind, for mental holism is quite often considered to be an obstacle to any such analysis.

---

17. Wittgenstein, "Philosophy of Psychology: A Fragment," in *Philosophical Investigations,* § 327 (235).

18. Blaise Pascal, *Pensées,* trans. A. J. Krailsheimer (Baltimore: Penguin Books, 1966), §§ 125–126 (32).

At the end of *The Mind's Provisions,* I wrote that once one recognizes the holistic character of mental concepts and thereby also recognizes the social and historical character of the human mind, one is immediately faced with a difficulty:

> When one wants to identify someone's thoughts, one cannot abstract from the historical context. So let us suppose that one wants to take the context into account: would we then be able to identify anything at all? The procedure of identification through the individuation of entities that are independent from one another does not allow us to identify *thoughts*. It remains to be seen whether mental holism does not in its turn rule out the discrimination of thoughts due to an inability to *distinguish* one thought from another. It therefore remains to be demonstrated that, if mental atomism is indeed incoherent, mental holism can be put forward in a coherent way.[19]

That passage formed the conclusion of a section that was summarized as follows in the table of contents:

> In what case are two people thinking the same thing and in what case are they thinking something different? Mental atomism proposes to identify thoughts through individuation: it assumes that thoughts can be counted one-by-one, as physical images might be counted. For its part, mental holism will have to explain how it plans to identify thoughts without individuating them: it will have to provide an identity criterion for thoughts.[20]

The chapters that follow seek to provide an answer to those questions. They take it as given that the identification of thoughts cannot take place through individuation and will seek to show that this identification is, in reality, a differentiation or a discernment. We do not ask whether two people have the same thought in the same way that we ask whether two people have the same car (whether the *token,* if they are co-owners of the same car, or the *type,* if they own two cars of the same model). The identity of thoughts is neither a token identity nor a type identity, for the type/token distinction applies only to the world of individuals.

---

19. Vincent Descombes, *The Mind's Provisions: A Critique of Cognitivism,* trans. Stephen Adam Schwartz (Princeton, NJ: Princeton University Press, 2001), 247.
20. Ibid., x.

When we ask whether two people are thinking the same thing, we are asking rather whether there is a discernible difference between what one thinks and what the other thinks. As long as such a difference is not in evidence, they are thinking the same thing. How can such a difference (if there is one) manifest itself? It must be able to appear to the individuals themselves, in a discussion between them, in a dialogical way. This is only conceivable within the context of common institutions that allow us to assign meaning.

PART II

The Anthropological Holism of the Mental

4

The Question of Holism

4.1. What Is Meant by Mental Holism?

The expression "mental holism" is frequently encountered today in texts in the philosophy of mind. The concept is a technical one in which the word "holism" does not have precisely the same meaning that it does in other fields—for example in the philosophy of biology or in social theory.[1] I will therefore begin by introducing it.

In fact, in discussions of mental holism, holism is understood in a way that is particular to American philosophy. The notion is nevertheless, as we shall see, still useful outside of the confines of that tradition. Given the

---

1. According to P. B. and J. S. Medawar in the article "Holism" in their *Aristotle to Zoos: A Philosophical Dictionary of Biology* (Cambridge, MA: Harvard University Press, 1983), 144–145, the word comes from the philosophy of biology. It appeared for the first time in a book published in 1926 by Jan Christian Smuts entitled *Holism and Evolution*. Here is the definition given by the Medawars: "Holism teaches that any whole, and especially a whole organism, is not a mere assemblage of its constituent parts but enjoys an integrity or wholeness by reason of the functional interrelations and interdependences of its several parts. The philosophical opinion against which holists profess to defend us is that which is practiced by the reductive analytical-summative mechanist who believes that an organism is a mere additive sum of its constituent parts, parts among which the functional relationship is wholly explicable in physicochemical terms" (144). The authors, who make explicit reference to Karl Popper's philosophical ideas, nevertheless see holism as a kind of speculation remote from real scientific work. We may retain from this that the common meaning of "holism" is aptly rendered by the adage: "There is more in the whole than the sum of its parts."

importance of the theme of holism within philosophy of language and mind, one would expect there to be a great many works devoted to the idea. Yet, although there has been much discussion of the thesis that semantic and mental concepts are holistic, not as much attention has been paid to the concept of holism itself. What is it about Quine's theses on language or Davidson's ideas about the mind that renders them holistic? It is strange that no elaboration of the notion of holism itself has ever been provided. Yet recently there appeared a book by Fodor and LePore meant to shake up the emerging American philosophical consensus on the holistic character of concepts relating to meaning and the mind.[2] Fodor and LePore attempt a principled critique of all of the versions of semantic holism in circulation among American philosophers. Their aim, it should be noted, is not to defend atomism directly but rather to rescue it from the discredit into which it had fallen and to do this by pointing out the numerous difficulties to which holism gives rise in this domain.

In its most basic sense, holism is primarily the rejection of atomism. With regard to language, holism is the refusal to accept that a language might be constructed by providing a sign for one thing, then another sign for another thing, and so on. The atomist reserves the right to refer to a *first* sign without any obligation to seek out a *second* one. She reserves the right to consider the first sign as a fully fledged sign. With regard to the mental, holism is the rejection of the idea that mental life can be built up out of psychical atoms (like the representative ideas sought by associationist psychology). In fact, mental holism and semantic holism are inseparable: holistic theories of mind are based on holistic theories of the sign. They transpose to mental acts such as representing what was originally put forward with regard to signs and to speech acts.

Here is what characterizes, according to Fodor and LePore, semantic atomism: "The meaning of an expression metaphysically depends on some punctate symbol/world relation, some relation that one thing could bear to the world even if nothing else did."[3] By this they mean that semantic

---

2. Jerry Fodor and Ernest LePore, *Holism: A Shopper's Guide* (Oxford: Blackwell, 1992).
3. Ibid., 260–261.

atomism defines the originary relation of meaning as one of contiguity, as a kind of contact at a given point between two entities (the sign and the thing), without having any dependence on what goes on at other points. For example, the word "dog" has semantic properties, and these properties have their explanation, in the final analysis, in the relation that exists between this word and dogs.[4] As for holism, it rejects such atomism and upholds the idea that the fundamental semantic relation is not one between a symbol and a part of the world but rather inheres in the relations among symbols and the roles that each of them plays relative to the others. For a holist, it is these relations within the system that underwrite the relation between a collection of signs and the world.

The outdated theory of representative ideas was atomistic in character. A representative idea is like an image. Like an image, the idea presents a content to the mind. Like an image, it presents this content by itself and does not concern itself with other ideas. The photograph in the album does not become less representative of what it depicts if it happens to be the only photograph in the album. Because the idea is a unit of representation, it is also independent of other ideas. Ideas can thus be counted. It follows that a mind might, like Condillac's famous statue, have nothing but a single idea.[5]

The broad outlines of holism, when presented in this way, will likely be familiar to French readers who will see at work an opposition that they know by other names. The holist point of view calls to mind the structural point of view in its insistence on the role of the system and the necessity for the sign to belong to a system made up of diacritical differences. However, this impression is only partially justified.[6] It is true that the principle of structural analysis insists on the consideration of systems, i.e., totalities. Though the word "holism" was not in use during the heyday of structuralism in the 1950s and 60s, those practicing this sort of analysis adhered to the thesis of a holism of language and mind. But it is by no means certain that the holism studied (and criticized) in Fodor and

---

4. Ibid., 33.
5. See Condillac, "Treatise on the Sensations," in *Philosophical Writings of Etienne Bonnot, Abbé de Condillac*, trans. Franklin Philip and Harlan Lane (Hillsdale, NJ: Lawrence Erlbaum Associates, 1982), 153–339.
6. Fodor and LePore, for their part, act as though the ideas developed by Saussure and the structuralists were related to those of American semantic holism. *Holism*, 237 n. 9.

LePore's book has much to do with these notions of structural analysis or of signifying systems.

4.2. Meaning Holism

In their book, Fodor and LePore remind us that, within American philosophy, the idea of mental holism was derived from semantic holism. One must therefore return to the philosophy of language to understand what is meant here by the word "holism."

Every philosophy of language that rejects a definition of semantic relations as the dyadic association of a word and a thing is holist. What makes a sensuous figure a sign is no longer a direct relation with the thing of which this figure is the sign but rather its integration within a language or its place within a whole.[7] In the early pages of their book, Fodor and LePore remind us of the grand principles whose authority is invoked in order to justify the holistic approach to language. First is Frege's context principle.[8] Then there is Wittgenstein's reiteration of the Fregean principle: "To understand a sentence means to understand a language."[9]

Fodor and LePore raise three principal objections to what they call semantic holism, which we might call the objections of obscurantism, relativism, and nihilism, respectively. They do not all have the same persuasive force.

1. *Obscurantism*: Holism about language leads to holism about mental representations. If there are psychological laws, they must resemble, formally at least, "the laws of the association of ideas" that psychologists referred to in the nineteenth century. Each time you think about X, you never fail to then think about Y. In order for it to be possible to put forward laws having this form, it must be possible to identify mental states (such as that of thinking about X or Y). But such identification becomes

---

7. Ibid., 4.
8. "Never . . . ask for the meaning of a word in isolation, but only in the context of a proposition." Gottlob Frege, *The Foundations of Arithmetic: A Logico-Mathematical Inquiry Into the Concept of Number,* 2nd rev. ed., trans. J. L. Austin (1950; New York: Harper Brothers, 1953), xxii.
9. Ludwig Wittgenstein, *Philosophical Investigations,* rev. 4th ed., ed. P. M. S. Hacker and Joachim Schulte, trans. G. E. M. Anscombe, P. M. S. Hacker and Joachim Schulte (1953; Oxford: Wiley-Blackwell, 2009), § 199 (87).

impossible if the meaning of a thought that comes to an individual depends on all of the other opinions of that individual. According to this hypothesis, no general laws of the form "whoever thinks of X will then think of Y" can ever be put forward.

This objection assumes that the aim of psychology is to put forward nomological generalizations applicable to beliefs and desires considered as internal mental states. If we do not share this assumption, the objection fails to be persuasive. Indeed, the authors recognize that not everyone would find it disadvantageous if it became impossible to develop a naturalistic version of the human sciences.[10]

The two other objections, both of which are borrowed from Michael Dummett, are more forceful because they concern everyone, not just members of the positivist school.

2. *Relativism*: If semantic holism were confirmed, we would have to assent to the Sophist's claim that it is impossible for two people to contradict each other. Either two people think the same thing, or their opinions have no relation to each other (they are "incommensurable"). This objection suggests that mental holism makes it impossible to compare thoughts.

Is it possible for me to agree with one (and only one) of the propositions of your theory? Can we be in agreement on a single point regardless of our views on the other aspects of the question under discussion? Fodor and LePore allude to discussions about theoretical revolutions.[11] Taking the famous example of the Copernican controversy, if each of us has a theory of the cosmos, can we be in agreement on what the distance is between the Earth and the Sun? Can we even be in agreement about what our disagreement is about? Can we be in agreement about the identity of celestial bodies? Holism dictates that my theory and your theory cannot share a proposition unless they share all of their propositions. Indeed, holism claims that propositions have no meaning by themselves but only in virtue of the entire discourse to which they belong.

The same objection could be expressed in terms of translation rather than in terms of the convergence of opinions. Can I understand your discourse if you speak a language different from mine? It can be said that I

---

10. Fodor and LePore, *Holism*, 16–17.
11. Ibid., 8–9.

understand one of the sentences you utter if I can translate it into my own language. The holist thesis would be, according to Fodor and LePore, that I cannot understand one of your sentences unless I can understand all of your sentences.

3. *Nihilism*: If semantic holism were confirmed, one might be able to say *that* someone believes or desires, but one would be unable to say *what* it is that he believes or desires. One would be unable to say what it is to believe one thing rather than another. But if one cannot state what a particular belief consists in (or what a particular meaningful expression saying one thing rather than another consists in), then it is as if there are no beliefs and no meanings to the sentences that are supposed to express such beliefs. According to Fodor and LePore, this is the kind of semantic nihilism one finds in the philosophy of Quine.

The core of the objection is this: if the notion of opinion is to have a meaning, one must be able to say what it is for someone to have the same opinion as someone else. Now, we can determine whether two people have both made a noise that we interpret as "yes" while standing in front of a sign reading "Do you believe that snow is white?" But we cannot determine whether they have understood the sign as presenting a sentence bearing the same meaning that *we* attribute to it, nor whether the noise "yes" means that they hold the sentence to be true rather than, say, that they have successfully managed to read what was presented to them.

These objections have the merit of soliciting the opponents of atomism to spell out the way in which they understand the "holistic" character of semantic properties or of psychological attributes. We have no difficulty granting that a philosophy of language and meaning that would have as its first consequence to render ordinary facts of communication mysterious would, by that very fact, refute itself. We cannot take seriously a philosophy of language that would have as a consequence to render extraordinary the fact that people speak to one another. Yet, according to Fodor and LePore, that is what would happen, leading, for example, to the following absurd dialogue:

Me (addressing a passerby in the street): Could you direct me to the nearest post office?

Passerby: Take the next right.

Me (to myself): If only the sentence that he just uttered had not come from him, I could understand it. Alas, I know what this sentence means within the totality of my language, but I lack any knowledge of this passerby's language! Since I do not understand all of his sentences, I cannot interpret this one. Moreover, this passerby's behavior is more than a little strange. He answered me as if he had understood my question, and yet, in virtue of semantic holism, he could not have understood it since he knows nothing of the other sentences in my language.

Evidently, Fodor and LePore's objections play on the opposition between *one* sentence and *all* sentences: "[M]eaning holism would require that if any one sentence in your theory occurs in my theory, then practically all the sentences that occur in your theory must occur in my theory."[12] For them, holism requires that we share all of someone's opinions if we are to share any of his opinions, or that we understand all his sentences to understand any of his sentences. It would not be possible to be in agreement on this or that point or to understand some passages of a text and not others. In other words, holism with regard to language does not consist, in their view, in noticing that I understand the passerby's answer to my question because he responds to me *in English,* a language that I also happen to speak. Holism as they understand it does not consist in emphasizing that language is a totality insofar as it is an organized linguistic system.

What, then, is their exact conception of holism? In their first informal presentation, they understand it in a way that would be acceptable outside the domain of American philosophy. For something to be a sign, it must play a role in a system, a language.[13] But when it comes time to provide a criterion that makes possible the separation of holistic properties from atomistic ones, at that point neither systems, parts of wholes, nor roles within a language are discussed. The criterion proposed is, rather, derived from *number.* The condition that makes a property a holistic one is that the thing by which the property is recognized cannot be the only one of its kind. In order for something to be a symbol, it cannot be the only symbol. Thus, whereas the initial informal definition put forward by Fodor and LePore had as one of its essential traits the dependence of parts on one another, in the more technical definition there is no longer any question of

---

12. Ibid., 9. Here the word "sentence" is understood as any meaningful utterance.
13. Ibid., ix.

such dependence (other than in the impoverished sense in which the property under consideration depends on a plurality of instances).

Fodor and LePore begin by distinguishing two different kinds of properties, which they call "holistic properties" and "atomistic properties." Of any property one can ask whether it is attributable to a single thing in isolation and thereby without any need for us to know whether there are other examples of this property or whether it is instead only attributable to a thing on condition that there exist other examples of the same kind. For them, a property is *atomistic* if it is not impossible for this property to be attributed only a single time. A property is *anatomic* if such attribution is contradictory. Once they have explained this distinction, they can then move on to introduce the concept of a *holistic* property.

They provide examples. Here is an example of a property that cannot be attributed only once to a single individual: being a *sibling*. The notion of a sibling is that of a relation among individuals who have a link of filiation with the same individual. A person cannot be a sibling all by herself. Here is an example of a property that may well be instantiated only a single time: being a rock. A rock remains a rock even if it happens to be the only thing in the world that is a rock.[14]

Having posited their distinction between the atomistic and the anatomic, Fodor and LePore make the holism of certain properties into a particular case of anatomicity: "Holistic properties are properties such that, if anything has them, then *lots* of other things must have them too."[15] It is clear that this definition is concerned with a *plurality* but not with a *totality,* i.e., a complex system. The authors posit no conditions regarding the relations that the samples (whose plurality is necessary) must have with one another.

For anyone familiar with the usually accepted notion of holism, Fodor and LePore's way of proceeding can only appear strange and convoluted. How can one purport to provide the distinctive feature of holistic attributes without mentioning the interdependence of parts within a whole, the unity proper to the whole, and its primacy over the parts, etc.? It is as if the authors wanted to retain the ordinary criterion (i.e., one cannot describe part A without investigating the situation of part B, and reciprocally, since these parts are reciprocally determined), but without

14. Ibid., 1–2.
15. Ibid., 2.

using the words "interdependence of the parts" or "links among the parts within the whole" and thus avoiding what is ordinarily felt to be at the center of a holistic conception whose very principle is that *there is more in the whole than the sum of its parts*.

In short, holism ordinarily is the idea that certain realities must be studied as differentiated totalities, i.e., as totalities in which all of the parts have a function by which the interdependence and cohesion of the whole is assured. What makes of something a sign is the function that it has within a system of signs (which, in turn, has a place within a social practice or an intentional activity). It is in this sense that one can claim that Wittgenstein developed holistic views on language in his later philosophy: a thing is not a sign by itself (in virtue of its intrinsic constitution) but rather only in a (linguistic and extralinguistic) context. Fodor and LePore make a vague allusion to this way of conceiving the matter in the opening pages of their book, only to follow up by treating holism as requiring a plurality: if there is a sign, there must be more than one of them, for the quality of signifying is a collective property that can only be ascribed to several signs taken together.

Why do the authors exchange a holism of the *system,* which they never take up again, for a holism of the *collection,* which is the only one they go on to discuss? Needless to say, the position that semantic properties were called "holistic" because they could only be possessed by a collection of utterances was not something Fodor and LePore arbitrarily adopted. The viewpoints that they go on to discuss (those of Davidson, Dennett, David Lewis, et al.) come out of a tradition and make use of a terminology that originates in an article by Quine (an article that, they are right to point out, did much to overthrow the then-dominant opinion, making "holism" ascendant in a tradition that was more inclined toward atomism). We will therefore turn to Quine's article.

4.3. Epistemological Holism

The reflections of Fodor and LePore on holism have their source and their motive in the famous article by Quine that critiques what he called "the two dogmas" of both classical and modern empiricism.[16] The first dogma

---

16. Willard van Orman Quine, "Two Dogmas of Empiricism" (1951), in *From a Logical Point of View: Nine Logico-Philosophical Essays,* 2nd rev. ed. (1953; New York: Harper Torchbooks, 1961), 20–46.

bears on the distinction between analytic and synthetic truths: the idea that there are truths the knowledge of which does not depend on observed facts but uniquely on the language used to state them. It is enough to understand the terms in which these propositions are formulated to know that they are true (the usual example being the proposition "no bachelor is married"). The second dogma examined by Quine maintains that every meaningful assertion must bear upon immediate experience or on a construction built out of materials taken from immediate experience.

In this text, Quine's subject is above all epistemology, and he takes up the classical problem of the relationship between theories and observations. But Quine also puts forward a holistic conception of language that one might well call "semantic holism." Fodor and LePore are right to stress that there is a difference between epistemological holism and semantic holism.[17] They are also right to say that Quine's article does not clearly distinguish the two. Epistemological holism corresponds to what Quine calls Duhem's "doctrine," according to which one cannot verify the hypotheses of a theory one by one. But this epistemological thesis is formulated in such a way that it might be taken as a thesis about language, about the way in which the propositions that make up the theory possess the meaning they do.

It would perhaps be best to go all the way back to Pierre Duhem himself to see in what way his doctrine might be taken to be holistic.

In Duhem's book *The Aim and Structure of Physical Theory,* one section is devoted to establishing the point that "an experiment in physics can never condemn an isolated hypothesis but only a whole theoretical group."[18] The reason for this is that the propositions of physics cannot be used separately from one another. In order to make the point, Duhem compares the sorts of logical contradictions to which a mathematician might appeal in an *argumentum ad absurdum* and the experimental contradictions that the physicist uses. Here is the usual conception, which Duhem seeks to criticize: when the physicist seeks to show that a proposition of physics is false, he constructs an experiment meant to falsify it. If the proposition were true, one ought to observe that a certain phenomenon

17. Fodor and LePore, *Holism,* 40–41.
18. Pierre Duhem, *The Aim and Structure of Physical Theory,* trans. Philip P. Wiener (Princeton, NJ: Princeton University Press, 1954), 183–187.

is produced. Now, it so happens that the phenomenon in question is not produced in the set conditions. Therefore, it is claimed, the proposition has been refuted.

Yes, agrees Duhem, the proposition in question has been refuted, but only if we take as irrefutable the theory that allowed us to construct the experiment and also as irrefutable the theory that allowed us to link the proposition in question to the prediction of a phenomenon (by saying that the phenomenon *ought* to be produced if the proposition in question is true), and, finally, also as irrefutable the theory by which we interpret the results of the experiment (in order to say that the results were not those forecast by the proposition).

> The prediction of the phenomenon, whose nonproduction is to cut off debate, does not derive from the proposition challenged if taken by itself, but from the proposition at issue joined to that whole group of theories; if the predicted phenomenon is not produced, not only is the proposition questioned at fault, but so is the whole theoretical scaffolding used by the physicist. The only thing the experiment teaches us is that among the propositions used to predict the phenomenon and to establish whether it would be produced, there is at least one error; but where this error lies is just what it does not tell us.[19]

How are we to understand the notion of "theoretical scaffolding"? People often refer—Duhem first among them—to a *system* of propositions. But in what sense of the word "system"? Not in the sense of a theoretical system that postulates its own parts, whether in Descartes's linear and deductive way or the circular deductive way of the Hegelians. It is not being claimed that, if a proposition is not confirmed by experience, *all* of the propositions of the system must therefore be false. The only legitimate conclusion is that *at least one* of the propositions of the theory is false. The system in question is therefore one that results from bringing together the propositions of the theory by means of conjunctions.

In sum, the physicist can never subject an isolated hypothesis to experimental test, but only a whole group of hypotheses; when the experiment is in disagreement with his predictions, what he learns is that at least one of the

---

19. Ibid., 185.

hypotheses constituting this group is unacceptable and ought to be modified; but the experiment does not designate which one should be changed.[20]

Duhem himself goes on to explain by means of an image the sense in which systems are here at stake. He draws a contrast between a watchmaker and a doctor: in order to fix a watch, the watchmaker is always able to take the machine apart, whereas the doctor has to guess, according to the observed symptoms, which diseased organ has to be treated. The physicist is like the doctor. He cannot take physics apart in order to verify that all of its parts are in working order. He will have to proceed as does a doctor who can only wonder whether it is the lung, the liver, the spleen, the stomach, etc.

Physics is not a machine which lets itself be taken apart; we cannot try each piece in isolation and, in order to adjust it, wait until its solidity has been carefully checked. Physical science is a system that must be taken as a whole; it is an organism in which one part cannot be made to function except when the parts that are most remote from it are called into play, some more so than others, but all to some degree. If something goes wrong, if some discomfort is felt in the functioning of the organism, the physicist will have to ferret out through its effect on the entire system which organ needs to be remedied or modified without the possibility of isolating this organ and examining it apart.[21]

What does all of this have to do with semantics? In fact, Duhem is not at all concerned in this chapter with issues in the theory of meaning but rather with questions in the philosophy of physics. Only a verificationist prejudice can make this theory—which bears on the ways physicists proceed to establish a result—into one of significance for semantics.[22]

It is true that Duhem does at points speak about the "physical meaning" or the "experimental meaning" of a proposition. So, for example, regarding the principles of mechanics, he remarks that they have no "physical

---

20. Ibid., 187.
21. Ibid., 187–188.
22. Paul Gochet proposed a distinction between *significance* [*signifiance*], which is opposed to the absence of meaning, and *empirical signification,* which is opposed to the lack of any possibility of something being given in experience. See his *Quine en perspective: Essai de philosophie comparée* (Paris: Flammarion, 1978), 23. For Duhem, what is at issue is only empirical signification, not significance.

meaning" in isolation. However, he adds, the principles of mechanics are nonetheless subject to experimental control to the extent that they play a role in the theory of mechanics. Poincaré had asserted that principles are devoid of experimental meaning. For example, the principle of inertia makes reference to a material point removed from the action of any other body (its motion is uniformly rectilinear). The principle of inertia thus has no empirical meaning. Against Poincaré, Duhem upholds that a proposition that escapes any sort of direct control can nevertheless be subject to an indirect control. In isolation, the principle cannot have a physical meaning. But taken as the foundation of a theory, it becomes controllable just like any other hypothesis, since what is contradicted by an experiment is always a theory, never an isolated proposition. "There thus disappears what might have seemed paradoxical in the following assertion: Certain physical theories rest on hypotheses which do not by themselves have any physical meaning."[23] It is clear that when Duhem writes "no physical meaning" he does not mean to say that principles, when isolated, become pure nonsense. Duhem is not saying that one cannot comment on a principle or translate it into another language or even state its truth conditions (provided this is not taken to mean its verification conditions). The principle of inertia says something, even if it says nothing on its own that would directly lead one to devise an experiment. The proof is that one can explain why the principle, because of what it means, does not lend itself to direct experimental control.

Moreover, Duhem emphasizes that the results of an experiment must be interpreted.[24] This does not mean that the sentence that provides the result is incomprehensible. Duhem is only pointing out that this sentence does not have the same consequences for an uninformed observer that it does for the physicist armed with a theory. It is one thing to observe the back and forth of a beam of light on a celluloid ruler, quite another to measure the electrical resistance of a coil.[25]

23. Duhem, *Physical Theory*, 216.
24. Fodor and LePore rightly point out that the very statement of the thesis on the holism of the confirmation requires that one be able to understand the sentence reporting the observation (e.g., "the litmus paper turned red") independently from the various physical theories from which the physicist might choose (Fodor and LePore, *Holism*, 42).
25. Duhem, *Physical Theory*, 145.

Quine brings these ideas together into what he calls Duhem's "doctrine." Recall that one of the objectives of Quine's article was to overturn the empiricist dogma of a distinction between theoretical statements and statements of observation. If we asked him what we are to understand by "whole" or by "system," his response would be that these should be understood as the totality of propositions, in the collective sense of the word "totality." Indeed, Quine avails himself here of a classical distinction between two logical forms, *distributive* predication and *collective* predication.[26] The doctrine attributed to Duhem is, then, that the predicates "is verified" and "is disconfirmed" are properly attributed to the propositions of the theory taken collectively and not distributively. Quine claims to have taken the idea from Carnap that "our statements about the external world face the tribunal of sense experience not individually but only as a corporate body."[27] The comparison of the whole of a theory with a corporate body, in the juridical sense in which this status is given to an establishment (such as a business or a college), shows that the status of this whole is that of a collective totality, i.e., of an ontological plurality treated, for the purpose at hand, *as if* it had the unity of being that a flesh-and-blood person does. A few lines further on, Quine offers this remarkable formulation: "*Taken collectively,* science has its double dependence upon language and experience; but this duality is not significantly traceable into the statements of science *taken one by one.*"[28] Here it is clear that science is nothing but the plurality of scientific propositions taken as a whole or considered as a single body. In other words, there are properties that all of

---

26. In the form of collective predication, a predicate is attached to several things taken together (collectively)—e.g., with regard to a lot of ten articles that each cost one hundred euro, one may say that "these articles cost (together) one thousand euro." In a distributive predication, the predicate is attached to an individual thing, even where the proposition is in the plural—e.g., "these articles cost one hundred euro (each)." Even though the adverb "together" [*ensemble*] is sometimes used to mark the collective character of a predication, one must not confuse what logic holds to be a collective subject and what mathematical set theory calls a "set" [*un ensemble*]. Claims about the collective are not claims about the set (which is an abstract object). For example, four apples taken together [*ensemble*] have a particular weight, but the set [*ensemble*] of these four apples weighs nothing. I will return to the nature of collective predication in the following chapter.

27. Quine, "Two Dogmas," 41.

28. Ibid., 42; I have italicized the turns of phrase that oppose the collective and the distributive points of view.

the units of which science is made up possess distributively (for example, that of being propositions expressed in this or that language), but there are other properties that they only possess collectively or corporately.

Until now, the entire discussion has been about epistemological holism, i.e., the conditions in which it is possible to verify theoretical propositions. We still do not know what about this is meant to support semantic holism, unless it is the theory that the comprehension of these propositions must also take place in conditions that exclude the possibility of proceeding distributively, piece by piece, article by article, element by element. How are we to understand this?

4.4. The Unit of Meaning

In several places Quine provided the elements of a somewhat fanciful history of semantics.[29] In the first period of theories of meaning, according to him, units of meaning were sought on the level of words or terms. Then, thanks to the work of Bentham and Frege, they were sought on the level of sentences or propositions. Finally, thanks to the refutation of the empiricist "second dogma" and therefore in virtue of semantic holism, we have come to understand that it is impossible to take sentences one by one to see whether their meaning is empirical or purely theoretical.

Recall that the second dogma bears on the meaning of assertions: an assertion is meaningful provided that it either bears on an immediate experience or on a logical construction built of immediate data. According to Quine, the refutation of empiricist semantics (which posited the above reductive equivalence) has as a consequence the impossibility of understanding a sentence on its own (by relating it to an immediate experience). The units of meaning are therefore to be found at a higher level than that of the sentence. What level? Epistemological holism referred to the level of the entire theory. Semantic holism refers to the level of language. Is a theory a language? It would be strange if it were. And yet, that is apparently Quine's view. The move from a holistic doctrine regarding the experimental confirmation of scientific propositions to one regarding the semantic properties of linguistic units is no doubt facilitated by the

---

29. See, for example, Quine's *Theories and Things* (Cambridge, MA: Harvard University Press, 1981), 7.

following equivalences: a theory is a set [*un ensemble*] of propositions (or, if you prefer, sentences), but a language is also a set of propositions (or sentences). Therefore, a theory is a language.[30] It is hard to believe that this unfortunate slippage is the sole reason that can be put forward in favor of semantic holism, which would then be reduced to a holism concerning discourses made up of propositions, i.e., theoretical discourses.

Why do I call it a slippage? Because the difference between a language and a theory is indispensable. Without it, it becomes impossible to say whether, in a conflict of opinions, the parties contradicting each other speak the same language (which is a condition for such contradiction). What one party puts forth is precisely what the other rejects. It must also be possible to share another's language in order to reproduce the opinions he holds that one does not share. There is, for example, a sentence from Molière that reads, "There is nothing truer than the bogeyman," yet it is possible to understand this sentence without as a result being forced to share Sganarelle's theory regarding the bogeyman's transgressions.[31] Here again arises the objection that holism carries relativism within itself.

The semantic myth propagated under Quine's authority contains, like many myths, elements of truth mixed with fictions in an arrangement meant to present something—here, a philosophy—as grounded in a history that is decisive, as one promised by all the work of the past. The grain of truth to be retained is the contrast, in the history of reflection on semantics, between doctrines centered on the word and those centered on the sentence. The element that is mere theatrics is Quine's evocation of a kind of inexorable ascent that can only lead one to seek the subject of attribution of semantic properties at ever-higher levels.

On the contrast between a semantics centered on the proposition and a semantics centered on the noun, a remark by the historian of medieval logic Norman Kretzmann might usefully be cited here. He points out that semantic theory passes through eras that correspond to the fate of logic within philosophy as a discipline.[32] When logic has pride of place in

30. Here, the word "language" should be understood as meaning "discourse." In France, philosophers influenced by structural linguistics have developed theories of discourse that also wanted to extend linguistic analysis to "meaningful units" on levels above that of the sentence, e.g., theories of narrative or mythological discourse.
31. Molière, *Don Juan*, Act III, Scene 1.
32. Norman Kretzmann, "Semantics, History of" in *Encyclopedia of Philosophy*, 2nd ed., ed. Donald M. Borchert, vol. 7 (Detroit: Thomson Gale, 2006), 772.

philosophy, reflection about the meaning of linguistic signs is carried out within the philosophy of logic; it is therefore conceived as a part or an extension of logical analysis. Logical analysis bears on the valid modes of inference from one thought to another and therefore on the expression of thought in propositions.

The philosophers lucky enough to engage in their activity in a climate in which the study of logic is valued have at their disposal a precious analytical instrument. They can draw from the resources of logic to express the conceptual differences that seem to them to require attention in this or that domain. In these periods, philosophy takes on a style that today we would call "analytic." This is what happened in the Middle Ages, and it was once again the case beginning in the nineteenth century, when logic again became a living discipline. By contrast, Kretzmann explains, during the period that runs from the Renaissance to the Enlightenment, logic is stagnant and even in decline. Epistemology is dominant among philosophical disciplines, and the question of the conditions for certitude (or the grounds for our claims to knowledge) is what preoccupies the thinkers of this period. This question eclipses questions about the conditions for meaning or for the truth of discourse. Beginning in the Renaissance, the keenest minds generally turned away from semantic theories organized around the analysis of discourse. Reflection about language and signs is instead guided by a different model, provided by iconic signs. Kretzmann claims that the period in which philosophy of language is conducted from outside the domain of logic—on bases that are iconic rather than linguistic—runs from roughly the middle of the fourteenth century to the middle of the nineteenth. I believe that this is an important observation. It suggests that the most fruitful period of modern philosophy *did not have a philosophy of language* as we understand the term today. From Descartes, Hobbes, or Locke to Hegel and Nietzsche, the point of departure for all reflection on language is not the concept of a sign used to *say* something but rather a sign conceived as figuratively *representing* something (in the way an archetype or a painting represents).[33] We have not seen the end of the consequences of this decisive point, especially in the

---

33. If the paradigm case of a sign is an image or an icon, the temptation will be great to conceive of the relation between sign and signified thing along the lines of a dyad: the portrait and the original, the painting and the thing. The temptation is reduced when the paradigm case of a sign is one that *says* something. It is true that there have been many

philosophy of mind, if indeed it is true that the philosophy of mind is largely subordinate to logic and semantics. In a sense, what we call *modern* philosophy (by which we mean the philosophy that emerges in modern times) is no longer our philosophy. It is not that we are in some post-philosophical age, as has occasionally been claimed, but that when we do philosophy, we do it in other conditions and with other assumptions. This is precisely what we were able to glimpse in my earlier book, *The Mind's Provisions*: the difference between the traditional doctrine of representational mind and the new cognitivist doctrine is that the former conceives of cognitive entities using as a model the iconic sign, whereas the latter takes up the linguistic model of the propositional sign.[34]

All of this confirms the importance of marking the difference between the era of philosophies for which the word was the unit of meaning and the era of philosophies that start from the sentence, the utterance that can be true or false. Should we say that we have now entered a third era in the philosophies of language? Just as it became accepted that words had no other meaning than one that contributes to the meaning of the sentence, we have come to understand, according to this view, that sentences are not autonomous units of meaning but fragments of a higher unit. The meaning of sentences should then be sought in their contribution to the overall meaning of discourse. And, indeed, why should the analysis of propositions be holistic (in the sense in which the Fregean context principle is holistic) while the analysis of discourse remains atomistic?

I believe that, all things considered, the meaning of propositions must be qualified as discursive, in the same way that the meaning of words is propositional (see also chapter 8, section 5, below). But in order to understand what that means, more will have to be said about what it is for a part to contribute to the meaning of a whole. What contribution is required from the parts? How do the contributions of the parts combine within an overall meaning? What is at stake here is the very notion of a unit of meaning. One may well wonder whether Quine has not thought of

---

attempts to construct dyadic or representationist theories of the proposition (by, for example, seeing the proposition as *an image of a state of affairs*), but even in such theories, the object signified by the proposition is not something that one might designate or point one's finger at.

34. Vincent Descombes, *The Mind's Provisions: A Critique of Cognitivism,* trans. Stephen Adam Schwartz (Princeton: Princeton University Press, 2001), chapters 4–12.

discourse as a kind of great sentence rather than as a unit or a whole at a higher level than that of sentences. When semantics relocates the semantic unit from the level of the word to the level of the sentence, it has effectively moved from one level to another. Words are parts of the *sentence*—they are not parts of some greater, higher-level *word*. A collection of words is not yet a sentence. What is the higher unit that bears the meaning of which sentences are the parts? If sentences are the parts, this higher unit has to be something other than a sentence.

4.5. A Collectivist Holism

"Semantic holism," we are told, is the theory according to which the unit of meaning is neither the word (which is a part of the sentence) nor even the sentence itself, but sentences taken as a group [*les phrases prises ensemble*], the totality of language that has been put forth. Yet the very notion of a "totality of language" remains obscure in the current context. To which totality have we been referred? At first we are tempted to think it is a meaningful totality, in the familiar sense of a totality that, by its organization, furnishes a context for each of its elements, so that the meaning of these elements is their positional value. Yet it cannot be a meaningful totality in this sense because there is nothing in Quine's holism that resembles such a thing. This comes out in Dummett's critique of Quine's article on the two dogmas of empiricism.[35]

Dummett notes that Quine had first given language (that is, theoretical discourse) the structure of a web. In the language of the theory, statements have locations: those on the periphery are more easily revised; those at the center are not, by definition, infallible, but one would only agree to modify them as a last resort and after having tried to revise all the others. Dummett believes that Quine in fact abandons this idea (without saying so) when he

---

35. Michael Dummett, "Original Sinn" in his *Frege: Philosophy of Language,* 2nd ed. (1973; Cambridge, MA: Harvard University Press, 1981), 584–627. Dummett devoted two other studies to Quine's semantics, both of which have been reprinted in his collection *Truth and Other Enigmas* (Cambridge, MA: Harvard University Press, 1978). My intention here is not to adjudicate between Dummett's critique and Quine's ideas, but to take from Dummett's commentary those elements that will shed light on what we are to understand by "holism," thereby helping us to know how partisans and critics of the so-called holistic thesis conceive of the relation between a whole and its parts.

puts forward the thesis of semantic holism, at which point all sentences are henceforth on the same plane. If there is no distinction between the center and the periphery, then what confronts experience is the entire theory. The holistic meaning of this thesis is that "a total theory must be viewed as confronting experience as a single undifferentiated block."[36] In other words, Quine's holism is a doctrine in which the notion of totality is understood as a whole that cannot be analyzed into parts. The totality [*le tout*] in question is more like that in a game of *all or nothing* [*tout ou rien*] than it is the totality of a system divisible into subsystems.[37]

On the other hand, if logic is itself part of this block that confronts experience, then the logical structure of theory has been abandoned: "[T]he internal structure of the theory, consisting in the interconnections of sentences with one another, is totally dissolved, and the theory becomes a mere featureless collection of sentences standing in no special relations to each other."[38]

At the same time, one might well wonder whether Quine is not asking us to see a theory as a single great conjunctive sentence (rather than seeking the meaning of sentences in a higher totality, above the level of the sentence). A prediction is either confirmed or not: we will see whether the litmus paper turns from blue to pink. If the paper remains blue, the theory as a whole will have to be rejected. It is therefore the theory that is either true or false, and the theory is therefore the bearer of meaning or is what would normally be called "a proposition." Just as a proposition can be true or false without us being able to say of any of its parts that it is true or false, here the theory is true or false without us being able to say that a sentence of the theory is true or false.

This is exactly what Quine claims in a more recent article: it is not the hypothesis alone that is rejected in the case of an experiment that disconfirms a prediction—it is the "conjunction of sentences" that the physicist used to derive by implication the empirical prediction from his hypothesis.[39]

---

36. Dummett, "Original Sinn," 597.

37. This point has also been made by Gochet, who cites a critique by Vuillemin on the same subject (*Quine en perspective,* 26). In reality, it might be said that theory forms a whole in the sense of a system made up of compartments. This amounts to saying that it is a whole differentiated into parts and not some monolithic block.

38. Dummett, "Original Sinn," 597.

39. Willard van Orman Quine, *The Pursuit of Truth,* rev. ed. (1990; Cambridge, MA: Harvard University Press, 1992), 13–14.

This amounts to saying that it is always possible (although not always advisable) to maintain the hypothesis and modify another sentence that forms part of the conjunction. Sentences thus are parts of one great conjunctive proposition and not parts of something that would be to the sentence what the sentence is to the word.

An *undifferentiated block*, a *collection devoid of internal structure*: these qualifiers teach us something. Quine's holism is a doctrine of the collective whole. When we are in a collectivist holism, we are quite far away from structural holism.[40] In the semantic holism carried forward by Quine's disciples and criticized by Fodor and LePore, the word "whole" is understood as a collective subject of attribution. So, when one says "the entirety of the theory," we should understand *all the sentences of the theory taken collectively*. These sentences in no way form a whole outside of the context in which attributes (such as those of being confirmed or disconfirmed by an experiment) are predicated. We are miles away from the search for a structure that would allow a definition of the whole as a system characterized by the internal relations among its parts.

4.6. Collectivist Holism and Structural Holism

Above, I wrote that Fodor and LePore, when seeking to describe holistic doctrines, did not make use of concepts that might have been thought unavoidable: system, complexity, parts, functions, structural relations. Worse, it seems that they sought to set aside any notion of a system and thereby also the notion of a structure to be defined based on the multiplicity under consideration. This becomes apparent if we examine more closely one of the examples given in the opening pages of their book. The work begins, as mentioned earlier, with a general classification of kinds of properties. The reader might have expected relational properties to be privileged, since they are the materials from which holistic properties are constructed. Yet there is nothing like this in the book. The authors of *Holism* go to great pains to emphasize that a relational property (which

---

40. The adjective "collectivist" is here taken in a purely logical sense (the attributes are the object of a collective predication). It should in no way be taken to suggest an affinity with political programs for the collective appropriation of the means of production. Something similar is the case for "methodological individualism," which is a nominalist philosophy and not some programmatic selfishness.

requires at least two terms) is not *ipso facto* a holistic property. Here is what they have to say about this:

> You can't be a cat owner unless there is a cat that you own, so being a cat owner is a relational property. But it's by no means obvious that you can't be a cat owner unless there are other cat owners. Patently, the cat you own needn't itself own a cat in order for *you* to own *it*.[41]

Their treatment of this example reveals the limits of the Quinean conception of holism. What I mean is that the authors show to what extent they remain unaware of the reasons one might have, in a given domain, to make use of the notion of an overarching totality. Nevertheless, it is important here to introduce a distinction. It is entirely correct of them to say that a relational property is not *ipso facto* a holistic property: there can still be relations in atomistic conditions. For example, the fact that I am seated next to someone in the metro is not sufficient for one to speak of a *couple* made up of me and my seatmate (other than in a purely extensional—and therefore nonholistic—sense of the term). On the other hand, it would be difficult to speak about holistic properties without saying that they are a class of relational properties: they are relations that have as their distinctive trait to depend on one another, i.e., to form a *structure*. For example, if being president of the National Assembly is a holistic property of Mr. X, this is because Mr. X has this status only because of the position that has been given to him by the others in the group. Another example: psychiatrists have proposed a "systemic" theory of mental disorders. If this theory is right, individual disorders should be studied as manifestations of disorders in the familial system; for example, the difficulties sometimes encountered in the relation between a young mother and her child may be a function of the nature of the relations among other members of the family.

Let us return to Fodor and LePore's example. Contrary to what they write, to be the owner of a cat is not above all a relational property, the relation being between a person and a cat. The relation in question defines a status relative to other people. To be the owner of any sort of thing is a relation between someone, the owner, and other people—for example, the inhabitants of a neighborhood in the case of a cat. Compare these two attributes: *being the owner of a cat* and *being a photograph of a cat*. In order for

---

41. Fodor and LePore, *Holism*, 3.

something to be a photograph of a specific cat, it is not necessary that there be other photographs of that cat, nor is it excluded that there be any; rather, it is immaterial. The attribute is thus, in Fodor and LePore's terminology, atomistic. In fact, nothing about *this* photograph is changed by there being (or not being) other such photographs. By contrast, if I am the owner of a cat, you cannot also be the owner unless we happen to be co-owners of the same cat. In other words, in order for someone to be the owner of a cat, there must be *someone else* who is not its owner. The juridical concept of property, like every concept of a status or an institution, is thus *holistic,* not because it requires a plurality of subjects of attribution of a given status (for example, being the owner of this cat), but because its attribution presupposes the prior application of another concept—that of status—and the concept of social status requires not a mere plurality of subjects, but a differentiated plurality of subjects. Far from receiving from the system the same characteristic trait, they will receive *different* positions.

It goes without saying that the attribute "owner of something" does not have as a metaphysical requirement that there be *other owners* of the thing or even of a similar thing. But it does have as a metaphysical requirement that there be someone whose status is *not to be the owner* of what rightly belongs to me. Legitimate possession of a belonging is a holistic attribute because it presupposes that an entire system of relations among persons and things has been put in place.

The juridical notion of property put forward by Fodor and LePore is essentially that of Locke, since it is a dyadic relation between an owner and a thing. Fichte, at least on this point, had a better view: property is a *creation* of the entire society, not a tie between a particular person and a particular thing that others need only take note of. The right that an owner has over certain things is a right, recognized by society, to exclude all others from using or occupying those things.

[N]o right to the property of things can take place without the right to keep all men from acting upon them. Whether others observe my right to property is revealed solely by whether they avoid this foreign activity. This right to exclude foreign activity is, it follows, the true seat of the right to a property of things.[42]

---

42. J. G. Fichte, *The Closed Commercial State,* trans. Anthony Curtis Adler (Albany: State University of New York Press, 2012), 132.

Contrary to what Fodor and LePore suggest, the relation between the owner and the thing owned is not dyadic. It is triadic: it associates a thing with two statuses—the status of being its owner or owners and the status of not being its owner.

In what follows, my task will be to draw out the consequences of this elementary fact: what makes the attribute of being an "owner" a holistic characteristic is not that one cannot posit the existence of an owner without positing the existence of other owners. It is, rather, that one cannot posit the existence of an owner of something without positing the existence of *nonowners,* i.e., people who agree (or who are supposed to agree) to be excluded from the possession (if not of the enjoyment) of the thing the ownership of which has been attributed to someone other than themselves. Only in such a system can someone call himself an "owner."

———≫•≪———

As we have seen, the idea of a holism of the mental provoked a variety of objections, some negligible, others quite serious. The most serious objection asks what holism implies about the possibility of comparing thoughts. That question must be asked: how we can say of two people that they think the same thing if we are unable to individuate thoughts?

In fact, I believe that atomism has been definitively refuted by arguments such as those of Wittgenstein: the intentions or thoughts of someone cannot be determined outside of any context, which means that states of mind are not states of the mind (in the sense in which the physical state of a thing is its internal state).[43] The main question is then, to my mind, about sorting out the consequences of holism, whether they be relativistic or not.

Nevertheless, before even beginning to undertake this task, it is essential that we ask what holism is *as such*. The authors of *Holism: A Shopper's Guide* wrote their book after having scoured all of the (American) philosophical literature on the question. The definition that they put forward in the glossary at the end of their book is this: "A property is holistic just in case if anything has it, then lots of things do."[44]

---

43. See the last chapter of my book *The Mind's Provisions,* especially section 3, 236–247.
44. Fodor and LePore, *Holism,* 258.

This definition, as has already been pointed out, makes no reference to systems, parts and wholes, functions or roles, or any of what is ordinarily meant by holism. Why must other things possess the holistic property? What is the reason for the interdependence of the parts that precludes studying only one of them without concern for the others? Nothing in the proposed definition allows us even to raise this question. In short, the authors began—as one must—by speaking of a *system* but immediately swap this notion for that of a *collective*. Worse, they have explicitly ruled out the possibility that apparently structural attributes be considered holistic.

It is worth recalling that, in the French anthropological tradition, structural or holistic analysis consists precisely in studying intellectual categories that are grounded in symbolic relations, where the latter are understood as relations of complementarity between two statuses (e.g., man and woman, nature and culture, young and old, master and servant, etc.).[45]

Is this just a dispute about terminology? After all, why should American philosophers not be able to give to a doctrine whatever name seems to them to fit its content best? But this reaction is superficial. *Holism* is the dependence upon one another of the parts of a whole. The *philosophical question of holism* is one of knowing how it can be that the attributes of a thing depend on another thing. How is it, for example, that an inscription's status as a sign depends on knowing whether there are other inscriptions having this same status? We have seen that there are two possible responses to this question. These two conceptions of holism diverge on the reasons for the *dependence* of a thing on things other than itself.

For Fodor and LePore, the reason one might have for claiming that semantics must be holistic is that meaning is collective in nature and therefore not elementary, not atomistic. In other words, the properties of A depend on the properties of B because they are members of the same

---

45. In a recent book, Marc Augé provides the following explanation of the way in which anthropologists understand the idea of a symbolic relation: "If what we call 'symbolic' is the represented and instituted relation to the other, the relation of complementarity that exists between a same defined as such by this relation and an other that is other relative to this same . . . we can also say that anthropology's primary object of study is the symbolic, provided we make clear that the symbolic, which presents itself as prior to every form of practice, is itself called into question by the historical practices whose evolution and mutations translate its efficacy and prolong its influence." Marc Augé, *An Anthropology for Contemporaneous Worlds,* trans. Amy Jacobs (1994; Stanford, CA: Stanford University Press, 1999), 56 [translation modified].

"collective," in much the same way that one might claim that football players must be on the same victorious team if the description "winner of the match" is to be applied to each of them.

Structural holism puts forward a different conception of the reason for the mutual dependence of the parts: something is a sign only if it must be related to other signs in order for any sort of meaning to be attributed to it. But it is not enough that there be a plurality of signs belonging to the same category. In order for there to be a proposition, signs that complement one another—in the way that nouns and verbs complement one another—must be chosen. Their dependence itself depends on the structure of the whole within which the parts complement one another.

I cannot determine whether the reason Fodor and LePore follow Quine's usage is that they endorse it or, rather, because they wanted to discuss a variety of doctrines developed by thinkers who have in common that they understand holism in the way Quine did. What I can do is to try to imagine the explanation that someone might provide in order to defend the conception that I find strange—i.e., that holism must be understood in the collectivist way. One might think it through as follows:

The collectivist holist will first concede that a relation such as "cat owner" is effectively a structural one if the relation between the owner and the cat systematically depends on another relation between the owner and non-owners, a relation defined by right. But this then means, he will add, that the right is something collective. To have a right is not something that Robinson Crusoe can enjoy for as long as he is alone. Right begins when Robinson meets Friday. Robinson and Friday are rights holders only collectively. As a result, structural properties can be reduced to collective ones.[46]

In other words, the structure is the structure of a collection of individuals. Or, better yet, structural relations are collective relational properties. It is always multiple things together (and not each thing independently of

---

46. One of the examples discussed by the authors of *Holism* could be taken as moving in this direction. The question is knowing whether *being a criminal* is a holistic concept. It is a juridical concept, and juridical attributes presuppose a world in which there are multiple agents. "So it's conceptually necessary that Robinson Crusoe couldn't commit a crime . . ." (Fodor and LePore, *Holism*, 109).

the others) that possess a structure. This is why, they might say, every holism is, in the final analysis, a collectivism.

Their defense, then, amounts to pointing out that they sought to give a purely logical definition of holistic concepts. What makes a concept holistic? This is a determination to be made by your philosophy of language (in the case of signs) or of mind (in the case of acts and dispositions of mind). But in what does the holistic character of such a concept consist? This is what they sought to spell out, and that is why they began with a classification of predicates into various classes (atomistic, anatomic, holistic). Thus, at the level of abstraction that they have chosen, any totality whatever will appear as a collective totality.

In chapters 5 through 9, I intend to show that: (1) structural properties are not collective properties, and (2) this is so even though they are holistic properties in the usual sense of the term (i.e., a property that consists in playing the role of a part in a whole).

My thesis might seem paradoxical. One might well ask: what can possibly have a structure, other than precisely a collection of elements whose relations are structural in character? I maintain, precisely, that there is nothing paradoxical or astounding about this thesis.

In the current state of philosophical opinion, collectivist holism often gives the impression of having the advantage of being both clear and consistent with logic. As for structural holism, it would seem to be condemned to obscurity, regardless of its relevance, and is taken to be the expression of a kind of Romantic temperament or an aesthetic view of things, a revolt against the rigors of a sober analysis.

It is therefore incumbent on me to clear away these false impressions through reflection on the conditions for the description of a whole—i.e., a holistic description. My investigation comprises two parts: it must begin with the question of holism as such (in chapters 5 through 7) before returning to the questions of holism of mind and of language (in chapters 9 through 11).

I will show first that collectivism is, at root, a pseudo-holism, for it never engages in any analysis of the relations between the parts of a whole (chapter 5). I will then seek to determine the conditions in which it is possible to speak of a meaningful whole (chapter 6). In order to do that, we will have to explore the logic of relations (chapter 7), which will allow us to define a meaningful whole as a system constituted by a relation that is, at the very least, triadic (chapter 8).

What then remains is to understand why the concepts of mind and of the sign are holistic concepts in the structural sense (chapters 9 and 10). This will allow us to answer the question with which we began: is it a consequence of holism that the identification of thoughts is impossible (chapter 11)?

5

The Illusion of Collective Individuals

Collectivist holism derives its concept of totality from the logical form of collective predication. My question here is, what is a collective totality? Let us take, for example, a team. It is made up of members who can be enumerated. But a team can also carry out work, win victories, and go places, just as individual actors can. A team would then be an individual of sorts, since properties of an individual kind can be attributed to it. What Péguy once called "the party of forty-year-old men" is not itself forty years old, but the sports team that won the victory is itself victorious—its members are winners only as members of the team (i.e., indirectly) and not each one on his own. The property of having won the game is collective, it is said.

Collective predications like these are entirely ordinary and legitimate forms of discourse. By contrast, the notion of a collective individual is obscure and even incoherent. On the one hand, the subject of a collective property is a plurality of individuals. On the other, it seems to lay claim to its own reality, distinct from that of its members. This intellectual problem is a genuine reason to be mistrustful of all forms of holism that appear to slide from a statement of the obvious (there is more in a group of individuals than in each of the individuals themselves) to an absurdity (there is more in a group of individuals than the group of individuals).

5.1. The Singular and the Plural

When writing in French, one must take note of whether the subject of the sentence requires that the verb be in the singular or the plural. In cases where both forms are permitted, there is no semantic difference between them. This is not always the case in English. In English, it sometimes happens that one is unsure, even when the subject is, from a purely grammatical point of view, singular. And in cases where both forms are possible, one might have reason to wonder whether using the plural rather than the singular suggests anything to the reader. One may say "The Cabinet is divided," but one may also say "The Cabinet are agreed." In French, one might well say that "le gouvernement est divisé" [the government is divided] but not that "le gouvernement est d'accord" [the government is agreed], for the latter would mean agreed with some other party and not that the ministers were in agreement among themselves. Fowler, who cites and recommends both English usages, explains them as follows:

Such words as *army, fleet, Government, company, party, pack, crowd, mess, number, majority,* may stand either for a single entity or for the individuals who compose it, and are called nouns of multitude.[1]

Such a linguistic explanation is the heir of an entire logico-grammatical tradition, right down to its theoretical vocabulary (e.g., *stand for, nouns of multitude*). To say that "the Cabinet (with a capital letter) is divided" is to make use of a form designating a singular entity that, on at least one point on the agenda, has become divided. Fowler explains that it is better to think of the cabinet as a unified whole if one is later to speak of its division (only what is first undivided and united can subsequently come to be divided). However, when one says that "the Cabinet are agreed," the plural is preferable because "it takes two or more to agree."[2] Similarly, "the party lost its way" but "the party lost their hats."[3] In French, this difficulty does not arise: a group of people may take the wrong path and get lost, but a

---

1. H. W. Fowler, *A Dictionary of Modern English Usage,* 2nd ed., rev. Sir Ernest Gowers (Oxford: Oxford University Press, 1965), 402.
2. Ibid., 403.
3. Ibid.

group can neither lose *its* hat nor *their* hats, for *un groupe* is singular and not the sort of singular entity that can have or wear a hat.

Everything Fowler says here about the agreement of the verb and the subject can be transposed to certain substantives in English—for example, the word "people." Bertrand de Jouvenel sees this fact as indicative of a philosophical originality that infuses the English language. Referring to a speech by Edmund Burke, he points out that the meaning is modified when, translating the English word "people" into French as "*peuple,*" one treats it (as one must in French) as requiring third-person singular forms. If the translator hopes to be faithful to Burke's thought, he will sometimes have to use what are solecisms in French: the people of these colonies *are* of English descent [*le peuple de ces colonies* sont (sic) *de descendance anglaise*]; the people must *themselves* possess the power to bestow *their* own money [*le peuple doit posséder* eux-mêmes (sic) *le pouvoir d'octroyer* leur (sic) *propre argent*].[4] Jouvenel explains this necessity as follows:

Throughout my translation, I have used the solecism "le peuple *sont*" [the people are]. This is because the English term "the people" requires the plural and the use of this plural has important consequences. Different cognitive ideas arise depending on whether "the people" are treated as plural or singular: one way presents a crowd of individuals while the other contributes to the personalization of the group.

The French (singular) form is less likely to lead to a distributive conception of freedom: the idea that the freedom of the people is the freedom of the individuals who comprise it. We will later see the influence of the French form on the Napoleonic form of the State.[5]

I will not enter here into the discussion about whether this linguistic difference reveals a difference in national ideologies or whether it is the language itself that molded the different ways of thinking. What interests me is that a stylistic problem arises in English and that, in trying to devise

---

4. [Translator's note: The point here is that French, unlike English, forbids using plural pronouns, adjectives, and verb forms with the noun *le peuple*, which is singular, in the way that Jouvenel says is necessary for the translation of Burke's thought into French.]

5. Bertrand de Jouvenel, *Les débuts de l'état moderne: Une histoire des idées politiques au XIXe siècle* (Paris: Fayard, 1976), 68–69.

a solution, the authors who have dealt with it are naturally led to two other problems, unavoidably highlighting the link between them. On the one hand is the *political* problem of knowing who is responsible, in the last analysis, for the collective work that is human life in common, i.e., social and political existence. On the other hand is the *logical* problem of the representation of an action whose agent is in the plural. The latter problem is known among philosophers as the classical aporia of the one and the many. Jouvenel, in the text cited above, raises the political problem. Yet it is remarkable that he avails himself of the logical distinction between the collective and the distributive in order to set in opposition two conceptions of freedom. In fact, the terms in which the political problem of the two freedoms is expressed come to us from Scholastic nominalism.

What all of this shows is that our subject is not a question of interest only to philosophers (and experts in proper usage and style). These difficulties were not, for example, unknown to sociologists.[6] Marcel Mauss, explaining the prospects for internationalism and arguing that it is a philosophical and religious idea rather than a social fact, writes:

A society is an individual; other societies are also individuals. Among them, it is not possible for as long as they remain individualized to build a higher-order individuality. Utopians generally turn a blind eye to this factual and common-sense observation.[7]

As Louis Dumont points out in his commentary on this text, Mauss's judgment raises a conceptual problem.[8] Moreover, the fact that this

---

6. In what follows, I will draw on some of the elements of my study on "collective individuals," which appeared in the volume *Philosophie et anthropologie* (Paris: Centre Georges Pompidou, 1992), 57–93. Reprinted in *Revue de MAUSS* 18 (2001–2002): 305–337.

7. Marcel Mauss, "La nation" (1920), in his *Œuvres,* vol. 3: *Cohésion sociale et division de la sociologie* (Paris: Les Éditions de Minuit, 1969), 606.

8. Dumont summarizes as follows the definition of the nation proposed by Mauss: "The nation is the political group conceived as a collection of individuals and, at the same time, in relation to other nations, the political individual." Louis Dumont, *Homo Hierarchicus,* 2nd rev. ed., trans. Mark Sainsbury, Louis Dumont, and Basia Gulati (1970; Chicago: University of Chicago Press, 1981), 317. He adds in a footnote: "It may appear that there is a logical inconsistency in the conjunction of the two aspects: how can a collection of individuals be at the same time an individual of a superior order?" (Ibid., 445 n 19.) This is exactly

problem arises is evidence, according to Dumont, that a certain limit of contemporary thinking has been reached, an intellectual and, at root, philosophical incapacity to conceive of totalities in terms that are not individualist or substantialist. What is Mauss saying in the above passage? Societies are like individuals to one another; therefore they cannot be federated within a "superior individuality" since to do so they would have to give up their individuality. Here "individuality" also means sovereignty, independence. But societies are themselves represented as collective individuals in that they conceive of themselves as made up of citizens (one is reminded of the famous frontispiece to Hobbes's *Leviathan* showing the biblical giant Leviathan as made up of a collection of human bodies). This raises the following question: how did societies constitute themselves as collective individuals without effacing the individuality of their members? In fact, Mauss's way of expressing his sociological thesis is questionable since it seems to concede an antisociological thesis to the opponent of sociology—namely, that *if there were* such a thing as society (and not simply *people*), there would be a totality into which the individuals were subsumed and in which they would be reduced to the state of organs or parts. In other words, if there is to be a society, it must be an individual made up of individuals and therefore a collective individual. But the notion of a collective individual contains within it a latent contradiction. On the one hand, we are supposed to imagine a multiplicity that retains enough diversity to justify the adjective "collective." On the other hand, we want to imagine an individual, something that presents itself as undivided and indivisible. This seems to mean something that has sufficiently

---

the question to which I hope to provide a philosophical answer in the present chapter. The answer will be that there is indeed an incoherence and that a collection of individuals can in no way be held to be "an individual of a superior order." In the rest of the footnote, Dumont emphasizes that the incoherence is not imputable to Mauss but to the ideology that Mauss is seeking to explain. This ideology is made up of both ideas: on the one hand, the individual is all there is (society is thus nothing but a collection of individuals), yet, on the other hand, the society that we form when confronted with other societies is the nation (meaning that it is not the village or the clan, etc.), and the reality of the nation is expressed by the fact that it presents itself, with regard to other nations, as a political individual. The State is thus presented, in this ideology, sometimes as an instrument of domination for the control of which individuals (whose interests may coincide or conflict with one another) struggle, while at other times as another name for all-encompassing society (i.e., the national State, center of collective identity).

repressed all internal divisions to justify the substantive "individual" (a contemporary with liberal/libertarian leanings will say "repressed"; a contemporary with liberal/authoritarian leanings will join the Hegelians in saying "overcome").

As a general rule, only after a methodological dispute has arisen in the social sciences do questions of individualism and holism come to be raised. What interests me is somewhat different: not the methodology of these disciplines but the logic used in this contemporary debate, which is the successor of the classical debate between nominalists and their realist opponents.

Normally, the notion of a collective individual elicits reservations or even condemnation that is at once intellectual and moral. According to the usual definitions, a collective being—or, more succinctly, a *collective*—is a group of people. One might say, for example, that a particular review is published "by a collective," and one might even specify the names of the people who make up this collective. But the turns of phrase that one uses strongly suggest that this collective plays the role of an agent. Indeed, this is the sense of Jouvenel's remark on the fact that French uses the singular in these cases. If one is to engage in reflection on the logic of collective description, it is important to notice that the verbs used to describe what the collective is or does are the same ones that would be used for an individual person. This has led some people to believe that a higher-order agent has been introduced, one that resembles us since it does the same sorts of things that we do. This agent is nevertheless of a higher order, as it is made up of individuals in much the same way that individuals are made up of "members." This line of thought gives the impression of a competition between individual actors and collective actors. As Jouvenel suggests, our reaction is not the same if the group is presented as a reality at our level (people, militants) as it is if the group is presented as a reality that can itself be "personified" (The People, The Party). People and militants are merely groups of individuals not unlike us, with the same weaknesses, but The People and The Party seem to have a higher reality and a higher authority (ubiquity, longevity, memory, wisdom).

The notion of a higher-order individual makes us uneasy for moral reasons. First, the superiority of the collective individual is that of something that is more powerful because it is bigger: several people can do things, if they do them together as a group, that a single person cannot. But we are loath to think that a superiority in terms of size is also a moral superiority, an authority. We do not see why the collective individual would be due our respect and loyalty or why its will should be imposed upon us.

It seems to me just as important to take note of a logico-philosophical reason for our dissatisfaction with the superiority of the collective individual. After all, is this single enormous actor—the collective individual—not simply a fiction? We have just seen that this impression of a trick, or a conceptual error, is not exclusively a problem for logicians and metaphysicians. Indeed, one might ask if logicians and metaphysicians have demonstrated the same kind of acuity in their attention to the logical implications of a form of expression as have the authors of the texts cited earlier.

5.2. The Logic of Collective Terms

The idea of the collective comes to us first from the logical tradition, which draws a distinction between two possible interpretations of a sentence whose subject is plural: the sentence can be understood in a distributive or a collective way. Since this is a traditional doctrine, the definitions and even the examples are the same from one textbook to another.[9] For our purposes here, we need only consult the article "collective" [*collectif*] in André Lalande's *Vocabulaire technique et critique de la philosophie* [Technical and Critical Philosophical Vocabulary].[10] The article refers to four usages of the word, among which only three will be relevant to us. Although I do not believe that this doctrine is entirely comprehensible, I will first attempt to set it out in its own terms.[11]

One must begin, I think, with the *adverbial* difference between two forms of predication. This distinction proves necessary when one considers certain predicates that would have no meaning if they were not collectively attributed. "The soldiers are marching" does not necessarily

---

9. Traditional formal logic is a logic of terms and conceives of the proposition as relating two terms (see Chapter 8, section 3, below).

10. André Lalande, *Vocabulaire technique et critique de la philosophie,* 18th ed. (1926; Paris: Presses Universitaires de France, 1996), 147.

11. What is incomprehensible about it is not, of course, any particular collective proposition but rather the theory of such propositions offered by traditional logic.

mean that they are marching together. "The soldiers are parading" does necessarily mean that they are doing it as a group.

This acceptation underlies meaning B in Lalande's entry on "collective" in the *Vocabulaire*.[12] Here are his examples: "The stars are numerous" (one cannot say of the North Star that it is numerous)[13] and "Peter and Paul are brothers" (together they are brothers). Yet Lalande's explanation of this form of predication does not make reference to the adverb ("together" as opposed to "separately" or "each on his own"). In these sentences, he claims, the predicate relates to the subject "taken in a collective sense" (rather than in a distributive sense). Just because the stars are numerous does not allow one to claim that each star is numerous. In short, the sentence is plural, but the plural subject of the sentence is treated as an undivided whole, the subject of a joint proposition.

Traditional logic thus explains the notion of a "collective term" beginning from the locution "together" or "collectively." But it does not appear to be interested in the adverbial nature of this locution. It maintains that a proposition is collective because of the special character of its subject: because the subject is taken collectively, it is a collective subject. Just as a singular term is a word that designates an individual, a collective term is a word that designates several individuals or, especially, a collection of individuals. This is the case with the grammatical subjects in Lalande's examples, "the stars" and "Peter and Paul."

But what is one to do with singular terms that designate groups or associations or corporations? A team is a collective actor, yet one can speak of it as singular (e.g., "the team has played well"). This is where our perplexities begin. Is a term that serves as the subject of a collective proposition required to present itself explicitly as plural? Or can it be a singular term that we happen to know refers to a collection of individuals? Lalande

12. Meaning B is that of a collective term "taken in a collective sense"—"said of a plural term or several terms together when they are subjects of a joint proposition." Lalande, *Vocabulaire*, 147.

13. Before Frege, it was common among logicians to treat predicates of number as signifying collective attributes. Thus, the property of being three would qualify the group of Athos, Porthos, and Aramis without, needless to say, being "distributed" among the three musketeers, since none of them is three "separately." Frege demonstrated the falsity of this philosophy of number. If a group were three, it would be *three groups* and not one group. What is three are then the king's musketeers with whom d'Artagnan was to duel upon arriving in Paris. This does not mean that Athos is three, but that "three" is the answer to the question "How many musketeers is d'Artagnan supposed to duel?"

opts for the second solution, which is his meaning A. Here is the totality of his explanation:

Collective, A. Used for a singular and concrete term that represents a plurality of individuals: "The School of Elea; the Roman Senate; the Institute" and, by extension, a proposition that has a collective term as its subject.[14]

However, a proposition about the School of Elea or the Roman Senate is, at least at first glance, a proposition with a singular subject. Why should the subject of this proposition be taken to represent several individuals? There is nothing to suggest that it refers to several schools or several senates but rather to *this* school, the School of Elea, or to *this* institution, the Roman Senate.

Finally, Lalande provides as meaning D a third use of the adjective "collective," of interest to logicians: some properties (in the logical sense of qualities or attributes) are collective in the sense that they belong to a group of individuals taken as such. Today we would call them "emergent properties." Lalande points out that this sense of the term is consistent with the sociological perspective that might examine, for example, "collective representations," i.e., representations developed by the group (as opposed to representations that can be attributed to a particular individual).[15]

Up to this point, nothing yet suggests why the perspective suggested by collective description ought to be considered *holistic.* We learn this at the end of Lalande's entry: in the course of criticizing innovations proposed by Lachelier, Lalande proposes that we "reserve the noun 'collective' for terms that designate a group of individuals considered inseparably as forming a whole."[16] As a result, for Lalande, collective terms such as those given as examples of meaning A (the Roman Senate, the Institute) are not just representations of a plurality of individuals but representations of totalities.

14. Lalande, *Vocabulaire,* 147.
15. I will leave aside what Lalande takes to be meaning C and which reveals the confusion that often affects philosophical terms once they enter into the vocabulary of the human sciences. According to meaning C, "collective psychology" is collective because its object is "a group of individuals that are similar insofar as they make up a whole." This definition is useless and evinces, moreover, the principle of the oft-noted obscurity of the notion of *social class*: is it because they are similar that the individuals under consideration form a whole? Or is it because they form a whole that they are bestowed by that whole with common features that make them similar to one another?
16. Lalande, *Vocabulaire,* 147.

That is, as he explains, they are wholes considered as undivided. Here we come to the notion of a collective whole as a collective individual.

To speak of a collection of things is to speak about several things, but to speak of that collection of things while specifying that it is to be *taken collectively* is to treat as a unity (in the sense of an undivided entity) what was at first presented as a multiplicity. In the vocabulary of post-Kantian philosophers, one might say that the concept of totality is the result of a combination of the point of view of the Many and the point of view of the One. Totality, we are to understand, is multiplicity posited as a unity. The two concepts of the one and the many must be "synthesized." But how can they be synthesized? This is the entire problem of thinking totality.[17]

By asking us to call "collective" a term such as "the Senate," even though the term appears to be a singular term, traditional logic asks us not to limit ourselves to the proposition but to cast our gaze beyond the language used to the thing itself. This thing appears to be made up of individuals. But why should a logician care about knowing whether the thing designated by the subject is simple or composite? In reality, the logical interest in saying that an expression such as "the Roman Senate" is a collective term is to point out that one can replace this phrase (which is a singular noun) with another: "the Roman Senators." And this equivalence is what interests philosophers. How can it be that the Senate is the same thing as the Senators, that speaking of the Roman Senate is a way of speaking about the Roman Senators? But things are not that simple, for the Roman Senators constitute the Roman Senate only if the words "the Roman Senators" are taken collectively.

This entire doctrine is muddled and further confuses a traditional logic of terms that was already obscure by adding to it the difficulties associated

---

17. Hegelians are right to say that such an operation of totalization is *self-contradictory*. If the only way of conceiving a totality were to carry out an operation synthesizing the many and the one in the conditions here described—i.e., apprehending many things as being only one thing without losing sight of the fact that they are many things and not one thing—one would be forced to conclude that there is no such thing as totality (since the very notion is self-contradictory) or that there are beings whose concept is self-contradictory. The difficulty that I am attempting to resolve is whether we are really caught in this impasse.

with the notion of totality. What are we to understand when we are told to carry out the synthesis of the one and the many? What is this *many* as a *one* or this *one* that we are not supposed to forget is *many*?

Compare the following statements:

—Merleau-Ponty wrote *La structure du comportement.*
—Russell and Whitehead wrote the *Principia Mathematica.*
—Erckmann-Chatrian wrote [*a écrit*: singular] *L'ami Fritz.*
—Émile Erckmann and Alexandre Chatrian wrote [*ont écrit*: plural] *L'ami Fritz.*

It is well known that the authors of *L'ami Fritz* adopted a collective name, i.e., the name of a collective author (of the same nature as the name "Bourbaki").[18] The fact that this collective name is made up of two patronymics that are precisely those of the two members of the collective author does not prevent the name from being that of *one* author, unlike the case where two authors sign with each of their names a work written together (as in the case of Russell and Whitehead). There is thus no other difference between the name "Merleau-Ponty" and the name "Erckmann-Chatrian" other than the difference between the real and the fictive: in both cases, the name designates an author (a singular reality) but this author (in the singular) can present itself as a natural person or a moral person (the collective author). In a catalogue, one entry is needed for Erckmann-Chatrian (as for Bourbaki), two for Russell and Whitehead.

But if this is so, it is difficult to see how there could be anything else in the reality signified by the collective name "Erckmann-Chatrian" than the reality of the two real people named Émile Erckmann and Alexandre Chatrian. It is true that these two real people worked together and that they took this name in order to indicate that the works were by neither one nor the other but by the two of them working collectively. However, the nature of their work cannot be expressed by positing a real collective subject to correspond to the collective name. For the collective nature of their work does not mean there are *three* novelists writing—the two real people plus their combination as a collective author.

---

18. [Translator's note: "Nicolas Bourbaki" is the invented collective name under which a group of French twentieth-century mathematicians published their works.]

Thus, according to the traditional doctrine, there is something more than multiplicity in a collective whole: there is whatever it is that allows us to represent this whole as a unity. Our perplexity derives from our inability to say what it is that has to be added. The collective whole that is the team, it is said, is more than the simple plurality of team members. There is therefore more in several things than the things that there are when there are several things. What more could there be? According to the traditional theory, what is added is their "unity," the unity that they have when they are posited in the form of a "total," a collection.

This response does little to clear up the difficulty. If there is more than the plurality when the plurality is considered collectively and if what is added is the unity that, combined with the multiple, makes it a whole, why not say that one is dealing with an individual *tout court,* a *singular* individual? The very expression "collective individual" is indicative of a conceptual difficulty, as if one seeks to posit more than a mere plurality without going so far as to posit a real unity. It is not surprising that such an intermediate entity eludes every attempt to find a place for it in the order of things.

Let us bear in mind this first conclusion: there are predicates that are collectively attributed and, in this sense, there are collective subjects of predication, but there are no collective individuals. Collective predication describes *ordinary individuals* even where it describes them collectively. Collective propositions are perfectly legitimate forms of description precisely because there are things that people do together, experience together, lay claim to together, and so on. But none of that allows us to posit a collective individual that does and experiences and lays claim to these things.

The idea that a collective predicative proposition bears on a distinct entity—the collective—arises out of a flawed understanding of what the collective subject of a predicate is. In the end, this analytical error can be explained by the tendency to confuse the subject of the sentence (which is a linguistic sign) and the subject to which properties are attributed (which is the referent, the thing or things the sentence talks to us about). Here we can draw a distinction between the *subject of predication* and the *subject of attribution*. Take, for example, the sentence "Socrates is walking." I propose that we call the "subject of predication" what one would look to in response to the question "Does this sentence have a singular term as its subject?" (yes, because the subject is the sign "Socrates"). The "subject of attribution" will accordingly be what one looks to in response to the question "Who is supposed to be walking, according to this sentence?" (Socrates himself is purported to be walking). We can then say that the "collective subject" of traditional formal logic is the subject of predication: a collective subject is simply a sign that plays a role in a proposition the predicate of which is collectively meant. This sign may take the form of a list of individual names ("Peter and Paul are parading") or of a plural common noun ("the soldiers are parading").[19] What about collective nouns, what Fowler called "nouns of multitude"? This is where the Fregean context principle is applicable: taken separately, outside of any proposition, the list or the plural noun signifies nothing. If the soldiers of the regiment are parading, the regiment is parading. In this case, the regiment is identified as the regiment of these soldiers and thus as an abbreviation for the list of the soldiers who make up the regiment. And, in this sense, it is impossible for the regiment to parade without the soldiers of the regiment parading.

We therefore come to the following conclusions. Can Sapper Camember parade without his regiment? The answer is "no." Can the sapper's regiment parade without the sapper participating in the parade? The answer is that one must make a distinction. If one has decided to understand a "regiment" as a plurality of individuals (i.e., if the word "regiment" is a "noun of multitude"), the answer is "no." Dictionaries tell us that a collective noun is a designation used for several individuals. In this case, the sapper will have to parade for his regiment to parade. The most impossible response of all, though, is one that claims that the sapper's regiment can parade without the sapper parading and can do so because the regiment is a collective individual. The fact that this entity is made up of individuals can in no way give it the power of doing without individuals in order to posit itself into existence.

But, in fact, we do not use the word "regiment" (or the words "Senate," "Institute," etc.) in this way. We say, and we want to be able to continue to say, that on this or that occasion Sapper Camember was unable to parade with his regiment. And if we understand the word "regiment" in this way, it is not a collective noun, i.e., not the designation of a plurality of

---

19. On the logic of lists and its importance for understanding the reference of terms in collective propositions, see Peter Geach, *Reference and Generality: An Examination of Some Medieval and Modern Theories,* 3rd ed. (Ithaca: Cornell University Press, 1980), Chapter 7, as well as his *Truth, Love and Immortality: An Introduction to McTaggart's Philosophy* (Berkeley: University of California Press, 1979), 64–66.

individuals. And it is in precisely this *other sense* that we speak, in everyday language, about collectivities and collective actors. What this other sense might be remains to be determined. One thing is certain, though: it will not be accounted for by the logic of collective predication.

It is not the philosopher's place to propose reforms of ordinary language, even where the terms in question derive from the philosophical lexicon and even when the discrepancy between the two idioms—the philosophical and the everyday—is a constant source of misunderstandings. It is unfortunate that a collectivity in the ordinary sense is not a collective whole in the logical sense. Yet that is the situation. The words "collective" and "collectivity" are too rooted in our language for us to imagine asking that they be taken in the logician's sense. All that one can ask is that the difference between uses of the word be clearly indicated. The logical collective is the one accounted for by the logic of collective predication. Collectivity in the historical sense is the one referred to by dictionaries and manuals when they tell us that some singular terms—such as "army," "company," "State," etc.—in fact signify composite or complex beings, wholes whose parts are individual people. Neither of these two collectivities presents itself as a collective individual. From the logical point of view, if the collective proposition bore upon an individual, it would be singular and not collective. From the historical or social point of view, collectivities are not collections of individuals precisely because their identity is not determined by a list of individuals.

It so happens that this last point is disputed by nominalist schools of thought, which appeal to logic itself in order to support their theses on social and historical entities. These schools do not believe in collective individuals, which is indicative of their above-average insight (if the average is represented by Lalande's *Vocabulary* and its successors). But they believe that historical totalities are just pluralities of individuals treated within language as unities. They therefore believe that the critique of the illusion of collective individuals must entail an ontological demystification of our entire social and political philosophy.

5.3. Methodological Individualism

When the category of the whole is defined as the synthesis of the many and the one, it seems as if the whole is a creation of language or of representation. Indeed, we are asked to begin with a plurality—thinking for example of several people—and to deem that these people constitute a higher-order unity to which a name is then given: the Roman Senate, the Institute. How is one to avoid concluding that this plurality becomes a unity in language only (i.e., only in virtue of the mode of representation that we have adopted)? One of the themes of the program known as methodological individualism is to stress that these fictions of ordinary discourse have no place in scientific discourse. If they are useful, we need not do without these fictive entities, provided we understand that they are only ways of speaking. For, in principle, one could do without pretending to invoke such impersonal or suprapersonal entities.

That is Max Weber's view.[20] The jurist or the legislator, whose ends are not knowledge, can without difficulty treat social organizations *as if* they were people. This amounts to using terms such as "the State," "the cooperatives," "public corporations," or "foundations" as if these terms designated individuals to which rights and duties, privileges, and responsibilities could be attributed. But sociology, to the extent that it is a science, seeks to make known what there really is. For the sociologist, there is neither the State nor the administration, but there are real people—individuals—whose activity (as functionaries or members of the public) is oriented as result of the representations they have of their place and their relations with other individuals (see Chapter 10, section 3, below).

The philosophy of mind corresponding to this nominalism is clear: social science is ontologically committed to *persons* (organisms) and *representations*. There is no need to refer, beyond them, to *institutions*. Speaking of representations allows one to avoid positing the existence of institutions. In other words, institutions will be accounted for by (individual) representations (e.g., the *administration* will be accounted for by the ideas of the functionary and the members of the public) and not the other way around.

Karl Popper saw clearly that what was at issue here was the old dispute about universals and nominalism. What he called "methodological individualism" (or "methodological nominalism") is the principle according to which the descriptive language of social science is one that makes use of singular terms, terms that designate individuals.[21] As a result, all other

---

20. Max Weber, *Economy and Society: An Outline of Interpretive Sociology,* trans. Ephraim Fischoff, Hans Gerth, et al., ed. Guenther Roth and Claus Wittich (Berkeley: University of California Press, 1978), 13–15.
21. Karl Popper, *The Poverty of Historicism* (1957; New York: Routledge, 2002), 126.

terms, those that seem to designate something but that do not designate individuals, do not have a directly descriptive function. They are, rather, abstract terms that serve to build up "theoretical constructions."

> [M]ost of the objects of social science, if not all of them, are abstract objects; they are *theoretical* constructions. (Even "the war" or "the army" are abstract concepts, strange as this may sound to some. What is concrete is the many who are killed; or the men and women in uniform, etc.) These objects, these theoretical constructions used to interpret our experience, are the result of constructing certain *models* (especially of institutions), in order to explain certain experiences—a familiar theoretical method in the natural sciences (where we construct our models of atoms, molecules, solids, liquids, etc.).[22]

By speaking of abstract objects, constructions, and instruments, Popper implies that the reality that we call "an army" or "a war" is of the same nature as the reality of, for example, what we call "the average Frenchman." There does not exist among things (*in rebus*) anything that is the thing we are talking about, but we give ourselves a (summary and hypostasized) indirect representation of it by imagining, in a fictive model, the principal properties that are of interest to us.

Popper forcefully sets in opposition the *concrete* and the *abstract*. What is concrete are people who can fight and die. What is abstract is the theoretical hypostasis of an entity such as an army or a war. When one says that the army is advancing, one means that men and women in uniform are advancing. If the army (or any other "social entity") were to have a real rather than a purely nominal status, it would have to be something like a concrete universal, i.e., a pure contradiction.

Popper believed that the "collective terms" used by social science could only be cleared up by a return to disputes about universals. Here is how he explains the difference between terms that are referential (which refer, for example, to men and women in uniform) and those that have no other value than that of allowing us to organize our experience (by highlighting repetitions, resemblances, etc.).

He explains that there are two kinds of terms. General terms (universals) are, for example, "energy," "velocity," "carbon," "whiteness," "evolution,"

---

22. Ibid., 125.

"justice," "state," "humanity." Singular terms (or individual concepts or proper names—Popper makes no distinction among them at this level of his analysis) are, for example, "Alexander the Great," "Halley's Comet," or "the First World War."[23]

The difference between the concrete term and the abstract one is the same as between the adjective "white" and the substantive "whiteness." According to Popper, there are two parties involved in the debate about universals. The *realist* maintains that all things that resemble one another in being white have something in common, namely whiteness. There is thus whiteness and therefore there is something (a universal object) whose existence is to explain how it is that white things are white. The opponent of the realist is the *nominalist*. Popper formulates the nominalist's position as follows, in terms that fit Popper himself since this is the position he embraces:

One party [the nominalists] held that universals differ from proper names only in being attached to the members of a *set* or *class* of single things, rather than to just one single thing. The universal term "white," for instance, seemed to this party to be nothing but a label attached to a set of many different things—snowflakes, tablecloths, and swans, for instance.[24]

One might also say that the nominalist position is, from a logical point of view, extensionalist: in order to give the meaning of the word "white," it is necessary and sufficient to determine the set of white things, i.e., the extension of the predicate "x is white."

How does this nominalist position apply to the case of abstract objects such as an army or a war? Are terms such as "the regiment" universals? No, that is not possible. One may debate whether a determination of the extension of the predicate "x is white" is enough for us to understand the meaning and function of the concept of whiteness. But whatever the answer to that problem, it sheds no light on the mode of signification of so-called collective terms such as "state," "army," etc. When the word "white" is attached to the set of white things, it is attached to each of them. But the word "army" certainly cannot be attached to each of the men and women in uniform.

23. Ibid., 24.
24. Ibid.

It also cannot be attached to the entire *set* or the *class* of these soldiers. Whatever the difficulties involved in determining what there is really when there is an army, at least one thing is easily established: the invocation of sets and classes does nothing to clear up the matter. Moreover, this is not Popper's position, since he refers to theoretical models and not sets. It is nevertheless worth spelling out why this response via sets and classes is excluded in advance, for Popper did speak about sets in the case of abstract terms such as whiteness. As a result, there are people who believe it possible to be methodological individualists by saying that social entities are pure abstractions because they are nothing other than sets or classes of individuals.

Nominalist sociologists who hold that social entities are sets are victims of an illusion that Frege exposed: they imagine a set (as mathematicians would call it) or a class (as early twentieth-century logicians would call it) as a kind of physical or "mental" gathering of elements. They believe therefore that a set is *made up of* elements that belong to it in much the same way that furniture is made up of a certain number of chairs, sofas, etc., or a village is made up of houses.

Frege provides the essential distinctions in his review of the *Lessons on the Algebra of Logic* by the mathematician Ernst Schröder.[25] He calls attention to the ambiguity inherent in an expression such as "class of objects." Sometimes we think of a class of objects as a gathering of certain objects (in much the same way that a "class photo" is a photo of all of the students brought together in front of the photographer's lens). At other times, the notion of class is taken in a logical sense in order to indicate the entire extension of a property (as when one wonders whether the class—that is, the set—of students having earned two first-class degrees this year is an empty set or not).

Frege stresses that one should make sure not to confuse the relation of inclusion (*Einordnung*) of a part to a whole with what the logician calls an element's relation of belonging to a set (or to a logical class). In the first case, writes Frege, the classes of objects involved are "collective wholes" (*kollektive Ganze*).[26] The example he gives is a wood, or forest. This tells us

---

25. Schröder's work appeared in 1890 and Frege's article in 1895. Peter Geach's translation, "A Critical Elucidation of Some Points in E. Schröder's *Vorlesungen über die Algebra der Logik,*" is included in Peter Geach and Max Black, eds., *Translations from the Philosophical Writings of Gottlob Frege,* 2nd ed. (Oxford: Basil Blackwell, 1960), 86–106.

26. Ibid., 87.

that he is here following the ordinary usage of the term "collective whole." A collective whole would not be, for example, "the trees" but rather "the forest of Fontainebleau." Whenever the whole is something like a forest or an army, we conceive of it along the lines of the relation between a whole and its parts, a whole that can be *directly* designated. By contrast, when we want to talk about the set of objects that fulfill a condition—for example, the set of points that fulfill a particular geometrical condition—we utilize a notion whose logical structure is entirely different. It does not involve observing a whole and discovering its parts. In fact, the procedure is as follows: one starts with a general term (for example, "point" or "tree") and one joins to this descriptive term a logical operator such as "the set of . . . ," "the class of . . . ," "the multiplicity of . . ."

It would be fundamentally confused to take a forest for the class of trees situated within the perimeter of that forest or, conversely, to take the set (or the class) of trees of a forest for the forest itself. If all the trees of the forest have burned down, there no longer is a forest; one would not say that there remains a forest without trees even though one can of course refer to the set of trees having survived the forest fire, which in this case would be an empty set.

With regard to our problem, the important point in Frege's article is this: it is possible to take a concrete whole as the object of one's inquiry and discourse without having to specify the elements that comprise it. This shows precisely that the forest as a "collective whole" is not a collection of trees (i.e., several things) but just a forest (i.e., a single thing divisible into various parts). If we adopt the standpoint in which a (concrete) whole is divided into parts, writes Frege, we have no need to use the words "individual" or "single thing."[27] In fact, division can continue infinitely. In order to divide, one need not seek out elementary (i.e., indivisible) particles. The concept of an *element* is thus also superfluous. Frege provides the following example: if we take as a multiplicity or manifold (*Mannigfaltigkeit*) the German army and if we define an infantry regiment as a domain—this is the term Schröder uses—within it, we are free to determine whether the "elements" of this plurality will be the battalions or the companies or the single soldiers (*die einzelnen Krieger*).

---

27. "Auf dem jetzt von uns eingenommenen Standpunkte brauchen wir die Wörter 'Individuum' und 'Einzelding' nicht" ["From the point of view we are now adopting, we do not need the words 'individual' and 'single thing.'"]. Ibid.

When analysis seeks to determine the parts constitutive of the whole, there is no need to ask *how many* parts the whole has in general but rather *what is the internal structure* of its composition (for example, the regiment/company/battalion schema). By contrast, when speaking of a class, the question of enumeration must be raised in terms of the predicate whose domain of application is being studied: how many cases are there of the property under consideration? One must, therefore, have determined once and for all the level of individuation of the elements.

The situation is thus exactly the contrary of what we had been told. When analysis bears on relations of part to whole, it is no longer the collective entities (in the ordinary sense in which they *are not* collections of individuals) that are suspect. It is no longer the (concrete) totalities that give the impression of being surplus to requirements, of being made redundant by individuals. Rather, it is the perspective of the individual that is unnecessary: the notion of the individual serves no purpose because every part that is part of the whole is itself a whole, and it is in no way ruled out that parts of the part may play a role in the whole.

Using a vocabulary that is not Frege's, we might say that the holistic point of view is that of the division of a whole into its parts. This division is carried out via differentiation, just as it is in an organism, which explains the recurrence of organicist metaphors in the context of this discussion. When one takes up this point of view, one is never dealing with individuals, i.e., the ultimate units of the order being considered. Analysis identifies parts that are themselves wholes. It follows that a regiment, if it is a concrete totality (e.g., a historical actor) should not be conceived as a collection of individuals in uniform. Although a holistic conception of concrete totalities may well be objectionable for other reasons that remain to be seen, the main objection to it cannot be that it hypostasizes a plurality of individuals into a collective individual, for collective individuals are not part of this conception. A noncollectivist holist and a methodological individualist will be in complete agreement on this point: *there are no collective individuals.*

How then can one be a methodological individualist? How can one maintain that an army is an abstract object? Popper's response is not that, in talking about what the army is doing, we have taken the decision to hypostasize a set of objects (in our language at least). What we hypostasize, in his view, is a structure, a set of relations. Social entities, for example institutions, are not concrete entities (such as a crowd in the street); they are "abstract models constructed to interpret certain selected abstract relations between individuals."[28] The reduction that Popper advocates is thus part of the family of eliminations proposed by the philosophy of logical atomism.

The story of logical atomism is instructive. It is an attempt at a contemporary nominalism, by which I mean a nominalist metaphysics that can be expressed in the forms of our logic rather than in those of medieval terminist logic. Logical atomism, which is the tool used by methodological individualism to reduce the social to the individual, allows us to speak of the relations that individuals have among themselves (whether naturally or by their own volition). But it does not allow us to bestow upon these relations a reality such that the relation can be posited *before* the individuals. There are thus no structured totalities if by that we mean concrete totalities whose reality inheres in their organization. There are, rather, individuals who may enter into various relations with one another. One may then consider these relations by abstracting from the individuals that bear them. This allows one to speak about the family, the administration, the Franciscan order, etc. But what is not permitted is to treat the hypostasis that engenders the abstract object as anything other than a description of individuals and their relations to one another.

5.4. Logical Atomism

Among the fundamental ideas that Bertrand Russell claims to have taken up the day he stopped being a neo-Hegelian is the principle of the reduction of complex beings.[29] Reduction, for Russell, does not mean dogmatic negation but the demonstration of the logical equivalence of two different ways of speaking. Armed with this principle, he seeks to show that everything that can be said about a complex whole can be said in an equivalent way without mentioning the whole (i.e., without having to act as if it

28. Popper, *Historicism*, 130.
29. Bertrand Russell, *My Philosophical Development* (London: George Allen and Unwin, 1959), 117.

truly existed), simply by speaking of its parts and their mutual external relations.[30]

In *The Principles of Mathematics* (1903), Russell puts forth what would become the guiding principle of logical atomism: all complexity is logical in nature; there is therefore no need to seek any other unity for a complex system than that of a (logical) combination of its parts.[31] The thesis that all complexity is logical in nature means that there is no real complexity that cannot be reduced by logical analysis. A (simple) reference to a complex object can therefore always be replaced by a series of references to simple objects and a (complex) description of their arrangement.

An application of this principle can be found in the second of the lectures that make up Russell's *The Philosophy of Logical Atomism* (1918). We give names to things that are manifestly complex—Socrates, Piccadilly, Romania, etc. But how can a complex or plural thing bear a proper name? Traditionally this is explained through the invocation of a link or unity among the parts of such complex systems: the parts are so closely linked that they form *one* thing rather than *several* things. Russell found this type of explanation unsatisfactory, seeing in it a type of thinking that, if taken seriously, would have to lead to "the philosophy of monism," i.e., the idea that "the universe as a whole is a single complex entity."[32] In other words, nothing will prevent philosophers from taking the step that common sense would resist: since the complex systems we call "Socrates," "Piccadilly," etc., have links and unity sufficient to give them the status of individual things, nothing prevents the universe itself being treated as an individual. Common sense might well object; the universe is not an individual but rather, as Leibniz would say, an aggregation of individuals. But common sense objections do not provide a philosophical reason to rule out the inference that moves from the cohesion of the parts to the individual unity of the whole. Here is what Russell sets against these views: *the complex presupposes the simple*. This means that when we appear to refer to complex entities (as if they were simple), we are in reality referring to

---

30. Ibid. An analogous principle can be found in Wittgenstein's *Tractatus Logico-Philosophicus,* trans. D. F. Pears and B. F. McGuinness (1922; New York: Routledge, 1981), § 2.0201 (7).

31. Bertrand Russell, *The Principles of Mathematics* (1903; London: Allen & Unwin, 1937), § 439 (466).

32. Bertrand Russell, *The Philosophy of Logical Atomism* (1918; New York: Routledge, 2010), 17.

simple entities that enter into complex configurations. From this derives the entire philosophical program of showing that one can eliminate the apparent mention of a complex entity. Anything that one might want to say about Piccadilly or Socrates ought to be able to be said without naming Piccadilly or Socrates and thus without creating the false impression that there is, beyond the constitutive parts of the complex system, the additional entity of the system itself. The program is thus to treat complex entities as logical constructions and therefore as fictions.[33] Russell here is in agreement with the early, but not the later, Wittgenstein.

Wittgenstein is in this regard an entirely exceptional philosophical figure, having moved in philosophy from an extreme atomism (in the *Tractatus*) to a form of holism. He began by embracing Russell's general position unreservedly, a position that, it will be recalled, was opposed to what he called not "holism," but the "monism" of the neo-Hegelians.

One might well use the word "holism" to characterize the main idea of the *Philosophical Investigations*—that intentional or psychological descriptions are contextual (though needless to say, Wittgenstein does not use terms such as "holism," "monism," "atomism," etc.). However, the holism of the later Wittgenstein bears no resemblance to the "monist" doctrines criticized by Russell. Wittgenstein's passage through the severe discipline of Russell's nominalism thus proved to be fruitful.

The "monism" attacked by Russell is a rationalist holism, derived more or less from Hegel and one that sets mere appearance and the requirements of reason in opposition. The holism of Wittgenstein's grammatical analyses in the *Philosophical Investigations* is, by contrast, entirely grounded in what is required for the description of our language and in the conditions under which we are able to speak about the forms of human life. Such a holism therefore *defends* appearances against the sorts of superior realities invoked by philosophers, whether the Single Whole of monism or the Atoms of pluralism.

It will be illuminating to look at the critique of his own *Tractatus* that Wittgenstein puts forward in the *Philosophical Grammar*. It is an error, he claims, to say that "a house is a complex of bricks and their spatial relations."[34] To say this would be to confuse a concrete object (made up of

---

33. Ibid., 17–18.
34. Ludwig Wittgenstein, *Philosophical Grammar*, ed. Rush Rhees, trans. Anthony Kenny (Oxford: Basil Blackwell, 1974), 200.

parts) and a complex fact (the fact that the bricks are arranged in a certain spatial order relative to one another). Yet this is precisely what the early Wittgenstein would have said, as can be confirmed by looking at his very first published philosophical text.

In 1913, Wittgenstein wrote a harshly critical review of a book in neo-Scholastic logic that had recently appeared.[35] He charges the author with various mistakes, which he numbers 1 through 6, after which he concludes by saying that the list could be continued. Mistake number 5 bears on classes and complexes, with these terms being understood in Russell's sense. This is made clear in the illustration that Wittgenstein provides of the distinction that the book he is reviewing failed to make:

Mankind is a class whose elements are men; but a library is not a class whose elements are books, because books become parts of a library only by standing in certain spatial relations to one another—while classes are independent of the relations between their members.[36]

Wittgenstein is here criticizing the author of the manual for little more than having adopted the traditional theory and therefore failing to take account of the difference between a set—today we call them "sets," where Russell spoke of "classes"—and a concrete group. Wittgenstein's two examples suffice to draw out this distinction. First is the class or the set of humans (in other words, the extension of the predicate "x is a human"): the elements of this class can be identified as members of it without our having to be concerned with their relations (i.e., with their neighbors or families, etc.). If one were asked to provide a list of the members of the set, one could do it in any order. Second is the collection of books that make

---

35. The book is Peter Coffey's *The Science of Logic* (London: Longmans, Green and Co., 1912). According to Arthur Prior, the work was a neo-Scholastic treatise that made broad use of the works of the Cambridge logician John Neville Keynes. See A. N. Prior, *The Doctrine of Propositions and Terms* (London: Duckworth, 1976), 38 n 2.

36. The review is reproduced in its entirety in Brian McGuinness's biography, *Wittgenstein, A Life: Young Ludwig 1889–1921* (Berkeley: University of California Press, 1988), 170. Peter Simons comments on this same passage on classes and complexes in his work on mereological theories, *Parts: A Study in Ontology* (Oxford: Oxford University Press, 1987), 147.

up a library (of course Wittgenstein's example should be understood in a material sense, i.e., as a group of books and not as an institution). What prevents us from taking a library as a class (or set) of books is that the books belong to the library only if they are physically part of it. Wittgenstein seems to mean that if the library were abolished and its collection broken up, there would still be the books but there would be no library.

Thus, in his review, Wittgenstein emphasizes the distinction underlined by Frege: the class or extension of a description is a logical totality, not a concrete totality. However, Wittgenstein does not take into account the other aspect of the distinction Frege draws. A relation of belonging to a set (class) requires that the level of individuation of the elements has been specified. By contrast, a relation of whole to part is not laid down once and for all: a concrete totality can be divided in various ways and parts can be found within parts. Thus, to say that the library is made up of the books in the library is to represent it as too much like a set. Let us suppose that the library in question is a complete collection of the "Pléiade Library."[37] Of what is such a collection made up? One might say that it is made up of *volumes* or of *books* or of *works*. In breaking up the library, one might separate Plato (published in two volumes) from the Pre-Socratics (one volume). Or, one might separate the first volume of Plato from the second. One might count Victor Hugo's *Poetic Works* as one lot (three volumes) and his *Complete Theater* as another (two volumes).

What is remarkable is that at the very moment when Wittgenstein sought to demonstrate the superiority of the modern over the traditional logician by pointing out the error of taking a class, which is an abstract object, for a concrete thing really made up of its elements, he falls prey to another error that he will himself bring to light later in his career. The error lies in taking a complex reality (e.g., a library) as a spatial arrangement of its elements. More generally, the error lies in believing that the *parts of a totality* are to be understood as *elements* having various relations among themselves and that these relations make them the components of a system. This error is that of the logicist who believes that a complex description of simple elements can serve as the description of a real complex whole.

---

37. [Translator's note: The "Bibliothèque de la Pléiade" is a deluxe set of volumes by canonical authors published by the Gallimard publishing house.]

At the time, Wittgenstein still believed that he could grasp the metaphysical status of a concrete totality through the Russellian idea of a "complex entity." For example, the fact that there is a library in a particular spot would be analyzed (metaphysically) as the fact that there is book number 1 and next to it book number 2 and so on until the end of the top shelf, then a second shelf of books and so on. *What there is* in the world when there is a library would have been described by identifying all the books and providing their respective positions.

In section 60 of the *Philosophical Investigations,* Wittgenstein derides this sort of decomposition. First he gives the perspective of the logical atomist:

When I say "My broom is in the corner," is this really a statement about the broomstick and the brush? Well, it could at any rate be replaced by a statement giving the position of the stick and the position of the brush. And this statement is surely a further analyzed form of the first one.[38]

The logical atomist's idea is that the second statement is philosophically superior to the first in that it reveals, through a logical analysis of the referent (the broom) the real meaning of what we say. Someone speaking about a broom is in reality speaking, whether he knows it or not, about a stick with a brush attached. There is nothing more to a broom than these two more basic objects *and* the fact of their being joined together. Wittgenstein has no difficulty showing that this putative analysis is useless. First, it cannot claim to teach us what we really mean. Someone who asks to be brought a broom has not expressed himself elliptically. Yet this would be the case if the true meaning of his utterance were rendered by the more analytic formula "Bring me the broomstick and the brush that is attached to it." Second, and more seriously, neither the broomstick nor the brush is a simple object. It follows that the original sentence (that appeared to be) about the broom is not about these parts either. One ends up unable to say *what* the sentence bears on, other than that it bears on the ultimate constituents, the monads brought together in a broom.

---

38. Ludwig Wittgenstein, *Philosophical Investigations,* rev. 4th ed., ed. P. M. S. Hacker and Joachim Schulte, trans. G. E. M. Anscombe, P. M. S. Hacker, and Joachim Schulte (1953; Oxford: Wiley-Blackwell, 2009), § 60 (33).

Logical atomism's failure to account for the real complexity of any physical system is glaring. It therefore leads to the following conclusion: if we understand the concept of composition according to the atomist's adage that "the complex presupposes the simple," then the complex beings we seek to analyze are not composite. Their complexity cannot be represented as an arrangement of elements. This confirms Frege's claim that, in an analysis of a whole into its parts, we need not use the words "individual" or "single thing."

What is the major flaw in the young Wittgenstein's definition? If a library is defined as a collection of books, one can only define a library as an ephemeral entity. The library would only exist at a certain time. Every time that a new work was acquired, the old library would cease to exist and a new one would take its place. One could never say that the library was expanding its collection. Thus, even if we take the notion of a library in its purely material sense, we still cannot apply logical atomism's theory of complex beings to it. In order to be able to recount the history of a complex being, it must be endowed with a measure of diachronic identity.

This point was worth making because it is more than simply a preoccupation of Russell and the early Wittgenstein. For theirs is not an idiosyncratic doctrine but rather the general orientation and profound drift of Western thought. We can confirm this by turning to texts quite far removed in time and spirit from early twentieth-century Cambridge philosophy.

5.5. The Diachronic Identity of Complex Beings

The tendency to present various metaphysical views as purely logical demands is not a new phenomenon. The authors of the *Port-Royal Logic* had already drawn a distinction, though not in these terms, between apparent speech (which bears on complexes of objects) and real speech (which bears on simple objects).

Arnauld and Nicole raise the problem of description in a chapter about propositions whose subject is, as they put it, "confused." This text is so typical of the intellectual stance that concerns us that it is worth citing at length:

Augustus said of the City of *Rome,* that he found it of Brick, and left it of Marble. So too we say of a Town, of a House, of a Church, that it was destroyed at such a time, and rebuilt at such another time. What then is this *Rome* which is Brick in one Age, and Marble in another? What are these Towns, these Houses, these Churches, which are destroyed at one time, and rebuilt at another?[39]

They then proceed to answer the question of the identity of the subject of attribution by criticizing the illusion of a self-identical subject:

Was this *Rome* which was of Brick the same *Rome* that is now of Marble? No; but yet the Mind forms to itself a certain confused Idea of *Rome,* to which it ascribes those two Qualities of being of Brick at one time, and of Marble at another. And when afterwards it draws it into Propositions, and says, for Instance, that *Rome* which was of Brick before *Augustus's* Time, was of Marble when he died; the Word *Rome,* which seems to be no more than one Subject, does indeed denote two that are really distinct, tho' united under the confused Idea of *Rome,* which hinders the Mind from perceiving the Distinction of those Subjects.[40]

A first remark must be made regarding this text: it is not the logician who can tell us whether Augustus is speaking about one thing or two things. What, then, can the logician tell us? He can tell us that our thought as it is expressed has something vague about it. He can then invite us to say more clearly what it is we want to say, which assumes that we will pick the form of expression that suits us from among several such forms that differ in their consequences. The logician who hears us say that Augustus found a city of brick and left a city of marble might ask us to choose from among several objects of reference (several "subjects") by pointing out the

---

39. Antoine Arnauld and Pierre Nicole, *Logic; or, The Art of Thinking: Containing (Besides the Common Rules) Many New Observations, That Are of Great Use in Forming an Exactness of Judgment,* trans. John Ozell (1662; London: William Taylor, 1717), Part II, Chapter XII ("Of Confused Subjects Equivalent to Two Subjects"), 172. [Translator's note: Descombes intentionally cites a critical edition that uses an older form of spelling and says this of his choice: "I reproduce the text of the critical edition, with its classical spelling, in order to illustrate one of the guiding ideas of this book: the identity of a thought or a signification has nothing to do with its material—including typographical—identity. This applies here to thoughts expressed in writing in a French language that we recognize as still ours, despite the variations." In order to approximate the effect of the illustration as best I can, I have chosen the English edition of 1717. Although there is an older translation from 1692, unfortunately it is abridged and does not contain the passages Descombes cites.]

40. Ibid 171–172.

THE ILLUSION OF COLLECTIVE INDIVIDUALS   151

following. If the name "Rome" applies to a reality consisting in a certain brick construction, then Rome is by definition the same thing as a thing made of bricks. For Augustus's urban renewal project to be carried out, then, this (complex) thing made of bricks will have to disappear.

But when Augustus says that he found a city of brick and left a city of marble, it would appear to be similar to saying that he found a poor and primitive city and left an opulent and dazzling one. It is therefore implied that, under his reign, the city of Rome underwent a transformation for which he is taking credit, moving from an unremarkable or undistinguished state to a magnificent one.

The authors ask: is the Rome made of brick the same as the Rome made of marble? But the question *as asked* has no unequivocal meaning, with the result that it is unclear how one should answer. Indeed, the identity criteria of a *city* are not the identity criteria of the *materials* out of which the buildings of the city are made.[41] The identity criteria of a city, in the historical sense, allow us to recount the stages of its growth: first the city consists of a few huts in wood and cob, then of houses made of brick, then of houses made of marble.

Do the authors want to know whether the city was the same material mass, the same system of edifices? The answer is obviously contained within the question—the city is not the same. But the question can also be taken in another sense: is the system constructed of marble and left by Augustus the same city as the system he found constructed of bricks? The answer is that it is the same city, namely the city of Rome.

This example from the *Port-Royal Logic* is interesting in that it reveals the necessity of raising the problem of diachronic identity. When we speak about Rome, are we trying to talk about the buildings as they happen to be or about the city? If we identify Rome and its material reality at a given instant, we will be unable to identify Rome after its reconstruction in marble.

The distinction that has just been drawn cannot be denied by means of a commonsense argument that says Rome is a city, not an idea. For the proposed distinction does not ask us to turn Rome into an idea; it tells us

---

41. See David Wiggins, *Sameness and Substance* (Oxford: Blackwell, 1980), on the difference between, on the one hand, "to be" and, on the other, "to consist in" or "to be constituted of."

that at every instant in history, the city of Rome is the same thing as certain edifices and that each of these edifices is the same thing as a certain collection of various materials (wood, bricks, etc.). Rome is always (at every instant of its history) a certain matter. But there is no matter that is, at every moment in history, the city of Rome. If there were, it would be impossible to change anything at all—to replace a wall or a cobblestone—without causing a discontinuous passage from one city to another or, as the authors of the *Port-Royal Logic* put it, from one subject to another.

The authors of the *Port-Royal Logic* also discuss collective attribution in cases where the collective is an entity that is not only historical but well and truly social. They begin, as is the rule in traditional logic, with collective terms considered as possible logical subjects.[42]

(1) The Names of *Body,* of *Community,* of *People,* being taken collectively, as they usually are, for the whole Body, the whole Community, the whole People, do not render the Proposition wherein they stand properly universal and much less particular, but singular. As when I say, *The* Romans *overcame the* Carthaginians; *the* Venetians *are at War with the* Turks; *the Judges of such a Place condemned a Criminal*; these Propositions are not universal; otherwise we might conclude of each *Roman* that he had overcome the *Carthaginians,* which would be false. Neither are they particular; for that Proposition means more than if I said, some *Romans* overcame the *Carthaginians* . . .

Arnauld and Nicole here raise what would at the time still have been called the "problem of supposition" (today we formulate this problem as one of reference). How is one to move from the terms that appear in the proposition to the individuals that these terms "supposit" (the individuals that they represent or whose places they take)? How does our discourse relate to the things it aims to speak of? In the case of so-called collective propositions, it appears that the general term "Roman" appearing in a sentence is not to be taken as universal. We say, "The Romans defeated the Carthaginians," but that does not mean that each Roman is a victor nor that every Carthaginian was defeated by a Roman. The authors deem there to be three possibilities: the proposition must be either universal,

---

42. As the text here ought to be cited in its entirety yet is too long to be cited in one block, I will divide it into two paragraphs. This division is not in the original text.

particular, or singular. Since it is neither universal nor particular, it must be singular. The text continues as follows:

(2) but they are singular, because we consider every People as a moral Person whose Duration is of several Ages, which subsists as long as it composes a State, and which acts in all that time by those of whom it consists, as a Man acts by his Members. From whence it is that we say, the *Romans* who were overcome by the *Gauls* that took *Rome,* overcame the *Gauls* in *Cæsar's* Time; attributing thus to the same Term of *Romans,* the having been overcome at one time and the being Conquerors at another, tho' in one of those Times there was not one Man of those that were in the other. And this shews the Foundation of the Vanity which every Particular takes in the noble Actions of his Nation, tho' he had not the last hand in them; and which is as much that of an Ear, which being deaf, should claim Glory upon Account of the Vivacity of the Eye, or Skill of the Hand.[43]

But if the collective proposition is singular, we are once again embroiled in the paradox we have been discussing throughout this chapter: the collective proposition about the Romans seems to speak about a reality distinct from each of the Romans.

This problem is a *logical* one. In these sentences, defeat and victory are attributed to the Romans. We would like to know who is being referred to. We are told that the Romans defeated the Gauls in the time of Caesar; the Romans were defeated by the Gauls who took Rome. Arnauld and Nicole think that these sentences have a special subject consisting neither of all the Roman citizens nor of only some of them. In fact, it will be said that, from the grammatical point of view, the subject ("the Romans") is the same, even though we know that different people were involved in the two episodes. Yet for this semantic problem, the authors provide a solution that is moral and political rather than one derived from logic.

Their solution is the fiction of a "moral person." This fiction is an "organicist" one in which citizens are treated as the "members" of an immortal person. If we reason according to this logic, what is to prevent us from adopting an "organicist" doctrine of the State or of society? In order to avoid treating the State as a great organism at the same time that we continue to speak of it as if it were one, we must simultaneously stress the unreality of the entity our discourse evokes.

---

43. Arnauld and Nicole, *Logic,* Part II, Chapter XIII, 187–188.

If Arnauld and Nicole had been around the Sorbonne at the beginning of the twentieth century, they might have questioned the "prelogical mentality" of the Romans and of those who repeat their forms of expression. In other words, rather than finding a solution in logic to their problem in the philosophy of language, they would dispute the "rationality" of those using such entirely ordinary sentences.

When the Romans together enjoy the quality of being the victors over the Carthaginians, it is obviously not as if the quality of being victors is distributed among the individuals. Yet a mutual dependence among them would seem to have been affirmed. Unfortunately, the nature of this dependence eludes us. Since Titus is Roman, he partakes of the victory even though he did nothing, and he so partakes in virtue of the link between him and those who triumphed in battle. The collective proposition seems to assume a bizarre reversion of merits. The great deeds of some result in badges of honor for all. How can a logician explain this equivalence between some and all? What is the "moral substance" (as Hegel put it) in which I = them and they = me?[44]

One has to wonder, though, whether we have not been led astray by seeking the logic of holistic propositions in the form of collective propositions. Consider Caius, a legionnaire who returns victorious from war. If Caius's great-nephew says "we were victorious," it is not as if he were saying "I contributed to the victory" nor is it as if he were saying "we were victorious together, Caius by engaging in combat and I, his great-nephew, by being a Roman." Any analysis of "collective identity" that calls into question the necessarily irrational identification of oneself with other people is more a reflection of its own flaws than of the feeling to be analyzed. What is wrong with the descendant of victorious ancestors saying this: "I am part of a glorious nation, for my ancestors were conquerors and that makes me not a conqueror but rather someone whose own actions must be measured against those of the champions to whom he owes his existence"? This is less a matter of gratuitously partaking of the merits of others than it is of not denigrating oneself in light of the example that they set.

44. G. W. F. Hegel, *The Phenomenology of Spirit,* trans. A. V. Miller (Oxford: Oxford University Press, 1977), § 349 (212) [translation modified].

6

The Order of Meaning

How is it that all attempts to constitute a concrete whole out of individuals fail? Are committees and teams not collective actors whose composition can be given by listing out the names of the individuals that make them up? It ought to be possible to account for such a simple fact.

The fact of a team's formation is quite ordinary, so it can only be our thought about this fact that is unclear. The question is not whether a group of people can form a team together but rather whether we have the right metaphysics of complex beings. The doctrines of collective individuals required us to think of a whole as *one* individuated thing made up of *several* individuated things. This doctrine is self-contradictory. The concept of an individual is of an independent being. An individual cannot therefore be made up of other individuals.

A team is a collective actor. Teams can in fact be identified by providing lists of their members. What is collective, then, is the action of several individuals and not the subject of that action. The collective character is part of the predicate; it is *adverbial*. There is a totality in such cases, but it is not to be sought in the category of the substance or the subject of attribution because it is the totality of an action.

The flaw of collectivist holism is to say nothing about the dependence of the parts on one another. Yet this dependence was at the origin of the very notion of a holistic attribute. Consider a sign. If it cannot be a sign by itself, it must play a role, and it can only play this role if other signs play complementary roles. Our question then becomes this: in what sort of whole can one conceive of such a mutual dependence of the parts? Structural holism offers the response that what is necessary is a real whole, and a real whole is one that precedes its own parts.

In this chapter I will seek to determine the conditions for a holistic analysis.[1] For collectivist holism, there are no totalities to be analyzed, for it is only concerned with collective—and therefore indivisible—attributes. Questions about the different properties that things possess insofar as they enter into a system simply do not arise for it. Holistic analysis, if such a cognitive operation is conceivable, seeks to recognize the properties that a thing possesses in virtue of its integration as either a part or a member within a system.

For logical atomists, the very notion of a holistic analysis is a contradiction in terms. They are not alone in this opinion. A good many people would define the holistic conception of things as the idea that analysis is impossible or forbidden, that the whole must be grasped only in its unity and not dissected into its parts.[2] It is my task to show that there is nothing extraordinary or romantic about the logic of an authentically holistic description. Before taking on that task, though, a word of explanation about structuralism will be necessary in order to avoid the conflation of the position I am defending with this or that version of what has been circulated under that name. For it so happens that there is nothing at all holistic about the most well-known versions of structuralism.

6.1. A Critique of Structuralism

When working in the history of ideas, one has the right to refer to French structuralism in the same way that one speaks of German idealism. Both expressions refer to currents of ideas that did in fact exist, but neither says anything about the coherence of those ideas. Philosophically, however,

---

1. I have borrowed the expression "holistic analysis" from Louis Dumont, *German Ideology: From France to Germany and Back* (Chicago: University of Chicago Press, 1994), 5. A holistic analysis is above all an analysis of the interdependence of the parts of a whole.

2. See, for example, the article "Holism" in P. B. and J. S. Medawar, *Aristotle to Zoos: A Philosophical Dictionary of Biology* (Cambridge, MA: Harvard University Press, 1983), 144–145.

there was not a single structuralism but at least three different ones. I will therefore avoid referring to structuralism, since schools of thought that diverge from one another in important respects can all lay claim to this designation.

I believe one must draw a distinction among *structural holism, formalism,* and the *doctrine of structural causality.*

By *structural holism* I mean a theory that holds that, within a given domain, we ought to study as a system the way in which things present themselves. This means, as Lévi-Strauss explained in *The Elementary Structures of Kinship,* that the whole is, in a sense, given *before* the parts.[3] To put this another way: the parts of the whole are only identifiable within the whole, so that one must begin with the whole (or with the relations among the parts) rather than with disconnected elements if one wants to describe those parts. Structural holism asks us to practice structural analysis as a form of holistic analysis, i.e., as a search for the relations that ground the system.

The various programmatic statements for structural analysis (which are not to be confused with work that applies such analysis in a particular domain) have often presented structuralism as, at root, a *formalism.* Structural analysis in a given domain consists in seeking a formal invariant, by which is meant a set of relations among elementary units of the same kind (whatever that kind may be). This set of relations is called a "formal invariant" precisely because we can find it in very different domains, allowing us to study it in the way a mathematician might, independently of the content or the matter that is organized by these relations.

By the *doctrine of structural causality* I mean the idea that activities are subject to formal constraints that are imposed by the way in which the system is constructed (by opposition to constraints that arise out of the materials used). This leads to speaking of an *action* of the structure upon these activities. Structural analysis, for the causalist, consists in adding to the linear causality of the event an efficient causality of form.[4]

---

3. See Chapter 3, section 2 of my *The Mind's Provisions: A Critique of Cognitivism,* trans. Stephen Adam Schwartz (Princeton: Princeton University Press, 2001), 51–54.

4. How did such disparate ideas manage to take on the appearance of a single program? Historians of ideas will have to explain this by the ideological circumstances. At the time, the weak point of the dominant worldview among historians or sociologists was the explanation of ideas by the play of social or historical forces. Yet the social sciences could not

* * *

These three versions of structuralism are not only separable, they are in fact incompatible with one another.

We should first note that the ideas of formal analysis and structural causality have no link to the holistic perspective. For *formalism,* structure is above all a formal invariant that is indifferent to the content from which it can be derived; it is not a reciprocal order that the parts must have in order to form a whole. Formalism is interested in the fact that two things can be considered to be mutually derivable via a transformation, a transfer of the form from one matter to another.

Thinking of the doctrine of structure as the study of such *isomorphisms* is entirely separable from the holist thesis. This can be easily confirmed. Indeed, a structuralism of this sort was developed on the basis of logical atomism, as one sees in Wittgenstein's *Tractatus.* We know that Russell, in his Preface, derives from the book the lesson that the notion of structure allows for the development of a general theory of representation. What is it that allows the complex sign "aRb" to represent the fact that a thing a is in a certain relation R with a thing b? It is that the sign itself is, according to this doctrine, a complex entity constituted by the fact that the sign "a" is in a certain relation to the sign "b"—the relation of being to the left of a sign "R," while the sign "b" is to the right of the same sign. The structuralist idea is moreover explicitly put forth in section 4.014 of the *Tractatus*: it can be said that the phonographic disk, the musical thought, the score, and the sound waves are all linked to one another by a semantic or "pictorial" internal relation in that they all share the same logical structure (*der logische Bau*).[5]

What prevents formalism from being a structural holism? It lacks an interest in the relations of dependence among structural properties, and

---

accept the response favored by most philosophers—that ideas come from individual reason. Structuralism seemed to promise a solution: ideas arise neither from the free self-positing of the thinking subject nor from external social forces but from an infrastructure of thought seated in the "structural unconscious" (see Chapter 9, section 2, below).

5. Ludwig Wittgenstein, *Tractatus Logico-Philosophicus,* trans. D. F. Pears and B. F. McGuinness (New York: Routledge, 1981), § 4.014 (23–24). On the meaning and translation of *Abbildung* and *Bild* and related forms in the *Tractatus,* see Jacques Bouveresse, *Le mythe de l'intériorité: Expérience, signification et langage privé chez Wittgenstein,* 2nd rev. ed. (1976; Paris: Les Éditions de Minuit, 1987), 210.

this is why this formalism reaches its limits when it tries to present its algebra of relations as a theory of meaning. Similarly, it has been pointed out that, in the *Tractatus,* Wittgenstein claimed to account for meaning by the isomorphism between language and the world. Isomorphism, however, is insufficient. It cannot explain why *language* describes the world. Why is it not, rather, that *the world* provides a description of the order of symbols in the propositions of language?[6] The same difficulty, it so happens, confronts the reader of Lévi-Strauss's important text on the work of Marcel Mauss: is language the signifier of which the world is the signified? Or is it rather that the world is the signifier of which our thoughts are the signified?[7] It is quite difficult to say one way or the other since the first interpretation applies to the author's discussion of linguistic symbols, while the second seems more appropriate when he talks about religious symbols.

Structural causalism was the inspiration for Lévi-Strauss's article on the efficacy of symbols; structural analysis could in principle reveal an isomorphism among realities as different from one another as a myth, a conscious experience, and a physiological process.[8] One could then uncover an efficacy of discursive processes on physiological ones. An efficacy of speech would be magical if it inhered in the words used, but it would be natural if it inhered in the shared structure of the three processes.

Structural causalism is a good example of something pointed out by Wittgenstein: it is a confusion to see rules as powers that influence the actions of people or to believe that rules have the status of causes allowing one to explain observed regularities in behavior.[9] In fact, if such rules are applied, this cannot mean that they constrain actors to do this or that;

---

6. This was remarked by Giancarlo Colombo, the Italian translator of the *Tractatus*, as mentioned by G. E. M. Anscombe in her *An Introduction to Wittgenstein's "Tractatus": Themes in the Philosophy of Wittgenstein,* 2nd ed. (1959; New York: Harper Torchbooks, 1965), 67.

7. "The universe signified long before people began to know what it signified; no doubt that goes without saying. But, from the foregoing analysis, it also emerges that from the beginning, the universe signified the totality of what humankind can expect to know about it." Claude Lévi-Strauss, *Introduction to the Work of Marcel Mauss,* trans. Felicity Baker (London: Routledge & Kegan Paul, 1987), 61.

8. See Chapter 5, section 6 of my *The Mind's Provisions,* 102–107.

9. See Jacques Bouveresse's study, "L'animal cérémoniel: Wittgenstein et l'anthropologie," *Actes de la recherche en sciences sociales* 16 (1977), especially 50–51. On Wittgenstein's differentiation of logical "must" and physical "must," see Bouveresse's *La force de la règle: Wittgenstein et l'invention de la nécessité* (Paris: Les Éditions de Minuit, 1987), 50–56.

rather, they are applied because people are intent on applying them. Why do people apply them, and up to what point do they apply them? They apply them if: (1) they want to *do things the right way,* in the case of rules that govern activities that are defined in other ways, such as the rules for cooking a pot roast; or (2) because they want simply to *do things at all,* in the case where the rules are constitutive of the activity, as they are for the game of chess. The theorist of structural causality confuses the rule that one has to follow in order to reason or to calculate with the rail that guides the locomotive, as if, when we follow a rule, we were guided by an inflexible model. We say of someone that he is reasoning and that he must therefore, according to the rules of logic, draw such and such a consequence from a given premise. We do not say that he is forced to do so. "[T]he laws of inference do not compel him to say or to write such and such like rails compelling a locomotive."[10] The determination is logical, not physical.

6.2. The Logic of Holistic Description

What is sorely lacking in all of the theories of complex beings presented in the previous chapter is the very notion of a real complexity of the composite or complex entity. There is no real complexity where there is no dependence of parts on one another. The theory that seeks to turn the complexity of *a complex thing* into the complexity of the *description of several simple things* is fated not to perceive this mutual dependence of the parts. By definition, simple things (monads) cannot depend on one another.

It is thus not surprising that these theories are incapable of telling us why the attributes of a thing A might depend on the attributes of a thing B. The reason for this failure is clear. These theories do not account for the mutual *dependence* of the parts of the whole because they do not even speak of the parts of the whole as parts. They take no account of the relation of part to whole or of whole to part. These two lacunae are in fact one and the same. Indeed, the only conceivable explanation for a dependence

---

10. Ludwig Wittgenstein, *Remarks on the Foundations of Mathematics,* ed. G. H. von Wright, R. Rhees, G. E. M. Anscombe, trans. G. E. M. Anscombe, 3rd ed. (Oxford: Basil Blackwell, 1978), I, § 116 (80).

of part A of a whole relative to another part, B, is that this part A needs part B in order to be part of the complex whole AB.

Collectivist holism and methodological individualism (using the resources of logical atomism) appeal to the logic of propositions in which the predicate is collectively attributed to several things. But, as we have seen, only the predicate is collective, not the subjects of attribution that are mysteriously transformed into a "collective individual." The predicate is collective because it is jointly attributed to several individuals. If these individuals were a single individual, the predicate would become an individual attribute, an emergent property.

In other words, until now we have been looking at the wrong chapter of logic. Try though we might, we cannot find the explanations we seek in the chapter on collective predication. It is equally fruitless to expect them from a "dialectical" recasting of the notions of the "one" and the "many." Rather, we need to look to the chapter that deals with questions such as these: is what is said of the whole also said of the parts? Is what is said of the part said of the whole of which it is the part? This is the chapter that will tell us the logical traits of a holistic description, one in which we seek to describe the whole in its parts and the parts within their whole.

Unfortunately, I cannot rely on the contemporary theories known by the name of *mereology*, theories that do bear on the relation between the part and the whole.[11] But they have two major flaws. First, at least for those that I have consulted, they do not restrict themselves to the study of discourse about real totalities. They also bear, unavoidably, on *surreal* totalities. Among the Polish mereologists and also in Nelson Goodman's work, wholes are constituted out of individuals. Take, for example, three individuals: a = the horse on which Henri IV triumphantly returned to Paris, b = Kamikitazawa Station in Tokyo, and c = the first performance in Paris of *The Rite of Spring*. For the contemporary mereologist, there is a whole made up of these three individuals—a, b, and c. Our goal, however, is to study real totalities. Indeed, and this is the second flaw of mereological theories, we are not concerned with developing a general theory of systems. It would be a mistake to believe that one can develop a system of

---

11. In his book *Parts: A Study in Ontology* (Oxford: Oxford University Press, 1987), Peter Simons demonstrates the importance of mereological questions and the limits of the theories that have been proposed on the subject.

concepts in the form of a general metaphysics, i.e., before and outside of every application within a particular domain.[12] What interests us here is the holistic analysis of meaningful and intentional totalities. Examples of totalities drawn from other domains are only valuable to us as analogies or as figurative resources.

In these matters, I look instead to the work by Peter of Spain entitled *The Summulae Logicales*.[13] It happens that in Latin the confusion between, on the one hand, a proposition bearing on a whole and its part and, on the other hand, a collective proposition is more difficult than it is in French or in English, because the same word is not used in both cases. When Peter of Spain discusses collective propositions, he explains the logical function of the word *omnis*. When he discusses holistic propositions, he explains the role of the word *totus*.[14]

The logical operator that corresponds to the Latin term *omnis* must be applied to a general term: the predicate is applied, for example, to *all men*. The logic of collective propositions should therefore be sought in a section of the chapter on general propositions. Indeed, a general term is what appears in the logical subject. One might find, for example, after the operator "all" (in the sense of *omnis*), "senator." It is said that "the Senate voted when all of the senators present voted."[15] Among general propositions one finds particular ones (e.g., "A certain senator voted against the bill.") and universal ones (e.g., "All the senators were present."). Finally, among universal propositions there are distributives, as in the example just given, and collectives: "The senators passed the bill" (meaning, as the logical treatise explains, not that each of them passed it but that the body of senators passed it in a vote in which all of the senators present participated).[16]

---

12. See the "Note on the Concept of Metaphysics" that follows Chapter 4 of my *The Mind's Provisions,* 78–83.

13. Peter of Spain, *The Summulae Logicales of Peter of Spain,* ed. and trans. Joseph P. Mullally (Notre Dame, IN: University of Notre Dame Press, 1945).

14. Peter of Spain distinguishes between *omnis* and *totus* at the beginning of the "Treatise on Distributions." Ibid., 63.

15. Or, more precisely: "The Senate voted when everyone present in the way of senators voted."

16. The example that the text provides of an illegitimate inference is: "All the apostles of God are twelve . . . therefore these apostles of God (*isti apostoli Dei*) are twelve." Ibid., 63.

Note that the description by distributive predicates necessarily precedes the description by collective predicates. In order to be able to say that the senators form a *group,* one has to have determined who the senators are. But the quality of being a senator is distributive. The fact that someone is a senator does not depend on some other person being a senator. The collectivist holist will perhaps say: you cannot be a senator on your own; there must be others. Fine. But each senator must be elected independently of the others. There are no candidates that are elected senator simply because others are or have been. The collectivist point of view thus requires us to start from the plurality of individuals. The idea that one might produce something indivisible out of this reality divided into individuals would no doubt appear far-fetched if we did not believe that it must, in fact, be possible since otherwise we would lose the possibility of talking about historical institutions such as the Senate.

As for the logical operator that corresponds to *totus,* it can only be applied to a singular term—e.g., "the whole of Socrates," "the entire house." The logician must first indicate that his study bears on the word *totus* taken as a term of logic. Peter of Spain notes that there are three meanings of *totus* in Latin.[17] Two of these uses are of no concern to the logician: one says that something is a whole in order to say that it has parts of which it is composed; one also says, in Latin at least, that a thing is "whole" when it is entirely finished or completed (*domus tota*). The third sense is that of the logician and figures in sentences such as "Socrates as a whole is white" (*totus Sortes est albus*). In this case, the word "whole" does not describe the real subject (the subject of attribution) but indicates the way in which the logical subject (the sign in the sentence) is disposed relative to the predicate. When such a logical operator is inserted into a simple proposition, the proposition becomes *exponible,* meaning that it acquires a complexity that requires further development. Here we might take our distance from Peter of Spain and say that the word *totus* functions as an adverb, comparable to adverbs such as "rarely" or "frequently." "The patient rarely goes walking": here the adverb does not serve to indicate a way of walking but instead specifies the way in which the predicate applies to the patient, i.e., rarely.

The difference between a whole taken collectively and the whole of holistic relations is then the following. When it is a question of *the whole*

---

17. Ibid., 127, at the end of the "Treatise on Exponibles."

of Socrates or *the entirety of Socrates,* it is not the same as the Latin *omnis Sortes*. In other words, it is not as if we had applied the quantifier "all" to a general term that would be the equivalent of the verb "to socratize" (as in Quine's theory of the elimination of proper names). The statement is not about all individuals who are identical to Socrates; it is about Socrates considered from two points of view—Socrates considered in any of his parts whatsoever and Socrates considered in this or that of his parts. The example given by Peter of Spain is that of the attribution of a quality: Socrates as a whole is white (*totus Sortes est albus*).[18] The meaning is that Socrates, considered in any of his parts whatsoever, is white. What then is the difference between "Socrates is white" and "Socrates as a whole is white"? In the simple proposition, one is not at all concerned with knowing in what way the quality belongs to the subject. For example, it is neither affirmed nor is it excluded that Socrates's body hair be white. It is not the task of logic to determine the way in which a person is white in color. The error of logical atomism, in its theory of simple objects, was to act as though a simple proposition of this type could only be truly acceptable if it bore upon a monad, an object devoid of complexity. Atomism acts as if we assume that, wherever the predicate is related simply to the subject and without specifying the way in which the subject is disposed relative to the predicate, the individual that receives the predicate is itself a simple object.

From the proposition "Socrates as a whole is white," one may infer that every part of Socrates is white (the sentence concerns everything that is a part of Socrates, *quaelibet pars*). What does this inference mean? The proposition regarding the whole establishes a direct relation between the predicate and the subject: Socrates receives the predicate himself and in virtue of what he is (*secundum se*). Socrates's parts, however, do not receive the predicate directly but, rather, obliquely. They are not described directly (as what they are in themselves) but as parts of a whole (*prout sunt in suo toto sive sub forma totius*). This is why the immediate inferences from "Socrates as a whole is white" are: (1) directly, a proposition bearing on Socrates himself considered in any of his parts; (2) indirectly or obliquely, a proposition bearing on any part of Socrates that one might choose.

18. Ibid., 91–95.

It is thus always the whole that is the subject of reference of the proposition, even when it is about its parts. The logical operator has as its effect to relate the predicate first to Socrates and only subsequently to what is described as a part of Socrates and whose being derives from the whole (*illud quod est pars non habet esse nisi ab eo quod est totum*). What better explanation for why holistic description is not a description by collective predicates? When one is interested in the whole of Socrates or Socrates considered as a whole, one is not concerned with whether all of Socrates's parts are together but rather with what Socrates is partially (i.e., in one or more of his parts) or totally (i.e., in any of his parts).

Peter of Spain's discussion of a sophism allows for a better understanding of this point. The sophism consists in the following reasoning: every part of Socrates is less than Socrates, and therefore Socrates taken as a whole or taken totally (*totus Sortes*) is less than Socrates, and therefore Socrates is less than Socrates. This sophism fails to note the difference between considering Socrates purely and simply (*Sortes secundum se*) and considering Socrates in any of his parts. This is a confusion between an absolute point of view (*simpliciter*) and a relative one (*secundum quid*). It is as if one claimed that Socrates considered as a foot (*Sortes secundum pedem*) is less than Socrates and that therefore Socrates is less than Socrates. Whence arises the solution to the sophism: it is true that Socrates taken in any of his parts (*totus Sortes*) is less than Socrates himself (*Sortes secundum se*). But one must not treat as equivalent the consideration of Socrates *tout court* and of Socrates considered in the relations between the parts and the whole.

This last example is instructive insofar as it shows that to speak of Socrates's foot is indeed to speak about Socrates as a foot, since it is to speak of Socrates insofar as he is, in one of his parts, a foot. We say that Socrates *tout court* is Socrates when he is not analyzed holistically and that Socrates *as a whole* is Socrates considered in his differentiation into parts. It follows that simple predication says less than does holistic predication, and this is what makes the latter exponible. If we say that Socrates is in the water, we are neither claiming nor excluding that he is completely submerged; but if we say that the whole of Socrates or Socrates as a whole is in the water, we are saying directly of Socrates and indirectly of each of Socrates's parts that they are submerged.

This discussion shows that the referent is not different in the following:

(1) Socrates is immersed in the water.
(2) Socrates is entirely immersed in the water.
(3) Every part of Socrates is immersed in the water.
(4) Socrates is partially immersed in the water.
(5) Some part of Socrates is immersed in the water.

All of these statements bear on Socrates; even those that bear on parts bear on parts *of Socrates*.

What, then, is a holistic description? It is, first off, a description of *one* thing *of a certain type* and not of several things of that type. For example, it is the grammatical analysis of a sentence, not of several sentences taken together, or the analysis of a discourse, not of a collection of discourses taken together. These things can then be considered in two different ways: without concern for their internal structure or by seeking to understand precisely such internal structure. Holistic description is the description of a thing taken in its complexity.

How is internal complexity to be understood? By taking the thing as a part. For example, a doctor examines at one and the same time Socrates and a part of Socrates. If he is examining a foot, it is not a severed foot but a living organ. A holistic description of a foot is the description of what it is insofar as it is *Socrates's* foot. What is special about this description is this: one would not say that "Socrates's foot has a thorn" but rather "Socrates has a thorn in his foot." Holistic description bears directly on the whole even where it seems to bear only on a part; what is said about something insofar as it is a part is always said "obliquely." This is why holistic predicates are predicates of the parts as parts of a whole. The parts are only what they are thanks to the whole, and it is in this sense that the whole precedes the parts.

6.3. The Material of Meaningful Totalities

The logical analysis that I have just sketched out bears only on the reference of holistic propositions. Whether one is speaking of a whole or a part of a whole, the reference is the same. Nevertheless, this logical analysis tells us nothing about how the parts are distinguished and how they are defined in relation to one another. The examples given do not rule out the parts being arbitrarily distinguished without concern for the articulations of the thing itself (e.g., Socrates might be half immersed in the water). Logical analysis was unable to provide an organizational principle and did not claim to be able to provide one. No general analysis would be able to do this since doing so assumes that the concept "part of a whole" has the same meaning in geometry, biology, the art of dramatic composition, the psychology of perception, etc. One obviously cannot expect to find the same relation between part and whole in the case of an organic whole (e.g., Socrates) as one would in a meaningful totality (e.g., a speech, a ceremony, a calendar, a kinship system, a piece of legislation, etc.). Our concern here is with the holism of meaning and of mind. We therefore must consider how parts are defined within a meaningful totality.

At the same time that Russell sought to provide an extensionalist definition of complex beings, he recognized that his definition did not cover all of the meanings of the word "whole." He then proposed a distinction between *aggregates* and *unities*. An aggregate is a whole that is entirely identified when its parts have been identified. "Such a whole is completely specified when all its simple constituents are specified; its parts have no direct connection *inter se*, but only the indirect connection involved in being parts of one and the same whole."[19]

What Russell called "unities" are totalities that are not eliminated by atomistic analysis. They are meaningful totalities, propositions.[20] Consider, for example, a comparative statement: "A is greater than B" or, more succinctly, "A > B." We can describe the statement by its elements: it is made up of three symbols, "A," "B," and ">." Yet we have failed to identify the sentence by identifying these symbols, since the same aggregate (the same collection) of symbols can be used to compose the contrary statement "B > A." It is therefore not enough to know all of the "parts" of the whole (i.e., to be able to identify them) to know the whole that they comprise

---

19. Bertrand Russell, *The Principles of Mathematics* (1903; London: Allen & Unwin, 1937), § 136 (140). It is clear that what Russell here calls "simple constituents" we have since come to call the "elements" of a set.

20. I will leave aside entirely the questions raised by Russell's idiosyncratic use at that time of the words "proposition" and "term." Ibid.

(i.e., the whole in the composition of which they participate). One might say that the *material description* of the sentence, which gives the elements out of which it is made, does not allow us to individuate or identify it.

Russell pointed out at the time a "paradox of analysis": a proposition is above all a unity, and this unity cannot be restored once analysis has taken it apart. He makes the following bizarre claim. "The verb, when used as a verb, embodies the unity of the proposition, and is thus distinguishable from the verb considered as a term, though I do not know how to give a clear account of the precise nature of the distinction."[21] Indeed, he does not provide an account, but he has given a clear indication of what the problem is. To take the verb as a simple term amounts to saying that the elements of the proposition that we want to identify are the symbol "A," the symbol "B," and the symbol "is greater than." Now, the itemization of these three symbols does not make a proposition. On the other hand, taking the verb as the bearer of the unity by which these three symbols form a meaningful discourse amounts to considering the verb *within* the proposition. In order to identify the proposition, one would obviously have to describe these elements in a different way, for example by saying something like this: "(1) is greater than (2) and (1) = A, (2) = B." But then there would have been no dissection of the proposition, no reductive analysis, since the elements would not have been apprehended outside of their relations within the proposition. This is why a material description is not sufficient.

The thesis of the *materiality of the signifier* is thus refuted, at least if that thesis is expressed as follows: to describe the material of the sentence is sufficient for the sentence to be identified. Russell's "paradox of analysis" makes clear why it is not sufficient. To identify a sentence one must of course know its elements, but one must also indicate the order in which they are to be taken. The elements of a sentence do not enter into the sentence as if it were a monolithic block. There is an *order of meaning* in virtue of which to write "A > B" is not the same thing as to write "B > A." What is required is therefore a formal description to complement the material description.

The paradox encountered by Russell brings to mind a profound discussion in Greek philosophy. In the *Theaetetus* (201d–206c), Plato alludes to a

21. Ibid., § 54 (50).

mysterious theory that Socrates claims came to him in a dream. The theory is roughly the following: what is a *logos* (a word that can be translated either as "discourse" or "proposition")?[22] A *logos* is a sequence or assemblage of names. A *logos* is made up of several names and therefore contains too many to be said to mean only *one thing*. *Logoi*, because they are made up of several names, instead allow one to talk about several things. In order to talk about a single thing, however, one would have to use only the name of that thing without referring to anything else. As a result, the "primary elements" of things (*prota stoicheia*) cannot be the objects of a *logos*, they can only be designated, in a nondiscursive way, by their names. As for composed things (ourselves and all that is visible), we can speak about them in discourse by appropriately bringing together the names of their elements. Expressing this theory in a philosophically correct way, it would appear to mean that there is a lexicon of names corresponding to simple things and an inventory, which may be recursive, of the combinations of names ("sentences") for speaking of the things that are made up of simple things.

In the heyday of logical atomism, it was felt that there was a parallel between these speculative ideas in the *Theaetetus* and the theory of "simple objects" that were held to be the real referents of our sentences.[23]

We know that in *The Sophist* (261c–262e) Plato provides reasons why a theory of the sentence as an assemblage of names is impossible. For as long as one lines up only names, there is no discourse and nothing is said, and the same is true if one lines up a sequence of verbs. In order to have a meaningful discourse (*logos*), one must compose one's sentence out of signs that are syntactically different. "Lion deer horse" or "walk run sleep" are assemblages of signs that say nothing, but "Theaetetus is seated" is entirely meaningful.

---

22. [Translator's note: M. J. Levett and Myles Burnyeat, in their translation of the *Theaetetus*, choose to render *logos* in the passages in question as "account," while pointing out in a footnote that it can also mean "statement," "argument," "speech," and "discourse." Plato, *Complete Works*, ed. John M. Cooper and D. S. Hutchinson (Indianapolis, IN: Hackett Publishing Company, 1997), 223.]

23. In the *Philosophical Investigations*, Wittgenstein cites the passage from the *Theaetetus*, claiming that Plato's "primary elements" correspond to Russell's "individuals" and to the "objects" of his own *Tractatus*. Wittgenstein, *Philosophical Investigations*, rev. 4th ed., ed. P. M. S. Hacker and Joachim Schulte, trans. G. E. M. Anscombe, P. M. S. Hacker, and Joachim Schulte (1953; Oxford: Wiley-Blackwell, 2009), § 46 (25).

Plato's speculation on language is one of the sources of the theory of formal causality. Referring to the theory in the *Theaetetus* and its influence on Aristotle, Elizabeth Anscombe speaks of a "logical theory of elements," a clear allusion to logical atomism.[24] A *physical* theory of elements would explain, in the manner of the Ionian philosophers, how things can be transformed into other things in nature (e.g., water evaporates, etc.). A *logical* theory of elements is a theory of the simple objects on which our discourse bears if it is to bear on anything at all. Socrates is therefore proposing such a theory when he asks in the *Theaetetus* whether a sentence is not a series of names each of which designates a simple object. This theory is *logical* because the problem of reference is posed within it. According to the theory, when we speak of a composite being, we are in reality designating the simple individuals of which it is composed.

Aristotle has several arguments to discredit the logical theory of material elements. Imagine that the composite has been destroyed, but not the elements that enter into its composition. Something would then be missing that prevents us from having before us the composite thing. And yet, by hypothesis, the elements are all there. What is missing is the composition itself.

He also uses the following argument (*Metaphysics,* VIII, 1043b). To insist that the whole, for example a syllable, be composed of multiple elements and their arrangement is to treat the form as a third material element. But the syllable BA, for example, is not made up of three elements, the two letters plus the fact that one comes before the other. It is made up of the two letters *taken in this order*. The form is therefore not a component that would have to be composed or "synthesized" with the materials. It is the order in which the materials must be composed. This order is a meaningful one: the letters A and B are only the parts of the syllable BA (which is itself meaningful when it is part of a word that means something within a sentence) if they are taken in a certain order. Considered in themselves and in their individuality, these letters are not the parts of the syllable BA. If they were, they could not also be the parts of the syllable AB.

The argument about syllables presupposes that we take seriously the *materiality* of these elements. It is not a matter of indifference that the

---

24. G. E. M. Anscombe, "Aristotle," in G. E. M. Anscombe and P. T. Geach, *Three Philosophers: Aristotle, Aquinas, Frege* (Oxford: Basil Blackwell, 1963), 48.

THE ORDER OF MEANING   171

word used in the entire discussion is *stoicheion,* which means "element" but also "letter" and "character." Letters are here the paradigm of the elementary unit, of the atom. Atomistic theories are in many ways the product of a reflection on syllables and their parts.[25] Anscombe invites us to imagine that we have a stock of wooden letters and that a child is playing at forming words with them. Such wooden letters are endowed with a distinct presence separate from their possible assemblage into a syllabic configuration. Aristotle's reasoning shows that something has to be added to them for a composite to result. But what has to be added is clearly not another building block, or one risks entering an infinite regression. It must therefore be something other than the building materials: the *order* in which the elements are to be taken. As a result, the present existence of the whole cannot be reduced to the present existence of the elements, since these elements can be given without the whole also being given (the elements can be given in *no order at all*).

It remains to be understood how the whole can, in one sense, be given without its elements being given. This point would appear more difficult to accept.

Reflecting on the example of the syllable BA, can one really claim, as structural holism does, that the (structured) whole is given, in a sense to be determined, *before* the parts? At first glance, we would seem to be obliged to say exactly the opposite: the whole is only given, in a clear sense, *after* the parts. As long as the letters A and B have not been placed in some order or another, there is neither the syllable AB nor the syllable BA.

This is entirely correct. Note, however, that until now we have been speaking of what could be called a typographical or morphological entity: the syllable BA. We did not have to think about the way in which this syllable is used in order to discuss it. Our goal, however, is not to study a simple arrangement of letters but to specify the conditions for a holistic analysis of meaningful totalities. We will therefore have to consider the syllable BA from the point of view of a meaningful totality.

This is where the analytic paths of formalism and structural holism part ways. What does a formalist analysis of the syllable BA tell us? It tells

---

25. On the model provided by the letters of the alphabet and its role in Plato and Greek thought generally, see Victor Goldschmidt, *Le paradigme dans la dialectique platonicienne* (Paris: Presses Universitaires de France, 1947), § 21 (66–69).

us that the group BA has as its structural description "B followed by A." At the same time, the group AB is described as follows: A followed by B. In other words, the two syllables have the same formal structure, namely a letter followed by another letter. The difference between them is therefore entirely material. In one case, the first letter is A and then B. In the other, it is the converse. But the difference between the two letters is a physical one, not just because they are materially individuated (they are two distinct pieces of wood) but because the difference between the forms of the two letters is physical. It could, for example, be mechanically recognized. It follows, the formalist analyst will claim, that structural description is a "physicalist" description. An order of meaning has been described in natural or physical terms.

Nevertheless, it is worth pointing out here that a dimension is lacking in this description, at least if we are studying syllables destined to form linguistic signs. Consider the example of a child who sets about composing the word BABAR out of wooden letters taken from a large box.[26] The structural description of this word (in other words, its orthographical and typographical description) shows that two Bs and two As will have to be used. Peirce's distinction between types and tokens accounts for the fact that the word contains—depending on which criterion one adopts— either three or five letters. To compose the word BABAR with wooden letters, one would have to find in the box the letter A (twice), the letter B (twice), and the letter R (once). The child draws from the box two letter Bs. But which of the two Bs is he to put in the first position of the word and which in the third? It makes absolutely no difference, and the same is true for the letter A.

By contrast, if we want to provide an authentically "physicalist" description of the word—by which I mean a description that refers only to physical operations on physical entities—each of the wooden pieces will have to be identified, and we will have to distinguish the four possible combinations in which the word BABAR can be spelled with two As, two Bs, and an R. The physical movements will not be the same when placing one or the other of the two letter Bs drawn from the box, and the same is true for the rest of the word.

26. [Translator's note: Babar the Elephant is a well-known character created by Jean de Brunhoff in the 1930s and featured in a set of widely-translated French children's stories.]

Thus, the five distinct places in the structural description of the word BABAR are places for individuals, but individuals whose individuality is indifferent. A letter B has to be put in the first place, but it does not matter which one. Any of the available copies will do. All that the composite requires is that the first and third letter be of the same "B" type. In other words, the structure in question here *is not concerned with individuals.* Instead, it sets down conditions regarding the types of the legitimate occupants of the various places envisaged. In short, the situation here is like that of the syntax of a sentence. The units of a linguistic sentence are not words; they are "parts of speech," as a grammarian would put it. These parts are distinguished at a level that is higher than that of the words that are considered to be the ultimate elements of the sentence (ultimate, that is, from the perspective of a syntactical analysis of the sentence). Similarly, the typographical units of a text are not letters in their material individuality but rather the positions along the written line.

As a result, the structure is not a form in the still-morphological sense of an arrangement of elements. The structure of a meaningful totality is a *form of forms.* That is, the elements can only enter the structure if they are themselves endowed with a form. It is not sufficient, in a case such as that of the syllable BA, to distinguish form and matter as one would for a bed or a statue in explaining that what makes this wood into a bed is the arrangement of the assembled parts and what makes this marble a statue of a god is the marble's configuration. Indeed, in the case we are considering, the material does not present itself as some sort of amorphous stuff (as the bed's wood or the statue's marble does) but is, rather, endowed with a morphology, which is what allows us to distinguish types of letters and several examples of the same (types of) letters. In a meaningful totality such as a syllable, three levels will have to be distinguished: the *whole,* the *parts,* and the *elements.* The whole is not made up of elements in the same sense in which it is made up of parts. The parts of BABAR are the typographical spaces that must be filled to obtain the word—in order to give it an actual presence—while the elements are the wooden letters.

The material assemblage is made up of wooden letters in the same way that Balzac's complete works fit in the twelve volumes in the Bibliothèque de la Pléiade, or the way in which these volumes might take up an entire shelf of the library of an apartment. But the word BABAR is clearly not composed of wooden letters, even when we are considering an assemblage created out of these elements by a child. It is composed of five slots or positions, in the same way that one speaks of a "slot" to refer to a job or a "position" for which one is recruiting.

Unlike Émile Borel's typing monkeys, a child in the process of constructing a word seeks from the outset to write a particular word with its particular spelling. If she spells out the word BAZAR rather than BABAR, it will be said either that she wrote the word "bazar" or that she got a letter wrong. It is true that we must wait until the work of composition has been nearly completed before we can understand what she is doing. It is nevertheless the case that, if we see that the child has written BABA and is still searching for a letter in the box, we can at least conclude that if she is writing BABAR, then the child must be looking for the letter R. As long as she has not found it, she will not have accomplished her project. She may well abandon the effort, or fail for want of the letter R, or prove unable to write BABAR and therefore change her mind and stick with the word BABA instead. But whatever happens, the meaning of each of these possibilities is determined by the *rule for writing* the word BABAR. It is for this reason that this rule is a truly structural description. It cannot be taken as a naturalistic or physicalist description of the structure. The structural description of a meaningful totality as such does not tell us what it is made of; it tells us how the word *must* be written.

But if this is the case, the whole must be given *before* the elements from which it is constructed have been chosen and arranged in the correct order. To say that it is given is to say nothing more nor less than that when the first letter B is put in place, it is the first letter of the word BABAR if it is already determined that the second letter must be A, the third B, etc. It is precisely in this sense that structural description bears on a rule and that it cannot be reduced to the observation of an external morphological fact or a regularity.

Whence the following result, which can be outlined in two points:

(1) *The concrete whole can only be given after having been constructed with the elements required for its production.* In order to compose the word out of wooden letters, one will have to obtain wooden pieces cut into the appropriate forms. Another example is the symbolic system of kinship. Imagine a kinship system in which two groups must be allied through marriage: the marriage can only be celebrated if the families in question have children to marry off. For as long as these children have not been

brought forth and raised to an appropriate age, the event prescribed by the system cannot take place.

(2) *The whole (with its parts) must be given before its elements* in the following sense: if the whole were not given before the elements, one would not be able to say that the elements had been meaningfully chosen. Nothing would then distinguish such a "structure" from a material assemblage. It follows that, when the syllable BA is given, the syllable BAR that completes it is also logically given as what BA lacks if BABAR is to be formed.

This solution is broadly Aristotle's: the letters are the material cause of the syllable, but the syllable is the formal cause of the letters (*Physics*, II, 195a). There is nothing subtle about this distinction, which puts forward nothing but what is presupposed by the fact that we are speaking of a syllable and its two elements (letters). The syllable is the outline of an order of meaning. What, then, is an order of meaning? Wherever a partial whole is given as such, it is so given according to an order of meaning. What is given is a whole (here, one made up of two letters) that lacks something else in order to be the whole it is supposed to be—the other syllables needed to make a word.

Consider a part of a dismantled whole. Is the material unit BA a part of the whole BABAR? That depends. The unit BA is not a part of the whole BABAR in the sense in which it is only that, since it is just as much a part of the word BAR. By itself it is therefore a part of neither the one nor the other.

But if we adopt a formal and intentional point of view, BA is indeed a part of BABAR. It is part of BABAR if it is the part that our typographer child has *already* composed of the complete word to be formed out of the wooden letters. However, in this case, what we are referring to as BA is no longer a material unit, for it so happens that our young typographer is not in the process of composing the word BAR or BAT or any word other than BABAR. The typographical unit BA, taken as a part of BABAR, requires the complement BAR. It would be an *error* to place an R or a T immediately after it. As a result, the syllable BA is a part of the word BABAR if it *already is* this word—if it already is the word not actually but in intention. More generally, a thing is part of the whole if it is a partial realization of that whole, i.e., if it is the whole given in a partial form.

In short, the composite BA is part of BABAR if the composite *is* the whole (the word) but only as the *partial* whole (the word incompletely reproduced)—i.e., if BA is the combination of B and A (in this order) with the aim of composing a whole that, when given in its entirety, is the word BABAR.

6.4. Form and Meaning

A sentence can be described in three ways: as a unit of meaning, as a composition of signs (belonging to the appropriate categories—noun, verb, etc.), and as an assemblage of elements.

One might, however, claim that the only materialism to have been refuted here is one that sought to explain signifiers by the properties of the material out of which they are made, as if it were the wood of the wooden letters rather than the form of the letters that ultimately explained the syllable.

In fact, it might be objected, it is possible to articulate the program for a materialism of the signifier on a different theoretical basis. Here is how. First, one accepts the conclusion just established: describing the material or the elements out of which the sentence is made is not yet to describe it in such a way as to identify it. A description of the sentence taken as a sentence must be a formal one. But, it will be pointed out, the formal description of the sentence in no way contravenes the principles of a materialist ontology. Indeed, the description of the sentence as a sentence, though formal and not material, refers only to the material elements of the sentence and their distribution, their mutual relations in space. Even where the formal description is no longer restricted to the material elements of the whole, it remains physicalist, i.e., it never goes beyond the resources of physical identification. The elements are physical, and their order is defined in a space oriented from left to right. At no point does the description make an appeal to meaning, which means that the description of a meaningful totality need not be intentional.

It so happens that the historical alliance between formalism and causalism in French structuralism was based precisely on the idea that the formal description of meaningful matter makes use of only natural and physical properties. The partisans of this theoretical program believed it possible to describe an order of meaning *without concern for meaning itself.* This led them to maintain that meaning is a derived reality, either an effect or an epiphenomenon.

Today, materialist psychologists also invoke distinctions of this sort.[27] Between physical matter and meaning there lies, according to this view, an intermediate level that is formal and physical: that of syntax. Physical description identifies material data. Semantic description is intentional in nature, but syntactical description separates form from meaning entirely, identifying an order among physical forms. Physical description is of the *hardware* of a thinking machine; syntactical description is of its *software*.

It might then after all be possible to develop in a coherent way a *materialism of the signifier*, provided one does not mix up the levels of description. Because semantics and syntax can be distinguished from one another, it is possible to describe signifiers without concern for what they mean. The advance represented by algebra, the partisans of this view will explain, was to attain a level of formal abstraction such that one was able to consider only *signifiers without signifieds*. This level of abstraction is that of what is called "formal thought." Taking note of this point, Jean-Louis Gardies also draws attention to its ambiguity:

What is distinctive about calculus is precisely the replacement of reasoning about the signified by operations on the signifier, the "reduction of the *theory of things* to the *theory of signs*" by means of symbols "so selected and perfected, that the theory, combination, transformation, etc. of signs can take the place of operations that would otherwise have to be done by concepts." The very term *operation* is moreover incorrectly used by Lambert; for an operation is a material transformation that can in no way touch the concept itself, but rather bears upon the sign's materiality, whether this sign is the small stone or *calculus* that gives the method its name, the elements of the abacus moved about by the child or the Asian accountant, or an ideogram subject to purely scriptural manipulation.[28]

Gardies takes careful note of the slippage: an operation upon symbols is mentioned, but this same word sometimes designates an intellectual activity (as is the case, for example, in arithmetical operations) and at other times refers to manipulations that produce material transformations (the movement of tokens, inscriptions, etc.). One thereby envisions a transference of

---

27. See Chapter 8, section 1 of my *The Mind's Provisions*, 165–167.
28. Jean-Louis Gardies, *Esquisse d'une grammaire pure* (Paris: J. Vrin, 1975), 56. The interpolated citations are from Johann Heinrich Lambert's *Neues Organon* (1764) as cited by Edmund Husserl in the first of his *Logical Investigations*, vol. I, trans. J. N. Findlay, ed. Dermot Moran (London: Routledge, 2001), 210 [interpolated translations slightly modified].

the operation of calculation from the head of the person calculating to the physical movements of signs considered as material elements. Lambert (at least as far as these isolated phrases are concerned) seems to be saying that there is a single kind of activity or operation that can sometimes be carried out with material objects and sometimes with concepts. This suggests a parallelism between *two processes,* one mental and the other physical. At first the two processes are simply associated: the human calculator has mental units in his head on which he performs operations analogous to those he carries out, simultaneously, on physical units (tokens, beads, letters). It is then observed that formalization spares us from having to concern ourselves with the mental process; calculation then inheres in the physical transformations of material signifiers. It follows that a machine constructed in such a way as to produce those transformations (as the result of a program) would be a machine carrying out a calculation on symbols.

The same ambiguity arises if we act as if we could speak of a single class of entities, signifiers, while sometimes treating them as signifiers that signify and at other times as signifiers that do not signify, having been "liberated" from their role as bearers of signification. Within a formalized language, as Gardies points out, "the signifier gains its autonomy."[29]

In reality, the description of a calculation (whether it is carried out in one's head or on paper) is an intentional description and not a physical one. Our misunderstandings of this point derive from a confusion between signifying form and mere physical configuration.

A distinction between two concepts of form is required here. In textbook Aristotelianism, the concept of form is explained by means of examples such as those of a statue or a vase. Here is a block of marble; will it be a god, a table, or a basin? This concept of form is morphological: marble cannot be given without taking on some configuration or other. A block of marble is cut in a certain way, and its external configuration is what makes it a statue of a god. In this case, there are no elements that can be arranged in different ways or identified, outside of any arrangement, within an initial disorder. The morphology of the individual is an intrinsic quality of that individual.

The concept of form that matters to us for the analysis of symbolic totalities is not of form as a quality of the thing. To provide a meaningful form is not to shape a material. It is, rather, to provide an order to units that are

---

29. Gardies, *Esquisse,* 57.

themselves endowed with a shape or morphology. Form is a *unit of order,* not a unit of life or of substantial being. Elementary units do not owe their existence to a structure. Thus, within a ceremony or a gesture or a meal or a ritual, what counts is the order of the elements, because it is this order that determines the meaning of the presence of each element that is in its place. These elements are therefore already formed and can be described in their morphology. Taken in isolation, though, they are not meaningful elements. And this is precisely the holistic thesis on meaningful totalities: *elements are signs only within the system.*

When logicians speak of the rules that allow one to recognize a "well-formed formula," they do so for artificial notations. Such notations are conceived such that every graphical unit represents a symbol and therefore a syntactical unit. This is also the aim of the philosopher seeking to introduce a semiformal notation allowing him to tell us that, for example, he will represent the sentence "The individual named *a* is the father of the individual named *b*" by the notation "R*ab*." In this notation, there are only three letters, and each of these letters is a syntactical unit. Notice, though, that things would be different if the sentence were represented by "R (*a, b*)," as is also often done. There would then be six graphical units, but the logical syntax would be the same as in the earlier case: a dyadic predicate along with its two arguments.

Lucien Tesnière, out of a concern for the autonomy of syntax, highlighted the deleterious consequences of the confusion between syntax and morphology among many linguists. Morphologists, as he calls them, misunderstand the difference between a syntactic structure and an external form, recognizable to an observer by its perceptible "markers."[30] The exterior form is perceptible or physical and might be mechanically recognized by a machine built to detect it. But syntactical form cannot be grasped mechanically and requires intellectual understanding.[31]

---

30. Lucien Tesnière, *Éléments de syntaxe structural,* 2nd ed. (1959; Paris: Klincksieck, 1988), 13 n. 1.

31. See the very first page of Tesnière's book: "3.—Every word that is part of a sentence ceases to be isolated as it is in a dictionary. The mind perceives connections between it and the words around it and the set of these connections forms the framework of the sentence. 4.—Nothing serves to indicates these connections. Yet it is indispensable that they be perceived by the mind; otherwise, the sentence will be unintelligible." Ibid., 11.

What is it to describe the syntactical structure of an utterance? In order to explain it, the distinction between syntax and semantics is not sufficient; one must also distinguish syntax from morphology. Let us start with the indifference of syntax to semantics. Tesnière proposes an exercise reminiscent of some of Jean Tardieu's poems, which were composed according to the principle of "one word for another." Tesnière calls the level of the syntactical description of the sentence the "structural plan." The "structural plan" and the "semantic plan" are independent of each other.

The best proof of this is that a sentence can be semantically absurd while being structurally perfectly well-formed. Consider the sentence "The green signal indicates a clear way," which has an intelligible meaning. If I replace each of the meaningful words with the next word in the dictionary of the same type, I am left with the sentence "The gregarious signatory indicts a cleavable weakling," which preserves the same structural schema but has no meaning (in this regard, see also the work of the futurist and surrealist poets).[32]

In fact, in order to carry out such a transposition, one must be capable of *syntactical discernment,* knowing to transpose "signal" into "signatory" and "green" into "gregarious," while above all not transposing the articles. The whole thing would not work if the move to the following word in the dictionary were carried out mechanically: "the" would be changed to "theanthropic," for example. The result would no longer be a well-formed formula, and the poetic effect of the contrast between the flawlessness of the structure and the inanity of the content would not come off. As Tesnière says, only meaningful words are to undergo the transposition. In other words, form and meaning can be dissociated, but in order to recognize the syntactical construction of the sentence, one must have retained something of the semantic perspective.

Such transposition is a transformation that preserves what Tesnière calls a "structural schema." Structure can therefore be defined by a syntactical equivalence between two entities that are materially different, by which I mean this: two sentences that do not share the same glossary of meaningful words. This concept of structure defined by means of

---

32. Ibid., 41. [Translator's note: I have used an English dictionary to transpose the English translation of Tesnière's first sentence rather than translating both sentences as they appear in the original French.]

transposition—and thus by formal equivalence—is the concept of an invariant. Structure cannot be provided for an isolated utterance but only for (at least) two utterances having the same structure. Or, one establishes an utterance and its structure, on the one hand, and a lexicon allowing one to make substitutions, on the other.

All of this is grist for the mill of theorists who ask that we recognize the existence and the specificity of "formal thought": in order to reveal the form—the "structural schema"—meaning must first be bracketed. Nevertheless, one cannot conclude that this syntax will be free of every consideration of meaning, nor that syntax is the study of the liberated signifier. The structural schema will be brought out only if the transposition is carried out correctly. And in order to do that, it is not enough to be able to recognize words by their exterior form (a task made easier in artificial notation by the assignment of a letter to each symbol); one must also locate the meaningful words, which implies that there are others that must be in the sentence but not so as to signify anything themselves.

Tesnière here borrows from Chinese grammar the idea that there are two kinds of words, "full" and "empty" words. The attribution of a semantic content involves only full words. Empty words "are simple grammatical tools whose role is only to indicate, specify or transform the category of full words and to regulate the relations among them."[33] Here again, Tesnière presents a stylistic exercise as a way of illustrating this distinction (and of showing that it is a familiar one): he provides a passage in the style common to telegraphic communication. "Thus, the telegram 'Arrive Paris tomorrow eight o'clock train' can be easily understood to mean 'I will arrive in Paris tomorrow on the eight o'clock train,' whereas, on their own, the empty words of this sentence would be meaningless: 'I, will, in, on, the.' "[34]

In short, materialists of the signifier ask us to accept that, at a certain level of abstraction, all of our words are empty words, signifiers whose function is not to signify but to make possible the constitution of a well-formed formula.

To this we would respond, following Tesnière, that syntax is not an order among words, a structure that is a kind of collective property of the

---

33. Ibid., 53. Philosophers have an analogous distinction in their technical lexicon: *syncategorematic* terms are those that have no intention and denote nothing.
34. Ibid., 54.

sentence's elements. It is an order defined among syntactical entities that Tesnière calls "nuclei."[35] In the sentence "Alfred is tall," there are three words but only two nuclei. Logicians would agree and therefore put forward a notation such as "*Fa*" (predicate-argument). But the clarity of the artificial notation should not lead us to believe that syntax is defined around letters (i.e., around units made to be identified one by one). Only in artificial notation do syntactical units coincide with graphical units in such a way that the syntactical correction of well-formed formulas can be reduced to a question of orthography.

In textbooks for languages with ideogrammatic writing, one learns to compose a sign by combining strokes. In such cases, one might refer to a physical structure or *morphology* of the sign. The structure of the sign might also be thought of as the relations among the strokes that make up the ideogram. This would be like saying that four bars are required to make a capital E—one vertical bar and, perpendicular to it and to the right, three horizontal bars.

Collectivism can only speak of structure by defining it as a mutual disposition of constitutive elements. On the one hand, the elements are individuals: they are perfectly identifiable. On the other hand, the elements, collectively, have an emergent property. For example, the four bars possess an emergent property when they are assembled into the graphical form E. Taken as a group along with their arrangement, they are the beginning of the word ENTRY. If one believes that a structure is a set of relations among elements that can be enumerated, one has put forward a structural collectivism.

Syntactical structure cannot be understood in this way. The syntactical point of view consists in starting with the sentence rather than the elements of the text of the sentence. Tesnière does begin, as everyone does, with a discussion of "words." The sentence, he writes, is an organized whole whose constitutive elements are words. However, a few chapters on, the reader has been prepared to reconsider this point of departure. Words disappear from the syntactical perspective and, along with them, the morphological point of view: "the word has no syntactical reality."[36] Soon after that declaration, the situation has been entirely inverted, for we have come to recognize that, integrated within the sentence, the word is no longer a *unit* (as it is in a

---

35. Ibid., 47–48.
36. Ibid., 48.

dictionary) but the *term of a connection*. After that point, only connections are at issue. The sentence has as its framework the connection between a superior term and an inferior one (a governing term and a subordinate one). The key concept is therefore not that of an assemblage of words but rather of a structure conceived as a hierarchy of connections.[37] In short, the prologue to structural syntax consists in inverting the textbook perspective. The word is highlighted only because sentences are thought of as being given in linear order, whether the order of the spoken chain or of the linear text. Yet the normal (pedagogical) order is not that of a recording, whether by a tape recorder or a typographer. Intelligible order consists in starting from the sentence: "The concept of the sentence precedes that of the word."[38]

The relation of subordination is not itself a term. But it is also not a property of the elements, e.g., the words one can find in the dictionary. Essentially, one should probably avoid speaking of the structure of a sentence (as if it were a collective property of a plural subject). Instead, it would be better to refer to the equivalence between two completely different sentences: "The green signal indicates a clear way" is, from a syntactical point of view, the same sentence as "The gregarious signatory indicts a cleavable weakling." The transposition of elements in no way changes the form, and this is because it leaves in place the relations of subordination among the parts of speech, the syntactical units.

This is the same principle of structural analysis that is applied to symbolic systems. What does the linguist's approach (the guiding principle of which has just been provided by Tesnière) have in common with, say, that of a historian of religions such as Georges Dumézil or an anthropologist studying kinship systems such as Lévi-Strauss?

Structural analysis has given rise to slogans that philosophers have been quick to understand in a dialectical or neodialectical way: for example, "there are only differences, not terms that differ." These slogans have rightly been criticized for being obscure or absurd; if there is a difference, there must be things that differ in some respect.

Structural analysis's powerful idea was never this incoherent differentialism. Indeed, such differentialism has little need to investigate totalities or real systems. The important idea is that of the different levels one must

---

37. Chapter II of Tesnière's treatise has as an epigraph this maxim by Vauvenargues: "The sovereign law is subordination and dependence."
38. Ibid., 25.

take up in order to grasp a difference or, better, a differentiation. Every differentiation requires a distinction between a superior and an inferior level. The superior level *measures* what appears on the inferior level. The superior level is where the whole is identified in opposition to other wholes of the same kind. Did he seek to write the word "vine" or the word "fine"? The inferior level is that of the elements allowing one to carry out the identification: if the first letter is an F, the word is "fine," assuming an error did not arise during the composition.

This idea is not one that has reached the broader public (which is more responsive to themes such as the putative disappearance behind structures of the author or speaking subject), but it was brilliantly brought to light in a work that, for many philosophers of my generation, served as the Bible for everything related to the philosophy of structural analysis: Edmond Ortigues's *Le discours et le symbole*.

Even when one is studying phonemes—i.e., at a level below that of properly semantic units—one must still set in opposition the material (phonetic) and formal (phonological) perspectives. From the material point of view, a word *is composed of* phonemes. Elementary units then appear as elements or building blocks. From the formal point of view, a word *is broken down into* phonemes. The word is not something to be constructed; rather its phonemes are to be uncovered.

Seeing things this way amounts to elegantly reformulating Aristotle's two types of explanation: letters are the material cause of the syllable; the order in which they appear is its formal cause. This point of view therefore consists in giving oneself a whole by giving oneself a *principle of differentiation*; in order for the syllable to be the first syllable of the word we want to write, the first letter has to be B and the second A, giving us BA.

The phonological approach is thus regressive. One seeks out elements, which means that one must already have words or semantic groups so as to uncover "the articulatory or acoustic conditions able to distinguish meaningful units from one another."[39] Here is what Ortigues concludes on this point:

"Form" implies "selectivity"; "function" implies "hierarchy." We must always account for these two types of relation. Thus, even in phonology where we are initially dealing

---

39. Edmond Ortigues, *Le discours et le symbole* (Paris: Aubier, 1962), 95.

only with discriminating units, our analysis still remained within the demands of architectonic synthesis since the very idea of a function implied a reference to semantic groupings; that is, *at the level immediately superior to that of phonemes (in the way that the alternation "fine/vine" gives rise to the alternation f/v)*.[40]

This is just Tesnière's point expressed in a different language.

In this chapter I have taken up the idea that structural holism is, ultimately, accurately expressed by the classic aphorism according to which "the whole precedes its parts." Such primacy of the whole over the parts would be incomprehensible if the goal were to reconstitute the effective, empirical production of the parts. The meaning of this primacy is that one must distinguish between the material perspective in which elements are identified—elements that must be identified in themselves since they can enter into different combinations—and the formal perspective. This formal perspective cannot be taken to be a simply morphological point of view, as those who seek the means of "naturalizing" semantics believe. It is necessarily an intentional point of view.

Unfortunately, we are not yet home and dry, because a formidable obstacle arises here. A distinction has just been drawn between an element and a part. Holistic analysis is not concerned with elements but rather with reciprocal relations of delimitation and definition among parts. But the distinction, according to this objection, is purely and simply unintelligible. If the parts are identifiable, they are elements and we return to atomistic analysis. If the parts are not identifiable in the way that elements are, they are also not distinct parts but simply the whole considered under various descriptions. Is this not what was suggested by the analysis of holistic propositions outlined above, that Socrates's left foot and Socrates's right hand are not to be distinguished, but rather Socrates considered in his left foot and Socrates considered in his right hand?

In late nineteenth-century philosophy, relations that precede and constitute their terms were called *internal relations*. The objection that I have just raised is that every doctrine of internal relations is doomed to obscurity and incoherence.

40. Ibid., 97 (italics mine).

7

The Logic of Relations

> There is no term which is so absolute or so detached
> that it does not involve relations and is not
> such that a complete analysis of it
> would lead to other things. . . .
>
> —LEIBNIZ

7.1. The Primacy of Relations Over Terms

The aim of this chapter is to seek to clarify the principle of structural holism by looking at the logic of relations. As we have seen, this principle holds that there is a primacy of the relation over the terms it relates. This primacy is obviously formal and not material. It is traditionally explained as follows.

A relation that precedes its terms is a relation that formally constitutes them as what they are. The precedence of these relations over their terms is expressed by means of a distinction between two classes or two kinds of relations, those that are external and those that are internal.

External relations are relations whose reality follows that of the terms, since they are exterior to the reality of those terms. The relation does not affect the things related.

The archetypal example of an external relation is the spatial relation. The reality of a thing does not depend on the reality of the thing that happens to be next to it. On the other hand, the reality of the relation of proximity requires that there be both the reality of a first thing as well as, near it, the reality of a second thing. The bureau's first drawer and its contents do not really depend on what is inside the drawer below it. If we empty the first drawer of its contents, the other drawers and their contents remain as they were.

Internal relations, by contrast, are those relations that cannot be changed without changing the reality of their terms. This can be expressed as follows: if the relation ceases to exist, the things related (the *relata*) cease to exist. The textbook example is the relation between spouses. If one is without a spouse, one ceases to be a spouse oneself.

It would seem, then, that any formulation of structural holism will have to appeal to the doctrine of internal relations. It happens, though, that this doctrine has been subject to a critique that has been both intense and effective. One may therefore well believe that this doctrine is a dead letter, leading to an impasse that has long been acknowledged. If the idea of a structural explanation were only a version of the "doctrine of internal relations" disputed and apparently refuted by Russell in the early part of the twentieth century, structural holism would not fare any better than collectivist holism. We would once again end up with a monism, a view of things that is unable to sufficiently distinguish the elements of the totality. In the collectivism known as "semantic holism," it is impossible to understand an isolated element, because it is only when they are all taken together that meaningful elements have semantic properties.[1] If it were true that structural holism amounts to a monism of internal relations, the same would be true of it because individuality would not exist.

Here it will be illuminating to go back to William James, whose "pluralism" preceded Russell's own conversion to such ideas. James criticized the doctrine of constitutive relations in a style reminiscent, within a European philosophical context, of the critiques of Hegelian rationalism cited by Karl Löwith in his work *From Hegel to Nietzsche*.[2] In a famous text, Russell explains how his rejection of neo-Hegelian monism led him to pluralism. For James, this revolt was a revolt by individual existences against all systems of constitutive relations. A system of relations cannot engender the only thing that exists—individuals. Here I will refer to his article "Absolutism and Empiricism."[3]

---

1. See above Chapter 4, section 3.
2. Karl Löwith, *From Hegel to Nietzsche: The Revolution in Nineteenth-Century Thought*, trans. David E. Green (New York: Columbia University Press, 1991).
3. William James, "Absolutism and Empiricism" (1884), in his *Essays in Radical Empiricism,* ed. Ralph Barton Perry (New York: Longmans, Green & Co., 1912), 266–279.

James's position is that there are many relative attributes, ones that place terms in a relation of reciprocal dependence. A spouse cannot be a spouse by himself; he can only be one if there is someone who is his spouse. But James places a condition on this: there must first be individuals to acquire these attributes (which are exactly what we now call attributes of a holistic type). What he takes issue with is thus the vision of a universe in which things would exist only by and in their reciprocal relations. For if this were the case, individuality would be mere appearance.

James sees in this doctrine a philosophy that imagines it is speaking about reality when in fact it never departs from an abstract point of view:

> In any system, as such, the members are only *members* in the system. Abolish the system and you abolish its members, for you have conceived them through no other property than the abstract one of membership. Neither rightness not leftness, except through bi-laterality. Neither mortgager nor mortgagee, except through mortgage. The logic of these cases is this:—*If* A, then B; but *if* B, then A: wherefore, *if* either, Both; and if not Both, Nothing.[4]

James here makes the objection that will later be made by Moore and Russell—that the thesis is trivially true, since it is true *de dicto,* true of things described as members of a system (e.g., no club, no members of the club; no seller, no buyer, etc.). His principal objection is that all of it remains entirely conceptual, for existence is excluded. Give me some thing A and I will give you the system AB formed by the constitutive relation of whatever system is under consideration (bilaterality of the body, mortgages, etc.). But you cannot make a really *existing* member arise out of just the requirements set by this logic of relations. The objection is therefore one with an existentialist accent. If a member exists, there are relations, but if not, there is nothing. The reason for existence is therefore not within the system. The system does not explain why there are, in fact, mortgagers and mortgagees, nor, more generally, why there is *something rather than nothing*. Philosophers who think that they can, by means of mediations, generate the absolutely or immediately given inevitably end up with purely conceptual productions, Platonic "processions" of a merely intelligible kind.

4. Ibid., 269–270.

THE LOGIC OF RELATIONS 189

Husband makes, and is made by, wife, through marriage; one makes other by being itself other; everything self-created through its opposite—you go round like a squirrel in a cage.[5]

We may have the feeling of not advancing because there is a kind of conceptual flaw in postulating a real system of relations among things that are at one and the same time mutually dependent (in order for the relations to form a system) and independent (in order to exist). The parts of the system depend on one another and are therefore constituted by their relations. The elements are by definition independent from one another. How is one to turn independent individuals into dependent parts?

7.2. The Axiom of Internal Relations According to Russell

Russell's objection is not an expression of the revolt of existence to the demands of the rational System that is supposed to posit itself by itself. Russell intends to take up a position within the terrain of logic, i.e., within the terrain of an analytic rewriting of propositions. A paraphrase is analytic if it brings out clearly the truth conditions of the proposition under consideration.

In fact, Russell conflates two doctrines, which he calls, respectively, "monadism" and "monism," under the heading "doctrine of internal relations." According to him, both schools flout the logic of relations.

Russell's criticisms ought to be of interest to us, since the two theses mentioned *resemble* ideas frequently put forth within texts carrying out holistic analyses.

The monadist school does not accept that relations are external to the terms they relate. It follows that one cannot determine what the term is without uncovering its relations to the rest of the system. Commonly, one might say that everything is linked, that everything is expressed in everything else. But structural holism, it would seem, says much the same thing: if relations are external to their terms, they are not structural relations.

The monist school sees relations as properties of the whole. This is what structural holism seems to claim when it uses a distinctive opposition to place the parts within the whole. The parts of the whole are not

---

5. Ibid., 270.

independent individuals but parts that are differentiated by an opposition that places them within a relation of difference.

Russell criticizes these doctrines for having failed to respect the logic of relational propositions and thereby having developed an idealistic theory of relations. The doctrine of internal relations *seems* to give a great deal of importance, and even preeminence, to the category of relations. In fact, as we will later discover, these relations are ideal. Russell thus presents himself here as a defender of the reality of relations against all those who have sought in one way or another to reduce relations to something nonrelational.

Here it is worth discussing the work in which Russell recapitulates his philosophical itinerary, providing a context for his philosophical writings.[6] In it he recounts how his conversion to logical atomism and realism began as a revolt against a doctrine that, at the time, was called "monism," the view that everything in the universe holds together and everything is linked to everything else so that one must treat empirical diversity as mere appearance that obscures the real unity of all that is. In short, in this latter-day version of Parmenides's revelation, the foundational truth is that reality is one. One of the consequences of monism is precisely that one cannot state particular truths. For example, one cannot say that grass is green. Even if such a statement is not properly speaking false, it is also not quite true, for only complete knowledge would be authentic knowledge.

Late nineteenth-century monism resembles in one respect what is today, in the United States, called "holism." In a totality conceived along monistic lines, the interdependence of the pieces is such that nothing can be detached so as to be examined on its own. In opposition to this doctrine, which he calls the "doctrine of internal relations" and whose main representative is Bradley, Russell puts forward his own "doctrine of external relations." Russell believes that monism is incomprehensible. Among his criticisms, the most interesting for our purposes is this one: the doctrine of internal relations has as a consequence that relations are unreal, for they are no longer relations (between two distinct terms) at all. Indeed, internal relations cannot relate one thing to *another* thing; they can only relate a thing to itself. An internal relation can only be posited between

---

6. Bertrand Russell, *My Philosophical Development* (London: George Allen and Unwin, 1959). In Chapter 5, "Revolt Into Pluralism," Russell cites extensively from his 1907 text that criticized "The Monistic Theory of Truth." I will cite this latter text as it appeared in *Philosophical Essays* (1910; New York: Routledge, 1994), 131–146.

the whole taken under one of its aspects and the whole taken under another of its aspects.

The doctrine of internal relations can be found, at least as far as Russell's argument is concerned, in an axiom expressed in two clauses. The first posits that "*every relation between two terms expresses, primarily, intrinsic properties of the two terms.*"[7] In other words, the relation is grounded in what the two terms are in themselves; it is engendered by the reality of the things related. To be given two things is also to be given their relation, and to be given one of the two is also to be given the other, in virtue of the internal character of the relation. The reader might here be led to believe that this is a moderate version of "monism," since it makes reference to two terms. As we will see shortly, this way of speaking is provisional and will be overcome within the axiom's second clause. That second clause claims that *every relation between two terms expresses,* "*in ultimate analysis, a property of the whole which the two compose.*"[8] This means that the relation is not an attribute of one or the other of the two objects it relates, but of the whole.

Before one can profess to have understood the tenor of these claims, it would of course be desirable to come to an understanding of the metaphysical concepts used—"terms," "intrinsic properties," and, above all, "relation." It is nonetheless easier to make clear the meaning of the axiom by looking at Russell's examples than by amassing a set of formal definitions. There are three of these examples: the relation between a lover and a beloved, the relation of anteriority between an event and another event, and the relation of matrimony between a husband and wife.

The first example, according to Russell, is meant to reveal what is plausible about the doctrine of internal relations. This might seem to be a concession to his idealist adversary, but the reader soon realizes that this is not the case. The example is provided by the verb "to love," which the logician treats as a dyadic relation: "A loves B." In this notation, which is Russell's, it would appear that the letters "A" and "B" replace proper names or the designations of individuals.[9] In this formula, we might understand that

---

7. Russell, *Philosophical Development*, 54.
8. Ibid.
9. In the traditional philosophical vocabulary, terms are sometimes concepts or signs in a proposition, and therefore universals, and sometimes things that are related, with the

the letter "A" is the name of Romeo (or takes the place of any of Romeo's names) and that "B" is the name given to Juliet.

In virtue of the first clause of the axiom of internal relations, the relation of love, which can be said to create a relation between a subject of love (A) and an object of love (B), must simultaneously express an intrinsic property of A and an intrinsic property of B. It remains to be seen what an *intrinsic property* is, though this will become clear in Russell's discussion of the example. It is not entirely impossible, he says, that this proposition expresses an intrinsic property of A. But one would then have to understand the feeling of love to mean something like an experiential state of A, the state of someone who feels love. Understood in this way, love is a quality of the internal experience of whoever feels love, and for this reason it is intrinsic to the person who loves. One could here draw a distinction between experiential love (which is a feeling, a state of the person) and dramatic love (which is an affair involving several people, as is the case in Proust's *Swann in Love*). An experiential love is not really a relation between one person and another. Even an atheist, says Russell, must accept that there are people who love God. Yet this interpretation of the verb "love" at once deprives it of any relational fact posited by a sentence such as "A loves B." If love is taken in an intentional sense (so that we can say that "A loves B" without asserting whether there exists any such B), then we are no longer dealing with a reality belonging to the category of relations but with an intrinsic quality.[10]

Before considering Russell's next example meant to illustrate an authentic relation, we should point out that Russell does not seek in this text to bring his example into alignment with the statement that he himself provided of the first clause of the doctrine of internal relations. His first example allows him to illustrate one aspect of the doctrine: A's love for B may well be the expression of an intrinsic property of one of the

---

relation meant to go from one thing to another, its term. When the relation is bilateral, both things are terms. But the things that are the two terms of a binary relation are individuals, not concepts.

10. Russell does not have anything else to say about the particularities of this example and does not raise the problem of intentionality here. This sketch, however, has all the elements of the controversy regarding methodological solipsism in psychology. See Chapters 10 through 12 of my *The Mind's Provisions: A Critique of Cognitivism*, trans. Stephen Adam Schwartz (Princeton: Princeton University Press, 2001).

related terms, a real property of the subject of love (A). But what, then, is the intrinsic property of the object of love (B)? He does not say.

I conclude that psychological verbs are not serious candidates for being expressions of an internal relation between two "terms" such as lover A and beloved B. Russell's concession proves to have been only apparent. He acted as if these were the sorts of relations—those that one might call "purely mental"—that a monist might point to in order to make plausible his metaphysical doctrine about the intrinsic character of relations. Yet, as we have seen, these mental relations can in no way be internal in the sense stipulated by Russell. Even in the case where the intentional relation can be expressed by designating two people by their names, we still only have *one* real relation: that which goes from A to its term in B. The only real relation is the property by which B is the one with whom A is preoccupied when he experiences feelings of love for B. In the other direction, the converse relation by itself is nothing more than a relation of reason, which means that the relation may well figure in our discourse but not in the reality of B. The fact of being loved is for B a real relation to her lover only if we change the concept of love signified by the verb: if, instead of reducing it to certain emotions experienced by A when he thinks of B, we take it in the broader sense of a conduct that includes, for example, immoderate consideration and attention given to the beloved person. By contrast, if we stick to the sort of intentional relation expressed by the verb "to think of"—the model of a great many analyses of intentionality—it is clear that that by attributing to a thinking subject the activity of thinking of someone, a reality is posited in the thinker, but nothing is as yet posited in the object of thinking (unless one thinks that there are psychic interventions that can overcome distance). This is the entire problem of intentionality and the reason why it is fitting to think of these verbs as being special in nature.[11]

Russell's second example is that of a relation of temporal anteriority: event A precedes event B.

The doctrine of internal relations would maintain that this relation—"preceding in time"—can be tied to an intrinsic property of A. Now, an

---

11. Intentional verbs are neither purely relational (transitive) nor definitively intransitive (monadic). They may nevertheless become indirectly transitive.

authentic intrinsic property is one that can be assigned to a thing without concern for other things, in this case without mentioning B. Russell rightly deems such an analysis to be impossible: it is impossible to reduce the relation of succession between two events to the intrinsic properties of the terms of the relation. A relation of order cannot be paraphrased by the conjunction of three nonrelational propositions (see above, Chapter 6, section 3). If we identify both of the events and the relation of anteriority, we do not know the order in which to place these events around the relation.

Finally, Russell cites a third example, which he describes as "extreme," while attributing it to Leibniz. A man living in Europe is married to a woman located in India. His wife has just died, but he is unaware of this fact. According to Leibniz, Russell writes, this man undergoes an *intrinsic* change at the moment his wife passes away. By contrast, Russell's own doctrine holds that the man undergoes an *extrinsic* change. At first glance this example appears to support pluralism by showing the paradoxical quality of the monism of internal relations. If the unfortunate man who unknowingly has lost his wife underwent an internal change as a result, there would be no need to go to India to ascertain what had happened to his wife; it would be enough to examine the man's state to know whether he was married or widowed. The monist will have to explain how it can be that the event of the death of the wife can bring about a real change in the husband, given that a real change can only be a change in his internal state, i.e., one that can be described without mentioning existences independent from that of the man in question.

The intellectual difficulty presented by this example is instructive. It is pointless here to invoke what are often lazily called "our intuitions," for common sense is never presented with this kind of problem. Everyone agrees that there has been a change: someone who was married (in the sense that there existed a woman who was his wife) becomes a widower. Is this an internal or an external change? It seems to me that our common sense does not provide us with any "intuitions" about this case. Rather, we are required to look at the two conceptual systems proposed and decide which better corresponds to what we *want* to say.

Russell may have described this example as "extreme" because it seems that it invokes some kind of action over a great distance. The idea is thus that what happens in India is too far away to have any effect on us.

Discussions of this kind of difficulty do not originate in Russell or even in Leibniz.[12] One has to go back as far as Scholastic philosophy and beyond, to Greek philosophy. By recalling this history, I do not mean to suggest that these sorts of difficulties can be resolved simply by reconstructing the historical vicissitudes of the philosophy of relations but rather that it is worthwhile understanding the sources of classical arguments in order to perceive the dispute's fault lines or in order to recognize the terrain on which these opposing arguments compete. In the case we are considering, the dispute bears upon the *reality* of relations, which is why it owes quite a lot to the nuances of the debate between realists and nominalists.

Indeed, we are here confronted with an antirealist argument put forward by William of Ockham.[13] Suppose a painter is whitewashing a wall in Rome; by doing this, he renders the wall similar to a white wall in London. His work produces a change in Rome (a wall there becomes white), but it also produces a change in London, for there is now a wall in the English capital that just acquired, thanks to the painter's action, a relation of resemblance with the Roman wall. But how can a natural (as opposed to supernatural) agent produce intrinsic changes in London if he is located in Rome? The English wall cannot be touched by the natural action of an agent situated in Rome. As a consequence, it is impossible to argue that the relation of resemblance is a reality (a *relatio realis*), because to do so would oblige us to maintain that this relation is real in Rome, where the agent can intervene and produce effects, but that it is not real in the other direction (i.e., when the white wall in London is rendered similar to the white wall in Rome thanks to the latter having been whitewashed). One might respond to Ockham that there was never a question of the painter producing the whiteness of the wall in London, but merely of rendering the white wall in London similar to a Roman wall. Ockham can answer this defense: it is too much to ask of the Roman painter that he produce a real change in London. There is not just the white wall in London, but all the white walls in the world. We would therefore impute too much power to the painter if we attributed to him the power of producing real changes in all of these walls merely by painting a wall in Rome.

---

12. Moreover, even in Leibniz, the discussion would appear to have been taken from an example given by Locke (see below, Chapter 7, section 4).

13. Marilyn McCord Adams, *William Ockham*, vol. 1 (Notre Dame, IN: University of Notre Dame Press, 1987), 223.

In fact, all of these arguments rest on a distinction between intrinsic and extrinsic changes, which we must now examine more closely.

7.3. Intrinsic Changes

An intrinsic change is a real change. An extrinsic change is what Peter Geach amusingly called "'Cambridge' change," in reference to the Cambridge philosophers of the early part of the twentieth century, such as Russell and McTaggart, who reflected on such problems from a logical point of view.[14] Geach means by this a change whose concept is defined using only logical resources (as opposed to physical or historical resources, which are concerned with real developments). But speaking of a change that can be defined in purely logical terms already shows the limits of the endeavor: either one is seeking to reduce physics and history to logic (in a kind of logicism run wild) or one agrees to talk about change only from the perspective of the change in the descriptive value of the predicates, e.g., what was once true has become false or the converse.

Indeed, the only idea of change that can be derived from logic is that contradictory attributes can be ascribed to a thing only if there has been a change somewhere. This does not tell us what, in fact, has changed. How, for example, can a car be both near and far away from where I am? How can it be true to say "the car is near me" and also true to say "the car is far away from me"? The logician's response is that it is not possible to say these things simultaneously but that it becomes possible if there has been a change—the car is first near and then far away. But this logical criterion cannot determine whether the car has moved or I have. Logical analysis registers that there has been a change (that relationships have been modified), but it does not allow one to specify the point at which the reality of the change was produced.

A "Cambridge" change is not the same thing as a pseudo-change: one does really move from one state of things where a certain description applies to an individual to another situation in which that description ceases to apply. *Something* has therefore changed. But is what has changed the individual to which the description is applied, or is it something outside of it? Is it the thing or its world? An answer is precisely what the logical concept of change does not allow us to provide. Thus the distinction

---

14. P. T. Geach, *Logic Matters* (Oxford: Blackwell, 1972), 321.

between the two types of change—intrinsic and extrinsic—betrays a desire to distinguish what happens to the *thing* itself from what happens in its surrounding *milieu*. If we had only a logical criterion with which to grasp these changes, our understanding of such change would be holistic in the *collectivist* sense of the term. One would apprehend the move from one overall situation to another but without being able to grasp what, at the level of the elements of the totality, is responsible for the change. Each situation would be given in a long description of a state of the world (or a conjunctive set of facts). These propositions, collectively, would determine a world. For example, the difference between one world and another might reduce to the fact that, in the first world, the car is near us while, in the second world, it is far away (while everything else remains the same). If we could find a satisfactory, purely logical concept of change, it would require us to believe that there is only one subject of every change: the world.

Extrinsic change is thus real but is rooted somewhere other than in the being under consideration. When Socrates ceases to be taller than Theaetetus and even becomes smaller than him, our description of Socrates's height must be modified, not because Socrates really became smaller but because Theaetetus really grew (see *Theaetetus*, 154a–155c).

If we now apply these considerations to the discussion of Russell, we can see that for the monism of internal relations every change in the relations between one thing and the others is a change that affects the thing itself and not just its external environment. For the pluralism of extrinsic relations, however, every change in the relations that thing has with other things is a change in its world and not a change in what the thing is intrinsically or by itself. To put this another way, the thesis of internal relations posits that *every thing is its world* because a thing changes whenever its world changes, whereas the thesis of external relations posits that *every thing is detachable from its world*.

It then appears that the whole problem is knowing whether one can separately describe what is the individual (the intrinsic reality of the individual) and what is the individual's world (the reality exterior to the individual). It is not surprising that this way of stating the question has given rise to great debates.[15]

---

15. For example, the Hegelian critique of the historical materialism of the circumstances exterior to the historical actor. See my *The Mind's Provisions*, Chapter 12, section 3.

The need for a distinction between these two types of change is justified. If the doctrine of internal relations has the effect of erasing the distinction, that fact alone refutes the doctrine for the very sort of "monism" with which it was charged by Russell.

Let us return to Russell's first example: we want to be able to speak about A who loves B unilaterally. Unlike the shared love of Romeo and Juliet, unilateral love leaves its object unmoved. If the love that A really has for B could on its own really affect B, any beloved person would be modified by the very fact of being beloved—to become an object of love would be an intrinsic change.

But what could the property of "being an object of love" bring to the reality of B? In a theory of "triangular" desires such as that put forward by René Girard, the property of being beloved can unleash effects on a third person, C.[16] In this theory of love as it is depicted in European novels, in order for a hero to be awakened to love and desire, the object to be desired must be determined for him by someone else based on a jealous rivalry. The fictional hero can therefore only love what is already *an object of love*: he can find nothing lovable unless the lovable is already beloved by someone else. By contrast, if the emergence of love within A were able to provoke a real transformation in B, A would be able to have a triangular love for B (positing as a condition on his love for B that B be already beloved) without any need for a third person C to confer the status as a desirable object upon B, since the desiring subject A himself would have already turned B into an object of love. Moreover, this point of logic is independent of every psychology and would be just as valid if the triangular feelings were not those of rivals but of mutual inhibition: e.g., if I could only love what *has not* been already selected by another subject as an object of love.

7.4. Individuality

I conclude that every theory of internal relations is untenable if it is presented as a theory of internal relations *between individuals,* i.e., between subjects of intrinsic change. The way in which the concept of internal relations is often presented is in reality unintelligible and gives rise to

---

16. René Girard, *Deceit, Desire and the Novel: Self and Other in Literary Structure,* trans. Yvonne Freccero (Baltimore: Johns Hopkins University Press, 1976).

critiques—and even derision such as that from the pluralist camp—that are entirely justified.

The difficulty we have in understanding internal relations often arises from the examples that we are asked to consider and the language in which these examples are presented, a language that mixes logical interests with considerations that are entirely foreign to logic. Individuals are mentioned: Mr. and Mrs. Smith. We are then told that there exists *between* them a relationship and that this relationship is very important, that it plays a substantial role in their lives, and that it therefore affects these two people down to their most intimate reality, so much so that it is declared that the relationship is *internal*. For if it were not internal, it would be superficial, inconsequential, like the fact of being seated next to a stranger in the metro. Yet the very language in which we are invited to posit this internal relationship indicates that it is rather a connection that is exterior to the reality of both parties since it is, as we have just said, "between them." A certain uneasiness follows: we are seemingly required to think of an *independent* existence as subject to a *condition*. On the one hand, by putting forward Mr. Smith as the first term in the spousal relation, we posit an independent existence, a unit of being (that we willingly assimilate to the *conatus* of maintaining its own being, with a wanting to be free). On the other hand, the existence of Mr. Smith—of Mr. Smith *as a spouse*, we are reminded, though the meaning of this extra information is not entirely clear—is now hanging upon the existence of a wife.

We are told of an internal relation between husband and wife, but these two people had to have married at some point and might yet separate. In other words, we are supposed to consider a relation that is at first presented as an *external* fact (since it is posited between two "objects," two "substances") and try to imagine it becoming *internal*. Predictably, we are unable to carry out this transformation, and from this failure we can draw a first lesson: the relation cannot be internal—i.e., constitutive of the reality of the terms related—if it is posited between terms that we conceive of as absolutes. Mrs. Smith may well bear within her very name her status as the spouse of Mr. Smith; she is nevertheless presented, even under this name, as a person and therefore as an absolute existence. There is therefore nothing with which Mrs. Smith can have an internal relation. Internal relations can only link relative beings, beings under a certain description—not elements but the parts of a whole.

There is then something worth sustaining in William James's objection. The "dialectic" of the concept of marriage may well posit the wife out of the husband and vice versa, but such positing is merely conceptual. James mocks such positing by mutual presupposition: just as the subject requires an opposing object in order to be able to posit itself as a subject, the husband cannot posit himself as a husband without presupposing that there is a wife as the complementary part within the totality formed by the couple. Yes, the dialectic moves from the posited term to the required term, but that does not create an internal relation between the individuals. Bastien was only able to marry Bastienne under one condition: that Bastienne be a person who existed autonomously and independently of the desire Bastien had to get married. In order for the husband to be a husband, he needs a wife, but he needs a wife who actually exists and not simply a correlative position.

There cannot be an internal relation between individuals. This is not a discovery but a simple reflection on the reasons we have for speaking of individuals. We individuate the members of the canine species: for example, we distinguish Fido from Rover. Fido is an individual; this is the way a philosopher expresses the fact that Fido is a different dog than Rover. In other words, the fact that there is a dog named Rover and the fact that there is another dog named Fido are two facts that are independent from each other. If Rover stops being a dog, and therefore stops being altogether (because he dies), that tells us nothing about Fido. Our concept of the individual is of a distinct existence.

If we could stop there, we would be able to embrace pluralism or logical atomism. Internal relations would be reserved for representations: they would be nothing more than relations of reason, not real relations.

However, we cannot stop there, for extrinsic relations must be exterior to something. To what? To individuals. But how are these individuals envisaged?

In the explanations that are often provided, it is said that internal relations are so called because they cannot disappear without the terms also disappearing. But what does "disappear" mean here? It can only mean the disappearance from a class or category. If Mr. Smith loses his wife, he disappears from the class of spouses, but he simultaneously appears within the class of widowers (until he remarries). The positing of an individual term ("Mr. Smith") distinct from the relative term ("spouse") is justified by the desire to be able to say *who* it is that changes classificatory categories.

In this sense, Mr. Smith is intrinsically a member of neither category, since he can cease to be one and become the other. In other words, the fact of being married or not is not part of Mr. Smith's *human* individuality. We therefore distinguish internal and external relations from the perspective of a specified individual, an individual understood according to the kind or type of which he is exemplary. When the husband loses his wife in India, it is not something that can be read in his face (for as long as he has not heard the news). From the point of view of his internal state as, say, his doctor would define it, the change is external. If Mr. Smith loses weight, the same doctor will see that fact as an intrinsic, real, change. But for the tax inspector, such a physical change is extrinsic, whereas the fact of Mr. Smith being widowed moves him into a different class of taxpayers.

Each time, then, one must specify the reality whose intrinsic change one seeks to understand. To change is to change under this or that aspect.

As a result, internal relations are internal to objects under a description. But the exact same thing is true of external relations. The same relation can be held to be internal or external depending on what point of view one adopts. In fact, as Richard Rorty once demonstrated, the entire controversy between the partisans of internal relations (idealists) and their adversaries (empiricists) is only conceivable in an intellectual tradition largely dominated by empiricist principles.[17] Indeed, the idealist or monistic partisans of internal relations are not asking us to view *some* relations as interior to the very reality of things. They see *all* relations as internal. They have a symmetrically opposite view to that of the empiricists, who maintain that *all* relations are external. Both therefore agree about the important question. This question bears on the intrinsic individuality of the individual: what relations does an individual object—Socrates, for example—have to maintain in order to be itself? What relations can it lose without losing what constitutes its individuality, without ceasing to be *itself* and not *another*? Some will respond that the individual cannot shed any relations at all, even those that appear to common sense to be the most exterior. If Socrates is sitting next to Theaetetus, he has to be seated next to Theaetetus in order to be *himself,* Socrates. Others respond that, metaphysically, the individual has no need of any particular relation, for it has

---

17. Richard Rorty, "Relations, Internal and External" in the *Encyclopedia of Philosophy*, 2nd ed., ed. Donald M. Borchert, vol. 8 (Detroit: Thomson Gale, 2006), 335–345.

not been written in the very nature of things that Socrates must be Greek or a human that necessarily must be seated next to Theaetetus.

The idealist philosophy of individuality is the opposite of that of the empiricists, but both sides accept the idea of considering the identity of an otherwise unspecified individual. If Socrates had not married Xanthippe, would he have been himself, Socrates? This question is only intelligible if one presupposes a criterion of identity: would Socrates have been *a different man* if he had not married Xanthippe? It is therefore only with regard to an individual described as a mere specimen of the human species that social status and relationships can be made to appear "external" or "inessential." By contrast, when the questioning is pushed a bit further to become "would Socrates be himself, Socrates, if he ceased being a human?" it becomes clear that we have crossed the boundary separating sense from nonsense. In order to return to sense, another identity criterion would have to be provided to replace the one that we have just withdrawn.[18]

The metaphysical controversy between idealists and empiricists appears to expand to the dimensions of the universe itself a conflict between two visions of social life: for the empiricists social relations are exterior to individuals, while for the idealists social relations are constitutive of individuals. But one thing has been forgotten—that there are no pure individuals to be constituted. Social relations are thus exterior to pure specimens of the human species but interior to individuals that have been specified or particularized by their status (see below, Chapter 10, section 4).

We have now arrived at the question raised by Leibniz in the epigraph to this chapter: are there entirely absolute terms?

7.5. The Logical Form of Relational Propositions

Let us return to Russell's example: is the reality of a man in London affected when his spouse dies in India? It is obvious that Russell sees this example as favorable to his position. He refers, in the text cited above, to an example from Leibniz without providing a reference. He may have had a specific text in mind. Nevertheless, if we consult the *New Essays on Human Understanding,* things appear in a different light. We learn that

---

18. On the need for an identity criterion, see my *The Mind's Provisions,* Chapter 12, section 3.

Locke presented an example that is logically equivalent to Russell's, but neither Locke's commentary nor Leibniz's opposing commentary trace the division between internal and external relations in the way Russell does.

Locke, at first glance, takes the position that Russell will later defend, since his example aims to prove that *every relation is external*. Yes, but for Locke relations are, as a result, unreal and reduced to comparisons carried out by the mind and thereby to representations. Russell, as we have seen, insists on the reality of relations. His criticism of monism as well as of traditional metaphysics is precisely that they both hold relations to be reducible to intrinsic qualities so that they have no other reality, according to the traditional point of view, than the reality of those intrinsic qualities. The misunderstanding is therefore total. For Locke, relations are external and therefore unreal. For Russell, they are only real if they are external.

Here is Locke's example and thesis:

5. *Change of Relation may be without any Change in the Subject.* The *nature* therefore *of Relation,* consists in the referring, or comparing two things, one to another; from which comparison, one or both comes to be denominated. And if either of those things be removed, or cease to be, the Relation ceases, and the Denomination consequent to it, though the other receive in it self no alteration at all. v.g. Caius, whom I consider to day as a Father, ceases to be so to morrow, only by the death of his Son, without any alteration made in himself.[19]

The relation between father and son is exterior to Caius precisely because the reality of Caius in no way depends on the reality of his son. Each of them has his own independent life. They are two distinct existences. This would not be the case were the reality of Caius affected by what happens to his son, for then one would have to say that what happens to the son (also) happens to him. There would then be only one subject of the change, and the two people would be mere aspects or "moments" of that subject. This would truly be what British Hegelians called a "metaphysical monism" (at least for this father and son).

Leibniz's response is to deny that there is a clear and easily discerned opposition between intrinsic and extrinsic changes. It is, rather, a matter of degrees. He offers the following commentary on section 5 of Locke's

---

19. John Locke, *An Essay Concerning Human Understanding,* ed. Peter H. Nidditch (Oxford: Clarendon Press, 1975), II, Chapter 25, § 5 (321).

text cited above: "That can be very well said if we are guided by the things of which we are aware; but in metaphysical strictness there is no wholly extrinsic denomination (*denominatio pura extrinseca*), because of the real connections amongst all things."[20] Leibniz thus concedes the validity of a division between "extrinsic denominations" and "intrinsic denominations" (i.e., descriptions drawn beginning with the milieu and the counterparts of the thing to be described versus descriptions that begin with the thing itself alone). Yet this division concerns only "things of which we are aware." A deeper analysis reveals that denominations perceived to be extrinsic were not purely or totally extrinsic. This is what our epigraph says. Here is the complete passage: "But there is no term which is so absolute or so detached that it does not involve relations and is not such that a complete analysis of it would lead to other things and indeed to all other things. Consequently, we can say that 'relative terms' *explicitly* indicate the relationship which they contain."[21]

What does Leibniz mean here? Is his reference to "real connections amongst all things" a way of introducing metaphysical monism in a surreptitious way, such that there would only be a single thing of which the different beings that we encounter in our experience and treat as individual substances would be—in the last instance, facets or "moments"?

There are two points to consider here. One concerns the possibility of clearly distinguishing the individual from his surrounding milieu (the absolute and the relative); the other concerns the possibility of positing individual concepts at all. The first of these postulates is that there are not just absolute and relative terms but, between them, intermediate terms. The second point is of interest only for a more radical doctrine that would hold that all absolute terms are really relative and that every substance is in relation with all of the others. This extreme thesis becomes meaningful as part of a discussion about possible worlds.

It suffices here to note that these are two entirely separable philosophies. The first maintains that some descriptions of a thing by its relations

---

20. Gottfried Wilhelm Leibniz, *New Essays on Human Understanding*, ed. and trans. Peter Remnant and Jonathan Bennett (Cambridge: Cambridge University Press, 1996), II, Chapter 25, § 5 (227).

21. Ibid., § 10 (228).

with its surrounding milieu have a real scope, that they allow us to know the reality of that thing (and not the reality of the things around it, as is the case with "Cambridge" changes). In the second of these philosophies, we postulate that there is an individual concept of every monad, that the concept of Julius Caesar includes everything that happens to Caesar, which requires us to adopt an entire doctrine of the individuation of possible worlds.[22] I will not discuss this second point, which would take us too far from our current concern with seeing whether the concept of an internal relation is inescapably nonsensical.

Does Leibniz mean to say that relations are reducible to intrinsic qualities? Russell bases his entire interpretation of Leibniz, indeed his entire rationalist metaphysics, on the idea that classical philosophers recognized only one valid analysis of propositions—one that can function in a syllogism and therefore clearly separates the subject of the proposition from the predicate. Hidé Ishiguro has criticized Russell's interpretation. She has convincingly shown that the Leibnizian analysis of relational propositions is in no way reductive. I will follow her demonstration in what follows.[23] Russell seems to believe that it is impossible to express a relation in the form of a proposition of inherence. But why should this be impossible? The reason cannot in any case be drawn entirely from the spatial imagery that suggests that if the relation is *between* the things, it cannot be a characteristic *within* the one and simultaneously *within* the other related thing.

Does Leibniz have a philosophical program of reducing relations? That is what appears to be the case when he says that "there is no wholly extrinsic denomination (*denominatio pura extrinseca*)." Is this a reduction? A reduction would entail replacing the relational propositions with propositions in which the things are described using absolute terms. Now, in the same

---

22. Julius Caesar choosing not to cross the Rubicon is not our Julius Caesar making a different choice from the one recounted in his biography but, rather, a *different individual* who bears an enormous resemblance—at least until this decision—to the historical person in our history books. There would then be an individual concept for each thing containing the entirety of its reality, including its contingent reality. See, in this regard, Leibniz's correspondence with Arnauld, *The Leibniz-Arnauld Correspondence*, ed. and trans. H. T. Mason (Manchester: Manchester University Press, 1967).

23. Hidé Ishiguro, *Leibniz's Philosophy of Logic and Language*, 2nd ed. (1972; Cambridge: Cambridge University Press, 1990), 101–122.

chapter Leibniz explains that this is not possible. This is the thesis cited in our epigraph on the implicitly relative nature of absolute terms.[24]

Locke provided two series of examples. For absolute terms he says this: "A *Man Black, Merry, Thoughtful, Thirsty, Angry, Extended*; these, and the like, are all absolute, because they neither signify nor intimate any thing, but what does, or is supposed really to exist in the Man thus denominated."[25] For relative terms, the examples are father, brother, king, husband, blacker, merrier, etc. All of these terms require us to consider something else that exists separately from the first and that is "exterior to the existence of that thing."[26] Leibniz rejects this stark division. For him it is impossible to describe the reality of a thing without a mixture of absolute terms (or intrinsic denominations) and relative terms (or extrinsic denominations).

Locke's first example is the color black. The color—and this would be true for any perceptible quality—seems at first to be the epitome of a simple given, an experiential atom and a phenomenological absolute. Yet the color of a surface can be analyzed as a modal-dispositional property, i.e., as the power a surface has, as a result of its texture, to absorb light so as to produce on our senses the impression of seeing a color. The explanation of what a color is involves reference both to light and to the observer's eye. It is true that here this reference is suspended or prevented from being really relational by the modal character of the description, which speaks of possible light and a possible observer.

As for the psychological examples, they are also dispositions of the mind rather than mental acts. A disposition can be defined only by reference to the exercise of that disposition and, what is more, only within the appropriate context. A man cannot show himself to be cheerful or morose in a world that provides no occasions for gaiety or sadness. He cannot prove to be sincere if he lives in a world in which, as a matter of policy, one never has any opportunity to lie. The description of a being by its dispositions is thus not an intrinsic description since it presupposes a world that includes such possibilities.

The category of dispositions thus provides us with an example of properties that are neither entirely intrinsic nor entirely extrinsic. It remains for

---

24. Leibniz, *New Essays,* §10 (228).
25. Locke, *Essay,* II, Chapter 25, § 10 (323).
26. Ibid.

us to consider the way in which Leibniz treats real relations. As we shall see, this involves analyzing the relations of things and introducing the reality of relations into the reality of the subjects related. But, contrary to Russell's claims, this analysis does not result in the elimination of relations in favor of intrinsic qualities (or of relative terms in favor of absolute terms). In order to understand this point, it will be useful to introduce the notion of a *derelativized* term or predicate.

Consider the example given by Locke in section 1 of the same chapter, where he introduces the concept of relations. There are two ways of thinking about Caius: as a man and as a husband. When I give him the "name" *man,* the mind understands nothing by the word "man" other than what really exists in Caius; it is thus an intrinsic denomination. When I consider him under the name "husband," "I intimate some other Person" (namely, his *wife*). In this case a second thing (Caius's wife) will have to be considered in order to describe the thing that interests us (Caius)—i.e., the denomination is extrinsic. Further on in his text, Locke explains the *ground* of a relation between two relational subjects or *relata*: "As in the above-mentioned instance, the Contract, and Ceremony of Marriage with *Sempronia,* is the occasion of the Denomination, or Relation of Husband."[27]

We might well ask where Locke derived the name of Caius's wife. Not from the denomination "husband": to know that Caius is married (rather than a bachelor) is to know that he has a wife, but that does not entail knowing who his wife is. One has to have learned it elsewhere. It is thus possible to know that Caius is a husband without knowing whose husband he is. The term "husband" is a relative predicate but one that presents itself linguistically as if it were an absolute term.[28] Derelativized predicates do not cease to be relative: Caius must have a wife in order to be a husband. But these predicates no longer include a reference to the term of the relation. To illustrate this point with a particular application, one might imagine that, for certain procedures, it is important to know

---

27. Ibid., II, Chapter 25, § 1 (319).
28. On the passage from a relation between two objects (a dyadic predicate) to a derelativized attribute (a predicate that is monadic in form but implicitly polyadic), see Willard van Orman Quine, *Methods of Logic,* 4th ed. (1950; Cambridge, MA: Harvard University Press, 1982), § 27 (167–174) and his *Word and Object* (Cambridge, MA: The MIT Press) § 22 (105–110).

whether Caius is married but not at all important to know whom he is married to. For example, only married men might be eligible for certain positions or exempt from military obligations.

Leibniz's conception of the analysis of relations thus has a first task to accomplish: to show that certain terms that appear to be absolute are in reality derelativized terms.[29] We can conceive of predicative expressions that in no way contain the name of anything other than the subject to which the predicate is attached but that contain, in a way that is more or less clear and visible, a *quantification over a universe of objects*.[30] For example, to say of Alceste that he is jealous is to say that *there is someone* of whom he is jealous yet without naming anyone other than Alceste.[31] Dispositional terms include only possibilities of relation. This would be the case, for example, for someone with a "jealous temperament." Derelativized terms are in fact relative, but the relation is left in obscurity. One thus faces a proposition of inherence ("Alceste is jealous") whose predicate is undeniably relative. We attribute this relation to the subject without thereby describing him in his relation with this or that named person.

The other analytical task concerns well-formed relational propositions. The analysis consists, here as elsewhere, in uncovering their truth conditions. The goal is to make explicit what must be true of individual A, the subject of the relation, and of individual B, the term of the relation, in order for the relation in question to obtain between them.

Must an analysis of these conditions on relational propositions necessarily lead, as Russell claims, to the elimination of such propositions in favor of propositions of inherence? This would be the case if all analysis were necessarily reductive or simplifying (i.e., eliminative). It is true that, in an analysis, something must indeed be eliminated. So, in Russell's theory of definite descriptions, what is eliminated is the appearance of the

---

29 In other words, as Ishiguro puts it, a proposition that appears to be of the form "fa" proves after analysis to be of the form "$(\exists \chi)\, fa\chi$". *Leibniz's Philosophy,* 110.

30. Ibid., 105.

31. This is the normal concept of jealousy that covers ordinary as well as pathological cases but not the solipsistic oddness (see *The Mind's Provisions,* Chapter 10) of someone who is jealous without being jealous of someone. And let it not be said "of a person who exists" as if there were other sorts of people, nor "of a person that he believes to exist" as if there were two sorts of jealousy in our psychological repertoire, one for real people and the other for imaginary ones.

logical unit as in, for example, the expression "the present king of France." In this case, however, the analysis does not so much simplify as complicate things. It eliminates the appearance of logical unity and simplicity in order to bring out a hidden complexity: "Someone is presently the king of France, and this someone . . ." Such an analysis, far from being a reduction, is an "expansion."[32] One might also call it, taking up again the name given to the logical analysis of exponible propositions, an "exposition" or "development."

Here is a first example of the technique used by Leibniz: "Paris is the lover of Helen." His analysis offers this paraphrase: "Paris loves, and by that very fact (*eo ipso*) Helen is loved."[33] What does *eo ipso* mean here? It is the mark of a logical connection between two propositions (i.e., two facts). This connector is not extensional. The analytical paraphrase says that Paris loves someone, that Helen is loved by someone, and that the second truth is due to the first. It is not because Helen is loved that Paris loves, but it is because he loves that she is loved. Such an analysis shows that the property of loving is authentically a relational property—the relation resists analysis.

Here is another example: "Titus is wiser than Caius."[34] The proposed analysis is "Titus is wise and as such (*qua talis*) is superior to the extent that (*quatenus*) Caius *qua* wise is inferior."[35] This analysis shows that the comparison presupposes a system of reference on the basis of which degrees of wisdom are defined. Titus's wisdom places him at a level higher than the one that Caius occupies in virtue of his own wisdom. Here the analysis in no way conjures away the relational character of the comparison, as is shown by the presence of the adjectives "superior" and "inferior." It is limited to clearing up the following point: to have a quality is necessarily to have it to *a certain degree*. In virtue of being wise, Titus is placed on a scale; it is enough that there be someone else at an inferior level for Titus to be superior.

Here is a further example: when one moves from "David is the father of Solomon" to "there is really in David a paternity and in Solomon a filiation," one's analysis distinguishes two relations (the relation of paternity

---

32. Ishiguro, *Leibniz's Philosophy*, 121.
33. Gottfried Wilhelm Leibniz, *Opuscules et fragments inédits,* ed. Louis Couturat (Hildesheim: Olms, 1966), 287; cited by Ishiguro, *Leibniz's Philosophy*, 121.
34. Leibniz, *Opuscules,* 244; cited in Ishiguro, *Leibniz's Philosophy,* 119.
35. Leibniz, *Opuscules,* 280; cited in Ishiguro, *Leibniz's Philosophy,* 119.

and its converse).³⁶ But there is no reduction of the relative to the absolute since both the paternity attributed to David and the filiation attributed to Solomon are relative terms. The properties attributed to David and to Solomon are undoubtedly relations, even if the predicates do not specify of whom David is the father and of whom Solomon is the son. Here again, a predicate such as "father," whose *grammatical* form is monadic, hides a linked variable. It is therefore, with regard to its meaning or from the *logical* perspective of its truth conditions, a dyadic predicate.

As a result, it is possible to maintain at one and the same time that there is but a single relational fact at play in both "David is the father of Solomon" and "Solomon is the son of David" and that this relational fact consists in a fact concerning David (father of someone) and a fact concerning Solomon (son of someone). The unity of fact posited by the logical operator *eo ipso* allows us to give the following definition of a structure connecting individuals in a system, for example a kinship system: the relations inherent in the various subjects form a relational system because they are inseparable from one another and they are inseparable because they all express the same relational fact.

Thus, Leibniz's examples show how relations can enter in different ways into the (intrinsic) reality of things. Four cases have been considered:

1. There is no relation but only a possibility of relation (*dispositions*).
2. There is a unilateral relation: the entire reality of the relation from A to B is in the subject A (*intentional relations*).
3. The relation is one of comparison (*measures, degrees*).
4. The relation is grounded in the fact that the relative terms (paternity, filiation) are inseparable, not merely in our representations of them, but in the reality of the things (*real relations*).

Only in the fourth case do we have the real connection that allows us to attribute to each of the linked terms a real characteristic that depends on the relation. This real characteristic can be expressed in a term that appears to be absolute but is, in reality, relational (e.g., "father," "spouse," etc.).

---

36. Ishiguro, *Leibniz's Philosophy*, 132–133. See Leibniz, *New Essays,* IV, Chapter 17, § 4 (479).

8

The Subject of Triadic Relations

8.1. Relations of Reason and Real Relations

Let us remind ourselves of what distinguishes a real relation from a relation of reason, looking to the work of Charles Sanders Peirce for an explanation of the distinction. Peirce not only gave a great deal of reflection to the traditional doctrines on the question but also established a new logic of relations that, although couched in an idiosyncratic terminology, has since been integrated into modern, post-Fregean logic. In mentioning this distinction, Peirce claims that it derives from medieval logic; but we will see that he has clearly modified the classical conception so as to be more in line with the solution he plans to provide for the age-old problem of universals. The traditional definition of a real relation is that it relates two real things and that it corresponds to a reality on both sides. Here is Peirce's explanation:

The medieval logicians (following a hint of Aristotle) distinguished between real relations and relations of reason. A real relation subsists in virtue of a fact which would be totally impossible were either of the related objects destroyed; while a relation of reason subsists in virtue of two facts, one only of which would disappear on the annihilation of either of the relates.[1]

---

1. Charles Sanders Peirce, *Collected Papers of Charles Sanders Peirce*, vol. 1: *Principles of Philosophy*, ed. Charles Hartshorne and Paul Weiss (Cambridge, MA: Harvard University Press, 1931), § 365 (190).

The *facts* mentioned in the proposed definition correspond to what would have traditionally been called the *grounds* of the relation. In the case of what Peirce calls a relation of reason, there are two distinct grounds. For example, if a white thing A resembles a white thing B, it is because A and B are white in color. If we destroy one of the two things, the resemblance disappears but the thing that remains will not have changed color. The relation of reason assumes *two facts*. One could say that the relation of resemblance is a relation between two things, one that is grounded in two distinct and independent facts: the fact that A is white has nothing to do with the fact that B is white, so the destruction of B in no way changes the color of A. Peirce gives another example: Rumford and Franklin were both American citizens (and resembled each other in this regard), but each of them still would have been American even if the other had never lived. Peirce continues: "On the other hand, the fact that Cain killed Abel cannot be stated as a mere aggregate of two facts, one concerning Cain and the other concerning Abel."[2] The relation of murderer to victim does not rest on two facts (or on an "aggregate" as Peirce calls it, taking up Leibniz's word for simple collections devoid of any *real connection*). There is but one fact—Cain's action of which Abel was the object—one that can be stated in two ways, either in the active or passive voice.

Some of the medieval logicians mentioned by Peirce might have said that resemblance is a real relation because it depends on two real facts and not on our minds. Our minds are not what make it the case that two white things are both white. When the second white thing is destroyed, the first remains white but nevertheless loses one of its attributes—the resemblance in color with something else. If it loses an attribute, it is changed when the relation is changed. These logicians are *realists*.

For their part, logicians with *nominalist* leanings would have denied the reality of *all* relations, based on a consideration that can be expressed precisely in Peirce's terms: every relation is established after a comparison between two terms. The argument would be as follows. In the first place, a relation that does not rest on two facts is not real. This excludes all relations that rest on a single fact on one side or the other. Thus, in the case of intentional relations, the fact that A is thinking of B does not mean that there is a real relation between B and A. What remains are relations that

2. Ibid.

correspond to a fact on each side. But since these relations rest on two facts, they can be expressed simply by stating the two facts. The two facts are real, but the relationship between these two facts is carried out in our minds or in our discourse. This relationship is then a matter of representation. Thus, every relation is reduced to a complementarity or a similarity in one aspect or another.

Later on, Locke will provide a psychologistic version of such nominalism:

Thus, when the Mind considers *Caius,* as such a positive Being, it takes nothing into that *Idea,* but what really exists in *Caius*; v.g. when I consider him as a Man, I have nothing in my Mind, but the complex *Idea* of the Species, Man. . . . But when I give *Caius* the name *Husband,* I intimate some other Person. . . .[3]

Locke thus agrees with Russell that the quality of being a husband is exterior to Caius's own reality. However, he does not draw Russell's conclusion that the relation is real but localized between the husband and wife, as the "axiom of external relations" would maintain. For Locke, this relation amounts to a comparison that the mind makes between two individuals. When Caius and Sempronia are brought together in thought, they present themselves to us as each having with regard to the other the quality of being a spouse. Their relation is thus exterior to their reality as individuals (or rather to their respective realities as individuals). As a result, the positing of that relation is a conclusion that we draw after having compared what was true of one individual with what was true of the other. In the case at hand, it is true of Caius that he participated in a ceremony that resulted in him being married, and it is true of Sempronia that she participated in the same ceremony. "As in the above-mentioned instance, the Contract, and Ceremony of Marriage with *Sempronia,* is the occasion of the Denomination, or Relation of Husband."[4] In short, every relation is a relation of comparison, as Locke explicitly states in this text: all things can enter into relations "for, as I said, *Relation* is a way of comparing, or considering two things together; and giving one, or both of them, some

---

3. John Locke, *An Essay Concerning Human Understanding,* ed. Peter H. Nidditch (Oxford: Clarendon Press, 1975), II, Chapter 25, § 1 (319).
4. Ibid.

appellation from that Comparison, and sometimes giving even the Relation it self a Name."[5]

This is where Peirce innovates. The relation of resemblance is, for him, the epitome of a relation of reason because it rests on no *positive connection* between the two things and fails to unite them in a system. Their destinies remain separate. To take Ockham's example of the two walls: if the wall in Rome, which was white, is repainted red, it ceases to resemble the wall in London, which has remained white. But the latter has undergone no intrinsic change (see above, Chapter 7, section 2).

The distinctive trait of a real relation is precisely that it is able to create a system out of the objects it relates. It can do this because it corresponds to a positive connection and not to a simple community of attributes (whether generic or accidental). Peirce here abandons the "Scholastic realism" that sees universals as monadic terms grounding relations of resemblance. He replaces it with a realism of relations seen as polyadic terms (though he does continue to refer to his own position as "Scholastic realism," perhaps in order to be able to continue to refer to the doctrines he rejects as "nominalist"). For Peirce, universals are not just universals of qualitative resemblance (such as the whiteness of white things) or of formal resemblance (such as the tokens of a single type), but also and above all universals of relation. The reality of the universal is not so much the reality of whiteness as it is the reality of the order, for example of the diachronic order called a "natural law."

A proposition posits a real relation that links two things if it expresses a *single fact*. The relations of the one to the other rest on this single fact: if one of the two objects is destroyed, the fact of the relation disappears and the relative attribute of the remaining object disappears with it. The remaining object thereby loses something. Let us return to Peirce's example. Cain killed Abel. If we learn that Abel is a fictional character, then Cain did not kill anyone and he ceases having to be considered a murderer. There is thus, in this example, a fact concerning Cain (he has killed and receives the relative characteristic "murderer") and a fact concerning Abel (he was killed and receives the relative characteristic "victim"). But these two facts are nothing but the two sides of a unique fact of relation. These two facts cannot be simply recorded and brought together in a

---

5. Ibid., § 7 (322).

simple aggregate using a conjunction. The relation is assuredly, in this case also, grounded in facts concerning the *two* subjects of the relation: Cain is a murderer; Abel is a victim. However, unlike a comparison of similar things, the two facts concerning different individuals are in fact unified—they are but different facets of a single fact. The fact of the murder is what constitutes Cain as a murderer and Abel as a victim.

It will therefore be said that the ground of a real relation is expressed by monadic predicates that are in fact derelativized dyadic predicates. A man is a murderer on condition that he is the murderer of someone. A man is a victim on condition that there be someone of whom he is the victim. Cain has a relation with regard to Abel: he is his murderer. Abel has the converse relation with regard to Cain: he is his victim. *Yet these relations are but a single relation.* Above, we were dealing with a relation between two facts—which could be symbolized by characterizations of the two objects, a and b: Fa, Fb—from which we concluded that there was a relation of resemblance (with regard to property F) between a and b. In the present case, we have first a relation aRb and only afterwards do we have the distinct facts that follow from it. These facts can be expressed by opposed and complementary predicates: Cain killed Abel; therefore Cain is the murderer, Abel the victim.

It is interesting to compare the way Peirce defines real relations with the solutions to the problem of extrinsic change given by Scholastic thinkers.[6] What happens when a thing A becomes similar in quality or size to another thing B, not because it has itself changed its qualities or size but because B has undergone an intrinsic change? It is certain that, in our example given earlier, the wall in London becomes similar in color to a Roman wall without having itself changed color. The realist school emphasizes its acquisition of a new property, the fact that its reality has been augmented by a new relation that it did not have previously. If there is now a resemblance that did not exist previously, the London wall must have acquired a *res,* a reality that it might also one day lose, either by ceasing to be white

---

6. Here I will be making use of the study by Mark Henninger, "Aquinas on the Ontological Status of Relations," *Journal of the History of Philosophy* 25, no. 4 (1987): 491–515.

itself or by ceasing to be the same color as the Roman wall because the latter will have been repainted in, say, red. This is not Aristotle's solution, one that was later taken up by Thomas Aquinas.

In Book V of his *Physics* (Chapter 2, 225b), Aristotle explains that there is no becoming in respect of relation. The proof is that the relations of a thing with others can change without the thing having changed in itself. This is Aristotle's answer to the Platonic paradox of the extrinsic change by which Socrates becomes steadily smaller than Theaetetus (*Theaetetus,* 155b–c) (see above, Chapter 7, section 2). A thing can, without changing intrinsically, lose or acquire relations (for example, relations of equality or inequality, resemblance or dissimilarity). Why is this? As Thomas Aquinas explains in his commentary, it is precisely because A remains white and thus does not change that it can "become" similar to B. This means that a white thing is already, by its very whiteness, similar to all white things. It has no need to become similar in the proper sense of the verb "to become," i.e., via a change. On the other hand, B must change color if it is to become similar to A. The same theory applies to all relations of measure: equality, inequality, proportion. Thomas Aquinas believes that this answer is a realist one. The relation of resemblance is neither a relation of reason nor unilateral (i.e., intentional). It is not a relation of reason because there are two poles, two distinct things that are related. It is not unilaterally real like the relation of knowledge to the thing known. It is real in that it corresponds on both sides to something real. It is real because it is grounded in the real. Is this to say that a relation reduces to the foundation that it has in each thing related (i.e., to the fact that each possesses a characteristic that justifies the relation)? No, we are not here reducing the relative (for example, the adjective "equal") to the nonrelative. Rather than a reduction of the relative to the absolute, it would be better to speak of the *foundation* of an actual relation in its principle, which is already relational in its own way. Thomas Aquinas expresses this by the image of the root: whiteness is the root of the relation of resemblance to white things, size is the root of the relation of equality among bodies having the same size as well as being, at the same time, the root of the relation of superiority over bodies of a smaller size, etc.[7]

7. "Unde dicendum est quod si aliquis per suam mutationem efficiatur mihi aequalis, me non mutato, *ista aequalitas primo erat in me quodammodo, sicut in sua radice,* ex qua

THE SUBJECT OF TRIADIC RELATIONS

Consider the following example: here is an object A; it is a wooden board one meter in length. I cut a second board B by using the first (A) as a measure. The first board A is extrinsically changed (i.e., without any real becoming) when it thereby becomes equal to the board cut using it as a model. Does realism of relations require us to say that board A is really changed even when it is clearly not and surely must not be changed in its length since it served as a measure? In what can it then have been changed?

Here is another example: as a result of the fact that I live at a given address, I am already, in advance, the neighbor of whoever may come to live next door. This explains how the person moving in actually becomes my neighbor in doing so, while I was already a neighbor (if not his neighbor) since I never moved. It was through not moving that I acquired the relation of being a neighbor to my new neighbor.

This solution inspired by Aristotle can be compared to Leibniz's view of comparisons (see above, Chapter 7, section 4). When Titus has a quality (wisdom), he has that quality in a certain measurable proportion, which means that he is in advance comparable to all of the people who have, will have, or might have had this quality to any degree whatsoever.

Is Peirce's proposed distinction preferable to that of the traditional realist school? Are relations of resemblance devoid of reality? A partisan of the tradition might raise the following objection to Peirce's view, asking us to consider two American citizens, Rumford and Franklin. If x is a fellow citizen of y, the resemblance between x and y is real. Indeed, Rumford cannot possess the property of being of the same nationality as Franklin if Franklin never lived. But Rumford cannot be an American citizen if he is

---

habet esse reale: ex hoc autem quod habeo talem quantitatem, competit mihi quod sim aequalis omnibus illis, qui eandem quantitatem habent. Cum ergo aliquis de novo accipit illam quantitatem, ista communis radix aequalitatis determinatur ad istum: et ideo nihil advenit mihi de novo per hoc quod incipio esse alteri aequalis per eius mutationem." [Hence it must be said that if someone by changing becomes equal to me, and I did not change, *then that equality was first in me in some way, as in a root* from which it has real being. For since I have a certain quantity, it happens that I am equal to all those who have the same quantity. When, therefore, someone newly takes on this quantity, this common root of equality is determined in regard to him. Therefore nothing new happens to me because of the fact that I begin to be equal to another because of his change.] Thomas Aquinas, *Commentary on Aristotle's "Physics,"* trans. Richard J. Blackwell, Richard J. Spath, and W. Edmund Thirlkel (London: Thoemmes Continuum, 2003), § 667 (italics mine).

not in advance the fellow citizen of anyone who is an American citizen. So if Franklin did live and if he was an American, then the relation follows, grounded as it is on both sides in the qualities of both men. The fact that the two men have something in common does not depend on our minds; each of them possesses in himself the *radix relationis*.

However, Peirce is right to hold that relations grounded in *action* or *passion* must not be treated in the same way as relations grounded in *quality* or *quantity*.

When Rumford is an American citizen, he is by that very fact the fellow citizen of any American. Similarly, when the tablecloth is white, it is the same color as all white things. But, when Cain is the murderer of Abel, he is certainly a murderer like all other murderers, but he is not the archetypical murderer, the murderer of all murder victims. The relative characteristic that interests us in the case of Cain is not "murderer" (implicitly, of someone) but rather "murderer of Abel." This relation would not obtain if we discovered that Cain did kill someone but that it was someone other than Abel. One can be a murderer (or a father, etc.) several times over. Each time, a different reality is considered. By contrast, a citizen is a fellow citizen multiple times, but only once is he a citizen.

Let us return to the example of the neighbors, which suggests the following remark: if I live in an apartment building in which there are two apartments per landing, I am in advance the next-door neighbor of whoever will become my neighbor by moving into the apartment next to mine. But the apartment next to mine may remain vacant. In this case, I find myself the bearer, by the very fact of living in my apartment, of a *radix relationis*, but I lack a neighbor that would cause a real relation to arise out of this root. This, then, is the sense in which one can speak of a relational reality of all of the properties that are intermediate between "intrinsic" and "extrinsic" denominations. *Dispositions* would then be aptly described as the roots out of which the relations to which they predispose the subject arise in the appropriate circumstances. Similarly, *intentional activity* is not yet a transitive act or a real relation: I may seek the thief without finding him. But there is something potentially relational about intentional activity. This would appear to be what the phenomenologists were referring to with their images of openness or "being-in-the-world" (similarly to the way one refers to "being at work" or "being on the hunt"): intentionality is not so much a relation of a subject to an object as it is the condition for such a real relation to result from an intentional act. An example would be an empty intentional relation, such as the situation of lookouts or watchmen who have nothing to report. If they have not seen anything, they are not in relation with anything. Yet we do not deny that they are turned toward the world, that they are "open" to the world. They are in an attitude such that, should something present itself—a sail on the horizon or a movement on the road—they will see it. This availability is "relational" without yet being a fact of relation.

8.2. The Irreducibility of Polyadic Relations

The preceding discussion on the possibility of reducing relations to intrinsic qualities can now be expressed in the idiom devised by Peirce. As we have seen in the examples studied by Leibniz, derelativizing a term does not turn it into an absolute term. Doing so removes only one part of the information carried by the initial relative term, but not the deeply relational nature of the predicate. For example, one can know that Cain is a murderer (of someone) without knowing whom he has murdered, just as one can know that Caius is married without knowing that he is married to Sempronia. The notion of a derelativized predicate has thus allowed us to grasp the direction that the logical analysis of descriptive language must take. A property that is monadic in form (e.g., "husband") can be a particular or derived case of a dyadic property (e.g., "husband of Sempronia") but not the converse. One of Peirce's great insights is that the same is true of the polyadic and the dyadic. The polyadic cannot be *reduced* to the dyadic. On the other hand, it happens that a dyadic term must be developed or made explicit in a polyadic term.

With dyadic relations, one can of course construct chains, for example genealogical chains (x begat y who begat z, etc.). But, by definition, a chain must be constructed by attaching one link to another. In a genealogy, x is the grandfather of z by virtue of being the father of y, who is the father of z. An authentic triadic relation is not a combination of two dyadic relations.

The passage from Two to Three requires precisely a *change of order* in the Pascalian sense; one must cross the infinite with finite means in order to move from the one to the other.[8] In other words, accumulating

---

8. Blaise Pascal, *Pensées*, trans. A. J. Krailsheimer (Baltimore: Penguin Books, 1966), § 308 (123–125).

points will never produce a line, and piling up lines will never produce a plane.⁹

In a text dating from 1896, Peirce introduces the distinction within the framework of a traditional treatise on formal logic.¹⁰ In this treatise, the three mental operations define three levels of description of the logical form of a thought: the *term,* the *proposition,* the *syllogism.* The treatise explains that the things we think about must be grasped in a simple apprehension (each thing being grasped through a certain general term), that these things must be linked by judgment, and that, finally, a syllogism must be constructed out of these judgments. Peirce begins with this logical triad but modifies it in the course of his exposition. The "term" later becomes the "verb" (or what Peirce elsewhere calls a "rheme"). To grasp a term (*apprehensio simplex*) is to use a verb without applying it to a particular subject—for example, speaking of what is human (of what carries out activities and operations of a human kind) without speaking about this or that particular person. This is the level of monadic predicates. We then move to a second traditional level, the level at which we consider a proposition. The proposition gives rise to the subject since, in order to have a complete sentence, the verb will have to be used to speak about something; we therefore move from the monad to the *dyad,* in Peirce's terminology. However, Peirce is immediately at pains to correct what is overly simplistic in this derivation, since the dyad requires an action verb, not a simple attribution. If there is to be a dyadic proposition, it must contain a transitive verb. In other words, there must be two logical subjects mentioned: the subject of the action and its object. As a result, one must introduce the polarity between the active and the passive. This polarity is a characteristic of the dyadic properly so called. If A kills B, there is the following dissymmetry: A does everything, while B does nothing and only undergoes A's actions. If B had anything to do with the action, we would be in an entirely different scenario, one in which B was having himself

---

9. "[A]n indivisible, multiplied as many times as we like, will not make an extension. Therefore it is not of the same kind as extension, by the definition of things of the same kind." Blaise Pascal, "Of the Geometrical Spirit," trans. O. W. Wight, in *Thoughts, Letters, Minor Works* (New York: P. F. Collier and Son, 1910), 435.

10. Peirce, *Collected Papers,* vol. 1, §§ 471–519 (253–276). On the theory of relative terms, see Charles Sanders Peirce, "The Logic of Relatives," in his *Reasoning and the Logic of Things,* ed. Kenneth Laine Ketner (Cambridge, MA: Harvard University Press, 1992), 146–164.

killed by A (it matters little here whether intentionally or by mistake). Peirce then provides his analysis of the couple made up of the agent and the patient of a dyadic action:

> Thus, there are in the dyad two subjects of different character, though in special cases the difference may disappear. These two subjects are the *units* of the dyad. Each is a *one,* though a dyadic one.[11]

The above example now leads us to the difference between an authentically dyadic action and a triadic action expressed by a dyadic proposition. Consider this example: A murders B. The concept of murdering is that of an intentional act, unlike the concept of killing, which is a brute description (i.e., a description that does not tell us whether the act was intentional or not). In order for A to murder B, A must do something *with the intention* of putting B to death, for example, by shooting a revolver in such a way as to mortally wound him. Thus the proposition "A murders B" is at first glance dyadic, since it uses a transitive verb. One might then be led to believe that murdering is a dyadic action like "pulling the trigger" or "plunging the dagger." It is not: this apparent dyad is, in reality, a triad. Every triad, Peirce says, can be reduced to a dyad on the condition that one of the three subjects is left unspecified. In saying that "A murders B," one implies that A does something to carry out the act (for example, he shoots a bullet from a revolver), but without specifying the means used.

What about authentic triads? Here is an example: A makes a contract with C. First off, this triad is in fact an implicit polyad that can be analyzed as follows. A makes a contract D with C, and the contract D gives B to C. This triadic statement speaks of a contract without saying what the contract concerns (i.e., without determining what A gives to C by the contract D). What is important to Peirce is this: (1) polyads of this kind can be reduced to conjunctions of triads; (2) by contrast, the triad cannot be reduced to a conjunction of dyads. Why should this be the case? Peirce gives the following reason:

> Now let us consider the triad, A makes a contract with C. To say that A signs the document D and C signs the document D, no matter what the contents of that document, does not make a contract. The contract lies in the intent. And what is

---

11. Peirce, *Collected Papers,* vol. 1, § 471 (253).

the intent? It is that certain conditional rules shall govern the conduct of A and of C. There is no positive fact in this; it is only conditional and intentional. Still less, if possible, is it any mere monadic quality. It has reference to conditions of experience, involving existence, involving dyadic fact. It may be said that it is a psychical fact. This is in so far true, that a psychical fact is involved; but there is no intent unless something be intended; and that which is intended cannot be covered by any facts; it goes beyond anything that can ever be done or have happened, because it extends over the whole breadth of a general condition; and a complete list of the possible cases is absurd. From its very nature, no matter how far specification has gone, it can be carried further; and the general condition covers all that incompletable possibility.[12]

Peirce here emphasizes the affinity between the intentional (in a practical sense) and generality. Practical intention is also intentional in the Scholastic sense: it has a formal object ("no intent without something intended"). Naturally the intentional object is an object-of; it is neither an individual object nor a singular fact but everything that fulfills a certain set condition. This is why intention contains a *universal*: all scenarios are in some way provided for, without having to be actually given or taken into account one by one.[13]

It follows that the "world of fact" contains no triads.[14] Beyond facts is the world of the possible. In order to find a triad, we must leave behind the positive (which corresponds to what is and what will be) and enter into the conditional (what would be). Does this mean that triads are zombies, fictions without force? Peirce answers that even if the positive world contains no triads, it can be *governed* by triads. According to him it would perhaps be better to say that it can *only* be governed by triads (and not by "brute force"). For our concerns here, this means that even if certain events can be given a physical description (by brute facts, i.e., dyadic facts), physical description does not render everything that actually happened. Thus it is possible to provide a physical description of the event of the signature of

12. Ibid., § 475 (255).
13. One cannot avoid being reminded here of what Wittgenstein says about the meaning of rules. See his *Philosophical Investigations,* rev. 4th ed., ed. P. M. S. Hacker and Joachim Schulte, trans. G. E. M. Anscombe, P. M. S. Hacker, and Joachim Schulte (1953; Oxford: Wiley-Blackwell, 2009), §§ 185–243 (80–95).
14. Peirce, *Collected Papers,* vol. 1, § 478 (256).

contract D by A and C, but this description does not yet tell us that a contract was signed between A and C. In order to say *that,* one must move to triadic propositions. To claim that one can render the meaning of what happened by a conjunction of dyadic relations (A signed the piece of paper D and C did likewise, etc.) is like claiming to replace a general conditional proposition by a list of possible particular cases.

Peirce maintains two things. The first is a logico-philosophical (i.e., metaphysical) thesis on plural relations: generally, they cannot be reconstructed out of dual relations (any more than relations themselves can be reconstructed out of qualities). The second is a thesis on the domain of being whose description requires that relations that are (at least) triadic be determined; plural relations have something mental or intentional about them.

Some of Peirce's formulations are somewhat misleading because they carry on a traditional way of expressing the relation between the whole and its parts. For example, in a text that the editors date from around 1894, he writes: "A *dyad* consists of two *subjects* brought into oneness."[15] This way of speaking emphasizes the *enumeration* of the individuals being spoken about. It is as unenlightening as the formulas promulgated by the theorists of the collective individual. The useful definitions of the dyad are those that are not limited to the mere enumeration of the individuals mentioned in the proposition in response to questions such as: does the proposition refer to one, or two, or more than two individuals? On its own, this criterion is insufficient.

Consider the proposition "Athos, Porthos, and Aramis are going to war." The proposition refers to the activities of three individuals but is nothing more than a monadic proposition. Nothing is changed in this regard if we add that they are going *together*: the proposition would then attribute a collective action to the three individuals, but it would remain a proposition whose verb is monadic. Now consider "Athos sees Porthos and Aramis." The proposition contains three names, but this time it is dyadic.

We must therefore draw a distinction between a proposition with a single plural subject and a proposition with two or more subjects. Using

15. Ibid., § 326 (163).

Tesnière's language, we might say that a *monovalent* verb (such as "to go to war") has only one agent, which can be singular or plural.[16] The same is true of the first and second agents of a transitive (or *bivalent*) verb. In order to have a *trivalent* verb, the sentence must be one that is complete only when provided with its three agents.

Here we must be careful not to confuse two senses of the word "subject." On the one hand, Peirce seeks to separate logic from Indo-European grammar. He therefore believes that, from a logical point of view, there are two subjects in a proposition with a transitive verb—namely, what the grammarian would call the subject (nominative) and the object (accusative). What is important here is the difference between the (verbal) predicative element of the proposition and the element that completes the predicate (the single or multiple subjects, depending on the number of slots that need to be filled). On the other hand, Peirce notes that the structure of the verb has to be taken into account, since it assigns the places to the logical subjects. The structure is the order in which the designated individuals have to be taken in order to complete the verb. Here is the example provided in Peirce's article on relative terms in Baldwin's *Dictionary*:[17]

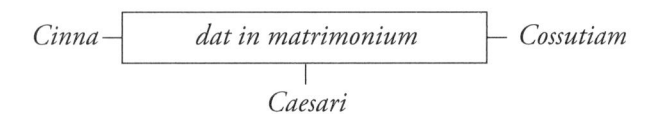

Cinna —| *dat in matrimonium* |— Cossutiam
              |
           Caesari

In this diagram, the relative term can be seen in the predicative expression within the rectangle, along with its three valences. It belongs thus to the meaning of the verb that, wherever there is an act of giving in marriage, we will find three (logical) subjects—one in the role of the donor, the other of the recipient, and the third of the person whose hand

---

16. Like Peirce, Tesnière derives his system of the valence of verbs from chemical models. See Charles Sanders Peirce, *Collected Papers of Charles Sanders Peirce,* vol. 5: *Pragmatism and Pragmaticism,* ed. Charles Hartshorne and Paul Weiss (Cambridge, MA: Harvard University Press, 1934), § 469 (321); Lucien Tesnière, *Éléments de syntaxe structurale,* 2nd ed. (1959; Paris: Klincksieck, 1988), 238.

17. Charles Sanders Peirce, *Collected Papers of Charles Sanders Peirce,* vol. 3: *Exact Logic,* ed. Charles Hartshorne and Paul Weiss (Cambridge, MA: Harvard University Press, 1933), § 636 (404).

in marriage is given. The order in which these subjects must be taken can also be shown using indices: the predicate will be d_{ijk}, where Cinna = i, Cossutia = j, and Caesar = k.

The three individuals now form a system. "By a system is meant an individual of which if anything is true, the truth of it consists in certain things being true of certain other individuals...."[18] We will therefore have to draw a distinction between the individual and the member of the system. Suppose that Cossutia is dark-haired. This fact has nothing to do with a member of the system; it is just a fact about Cossutia. However, the fact that Cossutia's hand is given in marriage involves a member of the system and is thus a fact relative to that system. To describe Cossutia under the aspect of her future marriage is not to describe a self-sufficient individual but a complete system in virtue of which this (holistic) trait belongs to her.

What then is the proper way of putting this? Should one say that the triadic relation has three subjects or that it has a single triadic subject? The issue here is not so much about pinning down a way of speaking but rather one of understanding what our way of speaking each time commits us to in the eyes of our interlocutors. Peirce handles this point in the following way.[19] The proposition "Cain kills Abel" has two subjects, "Cain" and "Abel." He explains that this means that it bears just as much on the bearer of the one name as it does on the bearer of the other. There is a logical equivalence in this regard between an expression in the active voice and one in the passive, the difference being purely stylistic. The fact that the word "Cain" is in the nominative does not give it any privileged status.

However, the equal status of the names in the sentence (Tesnière would call them the "agents") does not mean that the names are interchangeable: there is a difference between the role of agent and the role of patient, which reestablishes the rightful grammatical difference between subject and object. From this second point of view, we might say that the proposition

---

18. Ibid., § 637 (405).

19. Charles Sanders Peirce, *Collected Papers of Charles Sanders Peirce*, vol. 2: *Elements of Logic*, ed. Charles Hartshorne and Paul Weiss (Cambridge, MA: Harvard University Press, 1932), § 316 (180–182).

bears on a dyad. But what is a dyad? It is not exactly the same thing as a pair, explains Peirce, because a pair is nothing more than the conglomeration of the two individuals. The pair undeniably exists, which simply means that Cain exists and Abel exists. As for the dyad, it is made up of Cain as a first member and Abel as a second member of a dyadic system. It is thus an ordered pair, a *system*. In this case we would say that a dyadic proposition has a dyad as its subject and not two subjects. Yet it does not bear on a collective individual distinct from the two individuals named Cain and Abel. There is nothing more in a pair of subjects than the two individuals that make up the pair. In order to have a dyad rather than a pair, we do not somehow fuse the two subjects into a third subject, but must instead add the fact of the relation that involves them both: the action carried out by Cain and to which Abel is subjected. Only as such, under this description or, as Peirce says, according to this "mental diagram," do they form a dyad. The diagram is mental, but the relation is real—there is an actual murder and thus a murderer and a victim. What we add when speaking of a dyad rather than of two individuals is the idea that we are considering these individuals as the members of a dyadic system. Each of them is a dyadic unit; therefore each of them is the system itself considered within one of its members. Each of them is a dyadic unit because each is taken under a description: we are not speaking of Cain *tout court*; we are speaking of him insofar as he is a murderer. This is why, even though there are still only two individuals here, there is a dyadic subject, which is (equivalently) Cain taken in this relation to Abel or Abel taken in this same relation to Cain.

8.3. Are Triadic Relations Dialectical?

Here we come back to our point regarding relative terms that appear to be absolute (monadic). Leibniz showed how a term that appears to be absolute can in fact be relative. Peirce did more than just generalize this observation. He showed not only that an apparently dyadic term can in reality be triadic, but also that the triadic is as irreducible to the dyadic as the dyadic relative is to the monadic absolute. If a transition is possible from Firstness to Secondness and from Secondness to Thirdness, it is because the term under consideration was already implicitly part of the superior order.

This raises the problem of knowing whether such transitions between categories are dialectical, i.e., whether they belong to an intelligible movement that generates ever more complex categories. Can one, as a Hegelian might claim, deduce the categories by showing how some derive from others, beginning with a simple term that is supposed to contain within it the entirety of what is thinkable?

In reality, Peirce's solution is "analytic" and not "dialectical," since it consists, as it does for Leibniz, in bringing out the real complexity of the apparently simple and not in overcoming the contradiction inherent in the initial simplicity of the simple in a process of ever-greater complication.

The question of the dialectic is worth raising here, if only in order to respond to the suggestion that is often made that the natural sciences fall under logic as it was developed—as a formal logic—by logicians, but that the human sciences require *another logic*. Or, it is suggested, there is one concept of identity that serves to identify things and another concept of identity that would be required to speak about people and their deeds and gestures. The latter would be the sort of "identity in difference" mocked by Russell in his polemic against monism.[20]

In some ways, Peirce's demonstration could give the impression of bolstering such logico-philosophical dualism. Have we not just seen that, for him, intentional actions have a special form that can be distinguished logically? Do triadicity and the number 3 provide, for reasons yet to be determined, the logical form that is proper to the human domain—i.e., to everything that transcends the dynamic world of natural action (and for which only dualistic relations are required, according to the schemas of cause and effect or of the agent and the patient)?

Such ideas have been put forward, especially within French Hegelianist thought. For this school, the section from the *Phenomenology of Spirit* about the master-slave dialectic played a decisive role. Indeed, it is on the transition from consciousness to self-consciousness that, to use non-Hegelian terms, the transition from the natural to the cultural (or the prehistorical to the historical) hinges. And if there were a logical difference between the

---

20. Bertrand Russell, "The Monistic Theory of Truth," in his *Philosophical Essays* (New York: Routledge, 2009), 138.

description of the natural and the description of the intentional, would it not be precisely the difference between a two-term relation and a three-term relation? Indeed, the battle for recognition between consciousnesses—the struggle between master and slave—can, from a logical point of view, be categorized as a dual relation: there are two subjects confronting each other. From the perspective of these neo-Hegelians, the human dyad has something conflictual and morbid about it, as if the fact of a dyad could only mean that there are two candidates, two rivals for a single position (the position of the recognized being), and no rule with which to choose between them or assign them positions within an order. A curse thus hangs over dual relations: since each one is itself only via the other, neither of the two manages to posit itself for itself.

The humanization of the relations between the human animal and its partner (whatever it may be) assumes the introduction of a third party, a mediator. In order to make peace or to move from relations of reciprocal opposition to relations of reciprocal recognition, one must move from a duo to a trio. However, it is not enough to add a third party attempting to profit from the situation, as in La Fontaine's fable, for that would merely add another conflict to the existing conflict.[21] What is needed is a referee, a judge or a mediator, someone who is able to impose a rule of justice and thereby assign a portion of recognition to each of them according to what they are and what they have done. This mediator is Lacan's "Symbolic Third." Each has a place that is in some way legitimate (instead of being perpetually in play). Can such a philosophy of humanity—or, rather, of the humanization of the living—be given support by Peirce's logic of relations?

In fact, this is not at all the same sort of triad as in Peirce's analysis, where the third agent added to the first two is not a judge but a partner, the recipient of the gift or the victim at whom the weapon is aimed. The same is true of Tesnière's third agent, which is an indirect object. It is a beneficiary, not an arbiter.

In truth, an orthodox Hegelian would never countenance leaving nature to the sciences that are in conformity with a "logic of understanding."

---

21. See Jean de La Fontaine, "The Thieves and the Ass," in *The Complete Fables of Jean de La Fontaine*, trans. Norman R. Shapiro (Urbana: University of Illinois Press), 16.

What the Hegelian seeks to make manifest is a logic that will be valid for every conceivable domain, a logic of the conceivable as such and not simply a logic of the human sciences (the *Geisteswissenchaften,* as Dilthey later called them).

In any case, it is not my job here to adopt the perspective of an orthodox Hegelian and imagine the way he would go about showing that apparently dyadic relations are in fact triadic. Peirce might say: how he would go about reducing Secondness—the place of *hard facts*—to almost nothing.[22] It is however incumbent on me to explain why Peirce's triad has nothing to do with various responses that have been presented as *dialectical* in one way or another. It does not matter whether or not they use the word "dialectic." What does matter is that they believe that human relations, historical events, and intentional life outstrip the conceptual resources of a formal logic of understanding.

Let us begin with what seems to be an obsession or *idée fixe*: why Three? Here what is important is not the number 3 (rather than 4 or some other number). It is the fact that in every triadic relation there is a mental element, whereas in a dyadic expression of a relation to an object there is nothing indicative of a mental element even where there is one.

This remark allows us to respond to those who might be disquieted by Peirce's apparent insistence on constructing his doctrine of the categories (his metaphysics) on the numbers One, Two, and Three. Why these numbers? Such numerological speculation arouses suspicion in those who are struck less by the beauty of a construction in which everything has its place in one of three columns than they are by the arbitrariness of an artificial schema. These reactions seem to me to be entirely justified. Moreover, I would be reluctant to claim that Peirce is devoid of the sort of constructor's temperament that one finds among the great speculative philosophers of the early nineteenth century. Nevertheless, and whatever one may think of systematic concerns in philosophy, I believe it can be agreed that Peirce's logic of relations is not the product of his System but rather either its source

---

22. "Hegel [was] in some respects the greatest philosopher that ever lived. . . . but the element of Secondness, of *hard fact,* is not accorded its due place in his system." Peirce, *Collected Papers,* vol. 1, § 524.

or its pretext (the source out of which it develops, for those who admire the constructor's efforts at an architectonics, or the pretext for a staged performance, if one remains unmoved by such neo-Pythagoreanism).

Yet there is one observation that ought to satisfy those readers of Peirce who remain skeptical, as I do, about the formal procedures by which these categories have been deduced. The number 3 is not what matters here. In fact, Peirce could have given clearer expression to his thinking by saying: One, Two, and More than Two. Three does not appear in his list of categories as an extraordinary number endowed with special properties. Rather, a triad is simply a minimal polyad. In other words, the thesis of the irreducibility of Threeness to Twoness inheres in the following two points:

(1) Polyadic relations at all levels can be constructed out of triadic relations, whereas triadic relations cannot be constructed out of dyadic ones.
(2) The description of a dynamic action is a description of a local action that occurs through contact or direct transitive action and can therefore be carried out in a dyadic logical form, whereas the description of an intentional action is a description of the *undertaking* of an action at a distance by means of a local action, with the result that its logical form must comprise a multiplicity equal to at least three.

It seems to me that the word "multiplicity" in the preceding is taken in the same sense in which Wittgenstein uses the word in the course of raising the analogous problem of knowing whether a theory, for example Freud's theory, has the requisite "multiplicity" to explain what it seeks to explain.[23] This word, which has been borrowed from mathematics, signifies that relations can only be expressed if we have, so to speak, the necessary space for their establishment. In order to express a relation of superiority, I need only two terms (e.g., $a > b$). But to express proportions, I need at least three ($a/b = b/c$). More generally, the notion of multiplicity used here is the same one that Leibniz uses to reject Descartes's third precept on the ordering of difficulties from the simple to the complex. Yvon Belaval formulates this

---

23. See, for example, Ludwig Wittgenstein, *Wittgenstein's Lectures: Cambridge, 1930–32*, ed. Desmond Lee (Chicago: University of Chicago Press, 1989), 2: "A proposition must have the right multiplicity: for example, a command must have the same multiplicity as the action which it commands or prescribes."

well: "An order can appear only through a multiplicity that is sufficient for its manifestation; only then can synthesis be transformed into analysis as when in carrying on the sequence of squares 1, 4, 9, 16, 25, I will not fail to observe that the difference between successive terms is the sequence of odd numbers 1, 3, 5, 7 . . . , etc."[24]

Remaining within the dyadic, one can only deal with local actions. Every triad becomes accidental. In the causal chain A-B-C, the steps are all explained, but the fact that A is pulling on C is *accidental*. It just so happens that C is attached to B. Without this circumstance, which is external to the action of A upon B, there would be no action of A wherever A has no physical presence. By contrast, the intentional agent who pulls on the end of the chain attached to the bucket in order to draw water from the well is acting precisely where he is not. It is correct to say that his dynamic action is limited to the end of the chain in his hand. But it would be absurd to claim that his intentional action does not have the bucket of water as its object.

Of course, Peirce is proposing *one* logic of relations and not *two* such logics (one for natural relations and the other for semiotic relations). Triadic relations have a logical form. For example, the following consequences can be inferred from the proposition "A gives B to C": "A is the giver" (implicitly, of something to someone), "B is given" (implicitly, by someone to someone), "C is the recipient" (implicitly, of a gift given by someone). These inferences are in no way unthinkable for the understanding (*Verstand*); they entail no paradox or contradiction to be overcome. What is impossible from a logical point of view is to construct the triadic relation "A gives B to C" if one has available only the two statements "A gives B (to someone)" and "B is given to C (by someone)."

Nevertheless, there may still remain a suspicion that there must be some sort of kinship, and therefore a complicity, between Peirce's triads, which are those of ordinary language, and the dialectical triads constructed according to the Hegelian paradigm of intelligible generation: Being-Nothingness-Becoming.

Indeed, it turns out there is a reason that explains the emphasis both philosophers place on triads. It is one that is to be found in the fact that

---

24. Yvon Belaval, *Leibniz critique de Descartes* (Paris: Gallimard, 1960), 195. This is a comment on a text to be found in Leibniz's *Opuscules et fragments inédits*, ed. Louis Couturat (Hildesheim: Olms, 1966), 32.

traditional logical analysis differentiates among three levels of complexity in argumentation: the level of the term, the level of the proposition, and the level of argument or reasoning itself. In such traditional logic, questions arise as to the category to which the terms used (or "concepts") belong, as to the form of the propositions (or "judgments"), and as to the "pattern" (or "syllogism") of the argument itself. Peirce claims to have taken this triad as his point of departure in formulating his triad of categories. More specifically, he began with these triads and the role that such "triplicities" play in Kant's philosophy.

Both philosophers of Threeness—Hegel and Peirce—have something in common: both see formal logic (as it was at the end of the eighteenth century) as not so much "complete," as Kant believed, but rather as superficial and ineffectual. Obviously they part ways regarding the means for reforming logical thinking. However, they do share one criticism between them—that it is incomprehensible for a proposition to be constructed out of two terms or an argument (a syllogism) out of three propositions.

It is well known that Hegel criticized the theory of judgment presented in the treatises of his time. According to this theory, which derives more or less directly from nominalism, judgment consists in the linking of two terms (or of two "representations," as it was also put). Since there are two *distinct* terms in a proposition, they will have to be linked in order to obtain that proposition. The instrument by which this linkage is carried out, according to this theory, is the copula: the proposition states that man *is* mortal and this is why it is not a simple association of ideas (thinking about man and then thinking about the mortal). But how does the word "is" magically create a noetic unit (the proposition) out of the two noetic units with which it begins (the terms)? It is explained that the copula posits the following: what we are given to conceive in the first term (through the mind's simple apprehension of it) is what we are also given to conceive in the second term. Does this then mean that the two terms are two ways of thinking *the same thing*? Is the copula a sign of identity? No, the two terms are quite distinct. Man is not the only mortal being. Therefore, when I am given to think something by the term "mortal," I am in fact thinking something different than what I think when given the term "man." Yes, but if being mortal is not the same thing as being a man, what does our theory mean when it explains that the two terms are united within the proposition thanks to the copula? So far, the explanation of the link between the two terms has not gone beyond a simple association between two conceptual terms: what is man is also mortal.

In short, the very way in which traditional manuals in formal logic are organized (moving from terms to propositions thanks to the logical cement that the copula places between the signifying bricks of the terms) gives rise to an enigma of the copula, sometimes called the "enigma of the meaning of being." How, asks the rebellious student, can two terms be unified if they are different? They can of course be associated. But the manual refers to a *synthesis* and not a simple conjunction. The operation of the copula thus appears profoundly mysterious: anybody not inclined to believe every word that comes out of the mouths of professors must admit that their proposed explanation in fact explains nothing.

Hegel, we might say, takes the side of the recalcitrant student who claims to have understood nothing. In his eyes, the flaw in schoolbook formal logic is to have merely juxtaposed the two terms of a simple proposition. First we are told that they are only linked (and not identified with each other) in virtue of the copula, but then it is claimed that a higher logical *unit* has thereby been constructed (as if the fact that the two terms are distinct had somehow been overcome). The solution proposed by Hegel is to say that there are not *two* terms in an authentic judgment (in a "speculative proposition") but only *one*; the concept manifests itself in such propositions in a divided state, in opposition to itself. The passage from the "immediate" level of logical complexity to the next level therefore does not consist in adding a second term from outside, but rather in "letting" the first term divide itself into a subject and a predicate.[25] This division calls for a new manifestation of the initial unity in the form of a term that has overcome, by mediation, its internal contradiction.

From the perspective of a contemporary logician, Hegel's solution is remarkable in that it seeks the unity of the "signifiable complex" (i.e., of

25. This is illustrated, in a striking image, by the interpretation of the etymology of the German word *Urteil* (judgment): to judge (*urteilen*) would be to allow the "original division" (*ur-teilen*) of the thinkable to take place. See Georg Wilhelm Friedrich Hegel, *Enzyklopädie der philosophischen Wissenschaften im Grundrisse* in his *Gesammelte Werke*, vol. 20, ed. Wolfgang Bonsiepen and Hans-Christian Lucas (Hamburg: Felix Meiner Verlag, 1992), § 166 (182–183). [Translator's Note: An English translation is available as G. W. F. Hegel, *The Encyclopaedia Logic (with the Zusätze): Part I of the "Encyclopaedia of the Philosophical Sciences" with the Zusätze*, ed. and trans. T. F. Geraets, W. A. Suchting, and H. S. Harris (Indianapolis: Hackett Publishing Company, 1991), § 166 (243–245).]

the intelligible content of discourse) within the concept and, thus, at the level of our apprehension of the term. Here one can refer to the commentary on Hegel's *Science of Logic* by a philosopher well versed in contemporary logic, Dominique Dubarle:

After having given an account of the concept and its structures, Hegel, following the traditional order, treats of judgment and then the syllogism. His treatment of these is original from a logical point of view and calls for a certain number of criticisms. Hegel's originality consists in inscribing, so to speak, structures that are proper to judgment and the syllogism within those already laid out in his theory of the concept. Judgment becomes nothing more than an accentuated form of the concept or, more precisely, of its moment of internally divided particularity that corresponds to the duality of the subject and predicate in the moment of judgment. As for the syllogism, it corresponds in a certain way to the third moment of conceptual reality, the moment of the concrete singularity enfolding within itself the reduced, abolished and sublimated moments of previous mediating particularity.[26]

If this is the case, Hegelian logic appears to be an attempt to establish—within an inferential logic judged to be superficial—an infra-propositional logic that would be at work at the level of the term or of the "noetic unit."[27]

Peirce provides a solution that is precisely the opposite of the Hegelian one.[28] For Peirce, propositions are not constructed out of terms, nor are syllogisms (which he calls "arguments") constructed out of propositions in the way that walls are constructed out of bricks and houses out of walls. Far from seeking to give propositions and arguments the "accentuated

---

26. Dominique Dubarle, "Dialectique hégélienne et formalisation," in Dominique Dubarle and André Doz, *Logique et dialectique* (Paris: Larousse, 1971), 193.

27. As Ernst Tugendhat has shown, the idea of an infra-propositional logic is also that of a logic divorced from the requirements of argumentation. It holds that logical liaisons are established at a level *preceding* that of the statement and therefore also before any discussion of expressions whose meaning and appropriateness to their ends can be examined. The same flaw can be found in several contemporary philosophical movements that have declared that "propositional logic," or the "logic of identity," needs to be relativized and outstripped by a more powerful logic of the word or even the syllable. See Ernst Tugendhat, *Self-Consciousness and Self-Determination,* trans. Paul Stern (Cambridge, MA: MIT Press, 1989).

28. If the formula had not already been used, one might say that Peirce puts Hegel right side up again. This image is more appropriate for Peirce than it is for Marx in any

THE SUBJECT OF TRIADIC RELATIONS   235

form of the concept," Peirce does the opposite. He gives the concept the form of a proposition and the proposition the form of an argument. For Hegel, logic, when considered as a science of thought, is a science of the concept: *to think is to conceive.* By contrast, for Peirce, the key to what thinking is is the word "therefore": thinking consists in establishing relations from principle to consequence, and that is why it cannot inhere in any *act* or *state* or *intuition*.

It is therefore correct to say that Peirce makes use of the traditional logical triad: term, proposition, argument (or syllogism). But he does this while inverting it or, if you prefer, while removing its atomistic appearance.

In old logic textbooks we are told that a proposition is made up of terms (or, for nominalists, of names) and that an argument is made up of propositions. According to Peirce, this way of presenting things is misleading. A proposition cannot be made out of names, nor can an argument be constructed out of a combination of names. The error of the traditional order is to give a strong suggestion that there is a progressive construction that leads us from simple conceptions to propositional statements and from there to reasoning. If this were so, there would be only a difference of *complexity* between an argument, a proposition, and a term.[29] This is precisely what Peirce rejects: "It thus appears that the difference between the Term, the Proposition, and the Argument, is by no means a difference of complexity, and does not so much consist in structure as in the services they are severally intended to perform."[30]

What Peirce means by this is that the term is *already propositional* and the proposition is *already inferential*; the degree of complexity is thus the

---

case, since Peirce, like Hegel, works in the domain of logic or the conceivable. The groundwork for Peirce's overturning of Hegel was laid by the way in which Kant, despite following the traditional order, in reality subordinates the logic of the categories to the logic of judgments.

29. This is why it is tempting to see "terms," which this theory puts at the lowest level on the scale of intellectual complexity, as having been directly extracted from sensory experience by means of "abstraction." Peirce's attempt to invert the logical order consequently also deprives this empiricist doctrine of concept acquisition of one the reasons that made it seem plausible.

30. Charles Sanders Peirce, *Collected Papers of Charles Sanders Peirce,* vol. 4: *The Simplest Mathematics,* ed. Charles Hartshorne and Paul Weiss (Cambridge, MA: Harvard University Press, 1933), § 572 (462).

same. Rather than seeking to engender the complex out of what is believed to be simple, one must start with the complex (since all one will find is the complex in any case).

In another text, the same idea is expressed as a kind of Peircean version of Frege's well-known context principle: nouns should not be considered in isolation, for they have meaning only within the context of a proposition.

[N]o sign of a thing or kind of thing—the ideas of signs to which concepts belong—can arise except in a proposition; and no logical operation upon a proposition can result in anything but a proposition; so that non-propositional signs can only exist as constituents of propositions.[31]

Thus, it is not true, contrary to the way things are ordinarily presented, that propositions are "built up of non-propositional signs."[32] Peirce thus adopts a holistic philosophy of logic in that he refuses to build the whole up out of raw elements and sees parts as having no other status than that of parts of the whole. Terms (or concepts, such as "man" and "mortal" in the schoolbook example) are not names: they are general concepts and therefore are possibilities of determination to be applied to something within a proposition. "The truth is that concepts are nothing but indefinite problematic judgments."[33] For example, Peirce continues, the concept of man "necessarily involves the thought of the possible being of a man."[34] To grasp the concept "man" is not to contemplate an essence, it is to conceive what there would be in the world if there were a man. When we think by using only this concept (and nothing besides), what we do is to think about what there would be if there were a man.

In turn, a proposition is itself nothing but an argument of which one part has been left indeterminate. Just as a conceptual term is really what today is called an "open sentence" (e.g., to grasp the concept of man is to think that "x is a man"), so a proposition is an implicit argument. To put forward the proposition "man is mortal" is to posit the inferential principle "if human, then mortal." Peirce can then go on to develop his doctrine of the copula as an operator of what he calls "illation," or inference:

31. Ibid., § 583 (469–470).
32. Ibid., (470).
33. Ibid.
34. Ibid.

to say that "man is fallible" is to prepare oneself to say "Aristotle is a man and *therefore* fallible."

We have looked to Peirce to tell us what an order of meaning is from a logical perspective. Collectivist holism, as we have seen, is an attempt to talk about systems without mentioning their structure. But, by proceeding in that way, one is unable to speak even of a physical system. Signifying systems are of another order entirely. No description of brute (dyadic) facts can exhaust the meaning of a (triadic) intentional fact.

Collectivist holism has turned out to be a pseudo-holism because the only whole that it can claim to have brought out is the collective individual. Yet collective individuals have proven to be a mirage, the result of a faulty analysis of language. By contrast, an analysis of the facts of triadic relations allows one to speak about polyadic systems. A whole is here a polyad, for example a triad: we understand by "polyad" the system engendered by a relation that orders the logical subjects of the proposition, thereby indicating the status of each of the members of the system relative to the others.

With this foray into the logic of relations, my inquiry into holism as such reaches its conclusion. This is not because I can claim to have exhausted the subject but because the distinctions introduced should allow us to move to the second question asked at the outset: is a holistic view of the mind an obstacle to analysis? Can one speak of a holistic analysis of meaningful totalities? We will therefore turn toward what, in French structuralism, have been referred to as "the structures of the mind."

I will begin with the paradigm case of a triadic relation: the relation between *giver* and *recipient* established by the mediation of the *thing given*. This Peircean paradigm of the gift is also the point of departure for an entire anthropological school that thinks of itself as a science of the mind, an anthropology of the human mind and its intellectual structures. I will ask how the study of a social phenomenon such as the gift can pass for a study of the mind (Chapter 9). To answer this question is to decide on the sense in which the notion of an objective mind will be understood (Chapter 10). But if one can speak about an objective mind, then the question of the identification of thoughts must have been answered (Chapter 11).

9

Essays on the Gift

9.1. The Mediation of the Gift

The relation of the gift, which associates a giver (a donor) and a recipient (a donee) by means of a thing given is not one example among others of a triadic relation. It is, rather, the paradigm case in the Platonic sense, a model that allows us to understand by analogy other relations of the same type. It provides a schema that can be applied to a good many other cases. This can be observed if we consider the syntax of the verbs that Tesnière refers to as "trivalent." In fact, according to him, the verbs whose grammatical form is trivalent are either "verbs of saying" (i.e., declarative verbs) or "verbs of giving."[1]

Trivalent verbs are those that have three agents. The existence of such a class of verbs is easy to grasp in languages that have two kinds of passive construction. In the French sentence "Alfred donne le livre à Charles"

---

1. [Translator's note: Descombes's French text has a footnote here in which he cites Tesnière's list of the principal "verbs of giving" in French. A partial list of such verbs in English would include: to abandon, to accord, to administer, to ask, to attribute, to award, to bear, to cede, to concede, to confer, to confide, to delegate, to deliver, to distribute, to expedite, to give, to grant, to lavish, to leave, to lend, to pay, to procure, to promise, to provide, to refuse, to reimburse, to relegate, to relieve, to remove, to return, to sacrifice, to send, to steal, to transmit. See Lucien Tesnière, *Éléments de syntaxe structurale,* 2nd ed. (Paris: Klincksieck, 1988), 256.]

[Alfred gives the book to Charles], it is not immediately evident that "à Charles" is not an adverbial phrase (that might be left out) but a third agent (that must be implicit if it is not explicitly mentioned). The third agent is part of a system with the first (what is ordinarily called "the agent") and the second (the direct object). In English one can just as easily say "The book is given to Charles by Alfred" as "Charles is given the book by Alfred." The latter is a passive of the indirect object, or "third agent" as Tesnière calls it, and brings out the way in which the recipient or donee is an indispensable partner to the action signified by the verb. "From a semantic point of view, the third agent is the one for whose benefit (or detriment) the action is carried out."[2] It is she who receives the benefit or harm of the act.

So, what is the logic of relations that will be applied in the description of any gift whatever? On this point, a comparison of the responses given by Russell and Peirce will make plain the superiority of Peirce's solution.

In the lectures collected in *An Inquiry into Meaning and Truth* and in the course of discussing "atomic propositions" (those that are not formed by the logical combination of other, more simple, propositions), Russell is led to wonder how to analyze a statement of the form "A gives a book C to B."[3] The three letters stand for proper names, so we will have to imagine that the book has a proper name (as is the case for the manuscripts we have of ancient works or certain incunabula). Although Russell raised this logical question, he attempts to answer it in epistemological terms: what are the events that would allow us to say that we *saw* A give book C to B? We would have to witness, in his view, a succession of two events. If we are to establish on our own that A gives C to B, "we must see A and B, and see A holding C, moving C towards B, and finally giving C into B's hands."[4] Russell himself notes that his paraphrase of "I see A give C to B" leaves *intention* aside. But this amounts to saying that such a "phenomenalist" description cannot distinguish between a case where the observed transfer

2. Ibid., 109.
3. Bertrand Russell, *An Inquiry Into Meaning and Truth* (1940; New York: Routledge, 1992), 43.
4. Ibid., 44.

is intentional and a case where it is not. For example, the bookstore clerk puts book C into the hands of client B so as to allow him to decide whether to buy it.

Russell does grasp one aspect of the logic governing the description of the gift: it is an "atomic form," i.e., a fact that cannot be further broken down. The sentence cannot be cut up into distinct episodes that would then only have to be brought together. The scene of the gift inheres in a fact that can in no way be reconstructed as a conjunction of two more elementary facts. Russell believes that the atomic fact of the gift is dyadic: we witness, he says, the succession of two events. As is the case for every such succession, the relation by which A's setting down of the book precedes it being taken up by B is irreducible to a conjunction of two monadic facts (see above, Chapter 7, section 2). Russell wants to leave aside intention so as to have only a dyadic relation (of succession) between two dyadic relations (a relation of A to the book and a relation of B to the book). He could then determine *the relation of the people to the objects* without mentioning *the relation of the people to each other*. The relation between donor and donee would then become a simple logical consequence of two relations to the object. This is a form of description that would apply just as well to the transmission of a virus C from A to B.

Russell chooses to stick to a material description of the "brute facts" (one which is unusual in being "phenomenalist" rather than "physicalist"; this complicates his presentation but does not change the heart of the matter). Peirce's thesis on the triadic structure of the verb "to give" is that no description of the kind provided by Russell can succeed in reconstituting the reality of the event of the gift. This thesis is entirely justified. Russell has failed to analyze an example of gift giving; instead, he has provided an analysis of a kind of pantomime. His description would fit any operation that included, as one of its moments, the physical transfer of an object.

It follows that the description of an act of gift giving must be an intentional description. What are we to understand by this intentionality of the gift? According to Peirce, the mark of the mental is not intentionality as it is generally expressed in "Brentano's Thesis," i.e., as a binary or dyadic relation in which "all consciousness is consciousness of something." Rather, a triadic formula is required: all intentional consciousness is consciousness of the final (or intentional) relation of something to something else. Intentionality is the perceived or posited relation of intention between something (for example, these flowers) and something else (this person for whom they are meant). As he writes in a letter to Lady Welby:

> If you take any ordinary triadic relation, you will always find a *mental* element in it. Brute action is secondness, any mentality involves thirdness. Analyze for instance the relation involved in "A gives B to C." Now what is giving? It does not consist [in] A's putting B away from him and C's subsequently taking B up. It is not necessary that any material transfer should take place. It consists in A's making C the possessor according to *Law*. There must be some kind of law before there can be any kind of giving—be it but the law of the strongest.[5]

Peirce thus dismisses in advance what will later be Russell's solution. By leaving intention aside, a description that sticks to brute facts will leave *giving itself* aside. The succession of two dyadic facts is a relational fact. But it is an exterior fact that is unable to change the fact of setting down an object into a gift of that object or the fact of picking it up into the acceptance of a gift.

We can now see that there is little difference between failing to grasp the triadic nature of giving and failing to grasp a fact that presupposes an institution or a law. "*There must be some kind of law before there can be any kind of giving.*"

Triadic action, according to Peirce, always includes something mental. One might ask how we are to understand this mentalism. But it is not even really a mentalism if by "mentalism" is meant the replacement of real and public transactions by interior, psychical processes. What would be mentalist would be to seek in something given mentally the foundation of the relation between the two individuals. Person A sets object C down in front of himself, after which person B snatches up object C. How can one transform the physical operation of setting down an object in front of oneself into a gift that institutes a relation of donor/donee between oneself and the person before whom the object was set? The mentalist response is that what was not found in the sequence of physical movements that took place in the course of this operation should be sought in the respective heads of A and B. The presence in A's head of the thought "I am giving C to B" associated with the gesture of setting down C would be enough for

---

5. Charles Sanders Peirce, *Collected Papers of Charles Sanders Peirce*, vol. 8: *Reviews, Correspondence, and Bibliography*, ed. Arthur W. Burks (Cambridge, MA: Harvard University Press, 1958), § 331 (225–226).

these gestures to *constitute* the action of giving. That thought being present to the subject's mind would animate the gesture and give it its meaning (in a *Sinngebung*). But this way of speaking, which one often finds in phenomenological writings, risks leading us to see the actors in the action as interpreters of a natural event. "To provide meaning" is the task of a reader confronting a difficult text. The actor would then be not in the process of doing anything but, rather, attentively witnessing various physical movements (here is the text) to which she must give a meaning (here is the proposed reading of the text), a meaning that is her own if the physical movement is hers or that is someone else's meaning if the physical movement is one made by someone else in her direction.

Peirce's response is that it is impossible to make thinking about the gift inhere in a present event. To say that there is a law is to introduce (potential) infinity. The future is determined *regardless of what happens,* which shows that the determination in question is logical and not causal or physical. Not that all possible situations are foreseen, but they are logically anticipated. We do not know what the recipient will do with the gift he has been given. But whatever he may do, what he does will fall under one or the other divisions of a logical space that has just been determined. For example, if he wants to keep it he can, and if he wants to give it away he can. If the object were taken away from him without his consent, he would have been wronged, and so on. We determine the future while not knowing what it holds. This is why a mere collection of brute facts cannot provide *the multiplicity that is necessary for the manifestation of an intentional order.* In this, the similarity is obvious between Peirce's thinking on the originality of intentional relations and that of Wittgenstein on the irreducibility of rules to whatever may be presently given.[6]

A description of the operation of giving using only brute facts would be a description of a triadic action exclusively through dyadic operations. It would be an example of what Wittgenstein calls an "external description"—one that remains outside the story and thus fails to capture the meaning.[7]

---

6. This affinity was the subject of Richard Rorty's illuminating article "Pragmatism, Categories and Language," *The Philosophical Review* 70 (1961): 197–233.

7. Ludwig Wittgenstein, *Philosophical Remarks,* ed. Rush Rhees, trans. Raymond Hargreaves and Roger White (Oxford: Basil Blackwell, 1975), § 29 (68).

The consequences that flow from the physical act of placing an object in front of oneself in the presence of someone else cannot be explained by either the movement itself or any accompanying content present in the heads of the protagonists. The context that makes this act the action of giving something is an institutional one. This is the substance of a remark made by Wittgenstein in the *Philosophical Investigations*:

Why can't my right hand give my left hand money?—My right hand can put it into my left hand. My right hand can write a deed of gift, and my left hand a receipt.—But the further practical consequences would not be those of a gift. When the left hand has taken the money from the right, and so forth, one will ask, "Well, and now what?"[8]

Here again, what is at issue are the consequences of a physical gesture carried out in a historical context. By themselves, the physical gestures have determined nothing about the future: a movement has taken place, yet nothing follows from it for the status of the different partners in this scenario. What is missing? What is missing is a condition of otherness. Wittgenstein is contesting the mentalist doctrine of meaning: one cannot confer (or give) a meaning to a word or phrase—for example the psychological phrase "sensation of pain"—by mentally pronouncing this phrase while directing one's attention to the sensation. In both cases, events take place, but they do not take place in the context required for the meaningful consequences to ensue (in one case, the change in the status of a sum of money; in the other, the constitution of a noise as a meaningful phrase). As for giving, its condition is that there must be sufficient alterity between the giving and receiving subjects. In other words, giving can only take place within an *order of justice,* which can be established only among autonomous people.

---

8. Ludwig Wittgenstein, *Philosophical Investigations,* rev. 4th ed., ed. P. M. S. Hacker and Joachim Schulte, trans. G. E. M. Anscombe, P. M. S. Hacker, and Joachim Schulte (1953; Oxford: Wiley-Blackwell, 2009), § 268 (101). Wittgenstein makes use of a contrast between the verbs *schenken* and *geben* here. The vocabulary of giving is constructed around the first of these verbs: the right hand would like to effect a *Schenkung* in favor of the left hand and even provide it with a "certificate of donation," a *Schenkungsurkunde*. For the physical operation of transferring, the verb *geben* is used. Literally, this opposition is between an act of giving, whose mode of execution remains unspecified, and an action by which one hand *puts* the money in the other hand, in the sense in which one can place a coin in a hand.

* * *

Using a different terminology (which is no longer Peirce's), one might say that realism regarding triadic relations is a *holism,* which is opposed to both the *positivism* of dyadic relations (i.e., what there is can be reduced to brute facts) and to the *atomism* of monadic terms. In its most general philosophical definition, holism is the idea that the whole is not the result of the presence of the parts (i.e., the result of their collection) but that it is given before they are given in reality. Here this precedence of the whole over the parts can be understood as the presupposition of a rule in order for the very fact in question to arise: in order for A to be able to be described as giving C to B, the brute facts must be produced within the context of a rule of gift giving.

In order to be able to speak of a gift, there must be three "partners"—a thing given, someone to give it, and someone to receive the gift. But we also know that merely having three individual beings and indicating the relations among them is not enough to put in place a system with three partners, i.e., three members of a real system. For example, a chain made up of three links is not triadic as such: what would be triadic would be to move the third link using the traction of the second on the first. What is required is that the relation between two objects can only be given by passing through the third member of the system. The third object, taken as a member of the triadic system, can be called a *mediator.*

This amounts to saying that the triadic system can be grasped using any of its members. By setting one of the elements as the first member of the system, we can determine a second member that is present in support of a third member. Here is a table of the possibilities of relation among members 1, 2, and 3 of the system of the gift:

1	2	3
donor	gift	donee
gift	donor	donee
donee	gift	donor

This table represents the following triadic situation. Someone becomes a *donor* by tying himself to a *donee* through giving him a *gift,* and this presupposes that by this very fact there is something that becomes the *gift* by being given by its owner (the donor) to someone (the donee). *That* presupposes that there is someone who becomes a *donee* by receiving that same thing from the person who legitimately possesses it. This explanation invokes what Peirce calls, in language that is consciously Hegelian, a *mediation*.

Now consider things from the point of view of teleological action. This perspective always introduces a certain degree of generality in the determination of the means to be employed. Let us suppose that the goal of A is to become a donor with regard to B. He will have to give him something, but he can become the donor of something for B's benefit in several ways. Position number 2 in the above table is relatively indeterminate, and this introduces an element of freedom—and thereby also morality—into the relation. Similarly, C can only be given by its owner (A) and can only acquire the status of a gift by being given to someone, but this need not necessarily be B. Finally, the donee can only receive the gift from the owner of the thing given; he can receive a present from A in several ways (the possibilities noted above), and he can receive thing C as a present in several ways (either because A gives it to him or because A sells it to D and D gives it to B, etc.). In short, the triadic relations, once they have been derelativized by the fact of leaving indeterminate one of the members of the system, are the following:

—A gives something to B.
—A gives C to someone.
—Someone gives C to B.

If we choose to derelativize a second time these relations that are dyadic in form, we will end up with predicates of a monadic form but with a triadic meaning. There will then be two degrees of freedom since A, in order to become a donor, would have a choice of both the donee and the thing given (A gives something that remains to be determined to someone who has not yet been selected).

The fact that there are these degrees of freedom explains why the physical description of the gift is unable to model the fact that what is happening is actually a gift. The present can always have been given differently (even where the object given and the donee remain the same). The brute facts that one might adduce will never be enough to determine either that the situation is one of gift giving or what sort of gift it is. There is thus a dimension of the event that eludes mere physical description: the dimension of intention. This obviously does not mean that giving a gift is somehow immaterial, as if it were possible to replace the act of giving, which necessarily changes something in the world, with the simple intention of giving.

This mediation is not dialectical. It is not a transition that would raise us from the level of the dyadic to the triadic (e.g., from the simple to the complex). The triadic fact here is not the dialectical result of a synthesis overcoming the contradiction of an object C that, in order to be given by A to B, must be A's while also being B's, in virtue of something like the following eristic argument. "I cannot give what is not mine; I can only give what belongs to me. But if I give one of my things, it ceases to be mine. By ceasing to be mine, it ceases to be something that I can give. Therefore I can only give something on condition that I keep it." This sophism may appear stupid, but, like all sophisms, it has its depth and may be seen as a paradox. In this case, the sophism serves to remind us of the danger of conceiving of the system of the gift as a discontinuous series of operations. Later we will see how Lévi-Strauss locates a similar contradiction at the origin of human institutions.

We are at once within the triadic. Mediation here means that the triadic relation must be conceived as including both real relations (e.g., *this* specific thing is given to *that* specific person) and intentional relations (governed by rules). However, it is not possible to isolate real relations from intentional ones. For example, the donor must have possession of the thing to be given, so a real relation must have been established. But nothing is said about the form of physical transfer involved. Similarly, the triadic relation includes both links from person to person and from person to thing, but it is impossible to separate them. The people are linked by the mediation of the gift of the object, and the object is given (and not simply moved from its position) mediated by the tie between the people.

9.2. The Spirit of the Gift

The relation of the gift, like every triadic relation, is intentional. It contains, as Peirce says, a mental element. It follows that the study of a social phenomenon that puts gift relations into practice will by this very fact be the study of a mental phenomenon. The anthropology of the institutions of the gift can legitimately be called a *science of the mind*.⁹

But how can it be?

Within French anthropology, reflection about the customs surrounding the obligatory exchange of gifts has been of tremendous importance. The interest of the phenomenon and its particular forms is enough to explain the special attention given to it. It was nevertheless necessary for this interest to have been noticed and explained, which is what Marcel Mauss did in his famous *Essai sur le don* [Essay on the Gift].¹⁰

It goes without saying that social anthropology studies particular customs, some of which may seem quite exotic to us. The immoderation of the *potlatch,* for example, captures our imaginations. Mauss, however, stresses that these are institutions grounded in giving and that *we* also have customs relating to gifts and feast meals.¹¹ The diversity of usages and customs is thus not in itself an obstacle to their comprehension. If we can understand that a gift requires two operations (one on the part of the donor and the other on the part of the donee), we can, by extension, imagine a more complex rule that brings together a gift and a counter-gift. The relation will then link two operations within a rule: one prescribing giving to someone else, who will receive, and the other prescribing to the recipient to give back to the donor after having received.

It happens that Lévi-Strauss, in his commentary on Mauss's essay, explains that Mauss's theory requires modifications and that it can be corrected through an understanding of the logic of relations. As is well known, Lévi-Strauss's Introduction to *Sociologie et anthropologie,* the volume in which Mauss's main works are collected, is at one and the same time a

---

9. [Translator's note: *"Sciences de l'esprit"* is the French translation of the German *Geisteswissenschaften* and is one of several ways in French to refer to what, in English, are called "the human sciences." Descombes is emphasizing the link here between such disciplines and the mental, since *"esprit"* in French can just as easily be translated by "mind" as by "spirit." Accordingly, the title of this section could just as easily have been "The Mind of the Gift." In what follows I will usually translate *esprit* as "mind," in order to emphasize the relevance of Descombes's theses for the philosophy of mind. But the translation of *esprit* as "spirit" (as in Montesquieu's *The Spirit of the Laws* or Hegel's *Phenomenology of Spirit*) should also be kept in mind.]

10. Marcel Mauss, *The Gift: Forms and Functions of Exchange in Archaic Societies,* trans. Ian Cunnison (London: Cohen & West, 1966).

11. Ibid., 63–64.

tribute to Mauss's work, an original reconstruction of some of its main points, and a critique.[12] Mauss is held to be the precursor—but not the founder—of the new science that Lévi-Strauss believed to be emerging at the time of his writing. What Mauss is held to have lacked is a robust logic of relations that would have allowed him to reach the goal he was heading toward: a genuinely structural theory of social life ("to understand social life as a system of relations").[13] Mauss, unfortunately, thought of the problem of the gift or of magic "in the terms of classical logic," i.e., in the terms of an analysis that breaks every proposition down into three logical units (subject-copula-predicate).[14] We have already seen this opposition between a logic of inherence and a logic of relations. It is none other than our philosophical controversy on the reality of relations: are dyadic relations reducible to comparisons between monadic facts and triadic relations to comparisons of dyadic facts?

In Lévi-Strauss's *Introduction,* the two diagnoses go together. Social life is a tissue of relations, so there can be no sound sociology or social anthropology without a solid logic of relations. This allows Lévi-Strauss to present himself as Mauss's heir. Because Mauss was ahead of his time, he did not have access to our logic nor to what Lévi-Strauss believes to be a scientific discovery made by psychology and linguistics—the notion of an unconscious psychical life. If Mauss had had these theoretical resources at his disposal, doubtless he would have had an easier time saying what he wanted to say. At the end of his *Introduction,* Lévi-Strauss returns to his idea of an anthropology grounded in the idea that social life is exchange or communication and that this exchange is rendered possible by the presence in all humans of the same mental mechanisms (i.e., the unconscious structures of the mind [*esprit*]). He writes: "In fact, it is nothing other than Mauss's conception, translated from its original expression in terms of class logic into the terms of a symbolic logic which summarizes the most general laws of language."[15]

---

12. [Translator's note: Lévi-Strauss's text on Mauss figures as the Introduction to Mauss's *Sociologie et anthropologie*. This volume has not been translated in its entirety, but an English translation of the Introduction has been published in book form: Claude Lévi-Strauss, *Introduction to the Work of Marcel Mauss,* trans. Felicity Baker (London: Routledge and Kegan Paul, 1987).]
13. Ibid., 50.
14. Ibid.
15. Ibid., 64.

Thus, Lévi-Strauss criticizes Mauss essentially for having flouted his own precept as stated in *A General Theory of Magic*: "The unity of the whole is more real than each of its parts."[16] Instead of beginning with a whole treated as given before its parts, Mauss attempted to construct the whole by putting the various parts together, according to Lévi-Strauss. Remember that in the case of *The Gift*, the "whole" is exchange (in the archaic form of an exchange of gifts as opposed to market exchanges), while the "parts" are the three obligations by which the fact of *giving*—which is itself a social obligation—creates the obligation for the donee to *receive* (or else cause the donor to lose face) and also, subsequently, to *return the gift*, or risk losing face himself.

What is at stake in this discussion is our understanding of the very principle of structural holism. This principle states that in some sense the whole must be given before the parts. Yes, but given in what sense? Why does Lévi-Strauss think that Mauss was not sufficiently holistic in his approach in *The Gift*?

Did Mauss approach the phenomenon of archaic exchange with a mind to reducing it? Did he attempt to prove that the whole can be constructed out of the sum of the parts? This is Lévi-Strauss's claim regarding Mauss's procedures in *The Gift*: empirical observation provides the pieces where Mauss's theory "calls for the existence of a structure."[17] Mauss restricts himself to the elements given to experience—the three obligations—and seeks to reconstruct the whole of exchange out of these three obligations, i.e., out of what Lévi-Strauss refers to as "fragments," the "scattered members" of the structure.[18] Mauss, in short, asked himself why an object that was given and received must be returned. Failing to have first established the principle of exchange—the object was only given and received in order

---

16. Marcel Mauss, *A General Theory of Magic*, trans. Robert Brain (London: Routledge and Kegan Paul, 1972), 107 [translation modified]. Mauss means by this statement that, in a study of magic, one starts out with the feeling that one has brought together wildly different kinds of facts—some religious, some technological, others social or speculative, etc.—under a single label. Yet there is a system—i.e., a real whole—behind all these elements. It is therefore an error to follow the anthropologists of the nineteenth century by taking one element, for example the "Law of Sympathy," and seeking to reduce everything else to it.

17. Lévi-Strauss, *Introduction*, 46.

18. Ibid.

to be returned—Mauss borrows an explanation from those involved: if the thing given must not remain with the donee but must instead return to the donor from whom it came, this can only be because there is within it a *virtue* or *power,* a *spirit* that requires this return. Lévi-Strauss then cites (out of context) a sentence from Mauss: "We can . . . prove that in the things exchanged . . . there is a power [*vertu*], that forces the gifts to circulate, to be given and returned."[19]

Lévi-Strauss's criticism is surprising to say the least, for Mauss's descriptions repeatedly stress the mutual dependence, the solidarity, and the complementarity of all of the exchanges and operations. One need only cite the following text, from the end of the first chapter of *The Gift,* on the complementarity of the three operations of giving, receiving, and returning:

> In all these instances there is a series of rights and duties about consuming and repaying existing side by side with rights and duties about giving and receiving. But this strict mixture of symmetrical and reciprocal rights no longer appears contradictory if we realize that it is first and foremost a pattern of spiritual bonds among things which are to some extent parts of persons, and persons and groups that behave in some measure as if they were things.
>
> All these institutions express but a single fact, a single social regime and a single mentality: food, women, children, possessions, charms, land, labour, services, religious offices, rank—everything is stuff to be given away and repaid. In a perpetual interchange of what we may call spiritual matter, comprising men and things, these elements pass and repass among clans and individuals, distributed among the ranks, sexes and generations.[20]

To anyone who had just read this passage from *The Gift,* Lévi-Strauss's critique can only seem unfair. Can there be a more holistic approach than the one in evidence in the above text? Everything that such an approach requires can be found in it. First, Mauss stresses the relations of

---

19. Ibid. [translation modified]. For Mauss's original text, see *The Gift,* 41. This sentence appears in the context of an examination of the institutions of the *potlatch.* Mauss is emphasizing the impossibility of separating ideological and morphological facts. The section opens with this guiding idea: the obligation to exchange "is expressed in myth and imagery, symbolically and collectively; it takes the form of interest in the objects exchanged; the objects are never completely separated from the men who exchange them. . . ." Mauss, *The Gift,* 31.

20. Mauss, *The Gift,* 11–12 [translation modified].

complementarity among statuses, rights, and duties. Second, he draws a clear distinction between the principle of the system and the matter that is each time ordered and informed by it. Indeed, Mauss insists that, at root, any social situation will give rise to an application of the general schema according to which something must be given so that something will be given back, and in such a way that the statuses of the various parties are distinguished. The reason for exchange is therefore certainly not to be found in the specific nature of the different possible materials (food, women, children, goods, etc.). For example, the goal is not to easily acquire riches (by compelling others to give back to you). Third, Mauss refers to a "mixture" of the bonds among things and the bonds among people. This intertwining is consistent with what Peirce emphasized in speaking about an irreducible triadic relation: in every proposition containing a verb of giving, one will have a link to the thing and a link between people, and these two will be indissociable. Finally, the system is explicitly referred to as mental. It is more a state of mind—Mauss calls it a "mentality"—than it is a social operation.

It is true that Mauss refers to a "contradictory mixture," but this contradiction is only *apparent* and therefore a contradiction that exists only within inadequate descriptions of the facts. Mauss means that the external observer who comes to this form of exchange armed with his own practical categories (e.g., the economic, the political, the religious, etc.) will initially have the impression that the participants in exchange through gifts have mixed everything up and are incapable of making distinctions that *we* know to be essential. However, the contradiction disappears when the hasty initial interpretation is replaced by a comprehensive description (i.e., a description that allows us to understand because it encompasses the whole thing, in its entirety). The important thing for Mauss is that our distinction between people and things does not apply to the phenomenon in question. Within the perspective of the exchange of gifts, things are spiritual and people are material, which is a way of saying that one cannot proceed by considering, on the one hand, the relations of people to things and, on the other, the relations of people among themselves.

One can only conclude, contrary to what Lévi-Strauss suggests in his *Introduction,* that the source of the disagreement is not the principle of a holistic analysis of the three obligations. His critique of Mauss is not the one that he misleadingly puts forward. But what, then, is the source of the disagreement?

Mauss's description fails to satisfy Lévi-Strauss simply because Lévi-Strauss seeks to go beyond simple *description* in order to come to an *explanation*. Mauss seeks to provide nothing more than a description, and this is why he begins with what the participants in the gift or the potlatch say and think about the respective transactions. In other words, Mauss thinks that his job is complete when he has succeeded both in making clear the rule that the participants follow and in making it intelligible to us.[21] First, the anthropologist must state the rule as the participants understand it and in their terms. This explains Mauss's mention of *hau*—the spirit of the thing exchanged—which Lévi-Strauss finds unacceptable in a scientific inquiry. Within the perspective of an anthropology of meaning, the anthropologist must study the rhetoric of the participants. How do they express the obligations by which they consider themselves bound? What reproaches do they address to someone who fails to give or fails to give back or who does give back, but insufficiently? The investigator must report what the rules are in the very terms in which they are presented in the language of those who adhere to them. Otherwise, he runs the risk of replacing with a model of his own invention the reality for which he seeks to account.

Secondly, the anthropologist must render this unfamiliar system intelligible. He will do this by relating the form of exchange to our own forms of exchange. This allows him to see these two forms as particular cases of a formula that will have, at least to some extent, a universal anthropological status.

Lévi-Strauss, for his part, is opposed to the utilization of indigenous vocabulary in the anthropologist's description. These words can only appear if they are treated as documents to be explained; they are, of course, meaningful, but they in no way clarify matters. If we remove from the words (as they appear in Mauss's explanation) every semantic function, the system of the gift will openly appear to be an unintelligible phenomenon. What connects one obligation to another is a link marked X, a link

---

21. See Marcel Mauss, "Divisions et proportions des divisions de la sociologie" (1927) in *Œuvres*, vol. 3: *Cohésion sociale et division de la sociologie* (Paris: Les Éditions de Minuit, 1969), 222 and 224.

or element whose true nature remains to be determined. Lévi-Strauss proposes that we think of these indigenous words as empty signifiers, like algebraic symbols in that they appear in speech as placeholders to be replaced by an explanation that is as yet lacking.

It is immediately clear at what point the theorist of the structural unconscious diverges from the path of the pure social anthropologist. For Mauss, the obligations that the participants describe are precisely that: *obligations*. There is no need to seek (no more for the *hau* than for anything else) their explicative principle if by that one means seeking an *efficient cause* that will provide the explicative principle of an *obligation*.

By contrast, for Lévi-Strauss, the fact that the Maori see themselves as bound by obligations is an ideological fact whose explanation must be sought in another fact that will be explicative because it will not be ideological. In other words, one must move from the intentional to the natural, from ideological to brute facts, from triadic relations to chains of dyadic (causal) relations. Mauss's essay on *The Gift* would then have been limited in not having attempted to reach the underlying reality—one might well call it the "infrastructure"—behind the indigenous ideological epiphenomenon.[22] It is with just such a project of causal explanation that Lévi-Strauss seeks to counter Mauss's project for what we might call a "sympathetic" explanation.

Hau is not the ultimate explanation for exchange; it is the conscious form whereby men of a given society, in which the problem had particular importance, apprehended an unconscious necessity whose explanation lies elsewhere.... Once the indigenous conception has been isolated, it must be reduced by an objective critique so as to reach the underlying reality. We have very little chance of finding that reality in conscious formulations; a better chance, in unconscious mental structures to which institutions give us access, but a better chance yet, in language.[23]

What does it mean to "apprehend an unconscious necessity"? How does one go about *apprehending* an *unconscious* necessity? It would appear

---

22. On Lévi-Strauss's view of the underlying reality as an "infrastructure," see my *The Mind's Provisions: A Critique of Cognitivism*, trans. Stephen Adam Schwartz (Princeton: Princeton University Press, 2001), 258 n 17.
23. Lévi-Strauss, *Introduction*, 48–49.

that Lévi-Strauss means by this that the necessity that presents itself in a moral form to those concerned is, in reality, a "mental" necessity.[24] One might interpret this to mean that, if the necessity is mental, it remains within the order of ideas and ideals (i.e., obligations). But Lévi-Strauss would appear to be saying that we are no longer within that order since the structures in question are unconscious—i.e., unconscious psychical *mechanisms*.

One might understand this in the following way: there exists a psychological explanation that accounts for the fact that the Maori feel obligated to give when they possess or to give back when they have received. The feeling of having this obligation is conscious and therefore provides a motive, a reason to act. But the emergence of this feeling *must* have a deeper explanation, an explanation for which cannot be provided by the "indigenous consciousness" or the "indigenous theory." An authentic explanation will then be sought in the psychology of the intellect and, ultimately, in neurology.

This is more or less what Lévi-Strauss concludes after having related the *hau* (from *The Gift*) to *mana* (a notion studied in *A General Theory of Magic*). These notions are like the *x*'s in an equation, "floating signifiers" deprived of a signified. Their semantic value is similar to that of *abracadabra* in a magic trick, i.e., that of an unspecifiable operation that is such that it has the desired effect. The effect, however, is entirely specifiable. If we were to assess Mauss's explanations from this point of view, they do indeed leave something to be desired. Why is it shameful to keep what one has for oneself? Why is it preferable to give it away? Why is one obliged to give back when one has received? An answer transcribed using "floating

---

24. More generally, it appears to the participants in a deontic form, if we remember the three acceptations of "you must": logical, physical, deontic. Here is the general sense of this division. The ambiguity of an operator such as "you cannot fail to . . ." when applied to a verb is lifted when it is explained what the obstacle is. If failing to do the thing is meaningless or unthinkable, the obstacle is a logical one. If failing to do it is beyond our capabilities or those of any natural agent, the obstacle is a physical one. If it is contrary to the principles, ideals, and ends that the agent takes into account when concerned with maintaining his moral status, the obstacle is deontic, or moral in the broad sense. It goes without saying that "you must give back to the person who gave to you" is a deontic necessity. Lévi-Strauss seems to be saying that what the participants understand, deontically, as an obligation is in reality a natural or physical necessity (i.e., the intellect or the human brain cannot function in any other way than by representing the object as having to be given back).

ESSAYS ON THE GIFT

signifiers" would appear to be inadequate. It amounts to saying that the answer to these questions is this: because the thing possesses an *abracadabra* that makes it the case that it must go to its place with the donee, and also makes it the case that the donee must receive it, and that finally also makes it the case that the donee will never move beyond this gift until he has given a gift in return. Lévi-Strauss concludes:

> Exchange is not a complex edifice built on the obligations of giving, receiving and returning, with the help of some emotional-mystical cement. It is a synthesis immediately given to, and given by, symbolic thought, which, in exchange as in any other form of communication, surmounts the contradiction inherent in it; that is the contradiction of perceiving things as elements of dialogue, in respect of self and others simultaneously, and destined by nature to pass from the one to the other.[25]

The first sentence of this text calls to mind Lévi-Strauss's objection (raised in our previous discussion) to Mauss's way of proceeding: *hau* is a mystical cement, a pseudo-explanation. But there should be no need for such cement, because the entirety of the exchange is given along with the parts. Of course, the *hau* is also not unrelated to the reality to be accounted for. It is the "subjective reflection" and thus the way in which the reality in question is present in the consciousness of the actors in the exchange. This is where Lévi-Strauss's program moves from a structural holism to a structural causalism.

In short, Lévi-Strauss's critique comes down to this: Mauss seeks to explain a rule, but the force he invokes ends up explaining nothing. Lévi-Strauss's entire discussion of *The Gift* is thus precipitated and prepared by his rewriting of a question concerning a *rule* into a question concerning a *force*.[26]

---

25. Ibid., 58–59.
26. In a lecture from 1972, Lévi-Strauss returned to this question: should culture be explained by the action of the external environment upon a "plastic mind," or should it rather be explained by "psychological laws that are universal because they are innate and that everywhere give rise to the same effects regardless of history and of the particular environment"? His answer is that there is no need to choose between these two philosophies. The explanation will combine two determinisms: "[O]ne, imposed on mythic thought by the constraints inherent in a relationship to a particular environment; the other is a translation of persistent mental requirements which are independent of the environment. This reciprocal articulation would be hard to understand if human relationships with the

But why did he feel the need to rewrite the question? Without this rewriting, his entire critique loses its *raison d'être* since both the "mystical cement" and the irrational intrusion of the affective within the explanation disappear. The alleged flaws of Mauss's explanation are thus introduced into his text by Lévi-Strauss's postulate that holds that an obligation is not what it seems to be (an accepted rule) but rather a sense of constraint that is felt (in a mystifying way) as an obligation to be observed. This would be a little like a situation where we could only experience our biological needs in the form of an experience of a moral and social obligation to ingest and excrete. Lévi-Strauss seems to believe that the scientific method requires the anthropologist to see conscious rules, whose necessity is deontic, as manifestations of the effects of mechanisms whose necessity is natural or physical. But this reduction is a logical impossibility. Let us imagine that there are such constraints exerted upon thought. The autochthons who try to think differently are not able to do it; they are unable to *imagine* a situation in which the gift is not returned, in much the same way that we are unable to perform some mental operation that is beyond our abilities, such as memorizing a very long sequence of numbers. In such case, there would be no need to invoke a rule in order to prevent such a situation from arising.

To believe that Mauss was seeking a causal explanation but only managed to find a "mystical" one is to forget that Mauss is not offering a commentary on the Polynesians' physics (whatever that physics might consist in) but on their theory of *rights*. The notion of *hau* is a juridical one. The thing is animate rather than inert not because the participants have an animistic conception of inert things but because things are *integrated* within the system of exchange. What is "animate" is not the particular item in question—dried fish, pickled birds, etc.—but the thing as something given by such-and-such a person or family. This is a way of saying that the relation of giving is triadic and that one must never separate the relation to the object from the relation to the person. And this is precisely

---

environment and the constraints inherent in the functioning of the human mind arose from irreducibly separate orders." In the space of two sentences, "mental requirements" metamorphose into "constraints inherent in the functioning of the human mind." Claude Lévi-Strauss, "Structuralism and Ecology" in *The View From Afar,* trans. Joachim Neugroschel and Phoebe Hoss (Chicago: University of Chicago Press, 1992), 104 and 115 [translation modified].

what Mauss continually repeats. The notion of the *hau* is that of a juridical link among people, one that is created by the transmission of things: "[T]o give something to someone is to give something of oneself."[27]

One can therefore conclude that Lévi-Strauss's critique has entirely missed its target. He has failed to take into account the fact that, in a general way, things must be integrated into human society.[28]

Mauss demonstrated how to move beyond the apparent contradictions of the phenomenon by providing a superior description of it. The contradictions existed only within the unsympathetic accounts of ethnographers unfamiliar with the area or steeped in commonsense prejudices. Mauss was thus never tempted to dialecticize the phenomenon. Lévi-Strauss, on the other hand, proposes an explanation by way of infrastructures: not historical infrastructures (such as the conditions of material life), but infrastructures he calls "psychological" or "mental." The name given to this unconscious level of psychic functioning is "symbolic thought," a term that, surprisingly, is meant to fit both algebraic calculations and the elaboration of collective representations such as cosmological systems of classification, totemism, myths, etc.[29] The approach by way of "symbolic thought," as it has been invoked in this case, is striking in its dialectical

---

27. Mauss, *The Gift,* 10 [translation modified]. Mauss also writes: "If things are given and returned it is precisely because 'respects' or, we might say, 'courtesies' are given and returned. But, in addition, in giving them, a man gives himself, and he does so because he owes himself—himself and his possessions—to others" (Ibid., 44–45 [translation modified]).

28. Mauss writes the following in his study of magic: "[T]he magical value of persons or things results from the relative position they occupy within society or in relation to society. The two separate notions of magical virtue and social position coincide in so far as one depends on the other. Basically in magic it is always a matter of the respective values recognized by society. These values do not depend, in fact, on the intrinsic qualities of a thing or a person, but on the status or rank attributed to them by all-powerful public opinion, by its prejudices" (Mauss, *Magic,* 148). This notion of a place for every kind of thing is richer than what Lévi-Strauss proposes when he reduces the requirement for an order of things to a demand for a kind of tidying: each sacred thing must be in its place in order for the universal order to be maintained. See Claude Lévi-Strauss, *The Savage Mind* (1962; Chicago: University of Chicago Press, 1966), 10.

29. There may well have been a play on words at the origin of the entire Lévi-Straussian theory of the symbolic. Sociologists study social symbolism, while logicians work on

appearance. This thought overcomes its own *contradiction* in its immediately synthetic understanding of all things.

Thus, Lévi-Strauss's *Introduction* to Mauss's thinking would mislead any reader who believed (as Lévi-Strauss suggests one should) that the choice is between, on the one hand, the holism of the structuralist and, on the other, the anthropologist's impotent attempt at synthesis that was unable to make use of the progress made in the logic of relations. All of this is a façade. In reality, the reader faces a choice between two incompatible kinds of structural holism—one that remains within the autonomy of social anthropology, the other that seeks, in the last analysis, to reduce social anthropology to an "intellectualist psychology."[30]

Philosophically, the difference can be described as two different answers to the question "How can the whole be given before its parts are present?" The first possible answer is that this whole, when it is not actually given in the order of social life, is given *elsewhere*. It is present currently (*actualiter*) in such a way that it can play a causal role in a genuine explanation. Where can it be? In the mind, a mind that must be conceived in the *mentalist* way (and thereby be linked to action and to social life as a cause to its effect). The mental structures invoked in the text are causes, "psychological mechanisms." The regulation that they provide is that of a constraint, not a meaning. In this regard, Lévi-Strauss has been rightly upheld as one of the founding fathers of the "cognitive revolution."

A second possible response is that, yes, the whole must be given before its parts, but in the form of a *rule* rather than as a fact. The whole of the exchange is given before any gifts have been presented (to be received and given back), because there is an institution, a custom that has been established and passed on from generation to generation. An institution never consists in what is presently given. It can never be accounted for by a listing of brute facts (unlike the description that one might provide of a mechanism: this part acts on this other part and causes this effect, etc.).

---

symbolic logic, i.e., an algebra of logic. Therefore, it ought to be possible to study the religious symbolism of a society in the same way that one studies a "formal language"—i.e., without taking into account the fact that this symbolism embodies for the faithful the highest values and the most important realities, the source of life, and the power whose decrees govern us all. Algebraic thought, social thought, and religious thought would all be exercises in the same "symbolic" or "relational" thought.

30. Lévi-Strauss, *Introduction*, 65.

The description of an institution has as its grammatical mood, as Peirce would say, the conditional (*would be*) rather than the indicative (*will be*). What must be given before a transaction begins is the following rule: if someone possesses, then he must give; if he gives to me, I must receive; if I have received, I am obliged to give back. The future is logically determinate in all cases and no matter what may happen, but it is not causally determinate.

According to this second response, social anthropology practices a structural holism that chooses to understand the reality of the whole as the presupposition of the rule by every intentional or meaningful act: without the rule, there is no giving; therefore there is also no obligation to receive and give back. Mauss's *The Gift* is written in a descriptive style that would be satisfying to philosophers who, like Peirce, posit that the relation of the gift contains the infinite and therefore outstrips every attempt to reduce it to brute facts. It would also satisfy those who, like Wittgenstein, maintain that the rule is not an efficient cause of conduct (i.e., not a mechanism, whether psychological or not), but that it is a norm that people follow because they *want* to use it to guide them in life.

9.3. The Structures of the Mind

The preceding debate concerns the place of representations within explanation and thus the question of whether anthropological investigation bears on the way in which the people of a society conceive things or rather on the (internal and external) circumstances that make them conceive them as they do.

In a recent study, Maurice Godelier discusses this point, comparing the way in which Mauss accounts for the three obligations tied to gift giving—an archaic form of exchange—with Lévi-Strauss's opposed theory.[31]

Godelier makes two remarks regarding Mauss's theory itself. First, he notes that Mauss, after announcing that his essay bears upon "three themes from the same complex"—namely, the three obligations to give, to receive, and to give back—later writes that there is a fourth theme: gifts offered to the gods.[32] This fourth theme—the obligation to make sacrifices to the

---

31. Maurice Godelier, *The Enigma of the Gift,* trans. Nora Scott (Chicago: University of Chicago Press, 1999).
32. Ibid., 29.

gods—is not mentioned in Lévi-Strauss's critique. One might wonder why Lévi-Strauss ignores this religious obligation. Second, observers of societies that practice exchange in the form of gift giving have noted that almost anything can function and circulate as a gift, with the exception of certain precious objects that must be kept for oneself.[33] Mauss notes this difference among various objects: those that one consumes, those that are alienable and, finally, those inalienable objects that must be kept in the family and transmitted from generation to generation.[34] This fact also goes unremarked in Lévi-Strauss's interpretation. As a general rule, Godelier points out, Lévi-Strauss systematically ignores everything in Mauss's text that concerns the religious, the sacred, and hierarchical relations. His program at the time was to posit communication (along the lines of linguistic exchange) as the principle of social life. The social for him amounts to reciprocal exchange. Aspects of social life that do not fit into this definition are not taken into account. People exchange and communicate; they do not make sacrifices or faithfully hold on to *sacra*.[35]

Godelier is right: there is what would appear to be a systematic gap in Lévi-Strauss's descriptions and explanations. The status of magico-religious representations is never really acknowledged.

What is an anthropologist to make of these magico-religious representations? What role can they play in an anthropological explanation? Godelier

---

33. Ibid., 32.

34. Mauss, *The Gift*, 42. These inalienable objects are sacred possessions (*sacra*).

35. Godelier, *Enigma*, 22–23. According to Cicero (*De natura deorum*, III, 2, 5), Roman religion consists of two things: sacred rituals of offerings to the gods (*sacra*) and signs of the divine will (*auspicia*). On this point, see the commentaries by Georges Dumézil regarding *auguria* (divine signs) in *Idées romaines* (Paris, Gallimard, 1979), 95–96. Edmond Ortigues has shown the importance of this distinction that is entirely missed when one simply adopts the commonsense conception of the religious that sees it as the domain of the sacred or of spirits from the beyond. "When it is said that religion is the domain of the sacred, this is only roughly true. The Latins drew a distinction between *sacra* and *auguria*.... It would therefore be an error to think that religion can be reduced to a sacred solidarity that is ensured by a system of provisions and counter-provisions between the gods and men or between the ancestors and their descendants. There is more: there is the random nature of the Sign, the improbable event.... Inviolable and sacred solidarity is not closed upon itself, there are also unforeseen misfortunes, Signs from elsewhere." Edmond Ortigues, *Religion du livre, religion de la coutume* (Paris: L'Harmattan, 1981), 34. Religion is not just the sacred law of the ancestors; it is also *the Law and the Prophets*. God is not just the God of the fathers, but also he who sends signs and messengers.

believes that readers of Mauss's text confront a difficulty: the first two obligations have a prosaic explanation, but the third does not. Why give? In order to put the recipient into a relation of subordination (so the apparently disinterested gesture of the gift ends up being interested after all). Why receive? So as to avoid losing face and setting off hostilities. But why must the gift received be given back? Lévi-Strauss criticized Mauss for offering a religious reason to explain it; the thing possesses a special virtue or power. Godelier agrees with this criticism. Mauss provides an explanation in religious terms: the participants believe that there is a "soul of things" that compels things to return to those who first gave them. On this point at least, according to Godelier, Lévi-Strauss's critique is justified.[36] For it is not the case that the things exchanged move on their own under the force of the *hau*. Godelier's reading here is nothing more than a reiteration of Lévi-Strauss's interpretation—to my mind, a misinterpretation—of the role played by the notion of *hau* in Mauss's description.

Lévi-Strauss attempts to provide the "missing piece" of the theory by calling upon the unconscious structures of the mind. On this, Godelier believes that it ought to be possible to account for the potlatch without either relying on the religious beliefs of the participants or invoking mental structures. Religious notions do not explain the ties of obligation because they only offer "mystical cement," as Lévi-Strauss put it. But explanations by way of the structures of the human mind do not fare much better, as they have the flaw of being the same for all humans. It is difficult to see how such universal structures could explain particular and historical forms. In this, Godelier recapitulates the broad lines of Aristotle's criticism of Platonic archetypes: eternal forms cannot account for what happens in a world of generation and corruption; the Idea of a bed does not serve to explain how the tree becomes a bed, nor does the Idea of god explain how marble becomes a statue of god. What is missing from the principle of explanation put forward by Lévi-Strauss's structural anthropology is the provision of a particular historical and social context for the human mind.

This last critique is relevant. An anthropologist studying a custom is studying the human mind [*l'esprit humain*]. But he is studying the human mind within a *spirit of the laws* [*esprit des lois*] (Montesquieu) or an *objective*

---

36. Godelier, *Enigma*, 44–45.

mind or *objective spirit* [*esprit objectif*] (Hegel). The human mind is his object of inquiry to the exact extent that the Maori or Kwakiutl institutions are (always particular) manifestations of the human mind. He is therefore studying a human mind that takes the form for him of a social and historical reality, not a part of nature.

Yet even this critique concedes too much to the "intellectualist psychology" that Lévi-Strauss invokes as a science of the future. Godelier seems to admit that there might after all be a causal explanation via the structures of the mind, provided that the mind has been put in a position to act within a particular social form.[37] Explanation cannot be directly by way of the "structures of the mind," for to do this would be to forswear any possibility of accounting for the difference between one particular social form and another, one symbolism and another. But to make this claim is to concede that it is after all conceivable that formal psychology might provide an indirect explanation within the limits of the discipline.

Must we concede to the structuralist the right to present the principles of structural holism as also being those of a causalist philosophy of structures? Can we grant the hypothesis that *structures act*? We keep returning to this same point: how are we to understand *structures of the mind*?

The structures of the mind are Lévi-Strauss's response to the classical problem of the origin of human institutions. Such an origin cannot be insignificant, for the problem is not about explaining phenomena of mere gathering or gregariousness. Social phenomena have something intellectual or rational about them. Our problem is, then, one of "understanding how social phenomena may present the character of meaningful wholes, of structuralized ensembles."[38]

---

37. "Although it is legitimate to consider that human-ness cannot be reduced to consciousness and that, beyond consciousness there exist powers and principles that are continuously at work, it would perhaps be wise to take care when invoking unconscious mental structures to explain facts and behaviors that are *not* found in all societies or at all epochs, or which are found but do not have the same meaning or importance. *Something more* than the action of the unconscious structures of the mind is therefore needed to explain the transformations and developments which occur in the conscious productions of humans." Ibid., 24.

38. Claude Lévi-Strauss, "French Sociology," in *Twentieth Century Sociology*, ed. Georges Gurvitch and Wilbert E. Moore (New York: Philosophical Library, 1945), 520.

Two responses are excluded in advance.[39] One is the purely historical response that holds that human institutions are arrangements resulting from a multitude of historical circumstances. The other is the voluntarist response: human institutions are products of the individual reason of a divine legislator or of several people agreeing on social conventions among themselves. Lévi-Strauss seems to be saying that there are two other possible responses: Durkheim's, according to which such institutions are the product of a reason that is not individual because it is a *collective consciousness,* and the structuralist response, which holds that they are the product of a reason that is not individual because it is a *formal unconscious* that is the same in every human being. Durkheim's solution is to generate the symbolic out of the social; Lévi-Strauss's does the converse.[40]

Consider the explanation of kinship institutions. These institutions, which are sets of rules, are reduced by Lévi-Strauss to a principle. The principle of kinship systems is itself a rule (the prohibition of incest). This principle will then have to be explained by "certain fundamental structures of the human mind."[41] There are three such structures, according to Lévi-Strauss:

the exigency of the rule as a rule; the notion of reciprocity regarded as the most immediate form of integrating the opposition between the self and others; and finally, the synthetic nature of the gift, i.e., that the agreed transfer of a valuable from one individual to another makes these individuals into partners, and adds a new quality to the valuable transferred.[42]

These formulas are cryptic. In what way are these structures? And how are they structures of the mind? Lévi-Strauss speaks about rules here but, in the rest of his chapter, he treats "mental structures" as if they were mechanisms by which the "functioning" of thought could be explained. Even if we take the word "mechanism" in the most nebulous sense, we would still have to be able to apply it to something that resembles a

---

39. See my *The Mind's Provisions,* Chapter 3, section 2.
40. Lévi-Strauss writes that Mauss, like Durkheim, "still thinks it possible to develop a sociological theory of symbolism, whereas it is obvious that what is needed is a symbolic origin of society." *Introduction,* 21.
41. Claude Lévi-Strauss, *The Elementary Structures of Kinship,* rev. ed., ed. Rodney Needham, trans. James Harle Bell, John Richard von Sturmer, and Rodney Needham (Boston: Beacon Press, 1969), 84.
42. Ibid.

mechanism; there would have to be operations or series of operations that could be automatically set in motion by specific stimulations. Nothing in the statement regarding the three "structures" even comes close to resembling an operation, let alone a series of operations that could be set in motion by activating the appropriate lever on the machine.

There is, though, another more fruitful way of thinking about it: structures are mental schemata by which we attempt to make sense of situations and render them intelligible.[43] To grasp a mental structure would then have nothing to do with discovering calculations or automatic transformations of data. It would instead involve studying the response of a subject to a particular group of situations sharing some common features. For example, the common feature is that there arises an "opposition between the self and others." The response is to overcome this opposition through the application of the following general schema: where something appears at one and the same time as belonging to me and to someone else, introduce a formula of reciprocity such that, without contradiction, the thing can belong both to me and to the other person.

If this is what a mental schema is for Lévi-Strauss, the goal is to grasp the birth of a truly social order, i.e., a whole that is meaningful because it is structured. Lévi-Strauss provides a content for the abstract formulas above by presenting various situations. With regard to psychological mechanisms, he invites us to consider two children quarreling over a tricycle.[44] At first, each of them wants to have the tricycle for himself. As each comes to realize that this is impossible, each will demand equality (e.g., "if I cannot be supreme, we must all be equal").[45] So first we have the opposition between the self and others (the tricycle will belong to one or the other), then the resolution of the conflict through bonds of friendship (each gives up something and each will have the tricycle "in turn").

But a small analysis offered earlier in the book by Lévi-Strauss as a way of explaining the power of the "principle of reciprocity" provides the best clarification of the "fundamental structures" in question. In it, there is no

---

43. Ibid., 93.
44. Ibid., 85.
45. Ibid., 85. The citation is of the text from which Lévi-Strauss draws the example: Susan Isaacs, *Social Development in Young Children* (London: George Routledge and Sons, 1933), 223.

hint of a "psychological mechanism" to explain the "functioning of thought," but rather a situation from daily life: customers in a popular restaurant in Languedoc before the Second World War. Lévi-Strauss provides a brilliant analysis of a local custom (not really an institution, though), the exchange of wine.

The scene serves as a fable of the birth of a human order. Original chaos is represented by the initial situation: the diners come in one by one to eat alone at lunchtime in a restaurant offering a fixed-price menu. They are employees working in the area who do not have time to return home for lunch. The whole episode seems mundane. The restaurant is small, so the solitary diners are seated two to a table. How can civility be introduced into this uncomfortable situation? A diner takes the small bottle of wine served with the daily special and pours the contents not into his own glass but into that of his tablemate. "And his neighbour will immediately make a corresponding gesture of reciprocity."[46]

This anecdote captures both a manifestation of the human spirit itself along with its structures, but only because the uncomfortable situation described is too ephemeral for there to already have been a social rule to be applied in this case—"no ready-made formula of integration."[47] We can, as a result, represent the state of nature by the initial positions of the restaurant's customers and the ceremonial of the wine exchange as the operation by which we move from the state of nature to the civil state.

During my own experience of the working-class restaurants of Montpellier in the early 1970s, I was not able to witness the ceremony of the exchange of wine. However, I did learn that, in the Midi as in Paris, the problems diners face are not just the result of the cramped spaces but also of the lack of staff. It is difficult to get service. Although everyone will eventually be served, the vagaries of the kitchen and the numbers of customers mean that some will be served before others even where they all ordered at approximately the same time. In a situation of this type, the ceremonial of the exchange of wine would not be the somewhat arbitrary operation that Lévi-Strauss suggests, but rather a practical way of doing things. If I am served before my tablemate, I should compensate him, and to help him pass the time, I pour him some of my wine.

46. Lévi-Strauss, *Elementary Structures*, 58.
47. Ibid., 59.

In order to represent the birth of an ephemeral group through an application of the principle of reciprocity, Lévi-Strauss imagines people who have come to a restaurant to dine alone. It is not a communal meal served in, say, an inn. These diners are citizens who cherish their equality and bring forth an order of pure coexistence by means of the reciprocal exchange of tokens of consideration. Things would be different if Lévi-Strauss had considered the example of a group of people dining together. In that case, a table plan would have to be drawn up attributing places of honor, and there would have to be an order in which people were served. The rules that one would have to invent would be rules that assign different statuses to people: masculine or feminine, older or younger, guests or hosts, etc. Lévi-Strauss does not explain how the structures of the mind that he invokes might result in solutions to these sorts of problems of order. Once again, he turns a blind eye to anything resembling subordination or a relation of order.

Moreover, even in the sorts of uneasy situations that Lévi-Strauss conjures up, the difficulty raised is not simply that of coexisting but of knowing who will go first. These situations are of the sort where "for a short time . . . two strangers are forced to live together."[48] The social bond envisaged by Lévi-Strauss is nothing more than that: a short period of coexistence in a situation defined by a shortage of space with someone who means to get on with what he came to do "for himself" (for example, eat lunch). The customs or institutions outlined in the minor exchanges Lévi-Strauss describes are the means individuals use to attain their individual ends without bothering or being bothered by others. What is missing is a real society. However, even in these cases, reciprocity is not always the last word in the resolution of possible conflict. Two people are sharing, in another example given by Lévi-Strauss, a cabin on a transatlantic boat or a sleeping car.[49] But if it is a second-class cabin, the question will arise as to who will take the top berth. Does the principle of reciprocity require both passengers to occupy it in turns so that each spends half the night in it?

Oddly enough, the terms of Lévi-Strauss's conception of the social are not very different from those of Sartre. The persuasive little scenarios that Lévi-Strauss skillfully uses to illustrate his doctrine all have this in

48. Ibid.
49. Ibid.

common: they are stories about single people. Yet the goal is to get clearer about the institutions of family life.

It is as if Lévi-Strauss wanted to avoid having to write the words "relation of order." A relation of order is a nonsymmetrical relation: if A is taller than B, B is not at the same time taller than A. Hegelians use a familiar procedure for getting around this logical point. An alternative is stated: either the relation of order is unilateral (i.e., there is a relation of A to B but no relation of B to A), or it has a converse relation. Obviously, A's superiority requires a counterpart—the inferiority of B. The dialectic consists in asking us to conceive of this complementarity as a reciprocity. This can first be done on the formal level, by abstracting from the content of the relations: to the relation of A to B there is a corresponding relation of B to A. One can then do the same thing for the content itself through the dialectic of presupposition illustrated by the Hegelian figure of the slave who becomes the master's master. Since the superiority of A over B has as its *condition* the inferiority of B relative to A, it follows that A is (logically) *dependent* on B. At this point both have the same status (they have relations in which each is dependent on the other).

Lévi-Strauss's use of the notion of reciprocity is disconcerting. He seems to contrast reciprocity with unilaterality (rather than with relations of order). He says that to eat alone is to indulge in "unilateral consumption."[50] But what would nonunilateral consumption look like? The consumer would also have to be eaten by what he is eating! In fact, one encounters unilateral relations only in intentional relations: if A loves B, that does not create a link going from B to A (this is the unreality of the intentional passive). The relation is unilateral because there is no corresponding converse relation. The shopkeeper who sees me passing by would like to sell me something, but I never even saw him; his relation to me is unilateral. When a diner eats his bread, there is a converse relation: the bread is eaten. This does not make eating bread into a reciprocal relation.

Lévi-Strauss acts as if the social bond must always be one of reciprocity. But consider a professor and his student: the teaching is not reciprocal, yet the relation between them is still a social tie. By contrast, reciprocity does not in itself entail social integration. In the restaurant in the Midi, each

50. Ibid., 61.

diner is bothered by the close proximity of his neighbor, and *reciprocally*. Each is bothered while, at the same time, each bothers others.

As Louis Dumont points out, Lévi-Strauss carries out an extreme expansion of the notion of reciprocity, which he conceives as the solution to a conflict between individuals. But it would have been more in the spirit of structural analysis to stress the requirement for a distinctive opposition not between empirical agents (e.g., myself and someone else) but between statuses or categories.[51] For Lévi-Strauss, the last word in the sociological theory of the family is the prohibition of incest. The *raison d'être* of the entire system is, for him, the necessity of exchange. Admittedly, Lévi-Strauss is invoking an intellectual necessity rather than a basic need of the species (as a crude naturalism would have it). He nevertheless posits an agent faced with an entity made up of all the others (an entity that is a *collective individual*). When I renounce marrying my sister, I give something to the others and expect them to do the same.[52] According to Dumont, the fundamental notion here should not be the reciprocity of exchanges but rather the constitution of a kinship system out of the complementary opposition between relations of consanguinity and relations of alliance.[53] More generally, the fact that the domain being investigated is a universe of rules has this for a consequence: what is investigated is not so much the conditions of "the integration of groups in the society" (as a functionalist would claim) as it is the conditions of "the integration of ideas in the mind."[54]

Lévi-Strauss was right to seek to follow Durkheim in grounding the study of societies on the study of "objectified systems of ideas."[55] He was right to turn toward mental structures. But it was a mistake to go further and claim that the mental is made up of "unconscious psychical structures." Collective representations, which make up the objective mind

---

51. Louis Dumont, *Introduction to Two Theories of Social Anthropology: Descent Groups and Marriage Alliance,* ed. and trans. Robert Parkin (New York: Berghahn Books, 2006), 96–97.

52. This is formally the exact same logic that Lévi-Strauss applies to his car: he would gladly give up using it if everyone else would agree to do the same. See Georges Charbonnier, *Conversations With Claude Lévi-Strauss,* trans. John Weightman and Doreen Weightman (1961; London: Jonathan Cape, Ltd., 1969), 50.

53. Dumont, *Two Theories,* 64–65.

54. Ibid., 97.

55. Lévi-Strauss, "French Sociology," 528.

[*esprit*] of a society, must retain the normative character of rules. Rules only exist where people think that they must be—or that they generally should be—applied. Rules meant to be applied cannot be unconscious. They may certainly be difficult to explain or describe in detail. But the structures of the mind are more like the law, which all are presumed to know [*que nul n'est censé ignorer*], than they are like the laws of physics.

10

Objective Mind

It is now possible to move to the question of the consequences of the holistic stance on language and the mind [*esprit*].[1] Recall that the critiques of holism within the philosophy of mind had raised this crucial question: does a holistic conception of the sign not render mysterious the most basic facts of communication? I cannot understand any of your speech if I am not familiar with all of it. This amounts to saying: I cannot understand you until I have plumbed the depths of your mind, until I have become like you and, ultimately, until *I* am no longer distinct from *you*. It would be

---

1. [Translator's note: The title of this chapter in French is "*L'esprit objectif.*" The word "esprit," like the German "Geist," is notoriously difficult to translate into English, for both can be rendered by either "spirit" or "mind" (as well as by a couple of other possibilities that are not relevant here). Since these two words—spirit, mind—have different meanings and applications in English, the word *esprit* represents a challenge for the translator, as English forces us to choose between them. In most of what follows, I have chosen to translate *esprit* as "mind," in order to make clear that Descombes's argument bears upon questions in what, in English, is called the philosophy of mind. However, as Descombes makes clear, the very notion of "objective mind" or "objective spirit" comes out of Hegel's use of this concept, one that was at least partly inspired by Montesquieu's notion of *esprit* as deployed in *The Spirit of the Laws* [*L'esprit des lois*]. In contemporary translations of Hegel, this notion is usually rendered as "objective spirit." Accordingly, most of the occurrences of the word *esprit* in this chapter could have been translated by the English "spirit," albeit slightly less felicitously in my view. I urge readers to keep both senses of *esprit* in mind whenever they encounter the words "mind" and "spirit" and related forms (e.g., "spiritual").]

mistaken to think that this consequence is of interest only to one contemporary school of philosophers. If that were the case, one could avoid having to deal with the problem simply by avoiding debates in so-called analytic philosophy. I believe that it is not the case, however, and it is for that reason that I will try to present the philosophical problem of communication beginning from premises that are not those of analytic philosophy. These premises are clearly traditional, since they are post-Kantian.

10.1. The Origin of Language

It will be best to take as our point of departure a discussion that reflects a deeply felt difficulty. I will therefore begin with a remark made by Jean Paulhan about Jean-Paul Sartre's theory of language, one that can be found in Paulhan's critical essay on Brice Parain's philosophy of language.[2] The entire dispute bears on an episode recounted by Parain in an unpublished manuscript that Sartre cites and comments on in the course of taking on board one of Parain's ideas. That idea turns around the diagnosis of a particular "linguistic difficulty": words betray us because, far from serving to communicate our thought to an interlocutor, they are understood in a way that is that of the interlocutor himself and not in the way that *we* understand them. Here is the passage from Sartre's text as cited by Paulhan (who edits it slightly but not in a way that would change the point that is of interest to him). This passage brings the entire subject of discussion to a head:

In order to earn a little money, he [Parain] offered to give lessons to the children of a banker. The banker immediately investigated: who was Parain? In 1920, this meant: had he been in the army? and what had he done? What could Parain answer? That he had been a private? It was the truth. But what truth? No doubt about it, it was a social truth that took its place in a system of filing-cards, notations and signs. But Parain was also a graduate of the École Normale and an

---

2. Sartre's article is entitled "Departure and Return," and was reprinted in *Literary and Philosophical Essays,* trans. Annette Michelson (1944; New York: Collier, 1962), 133–179. It bears upon Brice Parain's *Recherches sur la nature et les fonctions du langage* [Investigations on the Nature and Functions of Language] (Paris: Gallimard, 1942). Jean Paulhan's commentary on both can be found in his *Petite préface à toute critique* [A Short Preface to Any Critique], 2nd ed. (1951; Cognac: Le temps qu'il fait, 1988).

agrégé. As such, he *should have* been an officer. "In saying 'private,' I am saying that to a worker I am a pal and to a banker a suspect . . . perhaps a rebel, at any rate, a problem and not a person to be given immediate confidence." And Parain adds: "If I said 'private,' I would think as follows: negligence at the beginning, honesty of being unwilling, despite advantages, to command, because I didn't think I was able to. . . . Won't (the banker) think: lack of dignity, liking for vulgarity, lack of patriotism? By telling the truth, I deceive him more than by lying." Parain therefore chose to say "lieutenant." Not in order to lie, but so as to be understood.[3]

The text is the elaboration of a paradox: it happens that one must lie in order to tell the truth. This paradox arises out of a conflict between two truths. These two truths are signified by the very same words. Indeed, the same response bears two significations, one that belongs to the author (the *normalien*) and one that belongs to the interlocutor (the banker).

Here we once again recognize the problem of communication that emerges in a holistic philosophy.[4] Indeed, the problem raised by Parain is the following: how can the banker understand the *normalien* if the latter gives only one response? How can the *normalien* make himself understood if he only has the right to one response? In the mind and the language of the banker, the sentences that the *normalien* might pronounce seem to have a place. But they only have that place from a material point of view, for each of them has a different meaning in the banker's "system of signs" than they did in the language of the *normalien*. The word "system" is Sartre's: "In which system did the word 'private' have a meaning? That of the banker or that of the soldier, Parain?"[5] The holistic approach to signs

---

3. Sartre, "Departure and Return," 141 [translation modified]. The passage is cited by Paulhan, *Petite préface,* 86. [Translator's note: The *École Normale* is among the most prestigious French institutions of higher learning. Its graduates are known as *normaliens*. An *agrégé* is one who has passed the French national competitive examination that qualifies one for a position as a teacher.]

4. See my *The Mind's Provisions,* trans. Stephen Adam Schwartz (Princeton: Princeton University Press, 2001), Chapter 12, section 3.

5. Sartre, "Departure and Return," 142. The reader will perhaps wonder how the speaker using the soldier's system can know the "unexpected repercussions" (Ibid., 141) of what he was about to say upon an interlocutor who uses the banker's system. One might say that, in this case, the speaker is bilingual. Parain is a peasant *and* a *normalien*. Sartre provides a different explanation, one that seems incompatible with the thesis of an unavoidable misunderstanding: that there is in reality only one available system, one language, and it is the system of the dominant classes. Those dominated are reduced to

(i.e., understanding a sentence presupposes that one knows with what other sentences it is given) would seem to ruin the possibility of communication. Since this would seem to be the case for every sentence, it is difficult to see how one might ever overcome endless misunderstanding.

This paradox calls for a solution. The solution will depend, for Parain as for Sartre, on a thesis on the origins of language. Parain adopts two opposing responses in succession: first, that man is the author of language; next, that God is. He calls these solutions "communistic" and "religious," respectively.[6] Sartre rejects both solutions as facile and seeks to provide a phenomenological solution—that the origin of language lies in the human subject's mode of being, which Sartre calls "existence in the presence of another."[7] He will therefore attempt to derive objective mind (i.e., language) from the subjective minds of the interlocutors.

By contrast, for Paulhan the problem raised by the two philosophers is a *false* problem. Paulhan's criticism is actually even more stern: it is a false problem typical of the way philosophers go about things. Once again, he says, philosophers begin by announcing their attention to develop a philosophy of language, but in the end, after having written a great many pages and discussed a great many subjects—love, power, inequality, the human condition, etc.—they manage to avoid talking about language and, indeed, show few signs of having thought about it at all. Paulhan calls for the philosophers of language to show a bit more diligence: if they introduce their ideas as a philosophy of language, it behooves them to talk to us about the same stuff that stylists, grammarians, and lexicographers do.[8] Their texts will therefore have to contain considerations on the meaning of terms, the equivalence between different forms of expression,

---

silence for the time being: "He had to choose either to manage with the system that had already been established or to be silent" (Ibid., 142). However, in the rest of Sartre's article, this notion of the relations of force that allow a banker to impose his language on a job seeker is no longer under consideration and is replaced by a conflict of consciousnesses that is part of the human condition, a conflict that results in the misunderstanding inherent in all communication.

6. Paulhan's commentary suggests that these might be two opposed religious solutions: "Thus, based on a single experience, Brice Parain is led first to an activist and arrogant doctrine, then to the opposite—mystical, contemplative—doctrine" (Paulhan, *Petite préface*, 88). The opposition between the active and the contemplative cuts across the category of the religious, as Max Weber demonstrated.

7. Sartre, "Departure and Return," 173.

8. Paulhan, *Petite préface*, 99–100.

the construction of statements, etc. One imagines that Paulhan would have approved perhaps not the theses but at least the approaches of the Scholastic authors of speculative grammars or contemporary philosophers in the mold of Frege and Russell.

Why is Sartre and Parain's problem a false one? Because, according to Paulhan, in Parain's vignette the words fulfill their mission. There is no betrayal by language, no linguistic disorder or disruption of communication.

Let us return to the example of the banker. Where is the betrayal by words, where are the shaky levers and the play in the gears described by Parain? At first glance, I cannot see them. The banker wants to know, simply, what Parain was; he hears, I imagine "a private." He is informed. What did Parain want to say or have to say? That he was a private? Well, he said it! Exactly and accurately. If I were looking for a case in which language worked perfectly, this one would fit the bill.[9]

Paulhan is right to reject the paradox. Parain would not have lied or spoken falsely by telling the truth (i.e., "social truth"). Paulhan is right, but only on condition that the banker wants to know Parain's status during the war *and nothing more than that.* The philosopher defending the thesis of a betrayal by language will respond that this is impossible. The banker is not seeking to learn this simple fact; he is asking the question in order to determine who Parain is. Only by means of an arbitrary abstraction can the two senses of the banker's question be separated from each other. What was Parain during the war? This does not just mean: was he a private or an officer? It also and especially means: can I trust you? The human relation (the relation from person to person) that is expressed in this second meaning cannot be separated from the first (literal and immediate) meaning. If we abstract from the intention of the question and the intention of the response, the phenomenon of linguistic exchange has been reduced such that our investigation takes place at a level removed from what speaking really is. Paulhan can claim that words mean what we say through them only if he has taken up an abstract point of view.

Sartre rejects such an abstract point of view; he praises Parain's approach by setting it off against that of a hypothetical linguist who conceives of his

---

9. Ibid., 89–90.

discipline in a way that other phenomenologists would call "objectifying."[10] "The linguist usually acts like a man sure of his ideas and concerned only with knowing whether the old and traditional institution of language renders them accurately."[11] Sartre then provides an example: a linguist is looking for a French equivalent of the German word *Stimmung*, "which supposes that the corresponding idea exists for the Frenchman as it does for the German and that the only question that arises is that of its expression."[12]

This study of language (reduced to the study of vocabularies) is one that Sartre sees as the study of an "anonymous" language, of language as it is "when spoken by no one."[13] Parain, on the other hand, is interested in language as it is spoken and thus in a particular situation in which a particular someone—a particular subject—is speaking ("What interests him is the language of this soldier, this worker, this revolutionary").[14] Sartre takes sides here, in favor of the *expressive word* that is opposed to the *institution of language* considered as something impersonally given. Both philosophers (Parain and Sartre) mean to repudiate what has since been called the "myth of meaning" (Quine). They denounce the illusion of "objective meanings." To explain the meaning of a word cannot consist in identifying anything whatever or putting one's finger on something and saying, "this is what the German word and the French word mean." In order to break free from this illusion, they invite us to return to the speaking subject.

As a result, Paulhan's position begins to seem simplistic. It is true that in the dictionary the word "private" means nothing more than *private*. But it means much more in the mouth of a *normalien* or a banker.

There can therefore be no other solution to the problem of making oneself understood to a banker than to direct one's intention, in the sense given to this idea by the moralistic theologians criticized by Pascal: we can change the moral description of our action by *deciding* that our intention while doing it was directed toward the good and that there was nothing

---

10. Sartre speaks of "an objective study of the medium of sound" (Sartre, "Departure and Return," 135), which is precisely what one will not find in Parain, a fact that Sartre applauds.
11. Ibid., 135–136.
12. Ibid., 136.
13. Ibid [translation modified].
14. Ibid [translation modified].

malicious in it.[15] Similarly, by declaring that he had been a lieutenant, Brice Parain undeniably tells a lie, but a lie that is merely *material* (it so happens that he was not a lieutenant). Moreover, his *formal* intention was to tell the truth. Formally, his response is therefore truthful, since only this falsehood can, according to him, communicate the truth (regarding his worthy character) to his interlocutor.

Yet Paulhan remains correct on this precise point. Parain's paradox, as recounted by Sartre, is a false problem. In order for the paradox to be a real paradox, the word "private" in the *normalien*'s mouth (in the particular circumstance in which it is being used, of course, and not generally or "anonymously") would have to be translated in the banker's idiom (in his idiom at that instant in the conversation) by "lieutenant" so as to mean, ultimately, "I am worthy of your confidence."

In fact, the notion of a literal meaning cannot be shed as easily as Sartre seems to think. Paulhan is right to reproach philosophers (or at least the two he is discussing) for their ignorance of this point: every theory of meaning must allow for the assignation of a literal meaning.[16] When the banker hears "lieutenant," he (perhaps) draws this conclusion: lieutenant during the war, therefore honest and worthy of confidence. This conclusion is not the one he would have drawn had he heard "private." Parain wants the banker to conclude: this *normalien* is an honest young man. Anticipating that the banker will think like a banker, he gives him a false premise so that the banker's reasoning will come to a conclusion that is materially true (or at least agrees with what Parain feels is a more accurate judgment of his moral character). This entire operation thus relies on the fact that the words first have a literal meaning. The word "lieutenant" in Parain's response, as in the banker's linguistic system, means *lieutenant*. It does not mean *worthy of confidence*. The response "I was a lieutenant" has a literal meaning and has one and only one such literal meaning. This is what Paulhan is pointing out—language here works perfectly.

No doubt the banker will derive various *conclusions* from Parain's response. And one might well say that there is nothing to stop him from

---

15. Blaise Pascal, Letter VII of *The Provincial Letters*, trans. Thomas M'Crie, in *Pensées, The Provincial Letters* (New York: The Modern Library, 1941), 402–417.

16. This conclusion has more recently also been advanced by Donald Davidson in his article "What Metaphors Mean" in his *Inquiries Into Truth and Interpretation*, 2nd ed. (Oxford: Clarendon Press, 2001), 245–264.

seeing these conclusions as meanings of the sentence within this particular context. When one asks what the question and response mean, one is asking what the people involved mean by them—what the questioner wants to learn and what the respondent wants him to know or think. In other words, a *pragmatics* of language can be put in place in order to determine what a given statement communicates (to a banker in a given interview) and to determine whether, in doing so, it transmits the speaker's intentions.

All of these points can be granted, yet none of that prevents the statement from having a literal meaning. The literal meaning will indeed be the starting point from which the banker will arrive at his conclusion, precisely the conclusion that Parain wants to prevent him from reaching too hastily. Because the word "private" perfectly fits the intention of a speaker who wants to say "I was a private," it is subsequently possible for interpretations of this fact to diverge. But what is then at issue is not the interpretation of the statement, rather the interpretation of a biographical fact: what should one think of a *normalien* who refuses to become an officer despite having the possibility open to him and, in the banker's view, the obligation to take it? Parain contests, reasonably enough, the principles of the train of thought he ascribes to the banker. But language is not in question here, and this is what Paulhan is rightly pointing out. Parain and Sartre blamed language itself rather than simply taking note of a difference between two systems of thought. Language has nothing to do with it. How did it happen that the charge was leveled against it? It is through a transfer that Paulhan compares to that carried out by "primitive kings" who condemned to death the bearers of bad news. "If language has not *created* the misunderstanding, it has at least *revealed* it in a place where it was not expected."[17] It is precisely because the words exchanged have been understood that disagreement can arise regarding the conclusions to be drawn. The disagreement bears not on the meaning of the words but, rather, on the meaning of the things signified by the words—for example, on the meaning of the decisions of Parain as a young man or on the way in which people ought to be judged.

How, then, is the problem of the origins of language raised? And, first of all, how is it that the fable of the *normalien* and the banker inspires Parain,

---

17. Paulhan, *Petite préface*, 94.

and then Sartre, to engage in reflections regarding the origins of language? Obviously, for philosophers, it is not about carrying out speculative paleontological research but rather about reflecting upon the nature and functions of language from a different angle.

The story Parain tells, in his view, is that of a failure of language as an instrument. Sartre says this: "Words were all about him, like eager servants. He had only to take them. And yet, no sooner did he want to use them than they betrayed him."[18] Here Sartre claims that Parain had an experience of being dispossessed: since words do not mean (on their arrival) what I wanted them to mean (on their departure), it must be that the instrument is not acting as my docile servant, for I have no control over it. Sartre also compares the general situation of man as a speaking being to that of people who suffer from having their very thoughts robbed.[19] These people complain that their thought has been diverted within them from its original meaning before it was even formulated. The same would be true of thought that has been expressed, with the difference being that the diversion takes place somewhere between the speaker and his interlocutor. "They're not so crazy. We all have the same experience. Words drink our thought before we have time to recognize it. We have a vague intention, we clarify it by means of words and suddenly we find ourselves saying something quite different from what we meant."[20] This is just what happens to Parain: the bankers "worm their way into him" and rob him, if not of his thoughts themselves, at least of his statements, his thoughts as they are expressed.

Opposing conclusions can be drawn from this experience. If language is a human institution, if man is the author of language, then the task will be to regain the control of words. This will involve expressing oneself in forms and with a tone such that the effect on the hearer is exactly what one hoped to produce. This is the "Leninist" solution and amounts in fact to abandoning all communication in language. Unable to make oneself understood to others, one seeks to direct them through "watchwords."

18. Sartre, "Departure and Return," 140.
19. Ibid., 143.
20. Ibid.

Sartre is well aware of the contradiction in this position: the individualist believes it possible to reunite with others by subjecting himself to "community discipline."[21]

The communist solution is doomed to failure. Far from restoring man's mastery of his instrument, it destroys language. Parain is therefore forced to the other solution: man is not the author of language and must therefore conform to it, accepting its law. Parain here outlines a solution that will be taken up again and again in later years: not knowing which way to turn, we still have the possibility of grounding an ethics in the "law of language" (as it will later be called), i.e., on honesty in the use of words. Indeed, language offers to individualists who have been disabused of communist artificialism palpable proof of a salutary discipline, for it is precisely when we agree to use words in their established meanings that our thinking is facilitated. This is, as Sartre emphasizes, a conservative solution in that one must endeavor to subject one's life to the superior order that is present in language itself (superior in that it does not come from us).

It is nevertheless doubtful that one could ever found anything other than a discipline governing expression upon the authority of language. How could the "law of language" ever constitute anything more than a purely linguistic community? For example, why would this law direct us to be faithful to the demands of the words "love" and "promise" rather than those of the words "crime" and "dishonor"? In what way could the order of vocabulary bear within it a morality? Does this not amount, once again, to refusing to recognize the autonomy that is proper to the task of expression in a language?

Parain's conclusions are not those of a philosophy of language in the sense demanded by Paulhan. They are nevertheless not entirely irrelevant, bearing as they do on the conditions of possibility for the institution of common meanings. Is it conceivable that an institution be controlled by individuals, and, especially, is it conceivable in the paradigm case of language, the institution in which such control is exercised?

---

21. Ibid., 152. This Leninist activism cannot fail to remind us of Orwell's "Newspeak" in his *Nineteen Eighty-Four*.

If there were only two kinds of response permitted—the "communist" one and the "theological" one—I believe that a transcendent origin is preferable to a human one.[22] The theological response is less foolish than the response that depends on a convention agreed among humans, not because it is, strictly speaking, in any way illuminating—in fact, it is not illuminating at all—but because it rules out the illusion that language has been *forged* by people in order to fill the need that they have to communicate with one another.

Sartre for his part rejected the need for a philosophy of language, either in the grammarians' sense or in the sense of a "metaphysics of language" like Parain's. Problems of expression are technical or logical problems with no philosophical implications. Not that Sartre rejects Parain's diagnosis: "language betrays me." Rather, it is Parain's explanation of this betrayal that he rejects. For Sartre, language "is only existence in the presence of another"; it is "the mere surface of contact between me and the Other."[23] Needless to say, if language has no more philosophical depth than a surface, there is no need for the philosopher to engage with problems of logical or syntactical construction.

How does Sartre manage to set aside language problems? He does it in two stages. First, he posits a sphere of the mind [*esprit*] in which language does not yet appear: the *cogito,* the silent act of self-presence. Then, he shows that the meaning of my intentions is betrayed in advance, even before they have been expressed, by virtue of the fact that others are others and are not me.

In the first part of his argument, Sartre seeks to show that neither society nor God is required in an account of language. Everything can be explained solely by positing an individual confronting another individual. In other words, Sartre seeks to derive objective mind (i.e., institutions) from subjective mind (i.e., consciousnesses). His solution is to place the word on the side of the object, giving it the same status as, say, an inkwell—the status of consciousness's opposite number (consciousness being, for Sartre, what I am when I am authentically myself). Consider an inkwell. How is it that I confront the same inkwell each time that I see it, rather than different inkwells? I must have *recognized* it. This recognition passes through the

---

22. The response is "theological" rather than "religious" because the language given to humans by the gods or by God is a human language, not a sacred one.

23. Sartre, "Departure and Return," 173–174.

sorts of "identifying syntheses" that phenomenologists have described. The same is true of the word. The linguistic sign must also be constituted by consciousness. The word has no privilege over the inkwell; it must also present itself through profiles and successive manifestations.[24]

In the phenomenologist's lexicon, to "objectify" something is to account for its diachronic identity. As soon as we raise the problem of the *same object*—of the relatively stable object—we must refer to the operations of consciousness by which objects are "revealed."[25] Language therefore forms part of what must be constituted, i.e., the world.

In this way, Sartre replaced the problem of the *identity* of the word with the problem of the *recognition* of the word through its sensuous appearance. He can then conclude that in linguistic matters consciousness is authoritative and not language (in the next section, I will say that he has substituted an objectified mind for objective mind). Sartre does not see the limits of his phenomenalism. In fact, such a reduction of the identity of the word to the consciousness of facing the same word is illegitimate. One might have the same word in unrecognizable forms, for example in the Roman alphabet, in Morse code, or in braille. Yet it is still the same word. Imagine that someone shows me a book in braille and tells me: here is Stendhal's *Le rouge et le noir* [The Red and the Black] in braille. I can easily *understand* that it is not only the same novel but the very same text, the same French words, yet without having the means to *recognize* anything at all.

When I understand a word, according to Sartre, I must be conscious of understanding it. No doubt he means something like this: when I understand a word, I am present so as to understand it; I am present to myself. The word is *before me* and therefore I am present to myself without having to say anything or use any words.[26] He therefore means that the philosopher has the right to proceed to the self-positing of the self within a sphere that precedes all language and all expression. As a result, what I have to say is also given in a silent self-presence before all language. It is afterwards that things go off the rails: at the moment of expressing myself, I use words—my words—which are also the words of others. At no point can I control language such that my words would have for others their original

24. Ibid., 170.
25. Ibid., 177.
26. Ibid., 171–172.

meaning, but I can always, for my part, return to the initial muteness of the *cogito*.

I know what it is that I want to express because I *am* it without intermediary. Language may resist and mislead me, but I shall never be taken in by it unless I want to, for I can always come back to what I am, to the emptiness and silence that I am, through which, nevertheless, there is a language and there is a world.[27]

Thanks to the trump card of the silent *cogito,* Sartre hopes to maintain his thesis (one he calls "humanist") that each of us is at the origin of language and, moreover, of the world—or, rather, of the meaning of the world as it is constituted by the successive appearances and profiles that are given to me.

In Sartre's dualist system, on one side there is the Ego, which is entirely self-identical but underdetermined. It is an *infinite* ego—in the sense that it is indeterminate and incomplete—since it must remain *before* language in order to coincide with itself: any kind of determination would be an alienation. On the opposing side, there is the Other [*Autrui*]. The presence of the other disrupts things since everything is taken from me, not by language but by the "existential" conflict between two subjectivities. Language is but the manifestation of this conflict. In this world perceived within the perspective of being-for-another, the ego is determined, *finite,* but also alienated.[28]

In a second part of his argument, Sartre reduces the problem of the meaning of words to the problem of the meaning of gestures that are observed by an onlooker who is not obliged to empathize with me. In Sartre's view, the "language sickness" diagnosed by Parain amounts to a fundamental feature of human existence:

If . . . when I speak, I have the agonizing certainty that words escape me and that they will take on elsewhere, outside me, unexpected aspects and unforeseen meanings, does this not mean that it is inherent in the very structure of language to be understood by a freedom other than my own?[29]

---

27. Ibid., 172.
28. Alain Renaut has pointed out the affinities between Sartre's philosophy of freedom and that of Fichte. See his *Sartre, le dernier philosophe* (Paris: Grasset, 1993).
29. Sartre, "Departure and Return," 173 [translation modified].

This is an excellent way of stating something that every thesis on the structure of language must take on board: it is part of the *structure* of language that the words I pronounce must be *understood* by a freedom that is not mine. In other words, there must be a relation between two freedoms, two powers of initiative. This allows us to come to the immediate conclusion that *the very structure of language* will slip away from any philosophy driven to the following admission: the world is badly constructed, for it is impossible for the words that I (freely) form to be understood in their meaning by someone else (freely) exercising her understanding by attending to what I say in a language that we both speak. But this is just what happens to Sartre's philosophy in this text. He thinks he can reduce the common language to existence in the presence of others, using the following rationale: as soon as there are others, the meaning of my gesture is no longer the meaning that I, author of the gesture, wish to give it; instead, it is the meaning that the other gives it (i.e., the same phenomenon of theft and diversion of thoughts, this time due to the simple presence of others rather than to words). Here is the example that Sartre uses to support his thesis:

Take, for example, the case of a woman who stands watching me shrewdly, full of hatred, without saying a word, as I move about the room. All my gestures are immediately alienated from me, stolen from me. They form a horrible composition of whose existence I am unaware. There, in the fire of her gaze, I am clumsy and ridiculous. . . . There you have language as a whole; it is precisely this silent and desperate dialogue. Language is being-for-another.[30]

It is worth noting that lack of understanding is a one-way street: the meaning of my conduct is deformed when stated by others, but the hateful meaning of the woman's gaze appears clearly to me. It is nevertheless strange, Paulhan remarks, to make claims about "language as a whole" based on a scene where nobody says a word. The philosopher's thinking must have somehow been "short-circuited."[31] This short circuit came about, I believe, when Sartre began by praising Parain for having avoided dealing with anonymous language, failing to notice that Parain was

30. Ibid. [translation modified].
31. Paulhan, *Petite préface*, 97–98.

thereby abandoning the position from which to discuss literal meaning and, ultimately, other (figurative) meanings of the words used.

The question that Paulhan addresses to the philosophers is thus altogether relevant: in putting forward your philosophy of language, in what way are you talking about the same thing as are the grammarian and the prose stylist? If language is truly what is being discussed, one condition must be fulfilled: meaning must be able to be detached from individuals so that language can be considered impersonally. If your philosophy deals with language, you must have recognized the possibility of isolating a level at which the words "private" and "lieutenant" mean the same thing for both the speaker and the hearer. This is the level of *common meanings*.

This presupposition is a condition *sine qua non* for your philosophy having anything to tell us about language. After granting it, every declaration against abstraction or the separation of the word from the idea and language from the individual, all of the condemnations of anonymity and abstraction are like a lawyer's dramatic gesticulating: they have no affect on the grounds of the case. Moreover, we have ourselves seen that the episode presented by Parain and then invoked by Sartre assumed that the two interlocutors were actually perfectly able to understand each other, that the *normalien* understood quite well what the banker was going to think, while the banker would have no difficulty drawing a distinction between, for example, "private" and "*normalien* and (yet a mere) private."

The question is therefore not one of knowing whether there are common meanings but whether our philosophy is up to the task of making room for them, of defining their status within our general conception of language and communication. What status should they be given? How is it that there is no conflict between two systems of signs but rather a conflict between two ways of thinking that manifests itself when the two thinkers speak to each other using the same language? Parain is right to say that neither of the interlocutors is at the origin of language. But to speak of a superhuman origin of language is pointless, nothing but a figurative way of reiterating that language is neither a personal system of expression nor a convention between two subjects but, rather, a social institution.

10.2. Objectified Mind

Sartre and Parain agree on at least one point: language is external to us in the same way that an inkwell is external to us. This idea may already be the germ of the "exteriority of the signifier to the subject" that later so exercised the structuralists.

Both of them talk about "transcendence" in this regard. But the notion is ambiguous because in principle what is at issue is an exteriority, yet the word "transcendence" implies something more than an exteriority—namely, a superiority and perhaps an authority. Parain writes:

> The fact that language is an entity exterior to us—even though, at first glance, it seems to be a manifestation of our existence—is already visible in the form in which it appears when it takes on its most solemn face: the book, i.e. an object similar to a tree or a house and as foreign to its readers and its author as the house and the tree are to the man who planted or built them. This is also visible in all of the monuments in which it dwells among us: the tablets, inscriptions, parchments, manuscripts, printed matter that make up libraries. . . .[32]

Merleau-Ponty criticized this manner of "objectifying" words. In a passage from the *Phenomenology of Perception,* he takes up the very same example given by Sartre: understanding the word *grésil* [sleet].[33] Sartre seeks to put the word before us like an inkwell (or like Parain's tree and house). He thus wants to "constitute" it from its "profiles" and "appearances." But, according to Merleau-Ponty, to do that is to confuse the *represented* word (which takes on the status of an object that I can inspect) and the word as it is *used*. The latter, insofar as it participates in personal expression, should be thought of as part of the constituting subject and not as part of the object being constituted. The word is a gesture, a form of corporeal presence (phonation, articulation), rather than an object.

Merleau-Ponty is right to find fault with Sartre's dualism. However, the invocation of the body's expressivity fails to provide a solution to the problem of the identity of the sign. Indeed, it appears that this identity can only be fully guaranteed by the gesture detaching itself entirely from the speaking body in order to become an endlessly transmissible text or the equivalent of one. And Merleau-Ponty is in no position to deny this point since this is precisely how he himself constitutes objective

---

32. Parain, *Recherches,* 7–8.
33. Maurice Merleau-Ponty, *Phenomenology of Perception,* trans. Colin Smith (New York: Routledge, 1962), 468. See also Sartre, "Departure and Return," 168–171. [Translator's note: In the English translation of Sartre's text, the word *grésil* has been rendered as "pellet."]

mind.³⁴ By that he means a cultural world or a society that is given to perception in things. "An Objective Mind [*un esprit objectif*] dwells in artifacts and landscapes."³⁵

This idea, Merleau-Ponty acknowledges, might seem paradoxical. He writes: "How can an action or a human thought be grasped in the mode of the impersonal 'one' [*on*] since, by its very nature, it is a first person operation, inseparable from an *I*?"³⁶ Here is how Merleau-Ponty introduces the notion of objective mind in the course of explaining that the lifeworld is not only physical but also cultural:

Not only have I a physical world, not only do I live in the midst of earth, air and water, I have around me roads, plantations, villages, streets, churches, implements, a bell, a spoon, a pipe. Each of these objects is moulded to the human action which it serves. Each one spreads round it an atmosphere of humanity which may be determinate in a low degree, in the case of a few footmarks in the sand, or on the other hand highly determinate, if I go into every room from top to bottom of a house recently evacuated.³⁷

How has Merleau-Ponty derived this concept of objective mind? All of the examples he gives make reference to situations of exodus or of desolation: roads with no travelers, streets devoid of pedestrians, churches abandoned by the faithful, material traces of a lost habitation. Here, the objectivity ascribed to objective mind tends to be confused with the materiality of the equipment and tools that remain after the disappearance of those who used them. What Merleau-Ponty retains from this notion is that it allows us to refer to a Mind or Spirit that is given not just *outside* of human subjects, but in their *absence*. In order to have a pure objective mind in Merleau-Ponty's sense, some form of human life must be given in order then to subtract from it everything that is a *subject*: what remains is then objective mind. Take a house without its inhabitants: what remains

---

34. What follows recapitulates an argument presented at a colloquium at Cerisy-la-Salle in June 1995 devoted to Charles Taylor. See my "Pourquoi les sciences morales ne sont-elles pas des sciences naturelles?" in Guy Laforest and Philippe de Lara (eds.), *Charles Taylor et l'interprétation de l'identité moderne* (Quebec: Presses de l'Université Laval, 1998), 53–78.
35. Merleau-Ponty, *Phenomenology,* 405 [translation modified].
36. Ibid.
37. Ibid.

OBJECTIVE MIND 287

are furniture, utensils, clothes. Take a city after a volcanic eruption or a tidal wave: what remains are ruins and relics. Such a concept of objective mind is ambivalent in nature. The meaningful thing is an insufficient residue, a simple trace (for the essential thing, the presence of subjects, is precisely what is lacking), but it is also an artifact and therefore a possible starting point for rediscovering the life or the thought that is deposited within it (for one can always, at least in principle, "reactivate the meaning" that has been lodged within material things).

The goal is to posit something in between (between man-mind and nature-matter), an intermediary category (that also seeks to mediate). Merleau-Ponty writes (implicitly against Sartre) that this must create a problem for a *dualist* philosophy that holds that there are "two modes of being": on the one hand "objects arrayed in space" or being-in-itself and, on the other, the mode of being of consciousness, i.e., of being-for-itself, which is aware of its existence and its states.[38]

The required intermediary is the human object. Objective mind, after having been introduced as the crystallized result of a human act—i.e., a subjective act that presents itself as the trace left behind in material things—now begins to look like an impersonal mind. This impersonal status of mind is engendered by the transition from the productive act to the product, from the operation to the result: a result that has *detached itself*. For example, the activity of writing results in a written page. Subjectivity expresses itself until a moment comes when it has expressed itself entirely. It has expressed itself so well that its expression has ultimately liberated itself from the subject that bore it, in order to coalesce into the form of a "speaking trace" that allows it to subsist in the manner of a thing.[39] Objective mind, in this acceptation, corresponds to the collections of a museum of archaeology or of popular arts and traditions. It is therefore possible to study mind in an impersonal form.

Contemporary textualism generalizes the notion of an objective trace by taking the archive, rather than an archaeological museum, as its model of objective mind. Because the pipe and the spoon must be understood and can only be understood through interpretation, they are texts in their own way. It will then be claimed that, in the human sciences, the given

---

38. Ibid., 407.
39. Ibid., 406 [translation modified].

presents itself as a *text* and its explanation as a *translation* or *interpretation* in the exegetical sense. Wherever the given has a textual aspect, we are in the domain of a hermeneutic science.[40]

Let us return to Merleau-Ponty's examples. The mind that is present outside of individual consciousnesses is above all a practical mind, a mind that manifests itself in gestures and behaviors the traces of which can later be uncovered. Various objects are mentioned as examples of such material traces of a spiritual presence [*une présence spirituelle*].[41] But there is an important distinction to be drawn among these objects. Some of them can be comprehended by all those who are able to mobilize within their own bodies the practical knowledge required in order to use the object. Understanding in these cases passes by an arousing of bodily techniques. One can say of someone who thus understands the object by imagining using it that he *imagines it in his body,* by opposition to a purely intellectual imagination in which one imagines such possibilities without awakening a corporeal schema or putting the body in a state of attentiveness. Someone who does not know how to swim the butterfly stroke, dance the polka, or drive a car can imagine doing such things in his head but not imagine doing them in his body.

Confronted with a pipe, I imagine myself smoking it: I imagine (in my body) grabbing the pipe, filling it with tobacco, bringing a flame toward the pipe to light it, breathing in the smoke without swallowing it, etc. The entirety of this exercise of the imagination is an outline of the human reaction to a human object by someone who grasps its practical sense. To understand in this way is to rediscover the subject—the pipe smoker— behind the bit of objectified mind that the pipe is. This pipe smoker is not a particular person, for example the historical owner of this particular pipe preserved in the archaeological museum; he is, rather, any such smoker, anyone who engages in this activity and knows the gestures involved.

However, in Merleau-Ponty's list there is one object that is of a different order: the bell. To understand the meaning of the bell, it is not enough to imagine ringing it or hearing it ringing. One has to imagine a little

---

40. I believe that this use of the term "hermeneutic" is improper. In order for the "texts" (in both the narrow and the broad sense) that come to us to have an authentic hermeneutic status, it is not enough that they be objects of a textual sort. They must also be received as forming a *bequest* requiring a response.

41. [Translator's note: "Spirituelle" is the adjectival counterpart of "esprit" and could just as easily be translated here as "mental" (i.e., of the *esprit* or mind).]

scenario, that one is in the place of someone ordering something by ringing the bell or in the place of someone who responds appropriately upon hearing the bell. In old apartments one sometimes finds a bell system linking the dining room with the office. In order to understand this fragment of objectified mind, one must grasp the *social relation* that gives it its meaning. I imagine myself seated at a table and ringing for the maid, or I imagine myself waiting in the kitchen for the masters to give me the signal to bring the next dish.

There is a difference in kind between the human meanings borne by objects such as a pipe or a plow and those borne by a bell. Smoking a pipe and plowing a field are human actions that call for certain techniques of the body and perhaps elicit them in the subject who confronts these objects. To ring for one's servant or to serve one's master on his signal are both behaviors whose correspondence to each other is not physical. Nothing in the bell or the noise it makes can determine, outside of an institution, the correct way to react. Here again, understanding requires imagination.[42] What has to be imagined is a two-person scenario, which means that one must imagine the gestures to be accomplished *by each of the two people*. What one must imagine is thus not so much gestures as it is the complementary social statuses involved.

Raymond Aron pointed out that Dilthey borrowed the expression "objective mind" from Hegel and modified the notion in doing so. Dilthey wanted to strip it of its speculative character so that it would no longer involve presenting the study of law, of ethics, and of politics as intermediate moments within the development of the idea of mind (between the first moment of "subjective mind" and the third moment of "absolute mind"). As a result, according to Aron, Dilthey broadens and redefines the notion. What the human sciences study are the manifestations of human life, of the life of individuals. Whence derives the concept's new field of application:

[L]anguage, mores, form (or style) of life as well as family, bourgeois society, the State, law and even art, religion and philosophy: all belong to objective mind.

---

42. Cornelius Castoriadis long insisted both on the necessary role of the investigator's imagination in his understanding of a foreign form of life as well as on what such a role presupposes: that the imagination is also at work in the institution of society. See his *The Imaginary Institution of Society,* trans. Kathleen Blamey (Cambridge, MA: MIT Press, 1987).

They are tangible realities into which life has deposited mind. From the most ephemeral word to the "bronze untouched by time," from the individual to the species, *everything given to the senses and able to be understood is the data for the human sciences [sciences de l'esprit].*[43]

This broadening of the notion obviously represents progress, even if it can also be claimed that Montesquieu had already understood the notion of a spirit of the laws [*un esprit des lois*] in the broadest sense (e.g., by including within the study of Chinese laws the study of Chinese religion). But one has the feeling that the notion of a "manifestation" or, even more, "expression" of life here fills two functions. The first is a function of helping to define the contents of objective mind; thus, the mind of Chinese civilization is expressed in its laws, in its worship, in its conception of the emperor. To speak of objective mind is to invite us to seek a meaningful totality within the manifestations of mind. This is the holistic aspect of the notion, which implies a thesis about mind [*esprit*] (which cannot be treated atomistically). But there is also an epistemological function of the notion, one that serves to indicate how the historian or sociologist is to carry out the reconstitution of the object to be known: objective mind is the given, the starting point, what it is that requires interpretation. The accent is placed on the solid, durable, and transportable aspect of the "traces" and "inscriptions." Aron writes regarding Dilthey's idea: "Surrounded by a real but inanimate past, amidst ruins, monuments, and books, man constructs the historical world because he gives life to these spiritual traces."[44]

However, something important would be lost if we remained confined within objectified mind as taken up by Merleau-Ponty, i.e., within what contemporary textualism calls the "text" to be interpreted. In the hermeneutic recasting of the Hegelian notion of objective mind—one that is meant to unburden it of its speculative missions within the system—something disappears or tends to disappear: we lose sight of the *normative* character of the facts that it must allow us to conceptualize. When objective mind inheres in the archives, for example in public records or collections of newspapers, we encounter texts but not what Hegel understood by

---

43. Raymond Aron, *La philosophie critique de l'histoire: Essai sur une théorie allemande de l'histoire,* 2nd ed. (1938; Paris: J. Vrin, 1950), 72 (italics in original).
44. Ibid.

the term "objective mind"—a totality that is meaningful because it gives a meaning to life and to action along the model of what Montesquieu called the spirit of the laws of a people.

As we have said, the notions of subjective and objective mind are Hegelian in origin. This historical note clears nothing up, of course, for such Hegelian notions are notoriously difficult to grasp without reproducing the entire system. Fortunately, in the case of this concept, we are not dealing with a purely Hegelian notion. In reality, Hegel used this notion as a way of integrating into the philosophy of mind the work of historians such as Montesquieu who moved beyond the level of simple narration. In fact, within the Hegelian system, the "philosophy of objective mind" corresponds to what, in the tradition, is called practical philosophy (the philosophy of law, of mores, and of the State). Hegel himself indicated that he found an anticipation of his idea of "objective mind" in Montesquieu's notion of a spirit of the laws.

What did Hegel take from Montesquieu? He took from him the holism that is inherent in the idea of a spirit or general intention of a system of laws and, more generally, of customs.

With regard to the historical element in positive right . . . Montesquieu stated the true historical view, the genuinely philosophical viewpoint, that legislation in general and its particular determinations should not be considered in isolation and in the abstract, but rather as a dependent moment within *one* totality, in the context of all the other determinations which constitute the character of a nation and age; within this context they gain their genuine significance, and hence also their justification.[45]

This reference by Hegel is invaluable because what interests us here is less the notion of objective mind as an orthodox Hegelian would understand it than it is the whole family of notions whose eponymous ancestor is the very idea of a spirit of laws and institutions. Among the members of this family, one might cite: Dilthey's objective mind or "meaningful

---

45. G. W. F. Hegel, *Elements of the Philosophy of Right*, ed. Allen W. Wood, trans. H. B. Nisbet (Cambridge: Cambridge University Press, 1991), 29.

totality"; Durkheim's "collective consciousness," the American anthropologists' "culture"; and the "symbolic systems" of structuralist anthropologists.

Within Montesquieu's work, we find the principal elements required to define objective mind. It is essentially a holistic principle. Montesquieu asks "in what way two different laws can be compared."[46] His example is the English and French laws against false witness: which is better? The answer is that these laws belong to systems, and one cannot therefore compare them in isolation. "Thus, in order to judge which of these laws is more in conformity with reason, they must not be compared one by one; they must be taken all together and compared together."[47] Montesquieu certainly does not mean this as a Quinian holist would—that one cannot compare a French law and an English law *at all* (i.e., that only the two bodies of legislation should be evaluated). He means that, when comparing a French law and an English law, one must always remember that one is in fact comparing a part of the body of French legislation with a part of the body of English legislation.

This is exactly the concept of a meaningful whole, a concept that Montesquieu will go on to extend beyond systems of legislation proper to mores and manners and, more generally, to what we would call the culture of a people. Montesquieu refers to a *total manner of thinking*: "Peoples, like each individual, have a sequence of ideas, and their total manner of thinking, like that of each individual, has a beginning, a middle, and an end."[48] To study a people or a society is to study just such a way of thinking.

Objective mind, taken in the Hegelian sense rather than in that of Dilthey or Merleau-Ponty, should be understood by contrast with the facts of the psychic life of individuals. The Hegelian sense therefore corresponds to what the Durkheimian school holds to be the object of sociology. Aron writes that the historical object "is not made up only of psychic events, but of *objective mind,* institutions and systems which control the infinite

---

46. Montesquieu, *The Spirit of the Laws,* ed. and trans. Anne M. Cohler, Basia C. Miller, and Harold S. Stone (Cambridge: Cambridge University Press, 1989), 608.

47. Ibid.

48. Montesquieu, *My Thoughts,* ed. and trans. Henry C. Clark (Indianapolis: Liberty Fund, 2012), 533.

plurality of individual actions."⁴⁹ Aron proposes to draw a distinction between the two notions in the following way:

> Let us give the name *objectified mind* [*esprit objectivé*] (to use M. N. Hartmann's expression) to what Dilthey called objective mind [*esprit objectif*], that is, all natural objects on which the mind has left its stamp: printed books, carved stones, painted canvas. Let us reserve the expression *objective mind* for what we often call *collective representations,* that is, for all the ways of thinking and acting which are characteristic of a society, judicial, philosophical, religious, etc. Man lives amid the remains of a past which again gives a sort of presence to those who no longer exist. He lives in a community both social and spiritual, within each individual, since it is shown by the partial assimilation of personalities, exterior to all since no one is the origin of the common practices, since no one has chosen the state of knowledge and the hierarchy of values which he has accepted and adopted.⁵⁰

Aron posits two conditions, which could be called the condition of *meaningful presence* and the condition of *exteriority to individuals*. These conditions may at first seem difficult to conceive. They roughly correspond to the following. First, the condition of a meaningful presence to the members of the group: people live within a community that is spiritual (in the sense of the German *geistig*). This means that their society rests on common ideas and values. Let us call ideas and values taken together by the name "meanings." Society rests on meanings that people must recognize. But also—and this is the second condition—these common meanings must be exterior to the subjects with regard to their origin, which is to say with regard to their authority and validity. To speak about an exteriority to individuals here is no longer a way of saying that the idea presents itself in the form of a material thing (in the same way that, for example, Plato's thought presents itself to us in the form of the twelve volumes of the Loeb Classical Library). Exteriority means that the idea presents itself to us as an established rule that depends on none of us in particular. It is not because I consent to it that a certain way of speaking is correct in French, and it does not become incorrect if I decide that I disapprove of it.

---

49. Raymond Aron, *Introduction to the Philosophy of History: An Essay on the Limits of Historical Objectivity,* trans. George J. Irwin (Boston: Beacon Press, 1961), 72.

50. Ibid., 73. The work Aron is referring to is Nicolai Hartmann, *Das Problem des geistigen Seins: Untersuchungen zur Grundlegung der Geschichtsphilosophie und der Geisteswissenschaft* (Berlin: de Gruyter, 1933).

Evidently, *objectified mind* corresponds to the fact that we live in a world that others lived in before us (these others are at first foreign to us). By contrast, *objective mind* is the opposite: it is not the trace of absent people within our field of perception; it is the presence of the social in the mind of each of us. It is thus in no way a relation to people foreign to us (that we would have to return to or rediscover and whose thoughts we would have to reconstruct based on the documents we have). On the contrary, it is a relation to familiar people that I have no need of returning to or interpreting because they are already present deep within me, in my language and my thinking. Objectified mind in Paris, for example, might consist in stumbling upon, in a building site, prehistoric traces of the first inhabitants of the banks of the Seine; we know almost nothing about these people. Objective mind in Paris involves knowing the map, the names of the streets, the metro routes, and the meaning that is typically associated with oppositions such as those between the Left and Right Banks and between the high-class neighborhoods and the working-class areas (these are oppositions whose borders change over time but without ceasing to express the same need for contrast).

As a result, the sociologist is led to restore something that was essential for Hegel: the precedence of the rights of objective mind over those of subjective mind. One might believe that this precedence is merely historical and therefore genetic and causal. It is much more than that. On this question, Aron writes:

One fact is for us fundamental: the community created by the priority within each individual of the objective mind over the individual mind is the historically and concretely primary datum. Men arrive at consciousness by assimilating, unconsciously, a certain way of thinking, judging and feeling which belongs to an epoch and which characterizes a nation or a class. . . . Biological individuality is given; the human individuality of the person is constructed, based on a common foundation.[51]

Objectified mind is the world minus the living presence of the subject. What remains are the subject's "objects," testimony of a bygone presence. The problem raised in this hermeneutic perspective is this: how does the historian-subject find *the subject of these objects,* working solely from the

---

51. Aron, *Introduction,* 71 [translation modified].

objects themselves? The subject of such human objects may well be an impersonal subject, an anonymous subject, but it is still always an individual. Seeing a pipe, I am referred back to the pipe smoker; seeing the hammer, I understand the carpenter because I know in my own body—with a knowledge that is corporeal rather than propositional—what the gesture of hammering consists in.

As long as the objects brought together as objectified mind (or, if you like, in the archaeological museum) refer only to an anonymous subject, they do not allow us to uncover the society with its institutions, ideas, and values. The hammer allows one to reconstitute the gestures of the carpenter or the shoemaker. In order to understand its role in these functions, we need not appeal to Durkheimian or Hegelian meanings (i.e., collective representations). This leads to the question: do we need such social meanings at all? Should we not rather congratulate ourselves on doing without them? Are notions such as "collective consciousness" or "the spirit of a people" not conceptual monsters that were long ago discredited?

To claim this would be to forget that alongside pipes and hammers there are also bells. Alongside tools that can perhaps be understood by the function they have in the manipulation of things, there are also the symbols and marks of social relations. It is therefore incumbent on the philosopher to explain why the meanings that allow us to understand symbols and marks are not metaphysical monsters at all but, rather, legitimate concepts.

10.3. The Spirit of Institutions

Objective mind: clearly this expression is not the most felicitous and lends itself to misunderstandings. The term is necessary here only because it is the one used by philosophers when they want to maintain that the social cannot be reduced to the nonsocial. This is why I have also taken it up in order to designate the system of ideas upon which the institutions of a society rest, what one could call, following Montesquieu, the spirit of institutions. How should we conceive of such collective ideas?

If two people have the same idea, or if they have the same opinion, we have no problem saying that they share that idea or opinion. Now this idea of *sharing* ideas and opinions is not as clear as one might hope. This can be shown by appealing to a distinction drawn by Charles Taylor between *intersubjective* meanings and *common* meanings.⁵² When a sociologist speaks of nothing more than the meanings shared by the members of a group, he fails to attend to an important difference between two different ways in which ideas can be held in common.⁵³

Intersubjective meanings correspond to phenomena of *consensus* among independent subjects. Taste is a good example. An opinion survey might show that the public leans toward a particular model of consumption, a particular way of dressing, a particular way of spending free time. This means that a good many people—in proportions to be measured by an empirical sociologist—express the same preferences, make the same judgments, and respond in the same way to a questionnaire they are asked to fill out, with each of them responding only for himself. In turn, this similarity of judgments of taste can be given an empirical explanation through the historical conditions of its formation within individuals (e.g., education, advertising). The harmony of judgments of taste is for an entire school of philosophers the paradigm case of a free agreement among human subjects. There is a convergence among the judgments that each individual freely forms, but this convergence is not fortuitous. Judgments of taste therefore have two remarkable characteristics. On the one hand, someone seeking to form a judgment of taste is seeking to exhibit her taste and not just demonstrate her own idiosyncratic reaction. She therefore believes that her judgment expresses something more than the particularities of an individual sensibility: it appeals, as is said, to a *sensus communis,* a human form of sensibility. However, the invocation of such a universal does not exempt the subject from forming her own aesthetic judgments. It is significant that each individual, despite claiming to have formed a valid judgment (one that therefore ought to command the assent of all who demonstrate taste, provided it is a well-formed and pure judgment of taste), insists on forming her judgment *herself.* Nobody accepts

---

52. Charles Taylor, "Interpretation and the Sciences of Man" (1971) in his *Philosophy and the Human Sciences: Philosophical Papers 2* (Cambridge: Cambridge University Press, 1985), 13–57. Here I will make use of several points from a study in which I discuss that distinction: see my "Is There an Objective Spirit?," trans. Daniel M. Weinstock, in James Tully (ed.), *Philosophy in an Age of Pluralism: The Philosophy of Charles Taylor in Question* (Cambridge: Cambridge University Press, 1994), 96–118.

53. Here the word "meaning" is meant to cover all of the intellectual and mental resources of the actors, from concepts to symbolic systems (for example, a calendar or a liturgy), to ideals and values.

the idea of deferring to an expert as one would for a scientific or technical question that was beyond one's competence. Nobody says: "The critic in my local daily newspaper said that this film that I have not seen was excellent; therefore I like this film."

These philosophers are inclined to refer to Kant's analyses in the *Critique of Judgment* precisely because it seems to them to contain the secret to authentic human relations, i.e., a relation that must, paradoxically, *bind* subjects who are *free* to one another. What they are seeking in Kant's book is what a Hegelian might call the bond between bonds and nonbonds, an agreement meant to be established in conditions in which all parties are fully independent so as to allow the universal of a human community to manifest itself.

Such a community—one produced by the free encounter of independent judgments—rests on a universal of resemblance rather than a universal of relation (see Chapter 8, section 1, above). Even if the idea of taste allows us to seek agreement, we must still wait until people have individually had the aesthetic experience to see if there is a consensus or not. This human community is thus an intersubjectivity. In other words, it remains a relation of reason: just as the white wall of London is, on account of its color, similar to all walls that will subsequently be painted white, similarly my judgment on the aesthetic value of the passing cloud in the sky is in principle communicable. If my emotion is authentically aesthetic, every human being who places himself in the aesthetic standpoint will have the same experience and will form the same judgment. However, I may myself constitute the entire audience for this ephemeral spectacle. Nobody else happened to raise their gaze toward the cloud in time, and now it has disappeared, gone forever. The relation to others posited by the judgment of taste is thus purely ideal; it is but a *possibility* of relation. This is why it is proper to speak here of a simple intersubjectivity and not of a society.

Taylor shows how the description of social life cannot limit itself to the distinction between two classes of meanings of which a person is capable: personal (idiosyncratic) meanings and shared meanings. A third class of meanings must be added, which could be called *common* meanings.[54] For example, two citizens living in different districts are thinking the same electoral thought if they both have the intention to vote for candidates of the same party. Citizen A votes Conservative and citizen B also votes

---

54. Taylor, "Interpretation and the Sciences of Man," 38.

Conservative. It is thus the same vote even though there are two different voters and they are voting for different candidates. These two voters *share* a political opinion. Nevertheless, what they share is an opinion that arises in each of them independently. The sharing of a political opinion therefore arises intersubjectively, from the convergence of two subjects, each of whom formed his judgment on his own.

Taylor then gives the example of a practice such as negotiation, which is an institution destined to allow the "parties" to agree after having moved through various stages of confrontation. If conditions are favorable, an intersubjective spirit will emerge. For that to happen, the partners in the negotiation will each have to recast the point that is the object of their negotiation in terms sufficiently close to those of the other party. But this very example, which is that of a cooperation, requires us to introduce *common* meanings, meanings whose commonality does not depend on an intersubjective consensus.

Fortunately, one can participate in an election (contested by different candidates from different parties) or in a negotiation without necessarily having to have opinions that match those of one's neighbors. By contrast, it is indispensable to share the representations or the thoughts on which these very institutions (elections, negotiations) are based. In order for the disagreement and the conflict of opinions even to arise as a disagreement or conflict within a *negotiation* or a *vote,* the participants must have the same representation of what they are in the process of doing (negotiating, voting). In fact, the two Conservative voters share with Progressive voters the same representations that allow them to express their disagreement in an election. These common representations are not "points of agreement" that we would discover by looking into their heads. They are *instituted* meanings that are not only *public* but also *social.* They are not identical by some sort of coincidence that could be explained by a similarity in life conditions and experience. They are inculcated within individuals in a way that makes it possible for the behavior of each of them to be coordinated and intelligible from the group's point of view.

The day of the vote, nobody is tasked with verifying that the voters who show up to vote have in their respective heads an appropriate representation of what they are supposed to do. It is probable that, in a large-enough population, some people will be participating in the vote in total ignorance of the conditions of the vote or under the illusion that they are doing something entirely different. These aberrations are necessarily exceptional; otherwise the institution would cease to exist. As a result, we can assume that there is an impersonal and general meaning of the practice, a meaning defined outside of the opinions of Peter or Mary and defined before Peter and Mary apprehended the practice.

The meaning of the practice thus does not belong to individuals either distributively or collectively. As Taylor puts it:

> The meanings and norms implicit in these practices are not just in the minds of the actors but are out there in the practices themselves, practices which cannot be conceived as a set of individual actions, but which are essentially modes of social relation, of mutual action.[55]

Here we find something like Hegel's objective mind:

> [W]e can think of the institutions and practices of a society as a kind of language in which its fundamental ideas are expressed. But what is "said" in this language is not ideas which could be in the minds of certain individuals only, they are rather common to a society, because embedded in its collective life, in practices and institutions which are of the society indivisibly. . . . They are, to use Hegel's term, "objective spirit."[56]

Therefore, in order to have objective mind, what must be added to intersubjectivity is the institution. The notion of intersubjectivity does not take us beyond a *dialogism,* i.e., the idea of a relation between a present self and a self yet to come. Peirce, the inventor of the idea that the subject cannot be Cartesian because it is dialogical, wrote that "thinking always proceeds in the form of a dialogue."[57] Yes, but a dialogue between what two parties? It is a dialogue between a *me* (at a point in time) and another *me* (at another point in time). It matters little whether the person to whom the thought is addressed is another person or the same person a bit later on. When I write a note in my notebook under tomorrow's date (e.g., "go to the travel agent to pick up the plane ticket"), my thinking is dialogical:

---

55. Ibid., 36.
56. Charles Taylor, *Hegel* (Cambridge: Cambridge University Press, 1975), 382.
57. Charles Sanders Peirce, *Collected Papers of Charles Sanders Peirce,* vol. 4: *The Simplest Mathematics,* ed. Charles Hartshorne and Paul Weiss (Cambridge, MA: Harvard University Press, 1933), § 6 (10).

"solitary dialectic is still of the nature of dialogue."[58] Peirce means by this that thinking is not given immediately and at once, that it is not the intuitive grasp by the mind's gaze (*acies mentis*) of a simple nature or a link between simple natures. To think is to posit a thought with a view to the inferences that will be drawn from it (by another self) or to draw the inferences of something that has already been posited (by another self). A philosopher of dialogism can obviously maintain that the dialogue of multiple parties must precede the dialogue with oneself, not just empirically but also conceptually. This observation is quite correct, but these are conditions on apprenticeship in dialogue, not conditions on thought itself. Thought is essentially dialogical, but it can be carried out in isolation from any real relation to another person.

In this regard, the notion of dialogism (which has been promoted by German philosophers seeking to renew critical philosophy by bringing pragmatics into it) takes us no further than the phenomenological notion of intersubjectivity. For it is quite remarkable that phenomenologists have assimilated the "constitution of others" (of the meaning of others to be given to certain phenomena) and the "constitution of a future self."[59]

What does the notion of an *institution* add to a relation between two subjectivities or two self-positings at different times or different points on Earth?

---

58. Charles Sanders Peirce, *Collected Papers of Charles Sanders Peirce*, vol. 5: *Pragmatism and Pragmaticism*, ed. Charles Hartshorne and Paul Weiss (Cambridge, MA: Harvard University Press, 1934), § 546 (386).

59. I can conceive, starting from my living present, a future present that I am not yet living through, and thus, by pushing this logic to the furthest extreme, a present that I will never live through (the present of others): "As my living present opens upon a past which I nevertheless am no longer living through, and on a future which I do not yet live, and perhaps never shall, it can also open on to temporalities outside my living experience and acquire a social horizon, with the result that my world is expanded to the dimensions of that collective history which my private existence takes up and carries forward" (Merleau-Ponty, *Phenomenology*, 503). Derrida, commenting on Husserl, made similar claims: "Before the 'same' is recognized and communicated among several individuals, it is recognized and communicated within the individual consciousness.... In a certain way, therefore, intersubjectivity is first the nonempirical relation of Ego to Ego, of my present present to other presents as such; i.e., as others and as presents (as past presents). Intersubjectivity is the relation of an absolute origin to other absolute origins, which are always my own, despite their radical alterity." Jacques Derrida, *Edmund Husserl's "Origin of Geometry": An Introduction*, trans. John P. Leavey, Jr. (Lincoln: University of Nebraska Press, 1989), 85–86.

Obviously, the word "institution" should be taken in the sociological sense, i.e., as designating what is specifically social in social facts. On this point, Mauss writes:

> What, in fact, is an institution if not a grouping of acts and ideas already instituted which individuals find before them and which more or less imposes itself upon them? There is no reason for the ordinary practice of reserving this expression exclusively for fundamental social arrangements. By institutions, therefore, we understand customs and fashions, prejudices and superstitions, just as much as political constitutions or essential legal organisations, because all of these phenomena are of the same nature and differ from one another only in degree.[60]

Institutions are thus not just large organizations (such as hospitals or parliaments). They are just as much conceptual systems. In general, according to Mauss, sociologists do not separate morphology from representations (i.e., ideology). Institutions are as much ways of thinking as they are ways of acting.[61]

What is it that indicates that a common meaning has an institutional character? What forces us to distinguish it? Its structural aspect. Intersubjective meanings do not demand that the "we" that is expressing them have a social character, or only do so indirectly (as when the point the two subjects have in common can be traced to the influence upon them of their respectively similar milieux). By contrast, authentic common meanings do not bring together two free subjectivities, but two partners who must do different things and whose roles or statuses are determined by an established rule, a social custom that they both follow.

Max Weber proposed that an action be deemed to have a social meaning when the actor takes others into account in his behavior.[62] A typical

---

60. Marcel Mauss and Paul Fauconnet, "Sociology" (1901), in Mauss, *The Nature of Sociology*, trans. William Jeffrey, Jr. (Oxford: Berghahn Books, 2005), 10–11.

61. Mauss writes in a text from 1906: "Calendars are social things as are festivals, signs and portents, just as are actions taken to ward off bad omens. All of these are institutions. The notions of the sacred, of the soul, of time, etc. are also institutions because they only exist in the mind of the individual clothed in the forms that they have taken on in specific societies. The individual receives them, through education, in traditional formulas." Marcel Mauss and Henri Hubert, "Introduction à l'analyse de quelques phénomènes religieux" (1906), in Marcel Mauss, *Œuvres*, vol. 1: *Les fonctions sociales du sacré* (Paris: Les Éditions de Minuit, 1968), 36.

62. For Weber, the activity of pedestrians who simultaneously open their umbrellas in the rain is not social: each of them is thinking of protecting himself from the rain (a

example of social conduct is avoiding bumping into other pedestrians in the street. In the evening, the music lover lowers the volume on his radio to avoid disturbing his neighbors. His conduct is eminently social, all the more so if no one notices that he is listening to music. Raymond Aron also provided this example: the professor speaks slowly and clearly enunciates his words so as to make it easier for his students to take notes.[63]

This Weberian definition of the social is obviously inadequate. It has only two conditions: consciousness of the presence of others and consciousness of one's interactions. But something else is missing: complementarity between roles. In Aron's example, what makes the professor's action a social action is not that he takes the students into account when speaking but that he is in the process of teaching. This immediately establishes a triadic system: he *gives* a lesson to students who *receive* it. Without the activity of the students who are studying a subject with the professor, he can talk as clearly and distinctly as he likes, but he is not teaching. Teaching is not something that one can do on one's own by imbuing one's acts and gestures with an intention directed toward others.

Castoriadis, in his criticism of Weber's definition, put his finger on the decisive issue: Weber fails to see that meaning for the subject is preceded by a meaning that is anonymous (of the kind that Sartre criticized)—i.e., "there can be no sense for a subject unless, in actuality, there is a sense that is for no one, unless there is a social signification and the institution of this signification."[64] What justifies the claim that "there can be none"? This is

---

relation of man to nature). What would be social would be to refrain from opening one's umbrella so as not to disturb one's neighbors (a relation of man to man). Similarly, "a mere collision of two cyclists may be compared to a natural event. On the other hand, their attempt to avoid hitting each other, or whatever insults, blows, or friendly discussion might follow the collision, would constitute 'social action.'" Max Weber, *Economy and Society: An Outline of Interpretive Sociology,* ed. Guenther Roth and Claus Wittich, trans. Ephraim Fischoff, Hans Gerth, A. M. Henderson, et al. (Berkeley: University of California Press, 1978), 23.

63. Raymond Aron, *Les étapes de la pensée sociologique* (Paris: Gallimard, 1967), 551. [Translator's note: The example does not appear in the corresponding passage in the English translation: *Main Currents in Sociological Thought*, vol. 2, trans. Richard Howard and Helen Weaver (New York: Basic Books, 1967), 228.]

64. Castoriadis, *Imaginary Institution,* 367 [translation modified]. Castoriadis has indicated that Hegel and Dilthey's "objective mind" corresponded to what he preferred to call the "institution." See his *Le monde morcelé* (Paris: Les Éditions du Seuil, 1990), 48.

not a claim in "social physics" but rather a conceptual and metaphysical claim. It is part of the very meaning of a social act to be linked by an internal relation to another, complementary social act. This is why Weber's "ideal types" are inadequate:

> The "ideal type" of Roman citizen refers *from within* to the "ideal type" of Roman woman, of religion and of law as these existed in Rome, etc.—and it is not the theoretical construction that can ever assure this intrinsic holding-together, this outside-itself immanent to each of these significations.[65]

In this text, Castoriadis is extremely critical of structuralism (by which he means a combination of formalism and structural causalism) but proposes a point of view that is precisely what I have been calling structural holism. Here is how he characterizes the deep historicity of meanings:

> [A]pparently similar "institutions" can be radically other, since, immersed in another society, they are caught up in other significations. To cite one massive and clear example, referring to an "ideal type" of bureaucracy in general cannot help but mask the critical differences between Chinese imperial bureaucracy, for instance, and the bureaucracy of modern capitalism.[66]

Here we find once again the idea that social relations have the characteristic of being relations internal to a system: the Roman citizen is the head of a household; the professor is the professor of a class. In short, they are dyadic units within a system of institutions.

10.4. The Subject of Institutions

I will now attempt to clarify this notion of the social subject as a dyadic unit of a system. In order to do this, I will make use of a general observation made by the anthropologist Louis Dumont.

It is often asked whether notions such as *person, subject, individual,* and *self* are Western notions or, rather, universal in scope. Every firm answer seems, at first glance, improbable. How could such notions be limited to the West? Do people from other intellectual traditions live in confusion?

---

65. Castoriadis, *Imaginary Institution,* 368.
66. Ibid.

Is it maintained that they are incapable of distinguishing what is mine from what is yours, Paul from Peter? Rare are those who would push historicism to such an extreme in order to say that there are people who do not make such distinctions. But the contrary response is no less absurd: are we to say that every human being sees himself as a self-conscious subject, endowed with both human rights and his own particular destiny? This is impossible, for we know that there is nothing universal about such ideas and that they only emerged over time. We know that they have a history whose stages we can recount.

Dumont calls our attention to the distinction between recognizing individual differences in one's own experience, on the one hand, and giving these differences a central place in one's conception of the order of the world, on the other. Every society recognizes, he claims, the empirical individual. But every society does not turn the human individual into a holder of rights or an *agent of institutions,* as he puts it. This remark is a general one, but it is made in the course of a presentation on Indian civilization, and it is from that civilization that Dumont derives the examples he uses to illustrate what he means.

In order to describe a society different from our own, for example Indian society, a distinction must be drawn between two levels of description—the empirical level (at which we find, naturally enough, particular human subjects) and the level of institutions (and therefore, first and foremost, of ideas). At the first of these levels, verbs are conjugated in different persons and everyone has a perfect understanding of the system of relations among them. But the second level is not organized around the notion of the individual person. Institutions are not related to individuals but to pairs of different agents. In this sense, the individuals of the empirical level are not visible at the level of values.

It is well understood that, empirically, Indians, like everyone else, distinguish particular human subjects or, as we customarily call them, "individuals." They conjugate their verbs in different persons and in daily life they recognize the personalities and characters of particular people with the greatest possible sensitivity. But if one studies their institutions—for example, the caste or, to take two other examples, land rights and kinship—one discovers that the particular man is not, strictly speaking, their subject. Analysis uncovers complementarities in each case that lead one to conclude that the true subject is a complex being, at the very least one constituted by a *pair of different agents.* The person is always captive within a relation that prevents him from emerging as an individual.[67]

Dumont provides several examples. For us, kinship is filiation, "that is, a *substantial identity* (transmission of the name)." But, for them, kinship is above all marriage, alliance, i.e., a relation that constitutes "a totality that can be symbolized by a pair of brothers-in-law."[68] Two men become relatives (e.g., allies) by each marrying the other's sister.

Here is how things present themselves to the investigator who seeks to describe the property regime in traditional India. Who is the owner of the land? Is it the State, the individual, the lord, or the farmer? According to Dumont, this notion of property is inapplicable. For us, the notion of property requires that all rights—or at least most of them—be retained by the same entity. For them, by contrast, the various rights are distributed among a variety of agents, all of whom have a relation to the land. Thus, in the region of Malabar, there are simultaneously two people with property rights. "If one absolutely insisted on finding an owner in this, one would have to take the pair, which generally comprises a man of high caste and a man of a low caste."[69]

Dumont suggests on the same page that we can begin to understand the difference between the Indian conception and our own using distinctions drawn from our own intellectual tradition. Thus we find in Hegel a distinction between *social ethics* and *subjective morality.*[70] Subjective morality is a universal morality: it speaks to everyone and therefore touches each of us in her indistinction or infinitude. Every person has rights. A social ethic, by contrast, is one of the "duties of one's status" [*devoirs d'état*] and therefore of special duties. "One is not simply a man; one is, depending on one's circumstances, a priest, a prince, a farmer or a servant."[71] Such an ethic is not addressed to the universal subject but to the "particular" (not only in Hegel's sense but also in the legal sense), to someone who incarnates only a part [*une partie*] of reality confronting other parties [*en face*

---

67. Louis Dumont, *La civilisation indienne et nous* (Paris: Armand Colin, 1975), 23–24 (italics in original).
68. Ibid., 27.
69. Ibid., 26.
70. These are possible translations of *Sittlichkeit* and *Moralität,* respectively.
71. Ibid., 23.

d'autres parties] in, for example, a trial.⁷² Particulars have special duties attaching to their statuses. What gives dignity and humanity to people considered as being particularized by their respective statuses is their complementarity with one another, the fact that they depend on one another, that together they form a totality. To understand what morality looks like in a civilization different from our own, or even in the civilizations of our own antiquity, one will have to understand that the social ethic is predominant, while common rights and duties (human rights and human duties) are quite vague and rarely enter into relations among people.

Human beings, in order to acquire an individual identity—to move from the status of *particular* to that of *individual*—must extract themselves from the various dyads of which they are a part, in order to posit themselves for themselves, not only as a matter of fact (which would be a banal occurrence) but as a matter of principle or as a value. They thereby acquire autonomy. Only then can the empirical individual appear on the level of collective meanings and institutions: he can appear as the "normative subject of institutions."⁷³

However, all of these anthropological examples ought to provoke us to raise an objection to the notion of objective mind as I have been presenting it, an objection that an attentive reader of this chapter will surely make. Dumont sets up a contrast between traditional societies and modern societies. He thereby invites us to ask this question: in the social life we are to describe, is the subject of institutions the individual or the pair of agents?

---

72. Translator's note: In drawing here the Hegelian tripartite distinction among individuals, "particulars," and universals, Descombes makes use of resources in French that English does not have. The noun "un particulier" in everyday French means "a private individual" and would, as he says, be used this way in a legal context. To translate it in that way, however, would lose the distinction he is making. For "le particulier" is also the French translation of Hegel's *das Besondere,* which is usually translated into English as "the particular." The particular in this sense is intermediate between the universal and the individual. Descombes here is using this notion to emphasize that particulars are what, in virtue of their "status," participate in a system of relations and that, following Dumont, the modern (human) individual historically "emerged" from such relations.

73. Dumont invites us to distinguish two different meanings of the word "individual": "(1) *The empirical agent, present in every society,* in virtue of which he is the main raw material for any sociology. (2) The rational being and *normative subject* of institutions; this is peculiar to us, as is shown by the values of equality and liberty: it is an idea that we have, the idea of an ideal." Louis Dumont, *Homo Hierarchicus: The Caste System and Its Implications,* 2nd rev. ed., trans. Mark Sainsbury, Louis Dumont, and Basia Gulati (1970; Chicago: University of Chicago Press, 1980), 9.

At this point, my entire argument in this chapter—and even in this book in its entirety—would seem to lead to a disconcerting conclusion. For, is the upshot of everything that has been said not the following: *the subject of a social action is a dyadic subject*? And if that is truly my conclusion, am I not ultimately saying that the only real society is a traditional one? Yet we are here in the West, not in the East Indies. Are we going to claim that all social life is of the Indian kind? Is not the normative subject of institutions in our society, as was just said, the human individual?

If my conclusions did not take all of this into account, the entire proposed demonstration would be reduced to absurdity, since I would have to first *rely on* Dumont's opposition between our own (modern) mode of thought and a traditional mode of thought, so as to ultimately reach a conclusion that would *erase* that same opposition.

The examples given above were meant to illustrate the fact that our notions of property or kinship are not applicable without modification to other societies. If this is the case, there is an opposition between our conception of the subject of social life and other conceptions—for example, the Indian conception. Now, this opposition is in no way called into question by the philosophical analyses that I have put forward. Moreover, it is not the philosopher's job to involve himself in the descriptions given by investigators: this precept is as valid for anthropological descriptions as for those in the natural sciences. What the philosopher *can* challenge is always another philosophy and nothing else.

But the comparative approach itself, which has given us these two examples of property and kinship, consists in showing that we can understand ideas that are not our own. In the cases at hand, we can understand them because we can conceive of people emphasizing certain aspects of social life that are also familiar to us even though we put no special value on them. Similarly, they recognize, outside of the aspects of the human that they idealize, other aspects whose existence they heed without placing them in the foreground in the way that we do.

I do not claim that the *subject of institutions* is always and everywhere a dyadic subject. I claim that the subject of the *institutions of social life* is always and everywhere a dyadic subject. For one must also account for the institutions of individuality. Every institution is social in its source and its transmission, but not every institution is meant to order social life. The discipline of a solitary or introspective life is itself an institution, merely an institution turned toward the self. It is convenient to refer to these as "spiritual institutions." Here one might first mention spiritual institutions of a religious nature, such as the rules of monastic life with its rigors and spiritual exercises. But one might also mention spiritual institutions of a nonreligious nature that arise from the dissemination of the instruments of spiritual progress to worldly men. Pierre Pachet has been able to show how the literary genre of the intimate diary is, in his remarkable formula, an "institution of the mind." This supremely individualistic genre was not the pure creation of one individual: it was a form that arose out of a movement of personalization and secularization of the idea of "spiritual work upon oneself."[74] Another institution of a spiritual nature is the work of modern art conceived as a form of self-realization. Such at least is how it has often been understood and presented by the artists themselves.

Again, these spiritual institutions can only maintain themselves in human society by entering into relations of complementarity with others. So, if the monk or artist in his capacity as monk or artist encounters himself in isolation, the monk who teaches and seeks charity or the artist who exhibits a work (rather than merely conceiving it) must return to be among others.

It follows that there is nothing contradictory about maintaining that the real subject of the institutions of social life is necessarily a dyadic subject while at the same time emphasizing that our own world is based on the idea of a form of human life that is held to be superior to mere social life. In our history, the idea was born and developed according to which there are demands that are higher than the duties attaching to one's status in society, and these higher demands are those of both personal freedom and the equal dignity of every human being (in virtue of the reciprocity between subjectivity and intersubjectivity).

There can therefore be no question of upholding the absurd idea that every society is traditional, such that our apparent difference and the organization of our social life according to different principles would be nothing but an illusion. In fact, we do live differently (even if we do not live entirely in the way described by philosophers of the Social Contract). From a philosophical point of view, the principle of this difference is indicated in Dumont's remark regarding the particular who, in a traditional society, remains "captive within a relation that prevents him from

---

74. Pierre Pachet, *Les baromètres de l'âme: Naissance du journal intime* (Paris: Hatier, 1990), 18.

emerging as an individual." The difference is therefore (remaining here at the level of principle) that, for us, the particular is not prevented from emerging out of the relation. He is *invited* to so emerge, to posit himself as an individual. In order to work towards this, he can call upon precisely the sorts of spiritual institutions that have been developed in our societies.

As a result, our conception of the relations among particulars is modified. We do not believe it necessary to incarnate them in a relation between a particular and an identified partner. It is, rather, sufficient that the relation be an impersonal one between a particular and anyone at all. For example, we can allow ourselves to see the relation of property ownership as being principally a relation between someone and something, a rights holder and a thing possessed, since for us the third term usually only comes into things in a negative way. From the logical point of view, the fact of my being the owner of this field entails no relation with any specific person. Only when someone claims to have rights over my field (or wants to rent it from me) does the relation between particulars emerge from the realm of the virtual to become established concretely.

Here is another example of the sorts of considerations that lead to a recognition of the dyadic character of the social subject of institutions. I will refer in what follows to the work of the historian and philosopher of right Michel Villey.

Villey disputes the idea that philosophers have always given an adequate account of our notion of property. The source of property rights cannot be the fact of occupation (the taking of possession of the thing by a subject exerting its will), nor can the source be work (as in the fiction of a first appropriation that is legitimated by work, followed by an uninterrupted series of legitimate transfers).

For Roman legal theory, outside of a small number of cases (relating to hunting and fishing) in which the community allows particulars to acquire rights by "occupation," all property rights can only be the result of a dividing up. Since such rights are a relation among individuals, they must flow from a source superior to the individual: law, custom or tribunals.[75]

75. Michel Villey, *Critique de la pensée juridique moderne* (Paris: Dalloz, 1976), 152.

Here as well it will be said that this concerns only Roman law and that we live in modern times. However, we have already seen that such an idea is not incomprehensible and, indeed, retains its relevance (see Chapter 4, section 6, above). The problem is then one of knowing whether Villey's claim bears only upon a peculiarity of Roman law or, rather, upon what makes Roman law exemplary of every conceivable system of law. It may well be that what is described is a trait that is constitutive of the very notion of property. But to determine whether this is the case we will have to push our analysis further, into the logical form of the attribution of a right.

When done properly, philosophy of rights requires that we conduct an analysis of juridical language, i.e., of the logical form in which rights are expressed. That is not a controversial idea. Now there is, as Villey notes, a great difference between attributing a comportment to a subject of attribution (e.g., "Socrates is walking") and attributing a right to a person.

As the term or end point of jurisprudential exertions, the "right" that the judge attributes to each party, once its proportions have been determined, is always a kind of quotient, the product of a quasi-*division* of things: "exterior" things are the object of divisions and, based on these divisions, of legal action. Before the judge there are always multiple litigants; never a man on his own, a single subject. It is time we got rid of the notion of a *right holder* or *subject of rights* [*sujet de droit*]. It is legitimate to speak about subjects in the domain of morality, provided that morality has comportments as its object. The acts that morality commands us or forbids us to carry out do indeed have "subjects." Rights, on the other hand, have no subjects, only beneficiaries.[76]

Villey seems to me to have been more attentive to the logic of legal statements than have many theoreticians of deontic logic. From a logical point of view, the attribution of an act or a moral duty is similar to the attribution of a quality: it takes the form of a predicative relation between a subject and its attribute. It is the attribution of a *monadic* predicate. But in the attribution of a right or obligation we must find, at a minimum, a *triadic* structure: a right (to something) is split between two people by the

---

76. Michel Villey, *Le droit et les droits de l'homme* (Paris: Presses Universitaires de France, 1983), 96.

judge. When Villey says that we must abandon the notion of a "subject of rights," he means of the subject conceived as that of a monadic predicate or a monovalent verb. This obviously does not mean that legal relations should be expressed by impersonal verbs in the way we do when describing the weather: e.g., "it is raining" [*il pleut*] or "it is windy" [*il vente*].

In order to give this examination of the subject of social relations its full scope, consider finally the example of the speech act considered as a social act. All of the theories of speech acts are pragmatics of language; they analyze the act within its context, which is necessary any time the words exchanged contain deictics (e.g., demonstrative pronouns). However, these theories do not all emphasize to the same degree the *social* character of the act, the fact that the context is above all one of social cooperation between two people. I am not interested here in the technical fine points of speech act theory but rather in something brought to light by Alan Gardiner, who was in many ways one of the founding fathers of the analysis of language as a speech act, an analysis that depends precisely on the distinction between *speech* and *language* (which Gardiner borrows from Saussure). As Gardiner puts it, "speech is a human activity demanding at least two persons possessing a common language and finding themselves in a common situation."[77]

But what does it mean to say that speech is a social act? Does it mean that speech acts are *collective* acts? Are they operations that cannot be carried out by a single person? Not at all. It may sometimes happen that a speech act is collective, as when several people speak together—for example when reciting a prayer or making a declaration as a group (e.g., a collective oath). However, most of the time, speech acts are not collective and are, indeed, highly personal in the sense that the speaker constructs his sentences as he likes without having to follow a text that determines what he is supposed to say. This individual act is nonetheless social, and that is what Gardiner stresses in an astute passage.[78]

Every speech act does in fact require two people, not in order to speak with a single voice (as a lone person) but in order to speak to each other (each speaking *in turn*). We will say that speech acts as such can never

---

77. Alan Gardiner, *The Theory of Speech and Language*, 2nd ed. (1932; Oxford: Clarendon Press, 1951), 7.

78. Ibid., 57.

be attributed to *one person*; there must be a multiple subject, a polyadic subject (and not just a plural or collective one). This multiple subject must exhibit a structure. For example, in a quiz show, there is a division of labor: one person asks the questions and the other is supposed to answer them.

Gardiner cites a profound remark made by Samuel Butler: "It takes two people to say a thing—a sayee as well as a sayer. . . . A may have spoken, but if B has not heard, there has been nothing said, and he must speak again."[79] Gardiner explains this as follows: "Speech is, of course, not the only human activity with at once a social aspect and an individual aspect. The relations of master and servant, or those of buyer and seller, are on much the same footing as the relations of speaker and listener."[80] A's action is an individual one; *she* decides to speak, to form her sentences, etc. But has she spoken? We will have to wait until we know whether B heard her; only when B has heard is A's action accomplished. Now A's action assumes free activity on B's part. It is not enough to hold forth; one must make oneself heard. It is not enough to write books; one also needs readers. It is not enough to offer gifts; one also has to get others to accept them. In all of these examples, the partners have different, but complementary, things to accomplish.

We have here brought to light, in an obviously basic form, how within social acts there is a relation between two *freedoms*. In doing so, we have conceded the point made in existentialist philosophy of language (see section 1 of this chapter): the structure we are describing is a structure of language only if it ultimately pertains to an instituted relation between two freedoms, between two partners whose actions are free.

The subject of social institutions, therefore, is neither the individual person nor a person somehow superior to individuals (i.e., a collective individual, the "system" seen as a great substance). What I have been calling the "subject of institutions" is an agent the model and rule for whose actions are provided by an institution.

There are institutions whose sources are social, but not their destination. These are spiritual institutions. They are social in the sense that the

---

79. Ibid.
80. Ibid., 65.

individual's activity conforms with a way of doing things that has been instituted outside of his control. Yet, in another sense, they are not social: they do not regulate the life of the particular but, rather, the transition from the particular to the individual, i.e., his liberation.

The institutions of meaning are social institutions in their origin (as are all institutions) and in their field of application. They regulate relations between particulars; they do not regulate relations between individuals. By definition, there are no intersubjective institutions, only conventions. An individual may think about others in deciding his own behavior. But if he wants to communicate his thinking to anyone, he must accomplish a speech act, and doing that entails the establishment of a social relation of interlocution.

Objective mind should not be sought within the category of individuated objects (in the way we do with things bearing the traces of human presence) nor in the category of subjects of cogitative and discursive acts (as if it were language itself speaking rather than the people when they open their mouths).

To have a mind [*esprit*] is to evince within one's conduct an intentional ordering power. An agent exhibits a mind when his conduct is organized according to a rational structure: his deeds and gestures are explicable by relations of intention. If the intentions revealed by his conduct are those of a particular attending to his own concerns, the mind manifested is a subjective one [*un esprit subjectif*]. If it is a social subject at work, the mind manifested in his conduct is also an objective mind [*un esprit objectif*].

Anyone accomplishing a social action exhibits at one and the same time a subjective mind (i.e., a capacity for individual action, aims that derive from oneself) and an objective mind (i.e., the ability, defined in the system, to coordinate one's action with that of a partner). The professor can demonstrate his originality by presenting an idea of his own, but if the lesson has been given—whatever its content—it must have been received; as such, it is a manifestation of objective mind.

II

Distinguishing Thoughts

11.1. Having the Same Thought

We can now return to the general problem: what is it for two people to have the same thought about a particular question or object?

Our question is one in the metaphysics of the comparison of thoughts. When someone wonders whether two people have the same thought, is the question analogous to wondering whether they have the same car? Or is it, rather, analogous to the question of whether they have the same internal state? Or, finally, is it an equivalence from the perspective of a system, similar to receiving the same grade on the same examination or the fact of living at the same address? Such questions are metaphysical because they bear upon the ontological category in which the comparison should be made.

The notion of a *proposition* is used to compare opinions. It is said that two people have the same thought (or are thinking the same thing) when they agree with each other about a proposition. Take, for example, the controversy surrounding Cornelius Jansen's five propositions, a controversy made famous by Pascal's *Provincial Letters*. These propositions were believed to express Jansen's thinking, some because they were citations of his work *Augustinus,* others because, although they were not literally present in the work, they distilled its tenor.

This arises also in textbook examples. A thought is expressed in a proposition—for example, the proposition stating that snow is white. John, having a thought he expresses by saying "Snow is white," and Karl who is having a thought he expresses by saying *"Der Schnee ist weiß"* are having the same thought that I have when I think that *la neige est blanche*.[1] This creates among us a psychological or noetic *resemblance*: by means of acts that are ontologically distinct yet similar, we think the same thing. One might say that we share a common opinion.

Does the notion of a proposition on its own provide a criterion for the identification of thoughts? If so, mental acts could be identified by referring each of them to a proposition. The idea of a propositional attitude was originally a translation of this conception of mental comparison. First, I identify in succession the proposition expressing John's belief, the proposition expressing Karl's, and the one expressing my own belief. Then, I compare these propositions. If I discover that they are *the same proposition,* I conclude that we have the same thought (regarding snow). In this case, having the same thought would indeed be something like having the same car. There would be but one car for three. But more precisely, the situation is rather like that of a single model of car for three people independently driving three materially distinct vehicles. The thoughts expressed in English, German, and French would be like cars registered in different countries but embodying a single archetype.

Can the work of comparing thoughts, then, be understood using the distinction between type identity and token identity (or, if you like, between specific and material identity)? If it proves to be possible, we can reduce the question "Do these two people have the same thought?" to a question of individuation much like "Do these two people drive the same car?"

In order to examine this point more closely, consider the way in which philosophy traditionally presents the triad that we might call "intentionalist" or "Austrian": we must distinguish, we are told, the *act* from both its *content* and its (exterior) *object*.[2] Indeed, these distinctions are required, as

---

1. If I have failed to draw a distinction between "sentences" and "propositions," it is not because I have forgotten that some philosophers believe they must be distinguished. Rather, it is that I do not believe that this distinction can be intelligibly explained, for reasons that I will provide below. I will therefore not use the word "proposition" to refer to an ideal entity associated with the linguistic entity known as the sentence. A proposition is nothing other than a sentence, a sentence constructed by someone precisely in order to *propose* his thought for someone else's attention.

2. In his article "On Propositions" (1919), Russell explains that there are three schools in the philosophy of mind. The proponents of what Russell himself calls an "analytic

is shown by the failure of all who have sought to do without them. The entire question is that of the meaning they are to be given.

These are the three dimensions by which discursive acts—and, by extension, all mental acts—can be compared. The extension has two phases: first, one notes the logical equivalence between the attribution of a *thought* to someone and the attribution in indirect discourse of a verbal *statement*; then the indirect discourse is brought back to its equivalent in direct discourse or quotation in virtue of the equation—which is itself legitimated by a style of sentence construction often found in biblical language—between "thinking something" and "saying something in one's heart."[3] This extension merely applies the principle of every analytic philosophy of mind: the criteria for the identification of mental acts are the criteria for the identification of an expression of those mental acts in a language.[4] In what follows, I will take it as established that to compare thoughts is to compare the expressions given to those thoughts. This in no way requires us to conflate thought and language; we are not comparing expressions that have actually been produced but rather expressions that could be given, in the right circumstances, to thoughts that have actually been thought by thinking subjects.

---

psychology" (Brentano, Meinong) draw a distinction among three elements in every representation: the act, the content, and the object. The realists (Moore and Russell himself, once he broke with the analytic psychological school) do without content. Idealists keep content, while abandoning the object *in fact* (even where they *claim* to retain it). The position that Russell calls "analytic" is that of every intentionalism. The position he describes as idealist calls to mind transcendental phenomenology, in which there is talk of an object, but only ever of an intentional object—i.e., a content and not an object in the sense that is relevant here. See Bertrand Russell, "On Propositions: What They Are and How They Mean," in his *Logic and Knowledge* (London: Routledge, 1988), 305.

3. Peter Geach, *Mental Acts: Their Content and Their Objects* (London: Routledge & Kegan Paul, 1957), 80.

4. The adherence to this principle is, I believe, independent of the various opinions one might otherwise have regarding the relative importance of the disciplines of semantics and psychology—or the predominance of either one over the other—within philosophy. The controversy surrounding this last point is of interest only to philosophers who, like Michael Dummett, see philosophy as a system comprising an order of precedence that is unavoidably linear and in virtue of which there is always a single point from which philosophical work must begin. See Michael Dummett, "Can Analytical Philosophy Be Systematic, and Ought It to Be?" in his *Truth and Other Enigmas* (Cambridge, MA: Harvard University Press, 1979), 437–458.

This is why, for the sake of clarity, I will substitute for the question of the identity of thoughts the question of the identity of the answers that people might provide in a public game, for example one set up by a weekly magazine. The rule of the game is that the right answers will be awarded a prize, with each player having the right to enter *one* answer to each of the questions on the questionnaire. The first question might be, for example, "What color is snow?" The winning answer will have been written in advance on a paper that is in the possession of a bailiff. In order to win, one must have sent in *a single* answer and one that is *the same* as that recorded in advance as the winning answer. We may well ask now, "What do the words 'one answer' mean?" and "What do the words 'the same answer' mean?" It appears that "to have given the same answer" can be taken in several different ways. In order to distinguish them, we will have to distinguish the content of the answer, the act of answering and the object. We will then say this:

1. Let us suppose that each of the participants in the game received only one answer sheet. Cicero is also called Tully, so any act by the one is also an act by the other. To ask whether Cicero's answer was received by those running the game is also to ask whether Tully's answer was received. It is sufficient that the first have been received for the second to also have been received. As a result, in one sense of the expression "the same answer," Cicero and Tully gave *the same answer* if, in looking first at what Cicero answered and then at what Tully answered, we look at the same piece of paper. In such a case, there is but *one* response, which is examined *twice*. One response means here a single (individual) answer sheet, for example an answer sheet on which is written *nix alba est*. The identity of the answers here is an identity of the *act* of answering.

2. The answers, and by analogy the mental acts, can also be compared with regard to their *object*. For example, Tully may have responded "white in color" to the first question in the game (which concerned snow), while Caius also responded "white in color" but in answer to the second question of the game, which concerned the color of the *toga praetexta* worn by the sons of patrician families. The two participants have given, in a sense, the same answer but to different questions, so their answers are in reality different (e.g., one of them may win without the other also winning). Answers formed by the same words can be different if they bear upon different objects.

3. Cicero and Titus have given the same answer if each of them independently provided an answer and these answers are equivalent. There are then materially two answers, but the two men answered in the same way, which means that Titus's answer is correct if Cicero's is correct and vice versa, or that Titus deserves a prize if Cicero deserves a prize for having given the right answer and vice versa. Two answers that have the same *content* can be considered to be identical.

The sense in which the identity of thoughts is of interest to us is the one where a thought is identified by its content. What is remarkable here, however, is the complete dissociation of the two questions of the *subject* and of *content*. The question of the subject is the question of who sent in the answer. The jury that receives the answers can understand and judge the answers without knowing who sent them in. As a general rule, the notion of a declarative proposition is that of a semantic unit that is either true or false—i.e., within our game, either a winning answer or a losing one—in virtue of what it says and not in virtue of the person putting it forth. The proposition has a meaning, and thus also truth conditions, regardless of who may have taken it on board.

If we could give *content* a comparable ontological status to that of the *object*—i.e., the status of an entity that can be individuated and counted—we could easily explain what we are seeking in comparing thoughts: we are looking to see whether the two acts have a single content, in much the same way that one can look to see whether two people have the same model or type of car.

By thinking of mental acts as "propositional attitudes"—i.e., as a relation between a thinker and a propositional content—we embark down the road of *individuating* thoughts by their content. One way of imagining this is as follows. Let us take a thinking subject A and proceed to "objectify" his *cogitatum*, his *noeme*, i.e., the content of his thought. Recall that such objectification consists in taking something that depends on a subject—e.g., his intention, his aims—and making it independent of that subject, in the way of material objects that do not depend on us for their existence where we find them. The very act of thinking, however, cannot be detached from the subject, for it depends on it ontologically. Yet, as we have seen, this is not the case for the content of thought.

DISTINGUISHING THOUGHTS

On its own, the content of a thought is never given as the content of the cogitative act of a subject A rather than of someone else, say, subject B. It follows that A's thought, considered in its content, can be *separated* from the subject. All one need do is consider A's thought (concerning snow and its color) to be a relation between A and a "propositional object" (here this would be the relation of approval of or belief in the proposition saying that snow is white). Henceforth, the object thought about by A is no longer the exterior object (snow and its color) but this thought content. The same operation applied to B's thought will extract a *cogitatum* from B's head or subjective mind. If the two operations by which A's and B's thoughts have been objectified end up producing the same object of thought (i.e., the same proposition), then A and B have the same thought—that is, they have the same relation to the same propositional object.

But what becomes of thoughts when they are no longer in the heads of thinking subjects? What form do they take? How do they exist?

The answer seems to be that objectified thoughts become signs, things endowed with meaning. No sooner is the subject's thought extracted from the act in which it was thought than it becomes a material object and therefore something like a *text* (whether in the narrow or the broad sense; see Chapter 10, section 2, above).

Once these two thoughts have been "objectified," they form an objectified mind, here given in the form of two texts (like the two answer sheets of Caius and Tully in our game example). Now we need only consider these two pieces of objectified mind: are they two tokens of a single type of object? Does the textual composition of the two texts match up point for point?

This procedure of comparison through objectified mind was basically the one we represented earlier with our model of a winning answer given in advance to the custody of the bailiff.

This is, then, the principle of the response given by *philosophies of objectified mind* to the problem of identifying thoughts with one another: subjective minds that started out unfamiliar to each other come together in the expression, the sign, or, if you will, the text. Obviously the act of thinking cannot be placed outside of the subject, but the *content* of its thought can be placed outside the thinking subject. There follows an operation of abstraction that bears upon the signifying objects produced by the objectifying expression (i.e., upon texts) and that will bring out the similarities and dissimilarities.

Perhaps, but this proves that the path of objectification leads to an impasse. Within the paradigm of the quiz game, there exists a model of the correct answer, which provides a standard of comparison. We know what the answers given by Tully and Caius would have to be in order for both answers to be winners and thus indistinguishable from each other. At the same time, we know that answers that deviate from the archetype are losers. The winners therefore are united in the sign, but the sign that unites them exists before their own signifying activity. We have thus presupposed that there was a common sign rather than engendering this common sign from the speaking subjects and their respective expressive activities.

If there is no preexisting list of answers that the speakers must reproduce, the question of identifying thoughts with one another is no longer solved in advance. In answering a question, two people might produce signs that are apparently different simply because they are responding in the same way but in conditions that differ. For example, they are responding in different languages.

This amounts to saying that the identification of signs is no longer an individuation because it is contextual. Individuation is an identification *in all respects*. Yet the identification of thoughts, like that of the signs of these thoughts, is an identification *in certain respects*. For example, we see the answers given in different languages as identical provided they have the same meaning. This means that we view them as indistinguishable within the context of answering the question asked.

Minds encounter each other in signs. Each of them expresses itself in a sign. If the two speaking subjects express themselves using the same sign, they are thinking the same thing.

But they do not meet within a sign that has previously been produced; they meet within a sign that each of them produces. In fact, each produces a sign. Are the two signs they produce the same?

We must, according to the individualist philosopher, "constitute" language starting from speaking subjects and constitute the common mind out of individual minds. Every other philosophy of language and mind appears odd and absurd: the sign expressing the thoughts would have to precede the acts of thinking; language would have to exist before its speakers themselves. Starting from speech in order to constitute the language spoken in that speech is not, according to this individualist doctrine, an optional choice that may be worthwhile (or not); it is a metaphysical necessity.

We necessarily witness the constitution of the institution out of independent acts: we must see common meaning arise out of the exchanges among subjects—for example, in an interview between a *normalien* and a banker. This is where this objection from phenomenologists and individualists has its greatest force: the sign cannot be made to precede the producers of the sign, nor can the proposition precede the people who express themselves by constructing propositions. Our game—in which ideal answers have already been recorded before the game even begins—cannot be taken to be a model of language as it really is.

Sartre and Merleau-Ponty did not make the task any easier by discussing such priority of speech over language at the level of *words*. Indeed, there is nothing paradoxical about saying that words precede the act of speech: the word "sleet" had already been used before Sartre took it up as an example of a linguistic sign. The point of their critique of an "abstract" or "objectivist" conception of the sign becomes clearer if we consider authentic speech, declarations, sentences that say something. In such a case, to insist that the sign be determined before its use is like asking that speeches be recorded before even having been written. Where would they have been recorded? In the office of what transcendental bailiff? Is there a model for all of the sentences I will ever pronounce in some heaven of propositions in themselves?

All of this amounts to saying that the very concept of objectified mind is necessarily the concept of a *result*. In order for there to be a morsel of objectified mind, a movement of objectification must have occurred and there must therefore have already been something to objectify: the act of a speaking subject and, by extension, the cogitative act of a thinking subject.

Otherwise, one would have to posit an impersonal abstraction preceding concrete personal acts. This would be like positing a resemblance before any things that resemble each other, whiteness before white things, bravery before acts of bravery, humanity before humans, in short, the abstract before the concrete. One would then have to assume the activity of an active intellect—to borrow a term from Aristotle's philosophy of mind (*De Anima,* III, 5)—distinct from individual intellects, that would bear this literal meaning, this abstraction. If objectified mind came before subjective minds, it would be as if texts were already there before the semantic activities of expression and drafting of which they are in fact objectifications. The library, instead of being the product of subjects expressing themselves, would be the real thinking subject, while individual authors would be reduced to the role of auxiliary causes, instruments used by the anonymous and transpersonal source of meanings.

In the quiz game, the participants are attempting to send in answers identical to the models that have already been produced and accepted (one might imagine, for example, the game reduced to a multiple-choice quiz with the input of the participants involving nothing more than checking a box for each question). This is why real verbal exchanges cannot be analyzed using this model of the game. We must compare with one another the actual signs produced and not simply assess their distance from a predetermined model.

If we could return here to an atomistic philosophy of the sign, we would need only to consider the two signs produced by placing them side by side. We would then see if they were truly identical, i.e., if they were interchangeable in every respect. But we have already recognized that it is impossible to proceed in this manner, for we will necessarily be comparing a sign within a system with another sign within another system. If only we had a *common system* at the outset, we would have the answer to the philosophical question; all the difficulties of identification would be empirical or factual and would not call into question the very principle underlying the comparison. For the individualist philosopher, the problem is whether it is possible to derive the common system from a comparison of two distinct systems. Can one begin with two idiolects and fuse them at least in part within a common language?

One thing emerges clearly from this discussion: if the establishment of a common system requires uniformity among the subjects whose acts are compared, we can only conclude that communication is *miraculous*. Before we reach such a paradoxical conclusion, it is worth trying out a different hypothesis: the traditional analysis is defective and, indeed, the source of such paradoxes.

* * *

The objection raised by the phenomenologist of the individualist school was that in the philosophy of language, one must begin with the personal expression (of a personal thought) and not with a proposition in itself. To this point, though, we have only considered examples of impersonal thoughts. When Karl says that *"Der Schnee ist weiß,"* he is performing a speech act and that act is his own. The content of his thought, however, could not be more impersonal. There is nothing in it that indicates that Karl is the one saying it rather than Herbert. Textbook examples are generally constructed according to this model: the line by which cogitative content (the noeme) is to be cut out so as to separate it from the subject's act is, as it were, already marked in outline form. In considering these sorts of examples we have, in a way, presupposed what we were supposed to produce: the possibility of bringing out a commonality between A's personal act and B's personal act. But the fact of analyzing these acts as though they were assenting to propositions (that we imagine have already been written and submitted for the subjects' approval) means that, from the start, we are in the realm of impersonality. Subjects giving the same answer are interchangeable: accepting one of the responses is the same as accepting the other, as if there had only been one answer given. We might as well say that our individual subjects were never introduced as subjects distinct from each another, but rather with features that were already impersonal.

In order to meet this individualist objection, we will have to turn toward thoughts that are irreducibly personal: how can one personal thought and another personal thought be identified with each other through their content?

11.2. The Identity of Personal Thoughts

Let us look at the first page of Flaubert's comic novel *Bouvard and Pécuchet*. Flaubert begins his story with two men strolling in opposite directions on the Boulevard Bourdon in Paris. They have distinguishing traits: one is tall, the other short; the tall one is wearing a linen suit, the shorter a frock coat; the former is wearing a hat, the second a cap.

When they reached the middle of the boulevard, they both sat down, at the same moment, on the same bench.

> To wipe their foreheads, they removed their hats, which each man placed next to him. The short man noticed the name *Bouvard* written in his neighbor's, while the latter made out the word *Pécuchet* in the cap belonging to the fellow in the coat.
> "Fancy that!" he said. "We both had the idea of writing our names in our hats."
> "I should say so! Someone could walk off with mine at the office!"
> "You don't say—I work in an office, too."
> At which point they looked at each other.[5]

Bouvard expresses himself in the first-person plural, which is a sign that the idea is shared by the two men and contributes to the resemblance that—notwithstanding the distinctive signs at first provided—becomes evident in the course of the story, rendering the two almost interchangeable: the same job, the same bachelorhood, the same boredom, the same vague desire to leave Paris.[6]

They had the same idea. However, this mental resemblance is compatible with the differing results. In Bouvard's hat is written "Bouvard," while the name appearing in Pécuchet's cap is, as one might expect, "Pécuchet." Thus the same idea, when it is put into practice, gives different results. From a strictly semantic point of view, the idea is therefore not the same, since the truth conditions of the statement "I have written my name in my hat" are different depending on whether the thought is being thought by the subject Bouvard or the subject Pécuchet. And yet it is perfectly legitimate to say along with Flaubert that Bouvard and Pécuchet had the same idea.

What, then, is Bouvard's thought? It cannot be enough to say that he had the idea of doing something, an idea that is carried out when the name "Bouvard" has been written in his hat. For this way of reporting Bouvard's thinking leaves out something essential, which is the *personal* aspect of the thought that came to him. From a logical point of view, the following three sentences clearly differ from one another:

---

5. Gustave Flaubert, *Bouvard and Pécuchet,* trans. Mark Polizzotti (Champaign, IL: Dalkey Archive Press, 2005), 3.
6. I say Bouvard expresses himself in the first-person plural, but it might well be the smaller man, Pécuchet, who is speaking and not "the latter," i.e., Bouvard. Flaubert skillfully maintains the ambiguity of reference here. This equivocation is the perfect illustration of the following fact: with regard to their shared idea, the two characters are indistinguishable from one another.

(1) I must write my name in my hat.
(2) I must write "Bouvard" in my hat.
(3) Bouvard must write "Bouvard" in Bouvard's hat.

For starters, the first sentence by itself does not say what name should be written in which hat. Taken out of context, this sentence is thus doubly incomplete and therefore unable to serve to identify Bouvard's thought. Only sentence 3 has truth conditions when taken out of context, but it is unlikely to identify the thought that occurred to Bouvard (since he must have thought of his hat as being *his* hat and not as the hat of *somebody named Bouvard,* the procedure he would have used for any hat other than his own).

Moreover, sentences 1 and 2 might express thoughts occurring to anyone at all—for example, to Pécuchet. Imagine that Pécuchet had written "Bouvard" in his cap: he would have had, in a sense, the same idea that Bouvard had insofar as Bouvard's intention was to write the name "Bouvard" in his own hat. But, in another sense, he would not have had the same idea as Bouvard, for Bouvard did not write "Pécuchet" in his own hat. There are thus several ways of understanding what it is to have or not to have the same idea.

The idea that occurred to both Bouvard and Pécuchet might be called a *reflexive personal thought,* a term that alludes to the logic of the "indirect reflexive pronoun" pioneered by Geach in his article "On Beliefs About Oneself."[7] The indirect reflexive pronoun is used by a narrator to report (in indirect discourse) the utterances of someone who spoke about himself in the first person. Where we say that "Paul will attend the meeting," Paul, speaking about himself, says "I will attend the meeting." This is why we do not report his words in the form "Paul said that Paul will attend." There is the following semantic difference: Paul could have said that Paul will attend the meeting without knowing that *he himself* is the person who must attend the meeting if Paul is to attend the meeting. Or, if such a case of amnesia regarding proper names appears too artificial, take the case of

---

7. P. T. Geach, "On Beliefs About Oneself" (1957–1958), in his *Logic Matters* (Oxford: Blackwell, 1972), 129. In what follows, I will be applying to Flaubert's text an analysis proposed by Geach in his "Teleological Explanation," in *Explanation,* ed. Stephan Körner (Oxford: Blackwell, 1975), 79–80.

Paul who, thinking he has disguised himself well enough to be unrecognizable, tells us, "Unfortunately, Paul will not be able to come to the meeting, but he asked me to attend in his stead, and I will be attending."[8]

In what way is the idea of writing one's name in one's hat a reflexive personal idea? What stands out in the passage is Bouvard's use of first-person plural personal pronouns ("we both had the same idea," "our hats") even though he is referring to different and independent mental acts by two different people. In order to speak in that way, Bouvard must place himself at a level of generality that abstracts from the particular subject concerned in each case without abstracting from the fact that the thought belongs to a particular subject, one that is different each time. Bouvard's act and that of Pécuchet can be identified by the same common feature. This common feature, this universal, is the concept of being oneself the one to whom a predicate must be applied.

Two levels can be distinguished:

1. the level of the *sentences* that express Bouvard and Pécuchet's respective ideas (these sentences are different since they identify different acts of writing in different hats);
2. the level of the *predicative structure* that is common to these sentences from the point of view of their intelligible content.

It is as if each of them had followed a general recommendation given to every employee: "Inscribe your name in your hat, as it may otherwise be taken from the office by someone else." Or, to put it in Fregean terms, each employee applying this instruction to himself provides an "argument" to this "function" and thereby determines the meaning of the resulting sentence (e.g., Bouvard will inscribe the name "Bouvard" in Bouvard's hat and Pécuchet the name "Pécuchet" in Pécuchet's hat). Similarly, a schoolteacher might tell the entire class, "Write your name on the first page of your notebook." Only one instruction is given, the same

---

8. In a review of Paul Ricoeur's book *Oneself as Another,* I attempted to show that the notion of an indirect reflexive personal pronoun allows one to justify several distinctions that philosophers of subjectivity rightly hold to be necessary but without thereby restricting individuality (*ipseitas*) to human beings. See my "Le pouvoir d'être soi," *Critique* 529–530 (1991): 545–576.

for everyone, which each student carries out, as do the others, by executing an action that is unique. In these examples, the general instruction retains a predicative or, if you will, "open" quality in the sense in which a predicate is an "open sentence," a sentence whose subject has not yet been determined (and here it is the task of the personal subject to recognize itself in the general figure of *oneself*).

In the example of the quiz game, the identification of thoughts expressed in the same way was made possible by the fact that the answers became interchangeable if we abstracted them from their subjects—i.e., if we saw it as immaterial that the phrase "snow is white" served to communicate the thoughts of two different people. In the case presently under consideration, there can be no question of seeing the two subjects as interchangeable in every respect, because the entire meaning of what is thought each time depends on the identity of the subject. What should Bouvard write? Since he is Bouvard, he must write the name "Bouvard." It is nevertheless possible to discover an identity of structure by assuming a higher level of abstraction, by formulating the common predicative structure of Bouvard and Pécuchet's ideas in a kind of general instruction. From the perspective of such an instruction, the two subjects are interchangeable. The instruction is addressed in the same terms to both of them and does not distinguish between them.

The difference between the identification of propositional thoughts, on the one hand, and personal thoughts, on the other, is this: the abstraction from the subject who is thinking the proposition "snow is white" has as a result that the thinking subject need not *identify herself* when accomplishing the act of thinking this thought. By contrast, the abstraction of the subject who applies to himself a personal predicate such as "x must write his name in his hat" does not exempt the thinking subject from an act of self-reflection or thinking about itself. It would not be enough for him to write his own name (which is not the same thing as affixing one's signature) if this were done only in order to make reference to the name's bearer. He must conceive of himself as he to whom the predicate applies.

The capacity for abstraction that allows someone to carry out such self-reflection is also what allows him to conceive that someone else can do the same. In other words and as idealistic philosophers have claimed, the subjective power exercised in self-reflection is at once an intersubjective power.[9] These philosophers were right to say this, at least if they meant by it something like this: someone who is able, as Bouvard is, to write his name in his hat is *ipso facto* able to recognize that Pécuchet had the same idea if he did the same thing. Someone who can say to himself "you must write your name in your hat" is also able to say "we had the same idea, to write our names in our hats."

But if this is the case, it follows that the intersubjective relation within which the two men consider and recognize each other *presupposes* another relation that we might call "dialogical," since it relates any subject whatever (self or other) to some other subject (self or other). To speak of a general instruction is to posit an instructor addressing new recruits. The recognition that leads Bouvard to see Pécuchet as an *alter ego* (and reciprocally) rests here on a relation of interlocution that we have compared to that of the teacher addressing a class in general terms to tell the students what to do, each for himself.

In order to identify thoughts with one another, there must be a relation of interlocution. But this is not a relation of interlocution between Bouvard and Pécuchet: *that* "we" of interlocution is precisely the one we seek to "constitute." Rather, it is the relation of interlocution that allowed *us* to assimilate Bouvard and Pécuchet's respective ideas.

It was within the context of the general instruction to "write one's name in one's hat" that Bouvard's idea appears to be identical to Pécuchet's. The identity that makes intersubjective recognition possible is the identity between a general instruction and a particular application of it. When the instructor says to everyone, "You must write your name in your hat if you

---

9. "Self-consciousness is faced by another self-consciousness; it has come *out of itself.* This has a twofold significance: first, it has lost itself, for it finds itself as an *other* being; secondly, in doing so it has superseded the other, for it does not see the other as an essential being, but in the other sees its own self. . . . [T]his movement of self-consciousness . . . has itself the double significance of being both its own action and the action of the other as well. . . . [The two extremes of the syllogism of self-consciousness] *recognize* themselves as *mutually recognizing* one another." G. W. F. Hegel, *The Phenomenology of Spirit,* trans. A. V. Miller (Oxford: Oxford University Press, 1979), §§ 179–184 (111–112).

do not want it to be taken from your desk," he is saying exactly what Bouvard understands as "I am going to write this word 'Bouvard' in this hat." It is only because Bouvard understands the application of the general instruction to his particular person that he can identify his idea with Pécuchet's.

It is therefore not the relation between oneself and oneself that is conclusive with regard to either the identity of thoughts with one another or recognition. The relation between oneself and oneself would be but a particular relation if it did not have a form analogous to that of the relation between an instructor giving orders and the individuals he addresses in a way that does not distinguish them. Bouvard is doubtless the source of the instruction received by Bouvard, whereas Pécuchet is the source of the instruction received by Pécuchet. Their thoughts are independent from each other. But in order to understand the universal that makes these thoughts comparable, we pass through the conditions of a general communication. Bouvard and Pécuchet's respective ideas can be identified with each other only because both ideas can be identified with what would be a general instruction addressed to both within a real relation of interlocution. Finally, the context within which such identification of thoughts can occur, in a holistic mode, would appear to be the context of a social activity such as the act of making oneself understood by someone.

We will now ask how thoughts can be identifiable with each other within a context that is holistic because it is provided by an institution.

11.3. The Thoughts of a Social Subject

It is a coincidence that Bouvard and Pécuchet had the same idea. However, this is not the case for what we might now call *social thoughts*. A social thought is a thought that fulfills the following condition: if the other does not have the same idea that I do, then I cannot have this idea either. Up to this point, we have been saying this: let us suppose that Bouvard had the idea of writing his name in his hat but that Pécuchet had the idea of putting his cap into his desk drawer, far from the other hats. In that case, each of them would have had his own idea, one that would differ from the other's idea. Each of them would have nonetheless had his own idea. The community of ideas arises from the comparison but is not a condition of the very identity of, say, Bouvard's idea.

Now let us consider a different case: the idea of a thinker A is such that someone else, B, must have this same idea, failing which, A does not have this idea. To introduce this new class of ideas, we need only extend our reflection on personal thoughts to a case of a polyadic predicate. Rather than an analogous operation carried out by two independent subjects, thinking here will have to become a single operation carried out by two subjects that belong to the same social dyad.

Consider two people, A and B, who have an appointment. First possible case: two employees who think "I have a meeting tomorrow at three with the director" have the *same reflexive thought,* by which each declares himself to be a member of the logical class defined by the extension of the predicate ". . . has a meeting with the director." Let us assume for this example that meetings with the director are always one-on-one meetings at a precise time. If two employees in these conditions have the same idea, then one of them must be wrong or the director's administrator erred in setting up the meetings. It is presupposed in our example that both employees cannot have the same appointment (i.e., they will not be received together). We therefore know in advance that at least one of the employees will necessarily be disappointed.

But now let us consider two people who have an appointment *with each other.* The first, A, says to himself, "I have an appointment with B." The second, B, says to himself, "I have an appointment with A." These thoughts had by A and B are obviously semantically different, which is clear from the fact that the actions each of them will have to carry out for the meeting to take place are different. But if we abstract from the subjects, we can, like Bouvard, express their thought in the first-person plural. A will say to himself, "We have an appointment (with it being understood that this means B and myself)." B, on the other hand, will say to himself, "We have an appointment (with it being understood that this means A and myself)." In this example "we" means in both cases the couple formed by A and B, but this couple presents itself differently in their respective thoughts.

These formulations reveal an identity between the respective thoughts of A and B, considered as members of a couple of social actors. Knowing who comprises the couple, we understand immediately that A cannot think what he thinks if B, for his part, is not *ipso facto* the subject of a complementary representation. The social relation of the appointment also serves to define a class, the class of people who have appointments with one another. In the case of reflexive thoughts, the identity consisted in this: Pécuchet had the same thought as Bouvard if he intended to do (for himself, i.e., for Pécuchet) what Bouvard intended to do (for himself, i.e., for Bouvard). The two characters had differing thoughts relative to the subjects to which they applied. Yet our analysis has brought out a common structure to these thoughts. They are *the same thought* when they are compared with each other in the abstract form of reflexive thoughts (e.g., "write one's name in one's hat"). In the same way, two people thinking that they have an appointment with each other are having different thoughts or, if you prefer, different beliefs regarding the sense in which to understand their relation to each other: B is the one that A must meet, while A is the one that B must meet. It is nevertheless acceptable to speak about *the same thought* if we take into account the fact that two *complementary* thoughts are involved.

It is not odd to say that the thoughts of A and B are the same even where they are expressed in differing ways, since this diversity of expression is precisely what their complementarity calls for. To speak of identity in such cases is no more unusual than is the move from the active voice to the passive or reversing the direction of a reciprocal relationship. If Romeo loves Juliet, then the thought that Romeo loves Juliet is, incontestably, the same thought as the one according to which Juliet is loved by Romeo. Aristotle's classic example can also serve as an illustration of this point: the road that goes from Athens to Thebes is also the road that goes from Thebes to Athens. One might therefore add that the thought that there is a road from Athens to Thebes is also, in a legitimate sense, the thought that there is a road from Thebes to Athens.

Here then is the decisive difference between thoughts that are common to two thinkers and a thought that is common to a *couple* of partners (i.e., between manifestations of intersubjective mind and objective mind): if Pécuchet had not had the same idea as Bouvard (who had the idea of writing his name in his hat), that can only mean that Pécuchet's idea was not to write the name "Pécuchet" in his cap; by contrast, if B never had the idea that he had an appointment with A, then A could also not have the idea that he had an appointment with B.

That conclusion may well seem unwarranted. It immediately provokes a stream of objections inspired by solipsism, the general tenor of which is this: how can what A thinks result in any conclusions whatsoever about what B thinks? Such a claim would amount to maintaining that A's idea determines what must be B's idea. This would seem to require some sort of telepathic action of A upon B. After all, it is entirely possible that one of them is wrong. It is possible that A *imagines* that he has an appointment with B and that he is wrong about it and even delirious. If A's thought were a social thought in the sense defined earlier—i.e., a thought that A has only if it is also one that B has—then all A would have to do is hallucinate something to force B to have the same hallucination. That would be a convenient way of securing appointments with people who are hard to meet: one would only have to think that one had an appointment with them!

In reality, the notion of social thought introduced earlier justifies none of these absurd consequences. But before answering such objections, one point will have to be conceded.

Consider a "Cartesian"-style argument meant to isolate the two characters, endowing each of them with an isolated mental sphere. A *believes* he has an appointment with B. What follows from this for B? The response is this: nothing at all follows for him. From this we can derive the following lesson: appointments should not be confused with apparent appointments. Let us compare that case with other reciprocal relations. If Caius is married to Sempronia, Sempronia is married to Caius. Now imagine the following idiotic exchange:

CAIUS: I am married to Sempronia.
INTERLOCUTOR: Ah, I see. But, tell me, is Sempronia also married to you?

In this situation, Caius's response cannot be "I do not know; you will have to ask her." Rather, his response will have to be "You must not have heard me; I just told you that we are married."

But let us imagine another scenario in which an elderly Caius's memory is failing so that he no longer remembers if he is still married to or divorced from Sempronia.

CAIUS: I believe I am married to Sempronia.
INTERLOCUTOR: Very well. But, tell me, does Sempronia believe she is married to you?

In this case, Caius's next reply might very well be that he does not know and that the interlocutor should ask Sempronia.

*　*　*

My thesis is that there are, beyond impersonal thoughts and reflexive personal thoughts, a class of social thoughts. The thesis is not that all anyone (say, A) need do is have the idea that he forms a couple with someone else (let us call him B) for there to exist a couple A-B. If that were the thesis, the doors to delirium would be open. A would only have to imagine that B is persecuting him for there to exist a couple in a relation of persecutor and victim.

The thesis I am supporting, in general, *does not bear upon* the phenomenological recognition of the facts concerning the subject and his partner (e.g., "Are we really married?" "Do we really have an appointment?"). I am not seeking in the lived experience of A some incontestable phenomenological datum whose sole presence would allow conclusions to be drawn as to the truth of his belief. I therefore grant that it is possible to be mistaken, that it is possible to be delirious, and even that it is possible to be delirious while wondering nervously whether one is delirious or not.

My point here is entirely different: in what sense should we speak about the same thought when two people think the same thing, since it is not in the sense in which we may be speaking about the same car?

In the above example, A's thought and B's thought are a single thought that each of them applies to himself. When A thinks that he has an appointment with B and when B thinks that he has an appointment with A, they do not have distinct thoughts that just happen to correspond as would be the case if, in Nice, A had the idea "I think I will send a postcard to B" while at the same time, in Paris, B had the idea "I think I will send a postcard to A." The two complementary thoughts about the appointment are two occurrences of the *same thought,* a single thought that arises *twice* (once for A and once for B) and that presents itself to each of them in different terms (according to whether the appointment is with A or with B).

The "Cartesian" argument about error and delirium has no bearing on this thesis. Imagine a delirious subject A: he wrongly imagines that he has a five o'clock appointment with B. Now imagine that, by some extraordinary coincidence, B is also confused and imagines that he has set up an appointment for five o'clock with A. One can of course claim that they are having the same delirium or that they have made the same mistake. But one cannot claim that they have an appointment with each other (as if one could make an appointment in a dream or in delirium). And if they have not made an appointment, they have no appointment, and therefore neither of them has *an idea of their appointment*. This pair of delirious subjects lacks a "we."

In other words, the example of the appointment is no longer that of a resemblance between two thoughts (to be analyzed according to the model of a resemblance between two white walls; see Chapter 7, section 3, above). The relation between the two thoughts is real (as in the case where Cain is the murderer of Abel on condition that Abel is the victim of Cain; see Chapter 8, section 1, above).

All of this can be put another way. The institution of the appointment only exists if people have ways of remembering that they have made appointments. To simplify things, one might provide them with an external memory just for appointments. The appointment has been made if it is put into memory, and it is put into memory if it is written in the diary. The thesis is that the same idea—"I have an appointment with someone who has an appointment with me"—is written in both diaries and that it is only *the idea that it is* if it is written in both diaries. Imagine now that the idea is written in one of the diaries but not the other. It is no longer the same idea.

This is why each of the two partners is ordinarily inclined, with regard to a particular appointment, to consult the other party's diary in cases where his own has been misplaced: the idea is the same, an idea that is only the same if it appears in both diaries.

Phenomenologically, "I have an appointment" and "I believe I have an appointment" are no doubt indistinguishable, as perhaps are also "I see a ghost" and "I believe I see a ghost." But what matters is that someone who discovers that the appointment he thought he had (having found it in his memory or in his diary) was not recorded by his counterpart should not say, "I had the thought that I had an appointment with B, but he did not have the thought that he had an appointment with me." What he should say is, "It seemed like I had an appointment with B, but I was wrong because I was the only one who thought so." In other words, *my* thought about the appointment is only *a* thought *about the appointment* if it is *our* thought about the appointment. The proof is that *my* illusion of having an appointment only presents itself (falsely) as a thought of *our appointment*

DISTINGUISHING THOUGHTS   335

through a claim to be *our* thought of the appointment. It claims this by accepting in advance to be subject to the proof of its identification through its double inscription (in both diaries).

This example of the appointment shows how the thoughts of two different subjects can be identified with each other within the context of a common system. Here we are no longer comparing two distinct mental systems so as to find resemblances that may result in the hypostasis of an objectified mind. We have an appointment if we have set one up according to the habitual practices. It is legitimate (and in no way obscure) to say that in this case what *we think* serves as a rule for what *I must think*. The subject "we" is not in this case a collective individual (e.g., a thinking crowd) but, rather, a social subject; it is each of us as a dyadic unit.

11.4. The Relation of Interlocution

Contemporary philosophers, following Quine, usually raise the problem of identifying someone else's statements in the form of a question regarding the possibility of "radical translation," which means a translation to be carried out in the absence of all of the usual conditions for translation work. Normally, to understand what people are saying in a foreign language, one must either learn this language from a teacher, or hire a bilingual interpreter, or arm oneself with a dictionary and a grammar. But what does one do if none of these means are available, i.e., if the language is "radically" unknown?

Quine's argument is often presented—and in the first place by Quine himself—as lending support to behaviorist linguistics. It seems to me that such a version of the argument assumes a dyadic conception of the semantic relation: to understand what a sign signifies or means is to relate it to something else. But what? What is the ontological category to which the signified belongs? One quickly realizes that the correlate of the sign cannot be the *idea*. We can identify signs through type individuation (e.g., by saying how it is spelled). By contrast, there is no way to identify ideas other than by either reproducing the sign that we were supposed to be explaining or by coming up with another, different sign held to be its equivalent (in a particular context and not, obviously, in every respect). It is thus impossible to place on one side of the verb "means" a designation of the sign (namely, its mention in quotation marks) and on the other a designation of the idea (or signified). To take signifieds to be individuals or entities is to fall prey to the myth of "objective meanings."

Since we have acknowledged that such objective meanings are chimeric, if we wish to preserve the dyadic conception of the semantic relation, the behaviorist solution is the only one left—i.e., associating the sign with an external circumstance (by means of a relation that is more or less causal). For example, the presence of a rabbit in someone's visual field would provoke the sonic emission of a sign, and we could begin with this dyadic relation in translating the sign emitted. The radical translator is supposed to observe that, in the circumstance in which he himself would be provoked to exclaim "lo, a rabbit," the natives react by producing the sign "Gavagai" and the translator notes this correspondence in his field notebook.[10]

If that were the meaning of the argument from radical translation, it seems to me that this argument would be devoid of interest and, indeed, ridiculous. It would exhibit the same error in principle as we found in Russell's analysis of the gift: seeking to identify a triadic fact (i.e., an intentional relation) by means of an accumulation of observations of dyadic facts (i.e., causal relations). If the argument from radical translation is generally considered to be an intelligible or even illuminating thought experiment, it is because it makes an appeal to relations other than natural ones.

In fact, in Quine's own work, the argument shows how an investigator forced to do translation work in the described "radical" conditions must ask himself in what circumstances of the *social* life of the natives it would be *appropriate* to emit the sign "Gavagai" so as to elicit in one's interlocutors a *response* such as "Indeed!" If the radical translator can only find a way to emit the sign "Gavagai" and have his use approved by the natives, he will have taken the first step in his acculturation. He will have succeeded in addressing the natives in their own language, in a language that he did not know but in which he has just made remarkable progress, for he will have succeeded in making it the case that a question has been asked in this

---

10. Willard van Orman Quine, *Word and Object* (Cambridge, MA: MIT Press, 1960), § 7 (29).

language. But making it the case that a question is asked in a language is more than simply asking a question, for I might ask a question without it being the case that a question has been asked—in the case, for example, in which nobody has heard or understood me. If a question has been asked, a speech act has been accomplished, a social act whose subject is the couple formed by a first member whose task is to construct the interrogative utterance and a second member whose task is to receive, in conformity with the local forms of address and customs, the sign produced.

As a result, the argument shows how an investigator placed in radical conditions would have no other solution but to establish a *bond of interlocution* with the natives, with himself in the role of the beginner and the natives in the role of listeners, correctors, and authenticators of his attempts to speak the native language.

In fact, the argument from radical translation brings to light the following: in order to explain what a sign means, one must move beyond all dyadic relations. The sign is given an *interpretant,* which can be the sign itself (as in the passage from mention to use), or its translation, or its paraphrase, or its development. Quine, then, rediscovered the triadic nature of the semantic relation. The relation of interlocution is the paradigm of a semiotic relation. Is "Gavagai" a sign and, if so, of what? It is the sign of the presence of a rabbit (the object) if it is to be translated by "lo, a rabbit!" (the interpretant). And, similarly, the object of reference is the event of a rabbit passing by if the sign emitted in this regard is to be translated into my language by the interpretant reporting this event. As for this interpretant ("lo, a rabbit!"), it is the interpretant of "Gavagai" if it assigns to this sign the intentional relation to the object to which it itself refers.

As a general rule, the relation of interlocution provides the context in which thoughts are identified with each other to the extent that such identification cannot be established unless the same thought is present twice: once on the speaker's side and once on the side of his interlocutor. Just as the relation of an appointment calls for the two people who have the appointment to have thoughts that are really complementary, when a question is asked there is a similar real complementarity between the thought expressed by the interrogative utterance and the thought expressed in the answer.

The act of thinking is rightly held to be supremely personal. Thinking, reflecting, and demonstrating intellective attention are all things that nobody else can do in my stead. The comparison of the thoughts that occur to different people is therefore a comparison among acts that are independent from one another.

The ontological independence of acts of thinking, however, does not prevent different people from thinking the same thing. It *must* not prevent it.

Here, individualist philosophers of mind run up against a problem: how can different subjects have identical thoughts? To speak about identical thoughts is to consider these thoughts—or, if you prefer, the signs expressing these thoughts—from an impersonal point of view. But it then seems as if, in order to compare the thoughts of two subjects, the two subjects must agree to renounce the distinctiveness of their thought.

In order for A to be able to understand and reproduce what B thinks, does he have to become B? Or does he have to return—at a deeper level than that of the appearances given to the consciousness of each of us—to the act of an impersonal universal mind that expresses itself sometimes through B's utterances and sometimes through those of A?

These individualist philosophers cannot grasp the impersonal portion within the personal. They conceive of the impersonal as the abstraction of a resemblance between two personal acts. In short, they know no universals other than relations of resemblance among monadic units, individual entities whose internal states are characterized by their intrinsic qualities. It goes without saying that such abstractions cannot precede concrete acts, unless we accept the idea of putting various conceptual monsters into circulation: e.g., the soul of the world, the speaking *id,* texts that write themselves, structures that commandeer the generative causality of actors, and so forth.

In order to understand the authority that objective mind has over subjects, the function of (impersonal) instituted meaning in the formation and communication of thoughts will have to be conceived in an entirely different way. The priority of the impersonal over the personal is not at all like the priority of the text over the reader or the copyist. It is, rather, the priority of a rule over the activity that it governs.

What makes a freely initiated act able to logically determine your reaction—whatever it may be—as being your response to my prompting are the established customs surrounding such acts. These customs are *institutions* in Mauss's sense: they are ways of doing and thinking of which individuals are not the authors. Individuals certainly are the authors of the *sentences* they construct, but they are not the authors of the *meaning* of these sentences, and this is exactly what is meant by an utterance's impersonal meaning. My interlocutor is wrong if he has not understood what I said in the same way as what *my sentence* means in the context. And I am equally wrong if I claim that what *I* said is anything other than what *my sentence* said in virtue of established practice (and any special conventions that we may have agreed between us to encode or distinguish our exchanges must themselves have been agreed upon in the common idiom).

These established practices allow us to decide what has been said—and therefore what has been thought—when someone makes himself understood by someone else. They are thus well and truly institutions of meaning.

Works Cited

Adams, Marilyn McCord. *William Ockham*. Vol. 1. Notre Dame, IN: University of Notre Dame Press, 1987.
Anscombe, G. E. M. "Aristotle." In *Three Philosophers: Aristotle, Aquinas, Frege,* by G. E. M. Anscombe and P. T. Geach, 1–63. Oxford: Basil Blackwell, 1963.
———. *Intention*. Oxford: Blackwell, 1957.
———. *An Introduction to Wittgenstein's "Tractatus": Themes in the Philosophy of Wittgenstein*. 1959. 2nd ed. New York: Harper Torchbooks, 1965.
———. "Under a Description." *Noûs* 13, no. 2 (1979): 219–233.
Arnauld, Antoine, and Claude Lancelot. *General and Rational Grammar: The Port-Royal Grammar*. Edited and translated by Jacques Rieux and Bernard E. Rollin. The Hague: Mouton, 1975.
Arnauld, Antoine, and Pierre Nicole. *Logic; or, The Art of Thinking: Containing (Besides the Common Rules) Many New Observations, That Are of Great Use in Forming an Exactness of Judgment*. Translated by John Ozell. London: William Taylor, 1717 (1662).
Aron, Raymond. *Les étapes de la pensée sociologique*. Paris: Gallimard, 1967.
———. *Introduction to the Philosophy of History: An Essay on the Limits of Historical Objectivity*. Translated by George J. Irwin. Boston: Beacon Press, 1961.
———. *Main Currents in Sociological Thought*. Vol. 2. Translated by Richard Howard and Helen Weaver. New York: Basic Books, 1967.
———. *La philosophie critique de l'histoire: Essai sur une théorie allemande de l'histoire*. 1938. 2nd ed. Paris: J. Vrin, 1950.
Augé, Marc. *An Anthropology for Contemporaneous Worlds*. Translated by Amy Jacobs. Stanford, CA: Stanford University Press, 1999.

Beaufret, Jean. "Note sur Husserl et Heidegger." In *De l'existentialisme à Heidegger: Introduction aux philosophies de l'existence,* 113–131. 1971. 2nd ed. Paris: J. Vrin, 1986.
Belaval, Yvon. *Leibniz critique de Descartes.* Paris: Gallimard, 1960.
Bell, David. *Husserl.* London: Routledge, 1990.
Blanchot, Maurice. "Literature and the Right to Death" (1949). Translated by Lydia Davis. In *The Work of Fire,* 300–344. Translated by Charlotte Mandell. Stanford, CA: Stanford University Press, 1995.
Bouveresse, Jacques. "L'animal cérémoniel: Wittgenstein et l'anthropologie." *Actes de la recherche en sciences sociales* 16 (1977): 43–54.
———. *La force de la règle: Wittgenstein et l'invention de la nécessité.* Paris: Les Éditions de Minuit, 1987.
———. *Le mythe de l'intériorité: Expérience, signification et langage privé chez Wittgenstein.* 1976. 2nd rev. ed. Paris: Les Éditions de Minuit, 1987.
———. *Wittgenstein Reads Freud: The Myth of the Unconscious.* Translated by Carol Cosman. Princeton: Princeton University Press, 1995.
Brandom, Robert B. *Making It Explicit: Reasoning, Representing, and Discursive Commitment.* Cambridge, MA: Harvard University Press, 1994.
———. *Perspectives on Pragmatism: Classical, Recent and Contemporary.* Cambridge, MA: Harvard University Press, 2011.
Brentano, Franz. *Psychology from an Empirical Standpoint.* Edited by Oskar Kraus and Linda L. McAlister. Translated by Antos C. Rancurello, D. B. Terrell, and Linda L. McAlister. New York: Routledge, 1995.
Breton, Stanislas. *Conscience et intentionnalité.* Paris: Vitte, 1956.
Castoriadis, Cornelius. *The Imaginary Institution of Society.* Translated by Kathleen Blamey. Cambridge: Polity Press, 1987.
———. *Le Monde morcelé.* Paris: Les Éditions du Seuil, 1990.
Charbonnier, Georges. *Conversations with Claude Lévi-Strauss.* Translated by John Weightman and Doreen Weightman. London: Jonathan Cape, Ltd., 1969.
Chauviré, Christiane. *Peirce et la signification: Introduction à la logique du vague.* Paris: Presses Universitaires de France, 1994.
Chisholm, Roderick. "Sentences About Believing." *Proceedings of the Aristotelian Society* 56 (1955–1956): 125–148.
Coffey, Peter. *The Science of Logic.* London: Longmans, Green and Co., 1912.
Condillac. "Treatise on the Sensations." In *Philosophical Writings of Etienne Bonnot, Abbé de Condillac,* 153–339. Translated by Franklin Philip and Harlan Lane. Hillsdale, NJ: Lawrence Erlbaum Associates, 1982.
Courtine, Jean-François. "Histoire et destin phénoménologique de l'*intentio*." In *L'intentionalité en question: Entre phénoménologie et sciences cognitives,* edited by Dominique Janicaud, 13–36. Paris: J. Vrin, 1994.
Davidson, Donald. "What Metaphors Mean." In *Inquiries into Truth and Interpretation,* 245–264. 2nd ed. Oxford: Clarendon Press, 2001.

Derrida, Jacques. *Edmund Husserl's "Origin of Geometry": An Introduction.* Translated by John P. Leavey, Jr. Lincoln, NE: University of Nebraska Press, 1989.

Descombes, Vincent. *Le complément de sujet: Enquête sur le fait d'agir de soi-même.* Paris: Gallimard, 2004.

———. "Les individus collectifs." In *Philosophie et anthropologie,* 57–93. Paris: Centre Georges Pompidou, 1992. Rpt. in *Revue de MAUSS* 18 (2001–2002): 305–337.

———. "Is There an Objective Spirit?" Translated by Daniel M. Weinstock. In *Philosophy in an Age of Pluralism: The Philosophy of Charles Taylor in Question,* edited by James Tully, 96–118. Cambridge: Cambridge University Press, 1994.

———. *The Mind's Provisions: A Critique of Cognitivism.* Translated by Stephen Adam Schwartz. Princeton: Princeton University Press, 2001.

———. "Pourquoi les sciences morales ne sont-elles pas des sciences naturelles?" In *Charles Taylor et l'interprétation de l'identité moderne,* edited by Guy Laforest and Philippe de Lara, 53–78. Quebec: Presses de l'Université Laval, 1998.

———. "Le pouvoir d'être soi." *Critique* 529–530 (1991): 545–576.

———. *Le raisonnement de l'ours et autres essais de philosophie pratique.* Paris: Les Éditions du Seuil, 2007.

Dubarle, Dominique. "Dialectique hégélienne et formalisation." In *Logique et dialectique,* by Dominique Dubarle and André Doz, 1–200. Paris: Larousse, 1971.

Duhem, Pierre. *The Aim and Structure of Physical Theory.* 1914. Translated by Philip P. Wiener. Princeton, NJ: Princeton University Press, 1954.

Dumézil, Georges. *Idées romaines.* Paris, Gallimard, 1979.

Dummett, Michael. *Frege and Other Philosophers.* Oxford: Oxford University Press, 1991.

———. *Truth and Other Enigmas.* Cambridge, MA: Harvard University Press, 1978.

Dumont, Louis. *La civilisation indienne et nous.* Paris: Armand Colin, 1975.

———. *Essays on Individualism: Modern Ideology in Anthropological Perspective.* Chicago: University of Chicago Press, 1986.

———. *German Ideology: From France to Germany and Back.* Chicago: University of Chicago Press, 1994.

———. *Homo Hierarchicus.* 1970. 2nd rev. ed. Translated by Mark Sainsbury, Louis Dumont, and Basia Gulati. Chicago: University of Chicago Press, 1980.

———. *Introduction to Two Theories of Social Anthropology: Descent Groups and Marriage Alliance.* Edited and translated by Robert Parkin. New York: Berghahn Books, 2006.

Fichte, J. G. *The Closed Commercial State.* Translated by Anthony Curtis Adler. Albany: State University of New York Press, 2012.

Findlay, J. N. *Meinong's Theory of Objects and Values.* 2nd ed. Oxford: Clarendon Press, 1963.

Flaubert, Gustave. *Bouvard and Pécuchet.* Translated by Mark Polizzotti. Champaign, IL: Dalkey Archive Press, 2005.
Fodor, Jerry, and Ernest Lepore. *Holism: A Shopper's Guide.* Oxford: Blackwell, 1992.
Føllesdal, Dagfinn. "Husserl's Notion of Noema." *The Journal of Philosophy* 66, no. 20 (1969): 680–687.
Fowler, H. W. *A Dictionary of Modern English Usage.* 2nd rev. ed. Revised by Sir Ernest Gowers. Oxford: Oxford University Press, 1965.
Frege, Gottlob. "A Critical Elucidation of Some Points in E. Schröder's *Vorlesungen über die Algebra der Logik*" (1895). Translated by Peter Geach. In *Translations from the Philosophical Writings of Gottlob Frege,* edited by Peter Geach and Max Black, 86–106. 2nd ed. Oxford: Basil Blackwell, 1960.
———. *The Foundations of Arithmetic: A Logico-Mathematical Inquiry into the Concept of Number.* 2nd rev. ed. Translated by J. L. Austin. New York: Harper Brothers, 1953.
Gardies, Jean-Louis. *Esquisse d'une grammaire pure.* Paris: J. Vrin, 1975.
Gardiner, Alan. *The Theory of Speech and Language.* 1932. 2nd ed. Oxford: Clarendon Press, 1951.
Geach, P. T. *Logic Matters.* Oxford: Blackwell, 1972.
———. *Mental Acts: Their Content and Their Objects.* London: Routledge and Kegan Paul, 1957.
———. *Reference and Generality: An Examination of Some Medieval and Modern Theories.* 3rd ed. Ithaca: Cornell University Press, 1980.
———. "Teleological Explanation." In *Explanation,* edited by Stephan Körner, 76–95. Oxford: Blackwell, 1975.
———. *Truth, Love and Immortality: An Introduction to McTaggart's Philosophy.* Berkeley: University of California Press, 1979.
Girard, René. *Deceit, Desire and the Novel: Self and Other in Literary Structure.* Translated by Yvonne Freccero. Baltimore: Johns Hopkins University Press, 1976.
Gochet, Paul. *Quine en perspective: Essai de philosophie comparée.* Paris: Flammarion, 1978.
Godelier, Maurice. *The Enigma of the Gift.* Translated by Nora Scott. Chicago: University of Chicago Press, 1999.
Goldschmidt, Victor. *Le paradigme dans la dialectique platonicienne.* Paris: Presses Universitaires de France, 1947.
Hacking, Ian. "Five Parables." In *Philosophy in History,* edited by Richard Rorty, J. B. Schneewind, and Quentin Skinner, 103–124. Cambridge: Cambridge University Press, 1984.
Hartmann, Nicolai. *Das Problem des geistigen Seins: Untersuchungen zur Grundlegung der Geschichtsphilosophie und der Geisteswissenschaft.* Berlin: de Gruyter, 1933.

Hegel, G. W. F. *Elements of the Philosophy of Right*. Edited by Allen W. Wood. Translated by H. B. Nisbet. Cambridge: Cambridge University Press, 1991.

———. *The Encyclopaedia Logic (with the Zusätze): Part I of the "Encyclopaedia of the Philosophical Sciences" with the Zusätze*. Edited and translated by T. F. Geraets, W. A. Suchting, and H. S. Harris. Indianapolis: Hackett Publishing Company, 1991.

———. *Enzyklopädie der philosophischen Wissenschaften im Grundrisse*. In his *Gesammelte Werke*. Vol. 20. Edited by Wolfgang Bonsiepen and Hans-Christian Lucas. Hamburg: Felix Meiner Verlag, 1992.

———. *Hegel's Philosophy of Mind, Being Part Three of the Encyclopaedia of Philosophical Sciences*. Translated by William Wallace. Oxford: Clarendon Press, 1971.

———. *Hegel's Philosophy of Mind: A Revised Version of the Wallace and Miller Translation (Hegel's Encyclopædia of the Philosophical Sciences)*. Translated by A. V. Miller, and William Wallace. Revised by Michael Inwood. Oxford: Oxford University Press, 2006.

———. *The Phenomenology of Spirit*. Translated by A. V. Miller. Oxford: Clarendon Press, 1977.

Henninger, Mark. "Aquinas on the Ontological Status of Relations." *Journal of the History of Philosophy* 25, no. 4 (1987): 491–515.

Husserl, Edmund. *Cartesian Meditations*. Translated by Dorion Cairns. The Hague: Martinus Nijhoff, 1960.

———. *The Crisis of European Sciences and Transcendental Phenomenology*. Translated by David Carr. Evanston: Northwestern University Press, 1970.

———. *Ideas: General Introduction to Pure Phenomenology*. Translated by W. R. Boyce Gibson. 1931. New York: Collier, 1962.

———. *Ideas Pertaining to a Pure Phenomenology and to a Phenomenological Philosophy, Second Book: Studies in the Phenomenology of Constitution*. Translated by Richard Rojcewicz and André Schuwer. Dordrecht: Kluwer Academic Publishers, 1989.

———. *Logical Investigations*, 2 vols. Translated by J. N. Findlay. Edited by Dermot Moran. London: Routledge, 2001.

Hyppolite, Jean. *Logic and Existence*. 1953. Translated by Leonard Lawlor and Amit Sen. Albany: State University of New York Press, 1997.

Isaacs, Susan. *Social Development in Young Children*. London: George Routledge and Sons, 1933.

Ishiguro, Hidé. *Leibniz's Philosophy of Logic and Language*. 1972. 2nd ed. Cambridge: Cambridge University Press, 1990.

James, William. "Absolutism and Empiricism" (1884). In *Essays in Radical Empiricism*, edited by Ralph Barton Perry, 266–279. New York: Longmans, Green & Co., 1912.

Jouvenel, Bertrand de. *Les débuts de l'état moderne: Une histoire des idées politiques au XIXe siècle.* Paris: Fayard, 1976.

Kenny, Anthony. *Action, Emotion and Will.* 1963. 2nd ed. London: Routledge, 2003.

———. Introduction to *Summa Theologiae,* Vol. 22: *Dispositions for Human Acts (1a2æ, 49–54),* by Thomas Aquinas, xix–xxxiv. Translated by Anthony Kenny. New York: McGraw-Hill, 1964.

Kojève, Alexandre. "The Idea of Death in the Philosophy of Hegel." Translated by Joseph J. Carpino. In *Hegel and Contemporary Continental Philosophy,* edited by Dennis King Keenan, 27–74. Albany: State University of New York Press, 2004.

———. *Introduction à la lecture de Hegel.* Edited by Raymond Queneau. Paris: Gallimard, 1947.

———. *Introduction to the Reading of Hegel: Lectures on the "Phenomenology of Spirit."* Edited by Raymond Queneau and Allan Bloom. Translated by James H. Nichols, Jr. Ithaca, NY: Cornell University Press, 1980.

Kretzmann, Norman. "Semantics, History of." In *Encyclopedia of Philosophy.* 2nd edition. Edited by Donald M. Borchert. Vol. 7. Detroit: Thomson Gale, 2006.

Lacan, Jacques. "The Function and Field of Speech and Language in Psychoanalysis." In *Écrits: A Selection,* 23–86. Translated by Alan Sheridan. New York: Routledge, 1977.

———. *The Seminar of Jacques Lacan, Book I: Freud's Papers on Technique 1953–1954.* Edited by Jacques-Alain Miller. Translated by John Forrester. New York: Norton, 1988.

La Fontaine, Jean de. *The Complete Fables of Jean de La Fontaine.* Translated by Norman R. Shapiro. Urbana: University of Illinois Press, 2007.

Lalande, André. *Vocabulaire technique et critique de la philosophie.* 1926. 18th ed. Paris: Presses Universitaires de France, 1996.

Leibniz, Gottfried Wilhelm. *New Essays on Human Understanding.* Edited and translated by Peter Remnant and Jonathan Bennett. Cambridge: Cambridge University Press, 1996.

———. *Opuscules et fragments inédits.* Edited by Louis Couturat. Hildesheim: Olms, 1966.

Leibniz, Gottfried Wilhelm, and Antoine Arnauld. *The Leibniz-Arnauld Correspondence.* Edited and translated by H. T. Mason. Manchester: Manchester University Press, 1967.

Lévi-Strauss, Claude. *The Elementary Structures of Kinship.* Rev. ed. Edited by Rodney Needham. Translated by James Harle Bell, John Richard von Sturmer, and Rodney Needham. Boston: Beacon Press, 1969.

———. "French Sociology." In *Twentieth Century Sociology,* edited by Georges Gurvitch and Wilbert E. Moore, 503–537. New York: Philosophical Library, 1945.

———. *Introduction to the Work of Marcel Mauss.* Translated by Felicity Baker. London: Routledge & Kegan Paul, 1987.

———. *The Savage Mind.* Chicago: University of Chicago Press, 1966.

———. "Structuralism and Ecology." In *The View From Afar,* 101–120. Translated by Joachim Neugroschel and Phoebe Hoss. Chicago: University of Chicago Press, 1992.

Locke, John. *An Essay Concerning Human Understanding.* Edited by Peter H. Nidditch. Oxford: Clarendon Press, 1975.

Löwith, Karl. *From Hegel to Nietzsche: The Revolution in Nineteenth-Century Thought.* Translated by David E. Green. New York: Columbia University Press, 1991.

Mallarmé, Stéphane. "Crisis of Verse." Translated by Mary Ann Caws. In *Selected Poetry and Prose,* edited by Mary Ann Caws, 75–76. New York: New Directions, 1982.

———. "Displays." In *Divagations,* 220–225. Translated by Barbara Johnson. Cambridge, MA: Harvard University Press, 2007.

Mauss, Marcel. "Divisions et proportions des divisions de la sociologie" (1927). In *Œuvres,* Vol. 3: *Cohésion sociale et division de la sociologie,* 178–245. Paris: Les Éditions de Minuit, 1969.

———. *A General Theory of Magic.* Translated by Robert Brain. London: Routledge and Kegan Paul, 1972.

———. *The Gift: Forms and Functions of Exchange in Archaic Societies.* Translated by Ian Cunnison. London: Cohen & West, 1966.

———. "La nation" (1920). In his *Œuvres.* Vol. 3: *Cohésion sociale et division de la sociologie,* 573–625. Paris: Les Éditions de Minuit, 1969.

Mauss, Marcel, and Paul Fauconnet. "Sociology" (1901). In *The Nature of Sociology,* 1–30. Translated by William Jeffrey, Jr. Oxford: Berghahn Books, 2005.

Mauss, Marcel, and Henri Hubert. "Introduction à l'analyse de quelques phénomènes religieux" (1906). In *Œuvres,* Vol. 1: *Les fonctions sociales du sacré,* 3–39. Paris: Les Éditions de Minuit, 1968.

McDowell, John. *Mind and World.* Cambridge, MA: Harvard University Press, 1994.

McGuinness, Brian. *Wittgenstein, A Life: Young Ludwig 1889–1921.* Berkeley: University of California Press, 1988.

Medawar, P. B., and J. S. Medawar. *Aristotle to Zoos: A Philosophical Dictionary of Biology.* Cambridge, MA: Harvard University Press, 1983.

Merleau-Ponty, Maurice. *Phenomenology of Perception.* Translated by Colin Smith. New York: Routledge, 1962.

Montesquieu. *A Defence of "The Spirit of the Laws."* In *The Complete Works of M. de Montesquieu.* Vol. 5. London, 1777.

———. *My Thoughts.* Edited and translated by Henry C. Clark. Indianapolis: Liberty Fund, 2012.

———. *The Spirit of the Laws.* Edited and translated by Anne M. Cohler, Basia C. Miller, and Harold S. Stone. Cambridge: Cambridge University Press, 1989.
Ortigues, Edmond. *Le discours et le symbole.* Paris: Aubier, 1962.
———. *Religion du livre, religion de la coutume.* Paris: L'Harmattan, 1981.
Pachet, Pierre. *Les baromètres de l'âme: Naissance du journal intime.* Paris: Hatier, 1990.
Parain, Brice. *Recherches sur la nature et les fonctions du langage.* Paris: Gallimard, 1942.
Pascal, Blaise. Letter VII. *The Provincial Letters.* Translated by Thomas M'Crie. In *Pensées, The Provincial Letters,* 402–417. New York: The Modern Library, 1941.
———. "Of the Geometrical Spirit." Translated by O. W. Wight. In *Thoughts, Letters, Minor Works,* 427–444. New York: P. F. Collier and Son, 1910.
———. *Pensées.* Translated by A. J. Krailsheimer. Baltimore: Penguin Books, 1966.
Paulhan, Jean. *Petite préface à toute critique.* 1951. 2nd ed. Cognac: Le Temps qu'il fait, 1988.
Peirce, Charles Sanders. *Collected Papers of Charles Sanders Peirce.* 8 vols. Cambridge, MA: Harvard University Press, 1931–1958.
———. "The Logic of Relatives." In *Reasoning and the Logic of Things,* edited by Kenneth Laine Ketner, 146–164. Cambridge, MA: Harvard University Press, 1992.
Peter of Spain. *The "Summulae Logicales" of Peter of Spain.* Edited and translated by Joseph P. Mullally. Notre Dame, IN: University of Notre Dame Press, 1945.
Plato. *Theaetetus.* Translated by M. J. Levett and Myles Burnyeat. In *Complete Works.* Edited by John M. Cooper and D. S. Hutchinson. Indianapolis: Hackett Publishing Company, 1997: 157–234.
Popper, Karl. *The Poverty of Historicism.* New York: Routledge, 2002.
Prior, Arthur N. *The Doctrine of Propositions and Terms.* London: Duckworth, 1976.
———. "The Ethical Copula." In *Papers in Logic and Ethics,* edited by P. T. Geach and A. J. P. Kenny, 9–24. Amherst: University of Massachusetts Press, 1976.
———. *Formal Logic.* Oxford: Oxford University Press, 1962.
———. *Objects of Thought.* Edited by P. T. Geach and A. J. P. Kenny. Oxford: Oxford University Press, 1971.
———. *Time and Modality, Being the John Locke Lectures for 1955–6 Delivered in the University of Oxford.* Oxford: Clarendon Press, 1957.
Proust, Marcel. *In the Shadow of Young Girls in Flower.* Translated by James Grieve. Edited by Christopher Prendergast. New York: Viking, 2004.
Putnam, Hilary. *Reason, Truth and History.* Cambridge: Cambridge University Press, 1981.
Quine, Willard van Orman. *From a Logical Point of View: Nine Logico-Philosophical Essays.* 1953. 2nd rev. ed. New York: Harper Torchbooks, 1961.

———. *Methods of Logic*. 1950. 4th ed. Cambridge, MA: Harvard University Press, 1982.
———. *The Pursuit of Truth*. 1990. Rev. ed. Cambridge, MA: Harvard University Press, 1992.
———. "Quantifiers and Propositional Attitudes." In his *The Ways of Paradox and Other Essays*, 185–196. Cambridge, MA: Harvard University Press, 1976.
———. *Theories and Things*. Cambridge, MA: Harvard University Press, 1981.
———. *Word and Object*. Cambridge, MA: MIT Press, 1960.
Rabelais. *Gargantua and Pantagruel*. Translated by M. A. Screech. New York: Penguin Books, 2006.
Renaut, Alain. *Sartre, le dernier philosophe*. Paris: Grasset, 1993.
Rivenc, François. "Husserl avec et contre Frege." *Les Etudes philosophiques* (January–March 1995): 13–38.
Rorty, Richard. "Pragmatism, Categories and Language." *The Philosophical Review* 70 (1961): 197–233.
———. "Relations, Internal and External." In *Encyclopedia of Philosophy*. 2nd ed. Edited by Donald M. Borchert. Vol. 8. Detroit: Thomson Gale, 2006.
Russell, Bertrand. *An Inquiry into Meaning and Truth*. 1940. New York: Routledge, 1992.
———. "The Monistic Theory of Truth." In *Philosophical Essays*, 131–146. New York: Routledge, 1994.
———. *My Philosophical Development*. London: George Allen and Unwin, 1959.
———. "On Propositions: What They Are and How They Mean." In *Logic and Knowledge*, 283–320. London: Routledge, 1988.
———. *The Philosophy of Logical Atomism*. 1918. New York: Routledge, 2010.
———. *The Principles of Mathematics*. 1903. London: Allen & Unwin, 1937.
Ryle, Gilbert. *Der Begriff des Geistes*. Translated by Kurt Baier. Stuttgart: Reclam, 1986.
———. *The Concept of Mind*. 1949. Chicago: University of Chicago Press, 2000.
Sartre, Jean-Paul. *Being and Nothingness: A Phenomenological Essay on Ontology*. Translated by Hazel E. Barnes. New York: Washington Square Press, 1956.
———. "Departure and Return" (1944). In *Literary and Philosophical Essays*, 133–179. Translated by Annette Michelson. New York: Collier, 1962.
Searle, John. *Intentionality: An Essay in Philosophy of Mind*. Cambridge: Cambridge University Press, 1983.
Simmel, Georg. *The Problems of the Philosophy of History: An Epistemological Essay*. 2nd ed. Edited and translated by Guy Oakes. 1892. New York: Free Press, 1977.
Simons, Peter M. "The Formalisation of Husserl's Theory of Whole and Parts." In *Parts and Moments: Studies in Logic and Formal Ontology*, edited by Barry Smith, 113–159. Munich: Philosophia Verlag, 1982.

———. *Parts: A Study in Ontology*. Oxford: Oxford University Press, 1987.
Smith, David Woodruff, and Ronald McIntyre. *Husserl and Intentionality: A Study of Mind, Meaning, and Language*. Dordrecht: D. Reidel, 1982.
Taylor, Charles. *Hegel*. Cambridge: Cambridge University Press, 1975.
———. "Hegel's Philosophy of Mind" (1983). In *Human Agency and Language: Philosophical Papers 1*, 77–96. Cambridge: Cambridge University Press, 1985.
———. "Interpretation and the Sciences of Man" (1971). In *Philosophy and the Human Sciences: Philosophical Papers 2*, 13–57. Cambridge: Cambridge University Press, 1985.
Tesnière, Lucien. *Éléments de syntaxe structural*. 1959. 2nd ed. Paris: Klincksieck, 1988.
Thomas, Aquinas. *Commentary on Aristotle's "Physics."* Translated by Richard J. Blackwell, Richard J. Spath, and W. Edmund Thirlkel. London: Thoemmes Continuum, 2003.
Tiercelin, Claudine. *La pensée-signe: Études sur C. S. Peirce*. Nîmes: Éditions Jacquéline Chambon, 1993.
Tugendhat, Ernst. *Self-Consciousness and Self-Determination*. Translated by Paul Stern. Cambridge, MA: MIT Press, 1989.
Villey, Michel. *Critique de la pensée juridique moderne*. Paris: Dalloz, 1976.
———. *Le droit et les droits de l'homme*. Paris: Presses Universitaires de France, 1983.
Weber, Max. *Economy and Society: An Outline of Interpretive Sociology*, 2 vols. Translated by Ephraim Fischoff, Hans Gerth, et al. Edited by Guenther Roth and Claus Wittich. Berkeley: University of California Press, 1978.
Wiggins, David. *Sameness and Substance*. Oxford: Blackwell, 1980.
Wittgenstein, Ludwig. *The Blue and Brown Books: Preliminary Studies for the "Philosophical Investigations."* 2nd ed. Oxford: Blackwell, 1969.
———. *Philosophical Grammar*. Edited by Rush Rhees. Translated by Anthony Kenny. Oxford: Basil Blackwell, 1974.
———. *Philosophical Investigations*. 1953. Rev. 4th ed. Edited by P. M. S. Hacker and Joachim Schulte. Translated by G. E. M. Anscombe, P. M. S. Hacker, and Joachim Schulte. Oxford: Wiley-Blackwell, 2009.
———. *Philosophical Remarks*. Edited by Rush Rhees. Translated by Raymond Hargreaves and Roger White. Oxford: Blackwell, 1975.
———. *Remarks on the Foundations of Mathematics*. 3rd ed. Edited by G. H. von Wright, R. Rhees, and G. E. M. Anscombe. Translated by G. E. M. Anscombe. Oxford: Basil Blackwell, 1978.
———. *Tractatus Logico-Philosophicus*. 1922. Translated by D. F. Pears and B. F. McGuinness. New York: Routledge, 1981.
———. *Wittgenstein's Lectures: Cambridge, 1930–32*. Edited by Desmond Lee. Chicago: University of Chicago Press, 1989.

Index

abstraction, 37–41, 43n53, 177, 319, 321–322; from subject, 326–327, 330. See also *epoché*
accusative case, 32
act, xv, 5, 12, 26, 32, 66, 315, 317; collective, 223, 311; discursive, 313–316; dyadic, 220–221, 230, 242; dynamic, 230–231 immanent, 33–35; intentional, xxvi, 12, 21–37, 48–49, 52, 57, 60, 62, 72–73, 79–82, 83, 86, 191–193, 198, 218–219, 221, 227, 230–231, 259; intransitive, 35; mental, xv, xxi, 5, 7, 13, 19, 23–29, 31, 34–36, 51, 59, 67–68, 79–82, 83, 96, 121, 206, 315–318, 321; physical, 22, 27–31, 34–35, 52, 78–79, 227, 241–243; real, 21, 32–35, 49, 57, 66, 72; social, 301–303, 306, 310–313, 329–330, 337; speech (*see* speech acts); teleological, 245; temporality of, 30; transitive, xxi, 25, 31, 33–35, 80, 218, 230; triadic, 221, 241–242
aggregates, 167, 212, 214–215
analysis: eliminative, 5, 143–145, 167, 207–209; expansive, 209; holistic, xxii, 90, 119, 156–157, 162–166, 171, 185, 237, 251–252; logical, 68–74, 111, 143–144, 148–149, 156, 166–168, 196, 207–209, 219, 231–232, 239; reductive, 95n, 168, 205, 208–209; structural, xii–xiii, xx,

xxii, xxv, 97–98, 119, 157, 159, 183–184, 268
Anscombe, G. E. M., xxvi, 62–63, 170–171
anthropology, xxiii, 119, 237, 247–248, 252; social, xii, xx, xxii–xxiii, 89, 247–248, 258–259; structural, xiii, xx, xxii, xxvii, 259–261, 292
argument. *See* syllogism
Aristotle, xxvi, 62, 170–171, 175, 178, 184, 216–217, 261, 321–322, 331
Arnauld, Antoine, 32–33, 48–49, 149–154
Aron, Raymond, xxiii, 289–290, 292–294, 302
associationism, xiv, xvi, xx, 6, 51, 87, 96, 98–99
atomism, xiv–xvi, xxiii, 6–7, 90, 96, 100–101, 102–103, 116, 118, 171, 185, 244, 322; logical, xxiii, 143–149, 156, 158, 161, 164, 167, 169–171, 190, 200, 235–236; mental, 6–7, 87, 90–91, 96, 100, 118, 290; semantic, xv–xvi, 96–97, 100, 119. *See also* holism; properties: atomistic
attitude: natural, 52–53; propositional, 67, 315, 318
Augé, Marc, 119n
autonomy, xxvi–xxvii, 200, 243, 306; of syntax, 177–181

Beaufret, Jean, 59–62
behaviorism, 87–90, 335–336
being: for itself, 37, 287; in itself, 287; in the world, 218; meaning of, 233
Belaval, Yvon, 230–231
belief. *See* thoughts
Bentham, Jeremy, 109
Blanchot, Maurice, 43
Bradley, Francis Herbert, 190
Brandom, Robert B., xv, xxix
Brentano, Franz, 7, 14, 25, 31, 34–35, 68, 76, 86, 315n2; on distinction between mental and physical, 26–28; School of, 21n26, 65; thesis of, 9–11, 12n, 14, 21, 23, 26–27, 30, 35, 65, 79, 240
Breton, Stanislas, 35n
Brunschvicg, Léon, 60
Butler, Samuel, 312

Carnap, Rudolf, 108
Castoriadis, Cornelius, 289n, 302–303
causalism: structural, 157–160, 176, 255, 262, 303, 338
causality: efficient, 253, 259; formal, 170, 175–176; material, 175
change: extrinsic, 194–201, 203, 205, 215–217; intentional, 36, 45; intrinsic, 194–201, 203, 214–216; logical concept of, 196–197; real, 33–35, 36, 45, 66, 194–195, 197, 201, 217; subject of (*see* subject: of change)
Chisholm, Roderick, 20–21
classes. *See* sets
cogito, 17, 280–282; as action outside oneself, 47–48
communication, 20, 100–101, 248, 260, 270–284, 322, 327, 329, 338
community, 152, 279, 293, 297
comparisons. *See* relations: of comparison
complementarity, xx, 119–120, 155–156, 200, 213, 215, 250–251, 267–268, 289, 302–306, 308, 312, 330–334, 337
computers, 6, 177–178
concepts, 8, 36–46, 191n9, 235–236; acquisition of, 235n29; criteria for possession of, xiv–xv; divided, 233–234; as indefinite propositions, 236; psychological, xiv, xvii, xxi. *See also* terms
Condillac, 97
consciousness, 23–26, 47–48, 52, 57–61, 73, 75–76, 79–80, 227–228, 240–241, 262n37, 280–281, 287; collective, xx, 263, 292, 295. *See also* mind: subjective; self-consciousness; unconscious
consensus, 296–297
content: of act, 315–318, 323; of painting 54–55; of perception, 56; propositional, 4, 318, 326; psychological, xvii–xviii, 7–9, 97, 318–319, 323; semantic, 180–181; of thought (*see* content: psychological)
context, 71n, 76, 81, 103, 115, 118, 145, 206, 243, 277, 311, 320, 329, 335, 339; historical, xvi–xviii, 91–92, 206, 243, 261; institutional, xxiv, 81–82, 89, 91–92, 243–244; linguistic, 86, 103; oblique, 4, 67–75
context principle. *See under* Frege, Gottlob
copula, 232–233, 236
culture, xxviii, 227, 255n26, 286, 292

Davidson, Donald, xiii, 89, 96, 276n16
denominations. *See* descriptions
Derrida, Jacques, 42–44, 300n59
Descartes, René, 11–12, 29–31, 33, 79, 105, 111, 230, 299, 332–333
descriptions, 3–4, 8, 19–20, 66, 149, 196, 219, 252, 257, 307; collective, 128–131, 134, 163–165; conditional, 259; definite, 71, 74, 147, 208–209; empirical, 304; vs. explanation, 252; external, 242; extrinsic, 204–207; formal, 168, 176; holistic, 121, 156–157, 160–161, 164–166, 225, 251; institutional, 258–259, 304; intentional, 3–6, 7–8, 12, 18, 21n24, 29–30, 50–54, 63–64, 73, 86, 88, 145, 176–178, 221–223, 227–228, 230, 237, 240–246; intrinsic, 204–207; material, 168, 176, 240; moral, 275; natural, 3–6, 12, 21n24, 23, 29–30, 52–53, 88, 172–178, 221–223, 227–228, 230, 237, 240–246, 258; phenomenalist, 239–240; physical (*see* descriptions: natural); psychological (*see* descriptions:

intentional); semantic (*see* descriptions: intentional); structural, 172–174; syntactical, 177, 180. *See also* "under a description"
determinism: causal, 259; logical, 242, 259
Dewey, John, xxviii
dialectic, 36–37, 77, 161, 183, 200, 226–231, 246, 257–258, 267; master-slave, 227–228, 267
differentiation, xvii, xx, xxii, 91, 103, 142, 165, 183–184, 189–190
Dilthey, Wilhelm, xiii, xix, xxviii, 229, 289–293, 302n64
discourse, xv–xvi, xxii, xxv, 17, 36–38, 42, 44–46, 99, 110–113, 152, 169; indirect, 4, 316, 325; order of, 42; theoretical, 110
dispositions, 7n4, 87–89, 206–208, 210, 218
dualism, 11, 29–30, 282, 286–287; logico-philosophical, 227
Dubarle, Dominique, 234
Duhem, Pierre, 104–108
Dumézil, Georges, 260n35
Dummett, Michael, 26–28, 34–35, 79, 99, 113–114, 316n4
Dumont, Louis, xii–xiii, xxii, xxiv, xxix, 126–127, 156n1, 268, 303–308
Durkheim, Émile, xii, xix–xx, xxiv, 263, 268, 292, 295

ego, xxvi, 17, 75, 282
elements, xiv, xxi–xxii, 121, 140–142, 146–149, 157, 170–176, 178–179, 182, 184–185, 187, 189, 236; of proposition, 16, 19, 167–173, 176, 181–185, 224
empiricism, xxiii, 39n44, 103–104, 108–109, 201–202, 235n29
entities. *See* elements; objects; terms
epistemology, xxviii, 103–109, 111, 239, 290
epoché, 51–55, 68, 73, 83. *See also* abstraction
equality, 216, 264, 266, 308
ethics, 279; social, 305–306
events: discursive, 36–37, 42, 46; intentional, 4–5, 11, 24, 37, 41–42, 43n53, 46, 48, 53, 246; natural, 4, 11, 222; real, 46; temporal relation of (*see* relations: temporal)

exchange, 248–261, 264–266, 268; linguistic (*see* communication). *See also* gift
expecting, 77–81
explanation, 252–259; anthropological, 260; causal, 253, 256, 258–259, 262; indigenous, 252–255; infrastructural, 257–258; psychological, 7, 254, 257–259, 262
extension, 116, 139–140, 146–147, 167, 209

facts: atomic, 240; brute, 222, 229, 237, 240–242, 244–246, 248, 253–254, 258–259, 336; dyadic (*see* facts: brute); ideological, 250n19, 253; intentional, 4, 6, 237, 246, 336; monadic, 240, 248; morphological, 250n19; natural, 4, 6; relational, 210, 214–217, 241; triadic (*see* facts: intentional)
Fichte, J. G., 117
Findlay, J. N., 10
Flaubert, Gustave, 323–324
Fodor, Jerry, xvii(n9), 96–104, 107n24, 115–120
form: of life, xvii–xviii, xxiv, 81, 90, 145, 289n; as morphology, 178–182; signifying, 178–179; as unit of order, 179
formalism, 157–159, 171–173, 176–181, 185, 303. *See also* structuralism
Foucault, Michel, 42, 44–45
Fowler, H. W., 124–125, 135
freedom, 245, 283, 308, 312
Frege, Gottlob, xiv, 10n, 56–57, 109, 130n13, 236, 274, 326; on concrete wholes, 140–142, 147, 149; "context principle" of, xvi, 98, 112, 135, 236
functionalism, xx, 268

Gardies, Jean-Louis, 177–178
Gardiner, Alan, 311–312
Geach, Peter, xiv–xv, 13, 88–89, 196, 316n3, 325
Geisteswissenschaften. *See* sciences: human
Gestalt theory, xx
gift, 237, 238–260, 263. *See also* exchange
Girard, René, 198
Gochet, Paul, 106n22, 114n37
Godelier, Maurice, 259–262
Goodman, Nelson, 161

grammar, 28, 32–35, 173, 224; philosophical, 34–35, 66, 72, 85

Hacking, Ian, 44–45
Hartmann, Nicolai, 293
hau, 252–257, 261
Hegel, G. W. F., xi–xii, xiv, xxiii, xxiv, xxvi, xxviii, 9n, 105, 111, 128, 154, 245, 294–295, 297, 328n; abstraction in, 37–40, 42–43, 48; critique of judgment, 232–235; critique of materialism, 197n; ethics vs. morality, 305–306; logic of, 227–229, 232–235; master-slave dialectic, 227–228, 267; monism of, 143, 145, 187, 203; objective mind, 261–262, 289–292, 302n64; totality in, 132n, 290–291, 294, 299. *See also* dialectic; mind: objective
Heidegger, Martin, 11n
Henninger, Mark, 215n
hermeneutics, xix, 287–288, 290
history: intentional, 36–46, 60; natural, 41, 44; positivist, 46; real, 45
Hobbes, Thomas, 111
holism, xii–xiii xvi, xx–xxiii, 66, 89–90, 95–97, 99–101, 103, 110, 113–121, 123, 128, 131, 142, 145, 154, 155–156, 158, 160–163, 165–167, 171, 179, 185, 188–189, 190, 236–237, 244, 250–252, 272–273, 290–292, 329; anthropological, xvi–xvii, xix–xxii, 9, 87–90, 249–250; collectivist, xxii, 101–103, 108, 113–116, 118–121, 123, 154, 155–156, 161, 163, 182, 187, 197, 237; epistemological, 103–109, 113–114; meaning (*see* holism: semantic); mental, xii–xiii, xxi, 3, 6, 77, 85, 86–91, 95–100, 118, 121, 167, 237, 270, 329; semantic, xvi–xvii, 96–101, 104, 109–110, 112–115, 119, 121, 167, 179, 187, 270, 272–273; sociological (*see* holism: anthropological); structural, xxiii, 115–116, 119–122, 156–158, 171, 185, 186–189, 249, 255, 258–259, 262, 303. *See also* atomism
human sciences. *See* sciences: human
Husserl, Edmund, 7, 11n, 17–19, 26, 31, 34–35, 42–44, 47, 49–53, 55–63, 65, 69, 73, 83, 300n59

idealism, xxiii, xxviii, 57–60, 190–191, 201–202, 315n2; classical, 59; phenomenological, 59–60, 64
idealities, *see,* object, ideal
ideas: representative, xiv, 96–97. *See also* associationism
identity, 202, 227, 232, 281, 285; of act, 317–318; collective, 136, 154; criterion, 91, 151, 202, diachronic, 149–152, 281; in difference, 227; human, 306; material, 150n39; of object, 317; of signs, 320–322; of thoughts (*see* thoughts: identification of); token, 91, 315, 319; type, 91, 315
imaginary, 41
imagination: bodily, 288–289; intellectual, 288–289
individualism, 127–128, 278–279, 303–309, 320–323, 338; institution of, 307–309; methodological, xix, xxii, 115n, 136–140, 142–143, 161; ontological, xix, 320–321
individuals, xxv, xxvi, xxviii, 91, 130, 134, 137–138, 141–143, 149, 187–188, 191n9, 197–200, 204–205, 225–226, 294, 303–309, 312–313, 339; autonomous, 306; collective, xix, xxii, 38, 123, 126n8, 127–136, 142, 155, 161, 223, 226, 237, 268, 312, 335; empirical, 304, 306; self-positing, 308–309; societies as, 126–128, 136–137. *See also* particular [*le particulier*]
individuation, 54–55, 141–142, 147, 200, 320; contextual, 320; of intentions, 90–91, 118, 315, 318; of possible worlds, 205; of signs, 320
inference, 111, 160, 236–237, 300
institutions, xii, xvii, xxi, xxiii, xxiv, xxv, xxvii, xxix, 9, 76, 81, 89–90, 137–138, 241, 246, 258–259, 280, 284, 298–304, 306–308, 312, 321, 339; of individuality, 307; as manifestations of mind, 262; of meaning, xxiv, 9, 92, 243, 258, 275, 278–279, 284, 298–299, 301–302, 313, 339; normative, xxiii–xxiv, xxv–xxvi, xxvii, xxix, 258; origins of, 262–263, 313; of social life, 306–308, 312; spirit of, 295; spiritual, 307–309, 312
instructions: general, 326–329

intelligence: artificial, 6
intentionalism, 7, 9–12, 17–18, 23, 47–48, 52, 65, 68, 83, 185, 315
intentionality, xvii–xviii, xxi, xxiv, 3–13, 19–30, 33–38, 41–46, 47–57, 60–62, 64, 65–81, 84–85, 90, 193, 218, 221–223, 228, 239–241, 313; as activity, 24; complexity of, 81; as criterion of the mental, 9–10, 23–24, 85; direction of, 275–276; formal, 276; irreducible to the natural, 5–6, 10, 52–57, 60, 65, 76, 246; in logical sense, 12–14; meaning-giving, 241–243; non-Cartesian conception of, 11–12, 79; in practical sense, 12–13, 222; as pseudo-relation, 68; as quasi-relation, 68, 76; in Scholastic sense, 222; of semantic terms, 12n9, 13–14; as state, 24–25; as structure of subordination, 80–81; as transitivity, 25–26, 31–32, 34–36, 48, 65–66
interpretant, 337
interpretation, xix, 6, 89–90, 277, 287–288; of experiments, 107
intersubjectivity, 296–301, 308, 313, 327–328, 331
intransitivity: of action, 34–35; of intention, 86; *See also* verbs: intransitive
intuitions, 42, 194, 235, 300
Ishiguro, Hidé, 205, 208n29, 209–210
isomorphism, 158–159

James, William, xxiii, xxviii, 187–188, 200
Jansen, Cornelius, 314
Jouvenel, Bertrand de, 125–126, 128
judgment, xv, 87, 220, 232–234; of taste, 296–297

Kant, Immanuel, xxvi, 49, 232, 234n28, 297
Kenny, Anthony, 25–28, 88n13
kinship, xiii, xxvii, 174–175, 210, 263–264, 268, 304–305, 307
Kojève, Alexandre, 37–40
Kretzmann, Norman, 110–111

Lacan, Jacques, 37, 40–41, 228
Lalande, André, 129–131, 136

Lambert, Johann Heinrich, 177–178
Lancelot, Claude, 32–33, 48–49
language, xxv, 42, 101, 320–321; authority of, 279; betrayal by, 271–283; constitution of, 320–321; distinction from theory, 109–110; exteriority of, 285; games, xvi–xvii; impersonal use of, *see* signs, impersonal use of; law of, 279; ordinary, 136; origin of, 271–273, 277–284; relation to world, 159; vs. speech, 311–313; structure of (*see* structure: of language); vs. thought, xiv–xv, 316; transcendence of, 285
law, xi, 75, 241–242, 269; comparison of, 292; of language (*see* language: law of); psychological, xiv, 98–99, 255n26; Roman, 309–310; spirit of, xi, 261, 290–292. *See also* rules
Leibniz, Gottfried Wilhelm, 144, 194–195, 202–210, 217, 219, 226–227, 230
Leninism: linguistic, 278–279
LePore, Ernest, xvii(n9), 96–104, 107n24, 115–120
Lévi-Strauss, Claude, xii–xiii, xx, xxiii, 157, 159, 246–268
lifeworld, 286
Locke, John, 111, 117, 202–204, 206–207, 213–214
logic, xiv, 110–112, 136, 196, 227–229, 232–237, 248; dialectical, 231–234; formal, 232–233; inferential, 234; infra-propositional, 234; intentional, 66–74; of relations (*see* relations: logic of); of terms, 12–14, 129–132, 143, 234; of tenses, 69
love, 191–193, 198
Löwith, Karl, 187

magic, 257n28, 260
Mallarmé, Stéphane, 43
mana, 254
materialism, 170–181, 184–185
Mauss, Marcel, xii, 126–127, 247–261, 301, 339
McDowell, John, xxviii

meaning, xiii, xxiii–xxiv, 56–57; common, 279, 284, 293, 296–299, 301, 320–321, 339; conferral of, 241–243; discursive, 111–113; as epiphenomenon, 176–177; experimental, 107; exteriority to individuals, 293, 302, 339; instituted, 298, 338; intersubjective, 296–299, 301; literal, 275–279, 284, 321–322; objective, 336; order of, 168, 170, 175–176, 237; speaker's (*see* pragmatics); unit of, 109, 112–113, 176
mechanism, xxiii, 258–259; psychological, 254, 256, 258–259, 263–265
Medawar, J. S., 95n
Medawar, P. B., 95n
mediation, 244–246
Meinong, Alexius, 315n2
mental data, 69
mentalism, 241, 258
mental states, 4, 98–99; identification of, 87–88, 98–99; intentional, xvii, 23–25; narrow, xvii–xviii, 99
mereology, 161
Merleau-Ponty, Maurice, 47, 285–288, 290, 292, 300n59, 321
milieu, 9, 12, 197, 204–205
mind, 5–9, 121–122; absolute, 289; impersonality of, 9, 287; intentionalist conception of, 7, 9–11; intersubjective (*see* intersubjectivity); objectified, xxiii–xxiv, xxv, 284–288, 290, 293–295, 313, 319, 321–322, 335; objective, xi–xii, xiv, xxi, xxiv, xxv, xxvi, xxviii–xxix, 9, 75–76, 237, 261–262, 268–269, 273, 280, 286–295, 299, 302n64, 306, 313, 331, 338; philosophy of (*see* philosophy: of mind); science of (*see* sciences: human); structures of, 237, 248, 258–263, 266, 268–269; subjective, xxvi, xxviii, 9, 75–76, 280, 289, 291, 294, 313, 319, 322
mind/body problem, 88
Molière, 84, 110
monadism, 189
monads, 148, 160, 164, 220, 338
monism, xxiii, 144–145, 187, 189–190, 194, 197–198, 201, 203–204, 227; *See also* holism

Montesquieu, xi–xii, 261, 290–292, 295
Moore, G. E., 188, 315n2
morality, 245, 305–306; of language, 279; subjective, 305
multiplicity, 230

names/naming, xvi, 15–16, 37–41, 57, 70–71, 74, 76, 86, 139, 144, 169
natural kinds, 42, 45
nature, 90, 227–228
necessity: deontic, 254n, 256; logical, 254n; mental, 253–254; moral, 253–254; physical, 254n, 256; unconscious, 253–254
Nicole, Pierre, 149–154
Nietzsche, Friedrich, 111
nihilism, 100–101
nominalism, 115, 126, 128, 136–140, 143, 145, 195, 212–214, 232, 235; dynamic, 44–46
normativity, xxiii, xxix, 76, 259, 268–269, 290; varieties of, xxvii

object: abstract, 108n26, 138–143, 147; of action, 315–317; complex, 143–145, 148–149, 167, 170; history of, 36–38, 43–44, 56, 66–67; ideal, 54, 59–60; immanent, 34–35, 55, 58–59; indirect, 228; intentional, 33–35, 48–64, 65–67, 72–76, 81, 85, 192, 222, 315n2; in logical sense, 14; mathematical, 42–44; of mental act, 22, 24–26, 27, 31, 35; natural, 55–58, 61; of perception, 48–61; of physical act, 27, 31, 50, 52; of proposition, 68, 74, 220, 224–225, 319; real, 17–19, 55–58, 61, 72–73, 319; simple, 144–145, 149, 164, 169–170; unreal, 18, 47–48, 57, 65
obligations, 249, 250n19, 252–256, 259–260; religious, 259–261
obscurantism, 98–99
one and many, 126, 132–133, 136, 161
opinions. *See* thoughts
Ortigues, Edmond, 184–185, 260
Orwell, George, 279n21
others, 282–283

Pachet, Pierre, 308
Parain, Brice, 271–280, 282–285

Parmenides, 190
particular [*le particulier*], 305–306, 308–309, 312–313
parts: distinction of, 166–167, 189–190; vs. elements, 173, 185, 189; mutual dependence of, 101–103, 119–120, 155–156, 160, 189; of whole, xii, xvii, xix–xxii, xxiv, 54, 95, 102–103, 112–115, 119–121, 141–143, 147–149, 157, 160–161, 163–166, 170–171, 173, 175, 185, 189–190, 199, 223, 236, 244, 249, 258. *See also* wholes
Pascal, Blaise, 90, 219–220, 275–276, 314
passion. *See* passive
passive, 33–34, 220, 238–239, 331; grammatical, 34; of indirect object, 239; intentional, 32–36, 41, 45–46, 47–49, 57, 60, 64, 65–66, 68, 70–78, 85–86, 267; real, 48–49, 77
Paulhan, Jean, 271–277, 279, 283–284
Peirce, Charles Sanders: on dependence of intentional relations on real relations, 14–20, 22, 66, 74, 76; dialogism of, 299–300; on gift, 239–242, 244–246, 251, 259; holism of, 234–237, 244; logic of relations of, xxiii, xxviii, 211–212, 214–215, 217–232, 246; triads in, 229–232, 235, 240–241, 246, 251; on types and tokens, 172
perception, 48–64, 69, 72–73
Peter of Spain, 162–165
phenomenology, xxiii, 42, 242, 285, 300, 321–323, 327–328, 333–334; existential, 47–48; idealism of, 58–64; on intentional objects, 47–64, 66, 68, 72–75, 83, 315n2; and intersubjectivity, 300; objectification in, 281; origin of language for, 273; teleology of mental acts in, 83; transcendental, 315n2
philosophy: of action, xxvi, 62; analytic, xxiii, 56, 111, 270–271, 316; critical, 300; descriptive, 52; first, 50; of history, 36; of human sciences, xvii; of language, xv–xvi, xxviii, 98, 100, 111, 121, 136, 273, 279–280, 284; "linguistic turn" of, xiv–xv; of mind, xiii–xv, xviii, xxi, xxiv,
xxviii, 7, 61–62, 65, 121, 137, 315n2, 316; modern, 111–112; practical, 291; of psychology, 9.
Plato, 168–170, 197, 216, 261
pluralism, xxiii, 145, 187, 194, 197–198, 200
Poincaré, Henri, 107
Popper, Karl, xix, 137–140, 142–143
positivism, xix, 5–6, 99, 244
possible worlds, 204–205
poststructuralism, xii
pragmatics, 271–277, 300
pragmatism, xxviii
predication, 15–17, 19, 224, 310; collective, 108–109, 123–126, 128–132, 134–136, 161–163; derelativized, 206–207, 215, 219, 245; distributive, 108–109, 126, 128–130, 154, 162–163; holistic, 165–166; monadic, 215, 220, 245, 310; polyadic, 330; relative, 206–208; simple, 165
Prior, Arthur, 20, 66–74, 146n35
pronouns: indirect reflexive, 325–326
properties: anatomic, 102; atomistic, 101–102, 117; collective, 103, 120–121, 123, 131; dyadic, 219; emergent, 131, 161; holistic, 101–102, 115–116, 119, 121; intrinsic, 191–194; monadic, 219; natural, 176; physical, 176; polyadic, 219; relational, 115–117, 120, 209; semantic, 103, 110; structural, 120–121, 158
property (ownership), 307, 309–310; Indian conception of, 305; private, 116–118
propositions, 15–17, 19, 67–68, 110–115, 120, 167, 205, 220, 231–237, 314–323, 326–327; atomic, 239; collective, 129n11, 130, 134, 135n, 136, 152–154, 162; dyadic, 220–221, 223, 225–226; exponible, 163, 209; falsification of, 104–107; general, 162; holistic, 162–166; as implicit arguments, 236; individuation of, 167–168; of inherence, 205, 208; intentional, 68, 70–71; meaning of, xvi, 4–5, 70, 99–101, 104, 106, 109, 111; modal, 67, 70; monadic, 223; particular, 152–153; polyadic, 221; relational, 202, 205, 208; vs. sentences, 315n1; singular, 152–153; speculative, 233; triadic, 221–223; universal, 152–153, 162

Proust, Marcel, 53–54
psychology, xiv, xix, 7–10, 50–52, 69, 316n4; analytic, 315n2; descriptive, 52–54; of experience, 50–51; intellectualist, 258, 262; laws of, xiv, 5–6, 98–99; naturalistic, 5–6, 50–51, 60, 99
psychological attributions, 7–8
Putnam, Hilary, xxviii, 11n8

qualities, 27–28, 33, 164, 209, 218, 310; extrinsic, 206; intrinsic, 178, 192, 203, 206–207, 338
Quine, W. V. O., 20n24, 100, 164; history of semantics of, 109–111; holism of, xii–xiii, xxi–xxii, 89, 96, 103–104, 108, 112–116, 120, 292; on modality, 67; on "myth of meaning," 38, 275; on proper names, 164; on radical translation, xix, 335–337

Rabelais, 16n
realism, 128, 139, 195, 212, 214–217, 244, 315n2; Scholastic, 214, 216
reciprocity, 228, 260, 263–268, 332
recognition, 280–281
reference, 10n, 14n14, 17, 56, 67, 74, 152, 165–166, 170; opacity of, 67–68, 71, 73–75; subject of, 165
relations: as attribute of whole, 191; causal, 15, 18, 253, 336; of comparison, 203, 209–210, 212–215, 217, 248, 329; dyadic, xxiii, 20, 98, 111n, 117–118, 191, 219–223, 226, 228–231, 240, 244, 248, 253, 335–337; external, 28, 66, 186, 189–190, 199–203, 213; hierarchical, 260; human, 228, 297; intentional, 11, 13–23, 31, 34–35, 43, 48–51, 56–59, 65–66, 68, 71, 73, 76, 81, 83, 191–193, 210, 212, 216, 218–219, 242, 246, 267, 313, 336–337; of interlocution, 328–329, 336–337; internal, xxiii, 28, 66, 83, 185, 186–203, 210, 303; intersubjective (*see* intersubjectivity); juridical, 257; logic of, xxiii, 14, 122, 186–195, 211, 228–237, 239, 248, 258; mental (*see* relations: intentional); natural, 4, 17, 48, 51, 65, 231; of order, 194, 266–267; physical, 11, 15; polyadic, xxiii, 214, 219, 223, 230, 237; real, 15–20, 22, 31, 48, 51, 59, 64, 65–66, 68, 71, 74, 76, 81, 83, 193, 195, 200, 203, 207, 210, 211–215, 217–218, 226, 246, 300, 334; of reason, 193, 200, 211–212, 214, 216; reciprocal (*see* reciprocity); referential (*see* reference); of resemblance, 195, 212, 214–217, 321, 338; semiotic, 231; semantic, 20, 56, 98, 335–336; social, 202, 288–289, 295, 303, 313, 330; spatial, 145–147, 158, 186; structural, 120; symbolic, 119; temporal, 193–194, 240; triadic, xxiii, 56, 118, 122, 219–223, 225, 228–231, 237, 238, 241, 244–246, 248, 251, 253, 256, 336–337; unilateral, 267
relativism, 99, 110, 118
religion, 259–261
Renaut, Alain, 282n28
representationism, 39n44, 47, 58–59, 111
representation, 137–138, 158, 200, 203, 210, 213, 232, 259, 260; collective, xix–xx, xxiv, 131, 257, 293, 295; magico-religious, 260–261
rights, 309–310
Rorty, Richard, xxviii, 201, 242n6
rules, 244, 246, 255–256, 258–259, 263, 269, 301; vs. causes, 255, 258–259; constitutive, 160, 174–175; of gift-giving, 247, 252–255; irreducibility of, 242, 256; of kinship, 263; priority of, 338. *See also* institutions; law
Russell, Bertrand, 158, 227, 315n2; atomism of, 143–146, 148–149; formalism of, 158; on gift, 239–241, 336; on internal relations, 187–198, 202–203, 205, 207–208, 213; on "paradox of analysis," 168; on wholes, 167–168
Ryle, Gilbert, 87–89

Sartre, Jean-Paul, 266, 271–285; phenomenology of, 47, 56, 64; philosophy of language of, 271–285, 321
Saussure, Ferdinand de, xvi, 97n6, 311

Scholasticism, 11n7, 13–14, 35n, 88n13, 126, 195, 215, 222, 274
sciences: human, xii–xiv, xvii, xxii–xxiii, 4–5, 44–45, 227–229, 247, 289–290; natural, xiii–xiv, 5, 45, 227–228; social (*see* sciences: human)
Searle, John, 12n10
self-consciousness, 327–328
Sellars, Wilfred, xxviii
semantic opacity, 67–68, 70–76
semantics, 57, 106, 119, 316n4; history of, 109–113; autonomy from syntax, 177–181; naturalization of, 185
sentences. *See* propositions
sets, 108n26, 110, 140–142, 146–147
signified, 111n, 159, 177, 335–336
signifier: empty, 253; exteriority of, 284–285; floating, 254–255; materiality of, 168, 176–181; independence from signified, 177–181
signs, 38–39, 56, 119–122, 155–156; iconic, 111–112; identification of, 320–322; impersonal use of, 75–76, 275, 284; non-propositional, 236; personal use of, 75–76; propositional (*see* propositions)
Simmel, Georg, xviii
Simons, Peter, 161n
social bond, 266–267. *See also* reciprocity
societies, 126–127, 266, 297; traditional, 306–308
solipsism, 11n, 51n4, 73, 75–76, 331–333; methodological, xvii, 47–48, 51, 192n10
speech, 311–312, 320–321, 323; apparent, 149; priority over language, 321–323; real, 149
speech acts, xv, xxiv, 4, 96, 311–313, 337
spirit, 39; of laws, xi, 290–291; objective (*see* mind: objective)
status, xxix, 116–119, 202, 236–237, 243, 251, 257n28, 266, 268, 289, 301, 306
structuralism, xii–xiii, xx, xxii, xxiii, xxv, 97, 156–158, 176, 183–184, 237, 258–262, 285, 292, 303
structure, 116, 120–121, 142–143, 157–158, 249; as mental schema, 264; of language, 312; of mind (*see* mind: structures of); predicative, 326–327; syntactical, 179–183; unconscious, xxiii, xxv, 6, 157n4, 248, 253–254, 261–262, 268; universal, 261
subject, xxv, xxvi, 19, 24, 49, 64, 73, 287, 294–295, 301, 303–304, 308; as agent of action, 13, 86, 220, 225, 227, 318, 322; of attribution, 134, 150, 163, 318; of change, 49, 66, 203; collective, 108n26, 130–136; composite, 132; dyadic, 225–226, 304–309; empirical, xxvi–xxvii; grammatical, 224–225; impersonal, 323; of institutions, 304–309, 312; intentional, 9, 24, 73, 192; logical, 14, 152, 163, 220, 223–226, 237; multiple, 311–312; as patient of action, 32–33, 35, 48–49, 52, 56–57, 63, 225, 227; of perception, 37, 48–51, 73; of predication, 134–136, 165; of proposition, 14–17, 134, 165, 205, 220; of rights, 310; self-positing, xxvi–xxvii, 228, 281, 300; simple, 132; social, 303, 307–309, 311–313, 329–335; transcendental, xxvi–xxvii
subordination, 183–184, 267
supposition, 152
syllogism, 220, 232–236
symbolic, 41, 119n, 257n29
symbolic effectiveness. *See* symbols: efficacy of
symbols, 41; algebraic, 253; complex, xvi; efficacy of, xxiii, 159; meaning of, xvi; religious, 159; simple, xvi
syntax, 178–183; autonomy of, 179–181; vs. morphology, 179
systems, 77, 97, 101, 103, 105–106, 108, 119, 157, 161, 210, 225–226; dynamic, xxiii; mental, 251; natural, xxiii, nominal, xxii; normative, xxiii; of propositions, 105, 113–115; polyadic, 237; real, xxii–xxiii, 183, 189, 244; of signs, xxv, 97–98, 101, 272, 322; symbolic, 292

Taylor, Charles, xxiii, xxvi(n15), 295–299
techniques of the body, 288–289

terms, 186, 191n9, 220, 232–236; absolute, 202, 205–208, 219, 226, 244; collective, 129–136, 138–139; derelativized, 207–208, 210, 219, 245; dyadic, 219, 226; general, 138–139, 162; intentional, 3–4, 13–14; monadic (*see* terms: absolute); natural, 3–4; polyadic, 219; relative, 205–210, 224, 226; singular, 139; triadic, 226

Tesnière, Lucien, 179–183, 185, 223–225, 228, 238–239

textualism, 287–288, 290

theory: as collection of sentences, 113–115; indigenous (*see* explanation: indigenous); as language, 109–110, 113–114; scientific, 104–109

thinking, 235, 300, 318, 338; dialogical, 299–300

Thomas Aquinas, 216

thoughts: contextuality of, 82; distinction of, 81–82, 91–92; identification of, xviii, xxiv–xxv, 90–92, 100–101, 118, 122, 237, 314–335, 337–338; impersonal, 8, 323, 333, 338; personal, 322–330, 333, 338; reflexive, 325–326, 330–331, 333; social, 329–334; symbolic, 257

totality, xii, xvi–xvii, xxi–xxiii, 97, 101–103, 114, 116, 123, 127, 132–133, 136, 142–143, 155, 161–162, 183; collective, 108, 123, 131; concrete, 142, 147–148; indivisible, 114, 131–132, 134; logical, 147; meaningful, 113, 166–179, 237, 290–292; real, xxiii, 161–162; surreal, 161

transitivity: of physical actions, 28–29, 31, 34–35; of mental acts, 25–28, 31–32, 34–36, 65–66, 76, 78n, 80–81, 193n

translation, radical. See *under* Quine, W. V. O.

Tugendhat, Ernst, 234n27

unconscious, 248, 253, 257, 261; structural (*see* structure: unconscious)

"under a description," 62–64, 85, 185, 199, 201, 226

unities, 167–168, 171, 249

universals, 37–40, 45, 137–139, 152, 211, 214, 222, 338; of relation, 297; of resemblance, 297, 338

verbs: agreement with subject, 124–125; bivalent, 224; intentional, 4, 21, 25–28, 34–35, 66–68, 72, 76–77, 83–86, 191–193; intransitive, 28, 33, 68, 76–77, 85; monovalent, 224, 310; in Peirce's sense (*see* term); physical, 25–26, 28–29, 34–35, 52; psychological, 25–26, 191–193; semantic, 75; structure of, 224; system of, 83–86; transitive, 25–29, 31–32, 35, 66 76–77, 86, 220–221, 224; trivalent, 224, 238

Villey, Michel, 309–310

voluntarism, 263

Wallace, William, xiv

Weber, Max, 273n6, 301–303

wholes, xvii, 101–103, 112, 113n, 114–115, 119–122, 142, 147, 173, 184, 189–191, 223, 236, 237, 249; collective, xxi–xxii, 108, 115, 121, 131–132, 134, 136, 140–141, 145, 155, 161–163, 167, 237, 244; complex, 143–145, 147–149, 160–161, 166–167; concrete, 141–142, 155; given before its parts, xii, xx, 95n, 102–103, 134, 156–157, 165–168, 171, 174–175, 185, 244, 249, 258–259; meaningful (*see* totality: meaningful); monolithic, 114–115, 145, 156; as *omnis*, 162–164; as polyads, 237; real, 156, 161, 249n16; structure of, 120, 142, 158, 264; as *totus*, 163–166 190–191; as unity, 167–168, 171, 249

William of Ockham, 195

Wittgenstein, Ludwig, xiv, xvi–xvii, xxi, xxvi, xxvii(n), 90, 145–149, 169n23; atomism of early work, 145–149, 158; on gift, 243; isomorphism of language and world, 159; on expecting, 77–81; holism of, 98, 103, 118, 145, 148; "language games" in, xvi–xvii; on intentional acts, xxi, 20–22, 77–83, 242–243; on multiplicity, 230; on rules, 159–160, 222n13, 242–243, 259. *See also* form, of life